A major critical magazine for nearly fifty years, *The Dial* underwent profound changes in the period between 1912-1920 during which it emerged as the foremost voice of contemporary literature and the arts. Dr. Joost carefully plots the editorships of Francis F. Browne of the genteel tradition (Woodrow Wilson, Henry Blake Fuller, Harriet Monroe, H. M. Kallen, Archibald Henderson); Martyn Johnson of the new American literature of social and political liberalism (John Dewey, Thorstein Veblen, Harold Stearns, Bertrand Russell, Conrad Aiken and Amy Lowell); and Scofield Thayer and James Sibley Watson of the final and most famous years (T. S. Eliot, W. B. Yeats, E. E. Cummings, Marianne Moore, D. H. Lawrence and Hart Crane). E. E. Cummings emerges as one of the subtlest and most significant caricaturists of the early 1920's.

Thayer, in his consummate taste, recognized the importance of artists such as Bearsdley, Picasso, Chagall, Lachaise, Dehn, Gropper and others whose works are represented in this book by forty-eight illustrations.

editorial staff of *Poetry* magazine (1951-1954). In 1957-1958 he was Research Consultant at the Worcester Art Museum (where the *Dial* Collection is housed), under a grant from the Bollingen Foundation, and in 1963-1964 was a Fulbright lecturer in the Netherlands. His *Scofield Thayer and The Dial* was published in 1964.

THE DIAL, 1912 - 1920

YEARS OF TRANSITION

The Dial

1912-1920

by NICHOLAS JOOST

BARRE PUBLISHERS, BARRE, MASSACHUSETTS, 1967

Preface

IN the preface to *Scofield Thayer and The Dial,* I gave a brief account of the way in which I came to write that book; much the same is true of *Years of Transition: The Dial, 1912-1920.* Added to those circumstances are others: a growing public interest in *The Dial* and its times, and one's continuing interest in learning more about *The Dial* and its milieu and in sharing with others the resultant insights and discoveries. The impetus to write the present book thus derived from continued research, from reviews of *Scofield Thayer and The Dial,* and from talks given to such groups as the Friends of Literature (in Chicago), the Midwest Modern Language Association, the Midcontinent American Studies Association, and the New England College English Association.

An expression of gratitude is due the following institutions and persons for essential help in the writing and realization of *Years of Transition: The Dial, 1912-1920:*

Scofield Thayer's representative, Charles P. Williamson, for permission to use and to quote from the Dial Papers in the Worcester Art Museum and for permission to use photographs of pictures in the Dial Collection housed in the Worcester Art Museum and in the Scofield Thayer Collection housed at the Fogg Art Museum of Harvard University; and beyond such generous aid, for reading the typescript of this book.

The Worcester Art Museum, its Curator, Louisa Dresser, and her Assistant, Elizabeth Henry, for advice and aid generously given, for research facilities, and for reproductions of the pictures in the Dial Collection.

Dr. James Sibley Watson, Jr., for advice about *The Dial*, for reading the typescript of this book, and for permission to use his correspondence and to reproduce Hildegarde Watson's *A Drawing*.

Southern Illinois University, for a research grant, for released time from teaching one course during Spring Quarter 1966, and for research facilities.

Fredric R. Mosher, for correspondence about *The Dial* and for generously furnishing typescripts of unpublished material. Michael D. True, for correspondence about Randolph Bourne, for furnishing portions of his unpublished dissertation, and for reading certain chapters of this book in typescript. Francis Villemain, for lending books and making suggestions on the subject of John Dewey.

The Fogg Art Museum and its Associate Director and Curator of Drawings, Agnes Mongan, for reproductions of the Beardsley drawings in this book. Charles H. Cox, of the Photographic Service, Southern Illinois University, for reproductions of pictures and emblems. Mary Sue Dilliard, Laura Joost, and Mabel Murphy, of the Lovejoy Memorial Library, and Alan Cohn, of the Morris Library, Southern Illinois University. Alyse Gregory, for correspondence and correction. Edna Bryner Schwab, literary executor of Paul Rosenfeld, for permission to quote an unpublished letter by Rosenfeld. Malcolm Cowley, for permission to quote his unpublished letter. Helen Crosby, of Doubleday & Company, for permission to quote her letter about the Publishers' Sun-Dial and for furnishing pertinent material. James K. Folsom, for suggesting Scofield Thayer's interest in marooned individuals. Kimball C. Elkins, of the Harvard University Archives, for information relating to *The Harvard Monthly*. Sinclair Hitchings, Keeper of Prints, and Paul Swenson, Curatorial Assistant, both of the Boston Public Library, for assistance generously given. Mrs. Ernest Thayer Clary, for generous advice and for reading the typescript of this book. James F. Beard for the invitation that prompted the writing of this book. Laura Spudich and Kathleen Hartley, my typists.

Library of Congress, Newberry Library (for the use of letters in the Francis Fisher Browne Collection), Yale University Library (for the use of the Dial Papers housed there), Columbia University Library (for the use of the Randolph S. Bourne Papers), Houghton Library of Harvard University (for the use of unpublished material by Bronson Alcott), American Antiquarian Society, Worcester Public Library, St. Louis Public Library, University of Chicago Library, Missouri Historical Society, Mercantile Library of St. Louis, Duke University Library, and Lovejoy Memorial and Morris Libraries of Southern Illinois University.

Portions of this book have been published in somewhat different forms in *Journal of the Illinois State Historical Society,* *Midcontinent American Studies Journal,* and *Studies in Philology,* and for permission to adapt such materials to the needs of a book, thanks go to William C. Marten, Stuart Levine, and O. B. Hardison, respectively of those three journals.

To my wife, as always, I have gone for aid and encouragement.

* * *

Certain details of *Years of Transition:The Dial, 1912-20* contradict assertions and attributions made in *Scofield Thayer and The Dial.* I thank Mrs. Agnes de Lima for perhaps the most important correction, and in this book, as is correct, Randolph Bourne dies in the apartment of Mrs. de Lima. Dr. James Sibley Watson is responsible for the attribution of the writing for *The Dial* of "Sganarelle" to Gilbert Seldes rather than to himself (as was erroneously stated in *Scofield Thayer and The Dial*) ; Mr. Gilbert Seldes has kindly confirmed that he wrote as Sganarelle and has related his pseudonym to his interest, since 1913-14, in the *commedia dell' arte.*

The opinions expressed in this book are those of the writer

and of his acknowledged sources. Those who read the book in typescript offered many helpful corrections, emendations, and suggestions for improvement. As far as possible, almost all were incorporated in the text, and the resulting modifications have made for a more accurate work. Those same readers surely cannot be held responsible for the author's view of a period in American history, involving themselves in certain cases, about which all too little has been ascertained and which remains, if nothing else, an age of turbulent transition and controversy.

Nicholas Joost
Edwardsville, Illinois
February 1, 1967

Illustrations

In the following list of illustrations, [1] designates a picture or object in the Dial collection and not previously reproduced; [2] designates a picture or object in the Dial Collection and previously reproduced in *The Dial;* [3] designates reproduction for the first time from the Scofield Thayer Collection of drawings by Aubrey Beardsley in the Fogg Art Museum, Harvard University; [4] designates publication of a picture or object in the catalogue of the Exhibition *"The Dial* and the Dial Collection" held in the Worcester Art Museum, April 30 - September 8, 1959; and [5] designates previous reproduction in *The Dial.* Date indicates when illustration first appeared in *The Dial.*

Following page 80

The End of the Chicago *Dial* (August 15, 1918)
In Memoriam Randolph Bourne (January 1920)
House Advertisement (May 1921)
William Gropper, *Editorial Conference* [1,4]
E. E. Cummings, *S. T., S. W., G. S.* [1, 4]
Henri de Toulouse-Lautrec, *The Chap-Book*
Aubrey Beardsley, *The Savoy, "Contents" Page of the First Number* [3]
Aubrey Beardsley, *Don Juan, Sganarelle, and the Beggar* [3]
Aubrey Beardsley, *Black Coffee* [3]

Aubrey Beardsley, *Alberich* for Wagner's *(Das Rheingold)* [3]
Aubrey Beardsley, *Scene* from *The Scarlet Pastorale* [3]
Aubrey Beardsley, *His Book-Plate* [3]
Gaston Lachaise, *Three-Quarters Length Figure* [1, 4]
Gaston Lachaise, *Seated Nude with Upraised Arms* [1,4]
Gaston Lachaise, *Caligari* [2, 4] (December 1925)
Claude Bragdon, *A Drawing* [5] (October 1922)

Following page 160

Jean de Bosschère, *"Ou Irai-Je?"* [5] (May 1921)
Constantin Brancusi, *The Golden Bird* [5]
Marc Chagall, *Man and Woman* [1, 4]
Marc Chagall, *The Market Place* [2, 4] (February 1924)
Marc Chagall, *The Idiot* [2, 4] (November 1924)
Ivan Opffer, *Gilbert Cannan* [2, 4] (February 1920)
Hildegarde Watson, *A Drawing* [4, 5] (March 1928)
Richard Boix, *Walking Architecture* [2, 4] (July 1921)
William Gropper, *Second-Hand Romance* [2, 4] (November 1920)
Adolf Dehn, *The Violinist* [2, 4] (August 1924)
William Gropper, *Fox Trot* [2, 4] (May 1922)
E. E. Cummings, *Dancers* [2, 4] (August 1922)
William Gropper, *He — The One Who Gets Slapped* [1, 4]
Pablo Picasso, *Clown Resting* [4]
Henri de Toulouse-Lautrec, *Seated Clowness* [4]
E. E. Cummings, *National Winter Garden Burlesque I* [2, 4] (January 1920)

Following page 240

William Gropper, *Tightrope* [2, 4] (September 1922)
Maria Uhden, *Tumbler* [4]
Anne Merriman Peck, *The Zanfretta Circus* [2, 4] (September 1924)
Marie Laurencin, *The Little Dancer* [2, 4] (October 1927)
William Gropper, *A Line Syncopation: Male Dancer* [2, 4] (October 1924)
E. E. Cummings, *Girl with Swagger Stick, Dancing* [1, 4]
E. E. Cummings, *National Winter Garden Burlesque II* [2, 4] (January 1920)
Adolf Dehn, *Mura Dancing* [1, 4]
Adolf Dehn, *A Memory of Our Hungarian Lady* [2, 4] (February 1925)
Adolf Dehn, *Two Dancers* [2, 4] (August 1924)
Adolf Dehn, *Negress Dancing* [2, 4] (February 1928)
William Gropper, *A Line Syncopation: Negro Dancer* [2, 4] (December 1923)
Frans Maserell, *The Boxer* [2, 4] (March 1923)
E. E. Cummings, *Acrobat* [2, 4] (January 1922)
Hunt Diedrich, *Toreador* [2, 4] (April 1921)
Max Liebermann, *Polo Game* [2, 4] (December 1927)

x

Contents

An Introduction to THE DIAL *and Its Tradition*

THE tradition of *The Dial* is effectively viewed in the perspective of its fitful development, more a product of the total American past than a phenomenon of a particular year or era. The American tradition of *The Dial* incorporates the histories of four discontinuous American periodicals, *The Dials* of 1840-44, 1860, 1880-1929, and 1959 to date, as well as of other periodicals with *Dial* in their titles.

The first *Dial* was the Transcendentalist quarterly edited successively by Margaret Fuller and Ralph Waldo Emerson from 1840 to 1844. The second was an imitation of the original *Dial,* issued from Cincinnati for twelve monthly numbers in 1860 under the editorship of Moncure D. Conway early in his career as a clergyman of advanced beliefs. Its chief importance in the tradition of *The Dial* is that by appropriating the title with the expressed good will of Emerson, Conway established a precedent: *The Dial* as a periodical title became traditional, a title to use much as *The Spectator* also has been used for a number of periodicals since 1711.

Two decades later the last of the three American *Dials* of

the nineteenth century began publication, edited in Chicago by Francis F. Browne. Under its title, as time passed, were incorporated what amounted to three different, even sharply distinguishable, magazines; they shared only the formalities of a title, the continuous, consecutive numbering of volumes of issues, a record of continuous publication, and a continuing incorporation that involved the buying and selling of Dial Company stock. The last of these magazines, *The Dial* of Scofield Thayer and J. S. Watson, Jr., thus inherited its tradition and its name not only from *The Dial* of Emerson and Margaret Fuller, but also from *The Dial* of Francis F. Browne.

Browne's *Dial*, from its inception, gave specific expression to this continuity of a shared tradition.[1] The first number, for May 1880, contained one of the earliest essays on Emerson's *Dial*, by Norman C. Perkins.[2] The liaison between the two journals is expressed in the title of Perkins's essay, "The Original 'Dial' "; indeed, the essay infers the indebtedness of Browne's *Dial*, different as it was by intention and content, to *The Dial* of Emerson and Margaret Fuller. By such an acknowledgement to the still living Editor of the New England *Dial*, Browne at once paid a debt to a literary and intellectual pioneer and firmly placed himself and his magazine in the then dominant American cultural tradition of the flowering of New England. Unlike Emerson and Conway, Browne was no controversialist. He founded and published a *Dial* with the uncontroversial subtitle, *A Monthly Index of Current Literature*; and this subtitle did not belie the contents of the magazine. To be sure, founding and publishing the Chicago *Dial* involved risk, but this was a perfectly straightforward hazard of commerce. With Francis Browne as editor and publisher, *The Dial* continued for more than a third of a century to publish its gatherings of compendious notes on literary and publishing matters and serious reviews of current books. But with the Editor's death *The Dial*, too, succumbed to the imperative of change. In the summer of 1916 the review was bought by a journalist named Martyn Johnson, and, the better to succeed with his transformation of it into a weekly of radical opinion, in July 1918 Johnson moved his purchase to New York. Johnson's guidance brought editorial vicissitudes and financial embarrassments for four years, and his *Dial* printed its last pages in November 1919. The new monthly *Dial* began publication in January 1920. As directed by Scofield Thayer and James Sibley Watson, it preserved the formal continuity and the corporate identity of *The Dial* begun in 1880; yet in its last and most brilliant incarnation, the magazine proved a vastly different phoenix. At the same time, it proved the generic phoenix after all: it remained, consciously, *The Dial* and bore witness to its origin, carrying on its masthead page the statement "founded in 1880 by Francis F. Browne."

Besides *The Dials* of 1840-44, 1860, and 1880-1929, between 1889 and 1897 in London Charles H. Shannon and C. S. Ricketts edited and published *The Dial: An Occasional Publication.* Their magazine of *Symboliste* persuasion and eccentric periodicity — it was issued in 1889, 1892-93, and 1896-97 in five hardbound numbers — seems to be the only extra-American instance of the use of *Dial* as a title for an English-language periodical.

Two nineteenth-century American periodicals have *Dial* as a part of their titles. *The Dial of the Old South Clock,* published daily from December 5 to 15, 1877, and again daily from December 5 to 15, 1879, was edited by Miss Susan Hale in Boston on the occasions of two annual church fairs, or bazaars, held for the preservation of the Old South Church. The lengthy title was conveniently shortened to *The Dial* by the editor in her writing, and of course the title has a derivation as obvious as it was intended to be. It remains a curiosity of journalism and little else. *The Dial of Progress* is extant in issues dating from 1890 through November 1904 and was published from Mt. Pleasant, Iowa. Edited by W. R. Cole, this weekly was the official organ of the Iowa Anti-Saloon League and bore for its motto, "The Saloon Must Go." As laudable in its aim as *The Dial of the Old South Clock,* and less decadent than the London *Dial,* this *Dial* of the Iowa Anti-Saloon League like them made only a minor contribution to the growth of the *Dial* tradition in America. Nowhere do *The Dial* of London, *The Dial of the Old South Clock,* and *The Dial of Progress* indicate an overt editorial awareness of the developing tradition of the American *Dial* and the significant contribution made by the journals bearing the title of *Dial* to the composite tradition. All of these successive *Dials* nevertheless used their common title with conscious awareness of its symbolic potentiality, and they all owed something of their usage to the first declaration of that symbolic significance in the original *Dial* in July of 1840.

The first issue of this *Dial*, edited from Boston by Margaret Fuller, printed on its outside back cover a prospectus, which gave the purpose of the magazine as that of furnishing "a medium for the freest expression of thought on the questions which interest earnest minds in every community."[3] *The Dial* would aim at "the discussion of principles, rather than at the promotion of measures," and its contributors would "possess little in common but the love of intellectual freedom, and the hope of social progress"; its pages would "promote the constant evolution of truth, not the petrifaction of opinion"; and its contents would "embrace a wide and varied range of subjects." Its literary criticism would be "just and catholic," while recognizing "every sincere production of genius"; its essays on philosophy would "attempt the reconciliation of the universal instincts of humanity with the largest conclusions of reason"; and its essays on religion would "reverently seek to discover the presence of God in nature, in history, and in the soul of man."

Further, the prospectus explained the significance of the dial in its use as title for a periodical. The prospectus held that *The Dial*, "as its title indicates, will endeavor to occupy a station on which the light may fall; which is open to the rising sun; and from which it may correctly report the progress of the hour and the day."

In the same issue, Emerson published an essay "From the Editors to the Reader" that, although written originally by Margaret Fuller, "he had rewritten . . . so extensively that he considered it his own."[4] Emerson too used the convenient metaphor of the title of the new journal:

> And so with diligent hands and good intent we set down
> our Dial on the earth. We wish it may resemble that
> instrument in its celebrated happiness, that of measuring
> no hours but those of sunshine. Let it be one cheerful
> rational voice amidst the din of mourners and polemics.

Or to abide by our chosen image, let it be such a Dial, not as the dead face of a clock, hardly even such as the Gnomon in a garden, but rather such a Dial as the Garden itself, in whose leaves and flowers and fruits the suddenly awakened sleeper is instantly apprised not what part of dead time, but what state of life and growth is now arrived and arriving.

The title of *The Dial* thus explicated by the prospectus and the editorial announcement would appear to have been a matter of a good deal of discussion in the fall and winter of 1839. As early as a meeting of the Symposium Club in September 1839, Margaret Fuller was expounding her views of the proposed journal and calling it by its name, according to the interpretation given by Col. Higginson to an entry in Bronson Alcott's papers: "Margaret Fuller, at a meeting of the 'Symposium' Club, September 18, 'gave her views of the proposed "Dial," which she afterwards edited.' This is the first instance I have found of the introduction of the actual title of the American periodical." Higginson gives the source of this quotation from Bronson Alcott not as coming from "Alcott's MS. Diary" but from "other memoranda by Mr. Alcott in my possession."[5] The qualifying clause "which she afterwards edited" sounds as though the passage had been written not in 1839 but either after Margaret Fuller had resigned the editorship of *The Dial* in 1842 or after its cessation in 1844.

In Alcott's manuscript journal of his thoughts and activities, the entry for September 18, 1839, which deals with the meeting previously mentioned, does not name the prospective periodical: "Our circle met this afternoon, at Bartol's Chestnut St. We discussed the subject of a *Journal* designed as the organ of views more in accordance with the Soul." After naming the persons present ("Francis, Alcott, Hedge, Wm. Channing, Dwight, Ripley, Parker, Bartlett, Russell, Robbins, Morrison, Shattuck, Miss Fuller"), Alcott concluded that "A good deal was said about our Journal, but no definite action was taken upon it: its idea and plan are not defined." The italicized word *"Journal"* is preceded by an asterisk, and in the bottom margin of the page of the entry is written "Dial.," in a hand that appears to be Alcott's but of a later period.[6]

A definite clue to the ultimate source of the title lies in Bronson Alcott's manuscripts. In his journal for February (undated, but 1840), he wrote the following:

I have been busy, from early morn till evening late, transcribing from my M.S.S. and classifying my collection, in the order of the Soul; attempting to realize in my work a symbol of her circuit through Nature and Man. To these papers I give the name of 'THE DIAL.' They are selections from my Scriptures during the last three or four years (including my Book 'the Psyche') and number nearly 2000 pages in MS.

At the end of March, of the same year, Alcott wrote:

I wrote much, and transcribed many passages from my M.S.S. for this my 'Dial', which wins more and more of regard as it shadows more broadly my life. A shapely volume it is already; but much remains yet to be written. —

And the next entry continues in much the same vein and concludes the page:

Ah me! the midnight flame has consumed my Dial. But yet the children of the Light are imperishable, exempt from the greed of the Flame. At my retreat in Concord, shall I not enkindle a purer light.[7]

In his journal, Alcott pasted the *Dial* prospectus, which is dated as published on May 4, 1840; and he noted marginally on the page that "This journal takes its name from a M.S.S. of mine of like designation referred to on Page 47 & 56 of this Scripture" (he habitually referred to his journal not only as his "Dial" but also, and precedently to the other title, as his "Scripture").[8]

In the first (July 1840) issue of *The Dial* were published the first fifty of Alcott's "Orphic Sayings," the first one of which uses the dial metaphor:

Thou art, my heart, a soul-flower, facing ever and following the motions of thy sun, opening thyself to her

vivifying ray, and pleading thy affinity with the celes-
tial orbs. Thou dost

the livelong day
Dial on time thine own eternity.

In view of his assertions to himself in his private journal, Bronson Alcott was strangely reticent on the point in public. When
Alcott publicly discussed the Transcendental Club and *The Dial,*
he made no mention of the genesis of the title: "The first time
The Dial was proposed for discussion was at the meeting of the
Club at Mr. Bartol's in 1839. There were present Messieurs
Bartol, Hedge, Channing, Ripley, Parker, Miss Fuller, and one
other [Alcott himself]. I may have omitted some whom I do not
now recall. I find no others named in my notes."[9]

Until the latter part of April 1840, Emerson himself wrote,
in his correspondence, of the prospective magazine simply as "the
Journal." He seems first to have used the name of *The Dial*
in a letter of April 20, 1840, to his brother, William, complaining of his anomalous connection with the magazine, which
brought him papers to read and judge, "which as I am not editor
but only contributor, I like not."[10] On April 22, Emerson wrote
Carlyle that he had very good hope that his friend Margaret
Fuller's "Journal — after many false baptisms now saying it will
be called *The Dial,* and which is to appear in July" — would
give his Scottish correspondent a better knowledge of the young
people of the Transcendentalist circle.[12] It is probable that Margaret Fuller and Bronson Alcott had been using *The Dial* as
a tentative designation prior to their persuading Emerson and
other participants in the venture that the title was the most fitting one for a Transcendentalist periodical, and probably the title
was due to Alcott's suggestion.

Alcott's "Orphic" thought was hermetic and platonist, and
he was an important member of the Transcendental Club, a
group of men and women who considered thought and art from
a platonist point of view. The title of *The Dial* was agreeable because it was consonant with a bias shared by members of the
group. As thinkers and artists, Emerson and his friends envisioned ideas in picturesque symbols.[12]

Emerson's fascination with the hermetic, platonist tradition is, of course, one of the pervasive aspects of his thought. See, for example, the close of "Intellect," with its recollection of "that lofty and sequestered class, . . . the high priesthood of the pure reason, the *Trismegisti,* the expounders of the principles of thought from age to age."[13] And Emerson held that "The world is emblematic. . . . 'The visible world and the relation of its parts, is the dial plate of the invisible.' "[14] In a poetic "Letter" written after the death of his first wife and prior to his second marriage, Emerson confided to his "Dear brother" the life, "Please, God, that I would lead," somewhere in "the mountain counties" of western Massachusetts amid "old woods" on a slope above a roaring river. Thither the poet proposed to bring his books, his "household gods," the "reliquaries of my dead saint" — the first Mrs. Emerson, we may assume — to dwell in "the door of her memory" and

> Then in the uncouth solitude unlock
> My stock of art, plant dials in the grass,
> Hang in the air a bright thermometer
> And aim a telescope at the inviolate sun.[15]

It is curious that both instances of Emerson's use of *dial* occur before the founding of his periodical and his revision of Margaret Fuller's editorial announcement in the July 1840 *Dial,* after which he seems never to have used the image again.

Undoubtedly the use of the dial image reflects the interests of the Transcendentalists not only in hermetic thought but also in another field, one closely related to platonist symbolism — metaphysical poetry, with its relation to the Renaissance and Baroque art of the emblem. Again Emerson's case illustrates the point. A favorite poet of Emerson was the seventeenth-century Puritan and metaphysical poet, Andrew Marvell, who united the visual emblem and the platonist symbol in his image of the dial in the final stanza of "The Garden":

> How well the skilful Gardener drew
> Of flowers, and herbes, this Dial new;
> Where, from above, the milder Sun
> Does through a fragrant Zodiack run;
> And, as it works, th' industrious Bee
> Computes its time as well as we.

How could such sweet and wholesome Hours
Be reckon'd but with herbs and flow'rs!

The new dial of the "skilful Gardener" has affinities with the Transcendentalist *Dial* on which the light would fall, open as it would be to the rising sun. Both suns were the same — the light of the One. Both dial images conduced to the leading of the contemplative life advocated by Marvell and Emerson.[16]

Whether Goethe's well-known use of the dial image influenced Emerson, Alcott, and Margaret Fuller in deciding on the title of their journal is matter for debate, despite William Wasserstrom's suggestion:

> Carlyle's way of describing nature's gift to intense artists who serve as heroes of culture, the gift Emerson called a transparency of eyeball and Henry Miller calls a cosmology of eye, is taken from no less a personage than Goethe. Carlyle says that Goethe himself had been led to this formulation by a study of Shakespeare in which he realized that Shakespeare's characters, " 'like watches with dial plates of transparent crystal,' " show the hour and simultaneously make visible its " 'inward mechanism,' " too. We realize, therefore, that Emerson's *Dial* displays Carlyle's prophetic vision of order in the heart of things, Goethe's image of harmony between men and culture, and Shakespeare's timeless, ceaseless yearning to advance on chaos and the dark.[17]

In the first place, Emerson's essay to the reader in the first number of *The Dial* explicitly rejects that dial which is "the dead face of a clock" — the kind of dial that the word dial-plate refers to — and specifies instead "such a Dial as the Garden itself." The eighteenth-century deistical and mechanical and therefore "dead" (rather than "organic") dial metaphor of Goethe is rejected for the metaphor of a dial that tells "what state of life and growth is now arrived and arriving." Second, Carlyle is superfluous here, and indeed impossible, as an influence. Emerson had defended Goethe's *Wilhelm Meister* against the objections of Wordsworth on August 28, 1833 (Wordsworth had read only the first part).[18] As Emerson then was familiar enough with *Wilhelm Meister* to make a defense of it, he must for years have been acquainted with the passage that Carlyle cited from Goethe's novel in his lecture on "The Hero as Poet," delivered in London on May 12, 1840. From the novel, Wilhelm Meister's warm defense of William Shakespeare, in Book Three, Chapter XI, is paraphrased by Carlyle to read: "His characters are like watches with dial-plates of transparent crystal; they show you the hour like others, and the inward mechanism also is visible."[19] Goethe used the word *Zifferblatt*, or "dial-plate" of a clock or watch, not *Sonnenuhr*, which is the German for "garden dial."[20] It is at least arguable that Emerson had such a precise difference as this in mind when he made his distinction to his readers, many of them familiar with Goethe's work. In any case, as Carlyle's lecture was delivered about three weeks after Emerson had penned the letter giving the title of the new journal, Carlyle could not have exerted even an indirect influence on the decisions to call the journal *The Dial*.

The Dial, furthermore, may owe its title not only to the Transcendentalists' appropriation of the hermetic and romantic symbolisms, their liking for metaphysical poetry and its techniques, their inheritance of the Puritan habit of symbolizing the visible world, and even their platonist sensibility, but also to their use of an available journalistic convention. *The Dial* is related, as the title of a periodical, to such precedent journalistic names as *The Times* and *The Sun,* and Philip Freneau's tri-weekly paper of 1797-98, *The Time Piece;* and all are, in turn, related to the seventeenth-century fashion of calling the early news organs diurnalls, e.g., Samuel Pecke's *A Perfect Diurnall* (1642-43). The emblematist tradition of these early titles is exemplified by *The Faithful Post* (1653-55), which carried in its heading the crude picture of an armed equestrian postman; this usage has had a lasting effect on periodical nomenclature. *Esquire,* *The Atlantic,* and *The New Yorker,* as they exist in the 1960's, have adopted identifying emblems as consciously as have, in times past, *The Faithful Post* and *The Dial. The Dial,* within this particular convention of journalism, was simply following precedent in taking a title rather closely related to the already existing *Times* and *Sun* but not hitherto used. In this instance the Transcendentalists made the best of several worlds.

Once its symbolism had been exploited by the Concord Transcendentalists, *The Dial* as title or part of a title was variously used by its several editors, and in most cases used by them for its latent symbolism. Pictorial emblems of dials were used by *The Dial of the Old South Clock,* in the 1870's; *The Dial: An Occasional Publication,* in the 1890's; and, in the same decade, the prohibitionist *Dial of Progress.* The first pictorial device — it is too matter-of-fact a representation to be called an emblem — of a dial to be published by any periodical with *Dial* in its title was the picture of the clock face, or dial, on the tower of the Old South Church of Boston, used as headpiece for each issue of *The Dial of the Old South Clock.* This picture of a dial has nothing in common with the image presented verbally by the prospectus of the Boston *Dial* in 1840, and it falls outside the tradition of the Fuller-Emerson *Dial* except as an irresponsible appropriation — and a wrenching — of what had become by 1877 a richly significant title. *The Dial: An Occasional Publication* (London, 1889-97) first used the sundial as a pictorial emblem on its cover. Vol. I (1889) has as its cover design a woodcut — by one of the two editors, C. S. Ricketts, and engraved by the other editor, C. H. Shannon — of a sundial on a pedestal in a garden with a tree in the background, the whole surrounded by a wall. Vols. II-V (1892-93, 1896-97) use a different cover; also a woodcut — and by the same hand — this design uses figures and architectural motifs juxtaposed for the sake of symbolic significance rather than scenic representation. The dial here is a wall dial placed in the upper left corner of the cover design. It may be the American *Dial* of 1916 vaguely imitated for its house advertisement the cover design of the London *Dial,* I (1889) ; otherwise I have not found any connection — indeed, no mutual reference, even — of the two periodicals. *The Dial of Progress* (1890-1904?) of Mt. Pleasant, Iowa, also used the device of the sundial; the face, gnomon, and hour markings are turned obliquely to the reader in this simple cut.[21]

There was, in contrast, a literary symbolism in *The Dial* founded by Moncure D. Conway, who pursued verbally the symbolic meaning of the dial that the Transcendentalist *Dial* indicated in its prospectus. "What do you think," he asked Emerson, "of our printing on the title-page as a motto, the Inscription on the Dial in the *Jardin des Plantes*: Horas non numero nisi serenas? — as giving the Idea that our Dial marks the more sane and lucid intervals of men."[22]

The symbolism of the title seems not to have taxed the editors and publishers of *The Dial* of Chicago from 1880 until late in 1916. Five months after the sale of *The Dial* by the Browne family to Martyn Johnson, a half-page house advertisement in *The Dial* for November 30, 1916, reproduces a woodcut of a sundial on a pedestal in a garden, backed by an arbor; in the Chicago *Dial,* this is the first emblematic usage of the Emersonian title. At the top of the advertisement is the motto *"The Literary Timepiece of America,"* which also refers to Emerson's interpretation of the dial symbol in the original prospectus. The second translation of the metaphor into an emblem occurred with the issue of June 28, 1917, when George Bernard Donlin was Editor. This sundial is a circular disc, and its gnomon is a quill sticking out at an angle from an inkwell; it was carried on the masthead until October 5, 1918, when wartime economies forced *The Dial* to use a more Spartan format.

In 1920 Scofield Thayer and James Sibley Watson adopted, as the heraldic emblem of their *Dial,* a stylization of a Georgian wall-hung sundial. Used on the letterhead of Dial stationery and as the headpiece of the first page of every issue, this dial was one of four designs made for the purpose, probably by Bruce Rogers (who with Thayer designed the magazine), the other three unpublished designs now being among the Dial papers. One may not assume in the emblematic use of the dial by Thayer and Watson that the title of their *Dial* connoted, by editorial intention, the manifold significance outlined in the prospectus of the original *Dial.*

In *The Dial* of Thayer and Watson there is no extended editorial comment on the significance of the dial as the emblem of and the title of their journal. The only metaphorical application is to be found in the editorial "Comment" for January 1921, written by Scofield Thayer. Here Thayer visualizes the emergence of the renovated *Dial* in the figure of an aging lady acrobat: "more or less coming up on her more or less renovated feet, clad in reassuringly genteel tights, she smiled stiffly at the world." Could two metaphors be more strikingly in contrast than Emerson's and Thayer's? One epitomizes the American Transcendentalist movement with its quasimystical worship of woods and fields and gardens, the very breath of American Romanticism. The other epitomizes the urban, antibourgeois rebellion of the 1920's with its self-conscious irony of the clown and the popular theater.

The emblem of *The Dial* of the 1920's was not so much a symbol as a simple journalistic identifying device, far from being the organic dial of the vegetation; nor did it connote for the new owners what the dial symbol so richly connoted for Emerson and Margaret Fuller, for Bronson Alcott and the readers of the original *Dial* of Boston and Concord. In the witty metaphor expressed by Scofield Thayer, one does not encounter the "prophetic imagination" housed in the figure of a clowness (Toulouse-Lautrec's famous lithograph immediately comes to mind; and Thayer owned the print). In her figure of burlesque one observes the artificiality of the decadent 1890's rather than the "organic" image of a garden dial. When Thayer and Watson appropriated the title of *The Dial,* they used it because it went with their majority ownership of the stock of the Dial Publishing Company. The fact remains that buying the title of *The Dial* meant, among other incurred responsibilities, participating in, and being responsible for, a particular journalistic family tree.

In the usage of the dial common to the various *Dials,* it is, to be sure, a natural symbol as well as a merely conventional one; but also it is a vital symbol. The dial is a natural symbol because, as the prospectus of Margaret Fuller's *Dial* explained, affinities existed between the two objects, the dial and the review. Both occupied stations on which the light might fall; which were open to the rising sun, of progress and of nature; and from which each correctly reported the progress of the hour and the day in meteorological and in cultural ways. Taken as an aesthetic convention by the editors of successive *Dials,* the dial became a convenient emblem for a kind of periodical — a conventional symbol.[23] As an emblem the dial became a vital symbol, too. It entered into certain activities, it emanated a peculiar *mana,* it was seen as possessing and communicating a kind of cultural vitality. For nearly ninety years the dial had a living significance in American letters.

And now to distinguish. The significance of the dial as a journalistic emblem exists totally within the frame of reference of the American liberal tradition, but that tradition underwent a change in the early years of the twentieth century. Much that had once seemed radical to the generation of the Transcendentalists had come to be taken for granted by their grandchildren around 1900. A new rebellion was brewing, and although involved in it were socialist principles familiar to the readers of Margaret Fuller's *Dial,* and aesthetic principles familiar to the readers of Emerson's essays, the success of the new rebels in art and politics would end in America the age dominated by the culture of New England. Significantly, Herbert Browne, son of the founder of the Chicago *Dial,* once remarked that *The Dial* of the 1920's was a magazine his father "would not have liked."[24] As one of the chief organs expressing the older ethos, *The Dial* of Francis F. Browne survived the revolution, but it emerged, with vitality undiminished, as the organ most brilliantly expressing the new ethos.

That ethos of the New Movement in the arts and letters of the period 1912-29 has become dominant in American cultural life. The two literary periodicals that have since July 1929 appropriated the title of *The Dial* are epigones in the tradition of their more brilliant progenitor. *The Dial* of the 1920's.[25] *The Dial: A Magazine of Fiction* was published by the Dial Press of New York (originally founded in 1924 by Scofield Thayer but as an entity distinct from the periodical he edited then), in three quarterly numbers from Fall 1959. In the concluding pages of an issue occurred reprinted material from *The Dial* of Thayer and Watson, such as an essay by T. S. Eliot or another of the contributors to Thayer's *Dial,* but the magazine existed primarily to print fiction by house writers such as Vance Bourjaily. It has been superseded by *The Dial: An Annual of Fiction,* a subseries of Apollo Editions under the aegis of the Dial Press. *The Poetry Dial* of South Bend, Indiana, began its life of quarterly publication in "Wintertime 1959" and is a quarterly printing verse in the tradition of the New Movement of the 1920's. It is indistinguishable from dozens of little magazines of the 1950's except by its appeal to the tradition established, in part, in the pages of *The Dial* edited by Scofield Thayer and by its use of garden sundials as distinctive devices carried on its front cover and advertising brochures. Chiefly the two recent *Dials* attest the importance of *The Dial* of Thayer and Watson to the New Movement and attest, also, the vitality of the tradition, itself, of *The Dial*.

The Chicago DIAL *(1880-1913) of Francis Fisher Browne*

E XCEPT for seven brief lines, *The Dial* for May 16, 1913, ap-peared its usual decorous self, an accustomed anomaly in that "noisiest and least spiritual of all great cities," as one of its editors, Waldo Browne, termed Chicago. But the announcement made in those seven lines was momentous for *The Dial* and of a certain importance even to people in Chicago, birthplace and home of the journal since its founding in 1880. Barred in heavy black at beginning and end and placed at the very front of the issue, came the news:

> Francis Fisher Browne, founder of THE DIAL, and its
> Editor from the first issue (May, 1880) to the present,
> died at Santa Barbara, California, on May 11, after a
> long illness. A sketch of his life and work, with a sup-
> plemental reproduction of a recent portrait, will be given
> in our next issue.[1]

The next issue of the fortnightly journal, for June 1, pub-lished a handsome photogravure portrait of its founder and editor, followed by Waldo R. Browne's obituary sketch and appreciation instead of the usual leading article. This in turn was followed by several columns of tribute from those who had known Francis F. Browne as editor and as friend. Most of the homage was anonymous, but William Dean Howells is credited as saying that none of Browne's friends "were more truly and proudly his friend than I, or could have valued him more for those spiritual, intellectual, and moral qualities which in their peculiar concord rendered him unique in his time and place." Fulsome and touching — and ringingly sincere — these many brief eulogies united in praising Browne for his qualities of the New England gentleman and intellectual and in lauding *The Dial* as "the purest literary journal in this country," established as it was "in the camp of the Philistines." Francis Browne was placed alongside "Mr. Alden [Henry Mills Alden, the venerable editor of *Harper's*], — the last representative of a long line of scholars and gentlemen of that elder, perhaps finer, day." The next encomium is equally specific: "More truly than Oliver Wendell Holmes, he was the 'last leaf' of that magnificent cluster."[2] It was an ominous epithet, more ominous undoubtedly than the writer intended it to be.

Browne's death marks the beginning of the end of a period, and not for his *Dial* only. The representatives of that elder and perhaps finer day, the flowering of New England, were already on the defensive against the vanguard of the New Movement, and the younger, more vigorous writers and artists would win the struggle for a wider freedom of expression and for popular acceptance of startlingly novel forms, in literature and the fine arts, in which to couch what they had to express; theirs too was the struggle for social justice and, a concept not easy to formulate, the fulfillment of a cosmopolitan sympathy for all cultures. Sympathetic though Francis Fisher Browne and *The Dial* had been to the struggle for social justice and an American culture with cosmopolitan breadth, aesthetically they stood for a tradition that by 1913 had largely lost its vitality. Editor and journal nevertheless had made positive and solid contributions to the rise of their city and the Midwest, and for that reason the Chicago *Dial* of Francis F. Browne is well worth describing in some detail.

The American tradition of *The Dial,* as it relates to the original quarterly *Dial,* incorporates the histories of three discontinuous periodicals, *The Dials* of 1840-44, 1860, and 1880-1929. Browne's *Dial* gave specific expression to this continuity of a shared tradition. The first number, for May 1880, contained one of the earliest of all essays on Emerson's *Dial,* by Norman C. Perkins. The liaison between the two journals is expressed in the title of Perkins's essay, "The Original 'Dial' "; indeed, the essay infers the indebtedness of Browne's *Dial,* different as it was by intention and content, to *The Dial* of Emerson and Margaret Fuller. By such an overt acknowledgement to the still living editor of the New England *Dial,* Browne at once paid a debt to a literary and intellectual pioneer and firmly placed himself and his magazine in the then dominant cultural tradition, that of the flowering of New England.

Browne was aware also that his *Dial* was the third of its name, not the second. Whether he knew of Conway's *Dial* when he founded the Chicago *Dial* in 1880, he did not say editorially; but in a lengthy review dealing with Moncure D. Conway's *Autobiography,* in *The Dial* for October 16, 1904, Percy F. Bicknell devoted a long paragraph to "the brief but honorable life-history" of Conway's "monthly magazine of the highest class," quoted extensively from Conway's account of his short career as editor, and concluded that "thus ended the brief course of the second of the three 'Dials' that figure in our literary annals." A second reference to Conway's *Dial* is made in the anonymously written obituary of December 1, 1907, "Moncure Daniel Conway": "He removed to Cincinnati in 1856, and it was there that he was married. It was also there that he edited 'The Dial,' second of that name, a monthly magazine which lived exactly one year." Casual these references may be, but they do show an awareness of the *Dial* tradition on Browne's part.

Moncure D. Conway established a precedent in 1860 by using the title of *The Dial* for another periodical, which kept alive the heterodoxy of the original. It would be difficult to select a journal more opposite in tone and purpose, if not altogether dissimilar in principles, to Conway's *Dial* than was its successor, *The Dial* of Francis Fisher Browne. Conway gloried in what he termed his "theological and philosophical heresies" at last inevitably given vent in his magazine — an ironic self-contradiction of what he termed *The Dial's* promise "to register only 'serene hours.' "[3] Browne founded and published a *Dial* with the uncontroversial subtitle, *A Monthly Index of Current Literature*; and this subtitle did not belie the contents of the magazine.

The adventurousness of the Transcendentalist quarterly and *The Dial* of Thayer and Watson was a quality basic to their foundation, to their continued publication, and in the men and women who founded and edited them. To be sure, founding and publishing the Chicago *Dial* involved risk, but this was a perfectly straightforward hazard of commerce.

Francis Fisher Browne was a Massachusetts Yankee and veteran of the Union Army, who after his demobilization in 1863, at the age of twenty, gradually made his way westward. In Rochester, N.Y., in 1867, he married Susan Seaman Brooks; they had six sons and three daughters, and widow and children survived him. Coming to Chicago the year he was married, Browne turned to the printer's trade that he had learned on his father's small New England newspaper; he also gained a literary bent from his father. William Goldsmith Brown had published two volumes of poems, among them "A Hundred Years to Come" and "Mother, Home, and Heaven," and Francis Browne, though not a poet, was a critic and reviewer of ability and a biographer as well, his most notable work being *The Everyday Life of Abraham Lincoln* (1886), whom he was said to resemble in appearance. Soon after settling in Chicago, in 1869, Francis Browne purchased a share in the *Western Monthly*, then just founded in Chicago. As chief and then, after the Great Fire of 1871, as sole editor, Browne transformed the *Western* into the *Lakeside Monthly*. According to the history of the *Lakeside* printed in *The Dial* for June 16, 1913, the *Lakeside Monthly* became a casualty of the depression of 1874, as well as of its editor's ill health, and for six years Browne was without a magazine of his own. Meanwhile, he had become an editor at the Chicago publishing and bookselling firm of Jansen, McClurg and Company, and in 1880, having secured the necessary financial backing from General McClurg, Browne founded *The Dial*; Jansen, McClurg and Company was the publisher.[4] During its early years, the magazine was owned by the publisher; after the summer of 1892, when Francis Browne purchased *The Dial* from Jansen, McClurg and Company, the Dial Company was organized as a corporation under the Illinois statutes. Browne was, of course, principal stockholder. William Morton Payne and Edward Gilpin Johnson became formally associated with Francis F. Browne in the editorship, while F. C. Browne, a brother of the Editor, and in charge of the business interests of the magazine since 1888, was appointed as business manager.

The first number of the new semimonthly *Dial* was dated September 1, 1892, and thereafter new numbers were issued on the first and sixteenth of each month. Two volumes a year were regularly issued. The corporate makeup of Browne's *Dial* is not known for most of its publication; not until the first "Statement of Ownership, Management, etc. of *The Dial*," in the issue of November 1, 1912, are there published the names of those owning stock in the Dial Company: Francis F. Browne, F. C. Browne (this member of the Browne family was no longer a stockholder when with the issue of October 16, 1913, the next annual statement of ownership was made), W. R. Browne, Rose E. Briggs, Mrs. Avery Coonley, Mrs. Sarah F. Gane, W. M. Payne, and Mrs. Coonley Ward.[5]

The Chicago *Dial* was so plain in appearance as to be nondescript. Issued in a self-bound cover, the quarto pages in their double columns seem more appropriate to *The New Republic* than to *The Dial* of Browne and Jansen, McClurg. In the beginning the contents appeared on the first page of each issue; after September 1884, the reviews, essays, and other material were sandwiched between pages of advertisements of Harper, Macmillan, Lippincott, G. & C. Merriam, Houghton Mifflin, and other publishers, and firms of booksellers and suppliers to the book trade and the reading public. Through the years the number of pages per issue varied, but more often than not it was apt to be twenty-four. Twelve monthly numbers sold for the annual rate of $1.50; special rates were given to groups. On September 1, 1892, this price went up to $2.00 a year, when *The Dial* became, according to its subtitle, *A Semi-Monthly Journal of Literary Criticism, Discussion, and Information*, published on the first and sixteenth days of each month. In an advertisement in the issue of November 1, 1893, for its offshoot, The Dial Press, the magazine stated that its typography — *"spoken of by The San Francisco 'Argonaut' as 'the journal de luxe among American literary periodicals' — is an example, in one direction, of the work done at this establishment."* Frank L. Mott describes the typography as "excellent," and the Chicago book designer Ralph Fletcher Seymour recalls that Francis Browne's "brother and an assistant, Mr. Gillespie, set its pages from type cast by Bruce Brothers eastern foundry. The face was good old Caslon."[6] This *Dial* looked easily readable and soundly serviceable, but to nobody could it seem a thing of beauty. Browne generally made no attempt to avail himself of the new processes in printing and the allied graphic arts.

Resisting the temptation, in the editor's words, "to bid for popularity at the sacrifice, in some measure, of the high ideals set for the journal at the start," *The Dial* did not achieve a mass circulation.[7] Browne never revealed his circulation figures to either of the directories that listed these and other statistics; in 1898 the round number the *American Newspaper Directory* could estimate was that the "largest" figure for circulation ever accorded *The Dial* was 5,000 in 1893, and in 1908 the same compilation could only note that "No definite and satisfactory statement has ever been secured from this paper, but it has been credited with exceeding 1,000 since 1899 and including 1906." Herbert S. Browne, a son of the founder and for years business manager of *The Dial*, once said that 5,000 was an approximately correct figure for the magazine's circulation and thus corroborated Rowell's estimate of 1898. To compensate for the absurdly small circulation, Herbert Browne cited the loyalty of *Dial* subscribers. *"The Dial* never had a large subscription list, but it was a list with a high rate of renewals. We used to use *Who's Who in*

America as one important source of subscriptions. The percentage of returns from this solicitation would have made us wealthy if we had been selling any kind of manufactured goods at a reasonable profit."[8] Such approximations can only with generosity be said to constitute statistics, but it is obvious from them that *The Dial* by both intention and accomplishment never attained anything approaching mass popularity. The editor considered his magazine to be a fit companion to the British reviews such as *The Athenaeum* and to *The Atlantic* in America, rather than to the mass magazines.[9] At any rate, one must remain content with these gleanings, for, according to Herbert S. Browne, the business records of *The Dial* were destroyed when Francis Browne's heirs sold the magazine to Martyn Johnson in 1916.

As *The Dial* had such a limited circulation, the editor could make sufficient profit to keep going only if he did not pay his reviewers, and Browne paid his reviewers with review copies of the books sent them for review. The result was that these reviewers were apt to be younger men seeking the opportunity to break into print, although, to be sure, Browne was able to attract and to secure the loyalty of other, mature scholars. The editor did pay for articles that were not reviews, but at a rate that has never been specified for the term of Francis Browne's editorship. In his practice, Francis Browne simply followed the good old editorial tradition adhered to by Emerson and Margaret Fuller, of paying little or nothing for contributions. The wonder is that both *Dials* were consistently of such superior quality.

Browne's monthly index of current literature existed primarily as an independent critical journal rather than as a publisher's advertising medium. Its contents mostly consist of reviews and of literary essays, which are either critical or historical in kind. The first number, for May 1880, is representative of Browne's policy, which continued the literary tradition of the original *Dial*. The leading article is a review essay by the distinguished librarian and historian, W. F. Poole, entitled "Hildreth's History of the United States," and it is followed by four similar pieces. After these comes the most interesting piece of all, Norman C. Perkins's "The Original 'Dial,' " an attempt, five years earlier than George Willis Cooke's first essay, to give a detailed account of the first *Dial* and its contents and contributors. Perkins's sketch is followed by brief notices of current books, which, unlike the longer articles and reviews, are unsigned: "The Literature of Music"; "Briefs on New Books," a series of paragraphs, each devoted to a short review; and three sections of professional and trade gossip, "Literary Notes and News" ("Mr. Longfellow's 'Evangeline' has recently been translated into Portuguese"), "Personal Mention" ("George Eliot's marriage to a Mr. Cross is announced by cable from London"; "Miss Emily Faithful will come to this country in September, and spend the Autumn and Winter in lecturing on 'Modern Extravagance — its Cause and Cure' "), and "The Library." Modestly appended to these columns is a prospectus, "Our Intent."

This prospectus points out that the general plan and character of *The Dial* "are well explained by the contents of the present number," and that the present "arrangement of departments given on our first page will be maintained, with such additions and improvements as experience may show will best embody the leading idea on which the journal is founded." Briefly stated, the idea was that *The Dial* aimed to become "an intelligent guide and agreeable companion to the book-lover and book-buyer" who wanted but was unable to keep informed of the character of the "vast literary current" constantly flowing around him. Further, following the "most approved English and American methods," the leading reviews of the new *Dial* would — and in practice they did — "frequently bear the signatures of their writers." The writing standard would be "known capability and fairness" of contributors, "whose judgments will carry with them the weight of the best available authority for the particular work treated."

What is most striking about the prospectus is its adherence to the uncompromising standards of Emerson and Margaret Fuller regarding freedom of expression: "The editorial comments will be made with conscientious freedom of opinion." This tenet was to be adhered to not only by Browne but also by the editors of

The Dial of the 1920's, who consistently battled the censorship of a later day and even opened their pages to John S. Sumner's rebuttals of their own stand. Browne nevertheless defines certain limits to *The Dial's* freedom; he goes on to distinguish between "literary criticism" and a destructive "literary cynicism," and the prospectus promises that *The Dial*, "while sensible of the obligation to reject the bad and false," would be "no less mindful of the obligation to conserve the good and true in literature." This positive aim surely adumbrates what the magazine of Thayer and Watson announced in one of their advertising circulars of 1920: "THE DIAL does not aim to educate, but the editors honestly believe that the publication of fine creative and critical work is an enterprise in civilization which will do something to stir America from the apathy of the imagination which has fallen upon it."

Browne's prospectus concludes with a few words on the "minor departments," those added "to give variety" to the journal's contents and "to complete its character as a compendium of current literature." Readers are assured that these pages will be "as fresh and piquant at possible" and that the monthly lists of books — *"all New Books, American and English, received during the month* [just past] *by* MESSRS. JANSEN, McCLURG & *Co., Chicago"* — "will aim to be complete and accurate."

From time to time during the next third of a century, the contents of the Chicago *Dial* varied slightly. Picking a date at random, one observes that by 1905 the minor departments now included only "Briefs on New Books," "Briefer Mention," "Notes," and "Lists of New Books." But it is obvious that the original plan and format of 1880 remained unchanged essentially for over three decades.

Nor were there great changes of a kind less apparent to the casual reader. In July 1892, announcing "The Dial — Change of Ownership," A. C. McClurg and Company, the successor to Jansen, McClurg and Company, stated that their interest in *The Dial* was transferred to Francis F. Browne, "who has been its editor and a part owner since its commencement." The change was no doubt occasioned by a conflict of interests between an

editor who wished to bring out what the announcement termed
"a high-grade and wholly independent journal of literary criticism" and a publisher "anxious to issue a useful house organ."[11]
This transaction meant only that Browne's direction would continue more strongly. As the retiring publisher promised, the
public would see little or no change in the content and format
of *The Dial*.

Relations with McClurg were cordial, and he remained one
of the writers for the magazine. Also in 1892 Edward Gilpin
Johnson and William Morton Payne, who had contributed steadily for many years, became associated with the editing of *The
Dial*. In 1901, Johnson left the staff, but Payne remained and
regularly reviewed new fiction and poetry until October 1915,
when he terminated his associate editorship after having sold his
Dial stock in 1914 to a new publisher-owner.

The respect in which *The Dial* was held for a quarter of a
century was due almost as much to William Morton Payne
as to Francis Fisher Browne. Like the owner, Payne was from
Massachusetts; born in 1858, he was self-educated beyond his
training in the public schools of Newburyport, Massachusetts,
and Chicago, where he lived after 1868. Payne taught in the
public high-school system of Chicago after 1876 and, before his
appointment as Associate at *The Dial,* was literary editor of the
Chicago Morning News (1884-92). As a literary critic, he was
chiefly concerned with modern literature, especially poetry, in
English, French, German, Italian, and Scandinavian; in fact, he
translated from the Norwegian Björnstjerne Björnson's *Sigurd
Slembe* (1888) and *Amljot Gelline* (1917). Payne also edited such
volumes as *American Literary Criticism* (1904) and Swinburne's
tragedy, *Mary Stuart* (1905). Despite his lack of formal university
training, he edited a volume of *English in American Universities*
(1895) and taught as a lecturer in English literature at the University of Wisconsin in 1900, the University of Kansas in 1904,
and the University of Chcago in 1904. The University of Wisconsin honored Payne with its LL.D. in 1903. A bachelor, William
Morton Payne was nevertheless a clubbable man, and was a
founder and chief spirit of the famous Cliff-Dwellers' Club in

Chicago, where he took lunch every day. The respect and friend-ship in which his contemporaries held him are exemplified by his appointment as chairman of the committee on the Philolo-gical Congress held in Chicago during the World's Fair of 1893, when he was only thirty-five; and for twenty-six years, from 1889 to 1915, Payne was secretary-treasurer of the Twentieth Cen-tury Club in Chicago.

For almost twenty-five years, William Morton Payne was the guiding critical force of *The Dial.* The importance he attached to his post may be judged by his collecting his leading articles written for Browne in three volumes: *Little Leaders* (Chicago, 1895), *Editorial Echoes* (Chicago, 1902), and *Various Views* (Chicago, 1902). These collections constitute a treasury of received literary opinion in the genteel tradition, and to read them is both educational and humbling for a later scholar and critic. Widely sympathetic and astute as Payne was, he could, and did, remark that except for Hawthorne the 1850's must be remem-bered in a survey of American fiction only for two new names destined to outlive their generation: *Uncle Tom's Cabin* and *The Virginia Comedians.* As for the 1840's and Melville, the fifth decade of the nineteenth century "was distinguished by nothing more noteworthy than Herman Melville's stories of the southern seas, which appeared in rapid succession during these years," Payne wrote in *Editorial Echoes* (p. 109). Few of Payne's critical judgments seem as wrongheaded as the pair cited here; yet even these were in accord with the then dominant attitudes and dogmas of American letters.

As the owner and editor of the journal, Francis Browne supervised the editorial work generally, and when, with increas-ing frequency, he wrote for his journal, he usually contributed leading articles. Among the distinguished contributors of the 1890's were Melville B. Anderson, Katherine Lee Bates, H. H. Boyesen, Chief Justice Melville W. Fuller, Joseph Jastrow, Fred Lewis Pattee, Felix E. Schelling, Richard Henry Stoddard, W. P. Trent, Frederick J. Turner, and Woodrow Wilson. They and their colleagues gave *The Dial* its dominant, academic tone. In 1892 the editor wrote that *The Dial* felt it had reason "to be proud of a list that includes the chief justice of the United States, presidents or professors of twenty or thirty colleges and universities, and many of the most distinguished private scholars in the country."[12]

Once master of his own publication, in the years after 1892 Francis Browne expanded his enterprise to a modest but substantial degree. He weathered the panic of 1893 with no ill effects, apparently; indeed, his reviewers regarded the entire phenomenon with optimistic detachment.[13] Instead of failing, *The Dial* constituted the nucleus of a buisness that established in 1893 the Dial Press. The Dial Press apparently always printed its books privately and never engaged in the commercial trade. It announced itself first in *The Dial* for November 1, 1893, as prepared to undertake the publication of *"Authors' Editions or Private Editions of meritorious works in any department of literature."* Services to be rendered to its clients included complete critical and editorial aid, even to distribution of copies to the press and elsewhere. Estimates would be given on application. The Dial Press, as distinct from the publisher of *The Dial*, apparently existed alongside *The Dial* as a means of supplying profitable work for Browne's composing room.[14] Here, also, under the direction of Francis F. Browne's younger brother, Frederick C. Browne, the type for both text and advertising pages of *The Dial* was set and was made into large "forms" to be printed in another part of Chicago by the Henry O. Shepard Company. The Dial Press of Chicago had no corporate descendant and probably was not itself a corporation at all. The present Dial Press of New York has been from its inception early in 1924 a venture in the business of competitive, trade publishing. Unlike its predecessor in Chicago, the Dial Press of New York was established by Scofield Thayer as a corporation completely distinct from *The Dial* that he edited; Thayer's correspondence with his business advisor, Herman Riccius (Riccius to Thayer: November 7, 1923. Thayer's letters to Riccius: November 14 and December 31, 1923, and January 5, 1924), makes clear the corporate distinction between the Dial Publishing Company, which owned *The Dial* and which had descended as it were from the firm established by Francis F. Browne, and the Dial Press newly founded in 1924.

A second periodical grew out of the success of Browne's *Dial. Trade Book List,* begun in 1895 and issued by the Dial Press, was a monthly sold in quantities to booksellers as a throw-away for customers. It was edited by Francis F. Browne until 1913 and then by Herbert S. Browne. A convenient biblio-graphical record, it shared little of the tradition of *The Dial.*

Another magazine, itself of great intrinsic aesthetic interest, did impinge on the growth and formulation of the tradition of *The Dial.* The relation of *The Chap-Book* to *The Dial* is so important as to necessitate at this point some account of the for-mer and of the precise bearing its publication had upon the history and the content and appearance of *The Dial.* In July 1898 *The Dial* absorbed *The Chap-Book,* which since 1894 had been "one of the few magazines of the nineties which can be called the predecessors of the little magazines of the twentieth century."[15] Founded in 1894 by Herbert S. Stone and Ingalls Kimball, when both were undergraduates at Harvard, *The Chap-Book* was started primarily as a means of publicizing the books of the young firm of Stone and Kimball and of promoting its sales. In October 1894, *The Chap-Book* moved to Chicago, where Herbert Stone lived, and in 1896 his new publishing firm, Herb-ert S. Stone and Company, became its owner and publisher. Stone was assisted in the editing at first by Bliss Carman and then, in Chicago, by Harrison Rhodes. Originally a small duodecimo pamphlet issued semimonthly and selling for a nickel, in Janu-ary 1897 the magazine was enlarged to quarto size "the size of the English weekly reviews"; at the same time it introduced as a prominent feature "the publication of criticisms of important new books."[16]

Like Browne, Herbert Stone was aware of the new currents of art and letters in America and Europe; unlike Browne, how-ever, Stone was interested in publishing the work of artists who were in the swim of things. Moreover — and it would be difficult to overstress the importance of this point in the development of the tradition of *The Dial* — Stone and his *Chap-Book* brought a welcome variety to the aesthetic fare of their decade. The tradition of New England culture was — at least as regards high art — primarily a literary tradition. From the date of Emerson's *Dial* to that of Francis Browne's *Dial,* this tradition dominated the American scene. Now, with Stone's *Chap-Book,* a new and conflicting attitude would compete for dominance. The three decades 1900-1930 would see the gradual defeat of the older tradition and the partial victory of the tradition that evolved during what Margaret Anderson in her memoir of the period called a Thirty Years' War. *The Dial* of Thayer and Watson sought to mediate these incompatible views, as it were to interpret them to each other, but the journal perforce paid tribute to the tradition first announced in American journalism by *The Chap-Book.*

Even in its later and more repertorial phase, *The Chap-Book* consciously provided an outlet for the more advanced art and writing of the 1890's. In its issue for July 1, 1898, appeared a photograph of Rodin's controversial statue of Balzac; and in 1897 Henry James's novel *What Maisie Knew* was serialized in the journal. A curious echo of the reproduction of Rodin's *Balzac* — which had been exhibited in the original plaster at the Paris Salon in 1898 — was the reproduction of the same plaster statue in *The Dial* for May 1925 as the frontispiece illustration preceding the lead essay, Hugo von Hofmannsthal's "Honoré de Balzac," in Kenneth Burke's translation. "Notes on Contributors" for that issue meticulously outlined Rodin's career and the furore over the *Balzac* but failed to mention the earlier reproduction in *The Chap-Book.*

Essentially, the avant-garde art and writing of *The Chap-Book* had two sources, both of them European: the pre-Raphaelite movement of Great Britain and the *Symbolisme* of France. With all their divergences, both movements united in their emphasis on form and their self-sufficiency, as opposed to the ethical bias of American nineteenth-century art. The first number of *The Chap-Book* had reproduced Aubrey Beardsley's self-portrait, and in later numbers Paul Verlaine's *Clair de Lune* was translated as "Moonlight" by Gertrude Hall, while his *Epigrammes* was given in the original French. At first the languors of *The Yellow Book* and the gothicism of the Kelmscott Press dominated the pages of *The Chap-Book* — the very title is evidence of the latter influence — but its editorial tastes were not content with pastiche. The native genteel tradition was admitted with such writers as Col. Thomas Wentworth Higginson and Thomas Bailey Aldrich; and of the decade's most adventurous trends, the editors represented *Symbolisme* with Stephane Mallarmé and the new naturalism with Stephen Crane. With continued publication, the magazine displayed an ever-increasing ambivalence toward these new aesthetic movements and productions. Finally, in 1898 the genteel tradition itself smothered in swirls of commercial-patriotic twaddle. Then, of course, Stone's experiment ended.

As an avant-garde publication, *The Chap-Book* anticipated *The Dial* of Thayer and Watson in several respects, not the least significant being a similarity of editorial tastes for certain writers and artists. Of the famous posters used regularly to advertise *The Chap-Book,* one, the *Irish and American Bar,* was by Henri de Toulouse-Lautrec.[17] Both Toulouse-Lautrec and Aubrey Beardsley were favorites not only with Herbert Stone but also with Scofield Thayer, who brought together major collections of Toulouse-Lautrec's lithographs and Beardsley's drawings.

A second similarity between *The Chap-Book* and the last *Dial* is that both magazines sponsored selections of prose that had appeared in their pages. In 1896 Herbert S. Stone and Company printed *Essays from the Chap-Book* and *Stories from the Chap-Book.* In 1898 the publisher issued *New Stories from the Chap-Book.* As a similar project, in 1925 *Stories from the Dial* was published by the Dial Press. The difference between the two sets of publications is that Stone and Company stood directly to gain, whereas *The Dial* could have gained nothing from its venture except the glow of self-approval, since the Dial Press was not financially connected with the magazine.

A third and more telling similarity of the two journals is

that despite the lapse of time and the revolution of taste that
had occurred between the 1890's and the 1920's, *The Chap-Book*
and *The Dial* both published the work of such writers and
artists as Max Beerbohm, Claude Bragdon, Anatole France,
Thomas Hardy, Yone Noguchi, Joseph Pennell, John Sloan,
and William Butler Yeats.

With superficially differing policies — *The Chap-Book*
espoused the "new," and *The Dial* the "best" of old and new —
the two magazines in their days stood for artistic freedom, freedom of imagination and of expression. In its final notice, in
the issue of July 15, 1898, *The Chap-Book* asserted that in its
earlier days, "the effort to put the public in touch with the
new and curious developments in foreign art and literature"
had brought upon the young magazine "considerable ridicule
and as well won for it much admiration"; moreover, its "habit
of free speech produced a curious movement among the young
writers of the country," a flood of little individualistic pamphlets,
in well-nigh every village and town, "frankly imitating the form
and tone of THE CHAP-BOOK." *The Dial* of Thayer and Watson
veered away from the advocacy of any ideology, and its editors
steered a course between the Scylla of the instructive, moralizing, and, to them, stodgy monthly and the Charybdis of the
little sheet issued by propagandists for some special ism in art;
rather, their *Dial* purposed to put the best of both the new and
the old produced in America side by side with the best of the new
and the old produced abroad. What was new in the 1890's had
often enough become *vieux jeu* by 1920; but if publication in
both magazines of, for example, France or Yeats exemplifies
sheer editorial perspicacity, it also instances the similarity of
taste and policy and the real continuity of aesthetic tradition
shared by Stone's *Chap-Book* and *The Dial* of Thayer and
Watson.

Still a further similarity exists. The interest of Stone in
the looks of his magazine and his incisive and witty "Notes" commenting on current literary life, these two aspects of the first
six volumes of *The Chap-Book* have strong parallels in the interest of Thayer and Watson in the looks of their *Dial* and in Tha-

yer's monthly pages of editorial "Comment." Both magazines, especially, advanced the cause of serious illustration — Stone with his posters mostly in black and red and white and with his black and white cuts, *The Dial* with its color and its black and white reproductions of the work of literally dozens of twentieth-century artists, as well as with its great folio *Living Art*. One such poster advertised in *The Chap-Book* for November 1, 1896 — Frank Hazenplug's *Living Posters* — foreshadows in its title Thayer's own *Living Art*. Moreover, the use of pictures in black and white by *The Dial* of the Twenties — not to illustrate passages of text but to give pleasure as art — constitutes a device for which Thayer and Watson were directly indebted to the pioneering work of *The Chap-Book*, its posters and caricatures and serious drawings.

Also, unfortunately, like *The Dial* of Thayer and Watson, Stone's *Chap-Book* never achieved mass circulation and the resultant profitable advertising, and it "must always have had deficits to pay."[18] In October 1895 it advertised an actual circulation of 12,206 and a printing of 12,500 copies; in 1896 the latter figure seems to have reached 16,500, but such a pleasant state of affairs did not last.[19] Attempting to break into a large and profitable market, Stone made material changes in the contents and appearance of his journal. He was not successful. *The Chap-Book*'s final numbers exhibit a dismal falling away of quality, and where Aubrey Beardsley's countenance once had glimmered, there later glowered the faces of admirals and generals of the Spanish-American War. *The Chap-Book*'s pictures became photographs, and its writing became, mostly, topical journalism.

In point of quality, Browne's *Dial* remained much the steadier periodical, and it consequently held the professional respect of the editor's colleagues as well as the continuing interest of the magazine's readers. In July 1898, Browne's promise, on announcing the accession of *The Chap-Book* to *The Dial*, that the latter journal would "in the main adhere to the well-defined aims and principles which have governed it for nearly twenty years and have given it the favor and support of the American literary public" could have only been reassuring to his subscribers, and to the world of American journalism. As printed among the back advertising pages of *The Dial* for September 1, 1898, the page of "Press Comments on the Passing of the 'Chap-Book' " ranged from the gloating of the *New York Times* to the barely perceptible regret of the *Boston Transcript. The Dial* never achieved a circulation comparable to that of *The Chap-Book;* yet its subscribers were so loyal that a consistent if limited circulation of about 5,000 copies seems to have been perennially assured, in contrast to the erratic policy and circulation of Herbert S. Stone's magazine.

Browne's announcement of his good intentions in accessing *The Chap-Book* was sincerely made. The poems in *The Dial* continued to be few and far between, all the same, and the literary reportage remained dutifully compendious. What is important to note is that the tradition of *The Chap-Book,* if submerged, stayed alive; the journal was a harbinger of *The Dial* that Martyn Johnson reorganized in 1917, and its hopes flowered in *The Dial* of 1920.

In 1906 Francis F. Browne expanded his business again. For a number of years *The Dial* had contained a helpful column, "Topics in Leading Periodicals," and apparently in the belief that a selective running bibliography of this kind would have a profitable periodical sale, Browne started *What's in the Magazines.* Despite its modest price of a nickel for each monthly issue and an annual subscription rate of only fifty cents, *What's in the Magazines* never caught on. For all Browne's professional expertise, he could not make *The Dial*'s offshoot pay its way. In *The Dial* for September 16, 1907, a full-page advertisement for the new journal reproduced its cover for October 1907; but this and other puffs did not suffice, and in 1908 *What's in the Magazines* ceased publication. Like Browne's earlier and more prosperous *Trade Book List,* his *What's in the Magazines* is not so much a part of the developing *Dial* tradition as of the history of American bibliography. Yet it is true that all the *Dials* from 1840 to 1929, save that edited by Moncure D. Conway, consistently tried to print comprehensive sections of brief reviews, or even of titles, of books.

Under Browne's editorship, *The Dial's* prime immediate, practical value lay precisely in its bibliographical comprehensiveness. The critical opinions of Payne and the various distinguished reviewers were, to be sure, of a more permanent, if a less tangible, value. But the financial security of Browne's *Dial* as the one solid business venture in all the history of the several magazines that have shared the name — a vital factor in the continuity and development of the *Dial* tradition — depended not on the aesthetic attractiveness nor the intellectual worth of its literary criticism but on its prosaic professional usefulness to librarians and teachers, scholars and book collectors, throughout the nation. A reading of *The Dial's* own advertisements month after month, year after year, from 1880 to 1915 bears out this contention. These displays consistently described their own pages as constituting "preëminently a book journal, published solely in the interests of the book class, — the literary and cultivated class, the class that *buy books.*" *The Dial*, one learns, "is more generally consulted and depended upon by librarians in making up orders than any other American critical journal; it circulates more widely among retail booksellers than any other journal in its class." It is, lastly (and least importantly to advertisers?), "the accustomed literary guide and aid of thousands of private bookbuyers, covering every section of the country," according to a house advertisement of August 1, 1910. The approach there is nothing if not businesslike.

Besides his personal and corporate prosperity, the chief fruit of Browne's absorption with books as a business was the slowly maturing series of annual holiday issues beginning in the mid-1890's and achieving climactic inclusiveness in the latter years of the founder's editorship. So successful did the device prove that two holiday issues, December 1 and December 15, were run each year. In their preholiday announcement of November 16, 1911, the editors announced, with a forthrightness in aggressive contrast to the magazine's usual gentlemanly reticence about circulation and financial statistics: "The most important issues of *The Dial* of the entire year — the two special Holiday Numbers — will be published December 1 and December 15 . . . . Advertising

Rate $40 per page." This full-page advertisement was repeated twelve months later. The approximately forty-nine special pages in the "holiday issue" for December 1, 1911, that were devoted to holiday advertising from seventy-five firms sold for about $1960; however, in the next issue, that of December 16 — not December 15, as advertised — the sixteen such special pages grossed only $640.

At first Lucy Monroe Calhoun assumed the task of reviewing for the special holiday issues. Then Edith Kellogg Dunton traveled each year from her home in Rutland, Vermont, to the offices of *The Dial* and spent a month or so helping review holiday books and working in Browne's Bookstore. As author of a juvenile series, Mrs. Dunton proved especially valuable in reviewing children's books, according to Herbert S. Browne.

Another business venture of these latter years of Browne's career was his attempt to revive the dying tradition of the Chicago firms that combined the selling and publishing of books in the decades after the Great Fire. Browne's Bookstore was the distinguished expression of this undertaking. With its rooms designed "through the cooperation of Mr. Frank Lloyd Wright as architect," Browne's Bookstore opened in November 1907 in time for the holiday trade, and *The Dial* for November 16, 1907, had a full-page spread with a cut of a line drawing of the main salesroom. Mr. and Mrs. Avery Coonley interested themselves financially in *The Dial* and Browne's Bookstore, and it may be that they influenced Francis Browne in securing Wright's services as designer of the bookstore, for the Coonley house, then being designed, remains the supreme expression of Wright's domestic architecture of his earlier career. Despite the talks and teas held in such novel and elegant surroundings — Wright's first interior design for a commercial firm — Browne's Bookstore did not attract a sufficient clientele. It moved away from its original location in an upper storey of the Fine Arts Building and then moved again and yet again, to no avail. At last on April 26, 1912, the sons of Francis F. Browne, who were also the managers of Browne's Bookstore, informed their stockholders that the enterprise must be dissolved. The proceeds of the sale of

Browne's Bookstore were used to pay off the debts of the Dial Company and to develop its other assets, *Books of the Month* and *The Dial* itself.

The two sons of Francis Browne never agreed about the motive that prompted their father to seek outside capital to supplement his own money and to sink these funds amounting to $75,000 in the kind of venture that had already proven itself unviable in Chicago. Herbert Browne held that his father's original motive in starting Browne's Bookstore was his hope of interesting wealthy Chicago society in *The Dial,* so that he might experiment with ways of increasing the magazine's influence. Waldo Browne disagreed, although he gave no reason beyond commenting that the bookstore was a calamity for *The Dial* and everyone connected with it. Perhaps Browne's *Dial* was uniquely successful financially because in it Browne, the torchbearer of culture, and Browne, the printer and entrepeneur, both served the same cause without mutual frustration.

The teas and the talks and the intellectual dinner parties that characterized this phase of Browne's work find their counterparts in the *Dial* tradition in the oyster dinners and the *conversazioni* of the Transcendentalist Club and Margaret Fuller, as well as in the weekly dinner parties at his flat above the *Dial* offices that Scofield Thayer gave, in season, during his period as Editor. But *The Dial* made money not as a result of the *conversazioni* held by Miss Fuller, not from teas amid Wright's décor, and not, in the final phase, from the meetings among the Beardsleys and Chinese furnishings of Thayer's Village apartment; *The Dial* made money as a result of the hard work done in Francis Browne's composing room, and only then was it profitable.

In these years concluding Francis F. Browne's long editorship of *The Dial,* new names appear as contributors. By 1911, Grant Showerman, Lane Cooper, and Carl Becker had become regular reviewers, and Archibald Henderson was a writer for the magazine of some years' standing. In 1912 Norman Foerster was reviewing Bliss Perry's *The American Mind,* and Louis I. Bredvold contributed an essay on Walt Whitman. In the first half of 1913 appear other familiar names, of scholars then vigorous but now deceased: Horace M. Kallen, Henry Seidel Canby, C. F. Tucker Brooke, Vida D. Scudder, Killis Campbell. Clearly, the typical writers for the Chicago *Dial,* until after the death of its founder and editor, were reviewers or critics by avocation, members of the academy whose writing, too, was academic. It would be unjust and indeed untrue to categorize these reviewers with the upholders of the genteel tradition; it is true, however, that Horace Kallen, alone of them, sympathized with the New Movement in the arts and letters and continued to review for *The Dial* when it changed its policy and openly espoused the cause of the vanguard.

Only faint echoes of the struggle against the genteel tradition ruffled this calm. The issue for June 1, 1913, containing the obituary of Francis F. Browne, published William Rose Benét's excited letter opposing the policy and content of Harriet Monroe's new *Poetry: A Magazine of Free Verse*; Benéts letter was another item in the *Dial's* continuing and many-sided epistolary argument over the new poetry. According to the correspondent, Vachel Lindsay's "General Booth Enters Heaven" had been the only poem of distinction cited by Harriet Monroe in her contribution to the debate; and as for Ezra Pound, *Poetry's* European correspondent, he could not really expect any serious artist to swallow *Contemporania,* the volume of poems constituting his "final jape." Such liveliness could not greatly unsettle the deliberations of *The Dial,* however. In the same issue, Professor W. H. Carruth of the University of Kansas protested the Nobel award to Gerhart Hauptmann for his novel *Atlantis* — a tale of love at once illicit and intercontinental — as an affront to clean art and clean morals. By printing Professor Carruth's letter, *The Dial* attacked inferentially Benét as well as Pound and upheld the growing assaults on its traditional standards.

The tradition Browne thus supported was not that of the young iconoclasts in America and Europe but was that of New England. It was not, of course, by any means fully identifiable with the New England tradition of the Transcendentalist group of the 1830's and '40's. The tradition of Browne's *Dial* upheld freedom of expression, and this position it shared with the tradition of

Emerson's *Dial*. But where Emerson had not only stood to one side of the dead and dry Scholars but also had stood — as he wrote in his journal on March 20, 1842 — apart from the Humanity and Reform Men who trampled on letters and poetry, Browne took his stand with the learned, the writers and teachers and scholars who conserved and channeled into an academic pattern the willful stream of Yankee romanticism.

Around the turn of the century, the Emersonian tradition as it had been adapted by the dominant academic and literary groups had become a well-established, even orthodox attitude. To *The Dial* Emerson possessed "literary genius of the first order," and, according to W. F. Allen in the issue for May 1882, in his obituary notice of Emerson, even to those "who do not recognize the importance of his work, as a thinker, he is nevertheless the greatest American author." Its obituary notice of Horace E. Scudder in February 1902 affirmed that to be the editor of *The Atlantic Monthly* as "Mr. Scudder was for a number of years, is not to be conspicuously in the public eye, but to those who know how to recognize real values, it is rather more of a distinction than to be President of the United States." As Waldo Browne wrote in the obituary of his father, in the issue of June 1, 1913, Francis F. Browne himself "belonged distinctively to the older editorial school, — the genial and scholarly and urbane type" that also numbered among its representatives William Dean Howells, Henry Mills Alden, and "that small but shining company of whom Curtis and Norton and Stedman are perhaps the chief recent exemplars," in sum, the men who inherited or were assimilated to the New England tradition of the academy and, in the words of Browne's obituary, "whose lives were given with quiet steadfastness to advancing the interests and enhancing the honor of culture in America."

Improvement of oneself and of society was indeed a basic aspect of *The Dial* of Emerson and Margaret Fuller, and in its expression of the great theme, the Chicago *Dial* carried on the tradition in a confident and austerely pedagogical fashion. Browne's *Dial* did not bother to sugarcoat culture's bitter pill. The few poems it published from time to time are mostly of

negligible quality, while the customary breadth and acuteness of
its criticism, reviews, and comment reflect the Editor's real intentions in advancing the interests and enhancing the honor of culture in America.

Indeed, representative examples of *The Dial*'s original verse
do not exhibit Browne's journal at its best. Such examples occur
in the issue for October 1, 1893, where the unsigned essay,
"Literary Tributes to the World's Fair," includes, with the
editors' approval, three new poems. Harriet Monroe there recast
her "Columbian Ode," which had been "the literary feature
of the opening" of the 1893 Exposition, as an untitled sonnet
("I saw a water-lily rise one morn"). This effusion is followed
by another "felicitous sonnet . . . from Prof. W. P. Trent, of
Sewanee College . . . . an unfeigned and spontaneous tribute"
to the group of Exposition structures:

> Where once the red deer, chased by wily foes,
> Sought the broad bosom of the peaceful lake,
> Behold a noble city bloom and break
> Into a flower of beauty! It arose
> As though from some enchanter's wand, and glows
> With supernatural splendor. . . .

The final tribute of this collection — which included prose by
Paul Bourget and Walter Besant among others — was Richard
Watson Gilder's poem, simultaneously published here and in the
October 1893 *Century Magazine*; entitled "The Vanishing City,"
it was "an eloquent expression of the feelings awakened in con-
templation of the early disappearance of the Exposition." The
sporadic occurrence of short sets of verses in various issues indicated a lenience of editorial policy rather than any lessening
of the purpose to publish a critical review and compendium
of current literature.

It is easy, under the circumstances, but mistaken to con-
descend to the Chicago *Dial* as a fruit of "the genteel vine,"[21] as a
complacent and Alexandrian end-product of what had once
been a virile and creative tradition. The Chicago *Dial* did not
pretend to be other than a critical journal, with a mild, limited
interest in printing an occasional poem; like most successful

periodicals, it had the amiable weakness of publicizing in its own pages the story of its achievements. Its self-satisfaction and its critical attitude were not narrowly provincial, however, and one concedes "its essential good sense,"²² in its view of foreign as well as American letters. In the issue of September 1, 1898, a leading article written on the occasion of Leo Tolstoy's seventieth birthday gave tribute to his indisputable "preëminence among the writers of his country" then living and placed him among a "list of the half dozen greatest writers now living anywhere in the world," specifically in the same company with "Ruskin, Swinburne, Björnson, Ibsen, and Carducci." Such an evaluation is consistent with the urbanity of Browne and Payne and their conscientious cosmopolitanism.

The *Dial* deplored "the occasional aberrations of taste and extravagances of enthusiasm that may accompany the new habit of looking abroad for the fresh inspiration or the fertilizing thought," when it thought the occasion right.²³ In its earlier years it was not hospitable to Walt Whitman's work, nor did it praise Stephen Crane freely. The associate editor, William Morton Payne, in his review of *The Red Badge of Courage,* doubted that much of the belated praise of Crane's book was deserved. But Payne's adverse opinion was based, let it be noted, on what he conceived to be the "rough-shod descriptive style" of the novelist's psychological probings, not on any distaste for Crane's naturalism; *The Red Badge of Courage* gives for its central character "a psychological history that is plausible, but hardly convincing."²⁴ The *Dial's* taste was conservative, as it admitted, but it was neither quibbling nor thoughtless.

This point is important. Browne's *Dial* may have seemed occasionally to be out of sympathy with the new Midwestern writers and the new schools of artistic experiment and naturalism, but the cause for its adverse judgment usually was not outright moral queasiness so much as aesthetic fastidiousness. The genteel tradition as exemplified by *The Dial* imposed the obligation to inspect the world as well as to judge it. Such an attitude would oblige William Morton Payne in his review of *The Damnation of Theron Ware* to own that while the scene "in which the first climax is reached may be reproached with touching upon the borders of the sensual, instead of remaining within the limits of the merely sensuous," Harold Frederic's book was "one of the most striking and impressive novels of the year, or of several years."[25]

Francis Fisher Browne was not, in any sense, a hidebound reactionary. In politics he supported Governor Altgeld; in the arts he supported the cause of Frank Lloyd Wright, whose work in designing Browne's Bookstore caused Margaret Anderson, many years after the proprietor's death, to call it "the most beautiful bookshop in the world." In a literal sense, Francis Browne supported the cause of the revolutionary avant-garde in the arts, for in June and July of 1912 Margaret Anderson worked in Browne's Bookstore as a book clerk at eight dollars a week. Miss Anderson founded one of the three or four leading organs of the New Movement in 1914, and her editorship of *The Little Review* was made possible, in part, through Francis Browne's kindness in hiring her. Adjacent to the bookstore where Margaret Anderson worked were "the offices of the *Dial,* a literary review founded by Edgar Allen Poe, which at this time was edited by Francis F. Browne . . . . I was soon taken on the staff of the *Dial,*" she asserted in her memoir, *My Thirty Years' War,* "and initiated into the secrets of the printing room — composition (monotype and linotype), proofreading, make-up. This practical knowledge was indispensable when I began the *Little Review.*" Miss Anderson supplied, to a line by Matthew Arnold, a missing word that Francis Browne could not recall, and the incident "made a friendship: I became his chief assistant — chiefly poetic." But soon she "could no longer stay on the *Dial* — our poetry society had become too lyrical for Mr. Browne, who one day had been moved to kiss me. He was full of sincere and touching apologies the next day, but I was as sincerely displeased as he was contrite." Miss Anderson departed to become "literary editor of the *Continental*" magazine and to a career far different from Francis Browne's. But he had been kind; indeed his kindness and his encouragement of a literary young woman are the only characteristic qualities he displays in Margaret Anderson's anecdote.[26]

Francis Browne's liberality of spirit, his urge to seek the improvement of the individual man and, through that means, the improvement of society, his critical insistence on excellence in letters and arts, these, along with the more tangible name of *The Dial* itself, constitute the basic legacy that was passed from Browne to the men who edited *The Dial* of the 1920's. This later *Dial* would echo Browne's prophecy of 1902 (in the essay just quoted on "Literary Cosmopolitanism") asserting "one of the clearest signs of the times" to be that "the spirit of cosmopolitanism is destined to influence, if not to control, the future development of the leading literatures of the world." And he added: "No people henceforth will be free to live unto itself in the forms and ideals of its literary expression, or to condemn the works of the alien. Despite the occasional aberrations of taste and extravagances of enthusiasm that may accompany the new habit of looking abroad for the fresh inspiration or the fertilizing thought, the current now sets everywhere too strongly in the direction of intellectual free trade to be in danger of checks or reverses. For good or evil — and we need hardly say that we hold it for good — the world is fast growing one in spirit, and this at a time when, as never before, the instinct of race is asserting itself as a force in the shaping of politics, and the arousing, among men of the same stock, of a common consciousness of their own distinctive character." By 1920 the time had come for the New World to influence the Old in the direction of literary cosmopolitanism; in August 1920, the new *Dial* of Thayer and Watson would comment editorially that if there was anything serious in the American war aims and American procedure during the first year of peace, "then what we are and what we think ought to be of the highest inspiration and encouragement to our former enemies. We cannot fail to aid the new countries we helped to create by showing them the fruits of culture and democracy."

II

The DIAL *under Waldo Browne and Lucian Cary*

T*HE DIAL* in 1913 was not alone in falling on difficult times. The new forces had gathered to struggle with the old tradition and, in the outcome, to dominate it and absorb it. As early as the 1890's, Chicago had been as it were a major arena of the struggle. There Louis Sullivan and his colleagues evolved a new architectural style and also adapted European *art noveau* for the ornamentation of Midwestern skyscrapers. The Chicago group of writers captured the greatness and the miseries and all the booming, coarse vitality of their milieu in the novel terms of a close realism undeflected by the imperatives of the old morality and influenced, rather, by the revolutionary sciences of the nineteenth century. That learning itself found a home at the University of Chicago, established in 1892 as an expression of intellectual adventurousness. In Chicago in the 1890's, too, *The Chap-Book* introduced new forms in art and writing, along with new authors and artists. Despite defeats and reverses, despite apathy and active hostility, the forces of the New Movement gathered to the bursting point by the end of the first decade of the twentieth century.

Harriet Monroe founded *Poetry,* in Chicago, in October of 1912, and the Armory Show opened in New York on February 17, 1913, and in Chicago on March 24. Later that spring, in Paris, partisans of the old, lush harmonies battled adherents of the new, harsh stridencies in the notorious riot at the premiere of Igor Stravinsky's *Le Sacre du printemps.* The noise, real and metaphorical, occasioned by these significant events was an omen: the years ahead to 1920 would be as turbulent in the arts as in the politics of the civilized world.

Unlike *Poetry,* dedicated as it was to the younger and more experimental writers, *The Dial* entered this period as a chief representative of the intellectually liberal but as yet aesthetically conservative group that then dominated American cultural life. *The Dial* emerged in 1920 as a leader still, but a leader of the New Movement in arts and letters rather than of the old and predominantly literary tradition in America. The story of these years constitutes, then, the story of *The Dial* in transition.

When Francis F. Browne died, the offices of *The Dial* were still in the Fine Arts Building, at 410 South Michigan Avenue, where the magazine had settled in 1899. According to Ralph Fletcher Seymour, the designer and engraver whose own studio was in the same building, it was known as the most desirable location for artists. The Fine Arts Building had been originally constructed as a warehouse and sales headquarters for Studebaker wagons at a time when farmers were still accustomed to buy their farm wagons on Wabash Avenue rather than on Michigan. As Seymour tells the tale, the farmers refused to walk a couple of extra blocks just to look at the Studebaker line, and the building became a white elephant. A promoter named Charles C. Curtiss secured the building and obtained permission to remodel it into a home for the arts. Curtiss reserved the top floor for painters. And, says Seymour, as a "primary qualification (perhaps just a trifle heartless) for admission as a tenant he required a high moral and financial standard"; still another "desirable but not essential)" standard for a prospective tenant was "a reasonably high aesthetic ability." Having admitted his tenants, Curtiss "browbeat them into compliance with his standards. Nev-

ertheless about all the artists with enough financial strength to
pay the rent gathered there." Musicians and workers in the
various allied arts filled the lower floors. "Two or three theatres,
book lovers and dancing schools and semi-public institutions took
space. Some of Bernard Shaw's plays had their first American
presentation in this building," when Maurice Browne's famous
Little Theatre occupied space in the building. Transients connected with all these aesthetic activities frequented its galleries
and rooms.[1]

Seymour's memoir suggests that there were some artists who
lacked the funds to pay for quarters in Curtiss' building; and,
truth to tell, there were, in Chicago in these years, two centers
where artists gathered. One was in the south of the city, a small
neighborhood for the young and not yet arrived or, at least,
only just arriving. Here gathered the youthful protestants against
the genteel; their leanings were Socialist or anarchist generally,
but their prime common motive was not so much the ideological
struggle as the struggle to liberate themselves. On Jackson Avenue this group took over a set of exhibition booths left from the
World's Fair of 1893; Floyd and Margery Dell and their friends
and hangers-on lived in these gay, makeshift quarters.

The other center, the Fine Arts Building, was less raffish
and more genteel; its inner group called itself the Little Room
and met for discussion after symphony or play. A visitor to a
studio or office in the Fine Arts Building could hobnob there
with the sculptor Lorado Taft, the painters Ralph Clarkson
and Charles Francis Browne, or such commercial artists as the
Leyendecker brothers. He might run into Hamlin Garland (who
was Taft's brother-in-law) or Henry Blake Fuller in the studio
of the cartoonist John McCutcheon up on the top floor or down
in Anna Morgan's school of dance and drama. The Browne
family, headed by Francis Fisher Browne, cut a considerable
figure in the life of the building. Not only were their *Dial* offices
there but also, in Seymour's words, their "very swanky bookstore,
for which Frank Lloyd Wright designed the furnishings. In
them he presented his advanced and surprising notions for the
use of oak plywood for tables, cabinets, and chairs, wall panelling

and benches. Society adopted the store as a rendezvous for tea drinking and for listening to talks by distinguished authors." Although the store was conceded to be a wonder, "it did not achieve the more wonderful record made by the magazine."² It was in this melange of activity that *The Dial* had its not altogether congruous place — the Wright furnishings did not match happily with what Seymour called the good old Caslon face in which *The Dial* was printed. And with Browne's absence, the incongruity would almost immediately become quite sharply obvious.

"The air is so full at present of utterances concerning Futurists, Cubists, Neo-Impressionists, and Post-Impressionists, that it seems wrong to add anything to the dust," wrote Edward Everett Hale, Jr. (as Edward E. Hale), in a review-essay on "Vincent Van Gogh: Post-Impressionist," which followed by a few pages the tributes to Francis Browne. Hale's temperance and his measured, qualified praise of Van Gogh — his sympathetic and yet coolly analytical appraisal — express the attitude of the old *Dial* at its best.

But other reviewers felt no such qualms about adding to the dust. William Morton Payne, in an unsigned leading article in *The Dial* for December 16, 1913, entitled "A Few Words about Moss," was concerned to answer a correspondent who had informed the editorial staff that "in his amiable opinion, THE DIAL no longer gives 'the time o' day,' and 'is getting mossgrown.'" Payne recognized the times for what they were, but his reaction was against this most ominous characteristic of "our unsettled modern thought," with its "apparent readiness to cast off all the political, social, and ethical moorings that hold it in its hard-won haven, and to steer an uncharted course into the unknown." Considering the "querulously intolerant mind represented by the [*Dial's*] correspondent," Payne pointed out that the *Zeitgeist* was now "as perhaps never before, obsessed by nightmares," and needed to be restored to "the normal condition of waking mental activity." The criticism called for by the situation was a criticism of the open mind, criticism in the broadest sense — criticism of the mind that "is opened wide on the side of the past, with its accumulated wisdom for our guidance, and which respects, because of the immense weight of its authority, the present institutions and ideals into which the thought of that past has become crystallized."³

In the issue for March 16, 1914, in another leading article, also unsigned, Payne more directly attacked the forces endangering what *The Dial* stood for. He was aroused by the spirit of the new poetry. When Harriet Monroe had first issued *Poetry: A Magazine of Verse* in October 1912, *The Dial* had ignored Miss Monroe and all her works, although she had been a contributor, at the time, of many years' standing. Payne's essay, "New Lamps for Old," noted the new poetry and *Poetry* with a vengeance. Commenting on the first lines of Carl Sandburg's "Chicago," which *Poetry* had published in March 1914, *The Dial* said that "The typographical arrangement of this jargon creates a suspicion that it is intended to be taken as some form of poetry, and the suspicion is confirmed by the fact that it stands in the forefront of the latest issue of a futile little periodical described as 'a magazine of verse.'" The anonymous critic went on to disclaim any kinship between the work of Sandburg and the "divine art which Wordsworth defined, and Milton and Tennyson exemplified." Although Edith Wyatt defended Sandburg in a letter to the Editor in *The Dial* for May 1, 1914, Payne was unrepentant.

Payne's attack on the new poetry and the new art in general does not at all accord with the reviews and leading articles that Waldo R. Browne, as interim Editor, was publishing at the time. For example, in the issue of January 16, 1914, appeared Amelie K. Boguslawsky's essay on "Ellen Key: Idealist"; of Miss Key, a controversial figure because of her notions about love and marriage (a phrase she used as the title of what Miss Boguslawsky termed "her most indignantly contested book") and socialism, one learns that "With two inspired women like Maria Montessori, who is freeing children's souls, and Ellen Key, fighting against our effete conception of the moral law, in the vanguard, we are slowly realizing our possibilities in making the most perfect development of the individual the basis of social advancement." And in the issue of April 1, an unsigned leading article entitled "When Swords Become Plowshares" decried the American "ill-starred experiment in imperialism" and the slow groping of the "civilized world . . . toward organic unity of purpose" and gave special mention to the American Association for International Conciliation, which distributed without price pamphlets of interest to "all who wish to have a share in the promotion of the victories of peace." A third indication of policy was a long review, "A Great Contemporary Novel," signed by "W. R. B." Waldo R. Browne here praised unstintingly Romain Rolland's *Jean-Christophe*: "with this work M. Rolland takes his place in contemporary literature as the spiritual and artistic successor of Tolstoy. He becomes the standard-bearer around whom will rally the idealistic forces of the new century."

Thus by the spring of 1914 the editorial policy of *The Dial* was splintered in two, because of its attachment to the genteel tradition in the arts and letters, especially in poetry, and Waldo Browne's advocacy of internationalism, democratic socialism, and Tolstoyan idealism. The problem caused by this split in the editorial policy was not solved for two years, when the Browne interests sold *The Dial* a second time, to owners hospitable to the new poetry, the new theater, the new art.

Less than a year after the death of Francis Fisher Browne, Waldo Browne decided to leave Chicago for life in rural England — though he contented himself with buying a country house, Hillside Farm, in Wyoming, in western New York state — and Herbert S. Browne felt that by himself he could not continue with *The Dial,* as he had not been trained as an editor. The brothers decided to sell *The Dial* and sought a buyer, in Chicago or elsewhere. Albert H. McQuilkin, editor of the *Inland Printer,* was interested in Chicago's cultural and literary progress and did not want to see *The Dial* leave town. He therefore persuaded its publisher, the Henry O. Shepard Company of Chicago, to buy the Browne brothers out.[4] The old stockholders, among whom were the children of Francis Browne as well as William Morton Payne and the creditors of the Dial Company, sold their holdings to the Henry O. Shepard Company, which now become sole owner and publisher; the Dial

Company temporarily went out of existence.⁵ The issue of May 16, 1914, saw the transference of ownership, and the embarcation of *The Dial* on a perilous transition — a process during which at more than one point the magazine was in danger of suspending publication. Payne now neither held any Dial Company stock nor wrote for *The Dial*. Waldo R. Browne, too, severed all relations with the magazine and left Chicago, but his brother Herbert continued to act as business manager, for the Henry O. Shepard Company.

The new editor was Lucian Cary. Before editing *The Dial*, he had succeeded Floyd Dell as literary editor of the radical, avant-garde weekly "Friday Literary Review" of the conservative, Republican *Chicago Evening Post*, then just past the peak of its short-lived but brilliant success and, in the words of George Test, "as close to an avant garde periodical as a book review supplement supported by a conservative Chicago newspaper could be." It had been established by Francis Hackett in 1908, and upon his departure in 1911, Floyd Dell assumed the editorship. Cary became editor with the issue of October 3, 1913.

Lucian Cary had contributed to the "Friday Literary Review" under both his predecessors, and when Dell had been literary editor, Cary and George Cram Cook had served as the two Associates. Cook, whose sympathies were outspokenly socialist, wrote the weekly "New York Letter" in the "Friday Literary Review" for Dell and continued to do so for Cary. Cary contributed major reviews of new fiction when he was Associate; for example, he wrote the full-page review of Theodore Dreiser's *The Financier*, illustrated with a portrait sketch of Dreiser, which started off the issue for Friday, November 22, 1912. He was, of course, in sympathy with the aims of the New Movement and, also, with the liberal-socialist attitudes of what Bernard Duffey has termed the "Liberation."

As literary editor of the "Friday Literary Review," Cary presided over a sharply reduced supplement to the *Chicago Evening Post*. A handsome, small magazine supplement of eight pages, containing much literary news of topical interest and selling by subscription for a dollar a year, had been reduced, late in

Dell's regime, to a tipped-in page that was much more limited in its range and that sold to subscribers for seventy-five cents for a year's copies. Cary's two Associates were his wife Augusta and Cook. Shan F. Bullock continued to send in the weekly news-letter from London, and Louis Untermeyer continued to review the new poetry. Augusta Cary wrote the brief reviews of current fiction, and the "Friday Literary Review" occasionally printed (or reprinted, as the case happened to be) poems by Rupert Brooke, Lawrence Binyon, Laurence Housman, Joel E. Spingarn, and others. Besides unsigned editorial matter, Cary ordinarily contributed the important review of the week. For example, on Friday, January 23, 1914, the "Friday Literary Review" printed his review of Holbrook Jackson's *The Eighteen Nineties,* and the issue was appropriately illustrated by two of Aubrey Beardsley's magazine illustrations, his design for the contents page of *The Savoy,* Vol. I, and his cover design for the *Yellow Book,* Vol. I.

On Friday, May 15, 1914, the editorial column of the "Friday Literary Review" — written by Cary's successor, Llewelyn Jones — had some complimentary words to say about the editor just departed:

"All the good literary editors go," remarked Mr. Lucian Cary when he saw Mr. Floyd Dell leave Chicago to engage in independent literary work in New York, and when he took the chair vacated by Mr. Dell.

Now Mr. and Mrs. Cary illustrate the thesis there laid down. Mr. Cary joins the editorial staff of our admired neighbor the *Dial.* Mrs. Cary, whose *causeries* on current fiction have been such a pleasant feature of the Friday Literary Review for the last few months, has undertaken the truly heroic work of editing a magazine devoted to that newest medium for the criticism of life — the moving picture.

The next month, in its issue for June 16, *The Dial* carried Lucian Cary's first review of "Recent Fiction," the signature, so to speak, of his editorship at *The Dial.* Cary was a young Midwesterner from Hamlin, Kansas. When he joined the staff of

The Dial, he had worked as a reporter in Wisconsin and Minnesota as well as in Chicago itself, yet he never gained full recognition for editing the magazine. Despite his never being listed as Editor on the masthead, however, the contents of *The Dial* bore the unmistakable stamp of his change. Later he wrote for the films, an easy transition from journalism for a man whose wife was an editor of a movie magazine, and he produced a series of light novels, such as *The Duke Steps Out* (1928), and books on guns, such as *The Colt Gun Book* (1961). In 1914, Cary must have seemed a surprising addition to the staid staff of *The Dial.* At the age of twenty-eight, he was very much in earnest as an advocate of the new poetry, the new theater, and the new freedom of the younger generation. True, he was far from being in accord with either Chicago's Jackson Avenue or New York's Greenwich Village; nonetheless, with his penchant for Freud and Dreiser, Cary was accepted by the vanguard in Chicago as one of its own.

His months as Editor are distinguished by two features. While neither was new to the *The Dial,* both are important, though for different reasons. For the first time, the leading articles broke with the well-established policy of Francis Fisher Browne's *Dial* and openly espoused the cause of the vanguard in the arts and in its social and political rebellion. Also, for the first time the column of "Recent Fiction" appeared in most issues. Previously fiction had been reviewed every month or every quarter by William Morton Payne. The policy inaugurated by Lucian Cary was that of reviewing fiction rather more often than once each month, so that in the latter six months of 1914 covered by the fifty-seventh volume of *The Dial,* eight reviews of the "Recent Fiction" were printed in the twelve numbers constituting the volume. When Waldo Browne returned as Editor, in 1915, he followed Cary's custom of more frequently printing reviews of the latest novels.

The importance to *The Dial* of these columns of "Current Fiction" is measured by the fact that the Editor himself wrote every one during his term. His first review of "Recent Fiction" appeared in the issue of June 16, 1914, exactly a month after the Henry O. Shepard Company became the new owner and publisher, and his final review of "Recent Fiction," marking the termination of his editorship, appeared in *The Dial* of February 1, 1915. To the historian the importance of Cary's reviews of novels is considerably lessened by the fact that most of the novels he commented upon are of little account. At the same time, one must keep in mind the extenuating circumstances that Cary was an employee of the Shepard interests, that Herbert Browne was still active on *The Dial* as a business manager, and that Cary in all probability was bowing to direction when he reviewed so many novels of at best ephemeral interest.

Nor was William Morton Payne's final "Recent Fiction" of 1914 more distinguished for the novels under review than most of Cary's columns, except by the mandarin style of the older man. For example, of H. DeVere Stacpoole, Payne remarked that "The exotic fictions of Mr. Stacpoole are multiplying rapidly, and exhibit a growing power which is making this writer a man to be reckoned with." And of Zane Grey's *Under the Light of Western Stars,* Payne concluded, "there is no lack of excitement in the narrative, which has also a considerable admixture of romantic glamour and poetic charm. It 'reads' from beginning to end and mingles a good deal of humor with its melodramatic plot." It is only fair to add that in his preceding review of "Recent Fiction," in the issue of March 16, Payne had commented on William De Morgan's *Ghost Meets Ghost,* Gilbert Cannan's *Old Mole,* Eden Philpotts' *The Joy of Youth,* A. E. W. Mason's *The Witness for the Defense,* Robert Hichens' *The Way of Ambition,* Mrs. Humphrey Ward's *The Coryston Family,* Edith Wharton's *The Custom of the Country,* and three lesser works.

The first novel Lucian Cary reviewed was Theodore Dreiser's *The Titan:* "if Mr. Dreiser has failed to draw his figure he has done some astonishing things with his background. No other writer's view of Chicago is so individual or so effectively presented. I confess, also, to enjoying his ironies at the expense of the pillars of society, though it is silly to pretend that the *liaison* was as well established in the Lake Shore Drive of 1886 as it was

in the French farce of the same period." Of Arnold Bennett's
The Price of Love, in the same "Recent Fiction," Cary concluded
that it "is an excellent example of what a first-class craftsman may
do with a little material. Mr. Dreiser has collected ten times as
many facts and attempted an infinitely more important task than
has Mr. Bennett, but Mr. Bennett has done precisely what he set
out to do, which is more than any one can say for Mr. Dreiser."

By all odds, *The Titan* was the most distinguished American
novel Cary reviewed as Editor. Reviewing Joseph Hergesheimer's *The Lay Anthony* in the issue of September 16, 1914, Cary
thought that the first chapters were surprisingly good but that
the author ultimately failed because he was "bound to move
his readers at any cost. He is not satisfied with the stuff he
has in his head; he must dress it up with the stuff that he has
found in yellow newspapers and in the speeches of romantic
social workers." In the issue of October 16, Samuel Hopkins
Adams was explained as being "familiar enough to readers of
'Collier's Weekly' but hardly to those who buy novels — or rent
them for three cents a day. . . . while Mr. Adams is neither deep
nor delicate he is readable, in the journalistic sense" (the novel
reviewed was *The Clarion*.) Bennett, Hergesheimer, and Adams
do not demand a great deal from readers, and most of the American and British fiction Cary reviewed was of far less substance
than *The Price of Love*, *The Lay Anthony*, and *The Clarion*.

On the whole, what substantial fiction Cary reviewed was
European. In the column of "Recent Fiction" in which the book
by Adams was discussed, Cary devoted his attention to a novel
he classed with Rolland's *Jean-Christophe* and Nexö's *Pelle the
Conqueror* as outstanding in the processions of novels in series
that regularly came over from Europe. This was Louis Couperus'
Small Souls, the first volume of *The Book of Small Souls*. Cary
admired Couperus because the Dutch writer had made "a direct
attack on a certain sort of bourgeois society"; yet he was "not a
tractarian in novelist's clothes" but an exceptional artist in prose
fiction. In contrast was Cary's review, in *The Dial* for December 1, of H. G. Wells's *The Wife of Sir Isaac Harman;* despite
the influence Wells wielded on the liberals of the day, Cary

refused to take Wells as seriously as he took Couperus. *The Wife of Sir Isaac Harman* was found to be immensely interesting, but Wells was aspiring rather than iconoclastic, and unconventional rather than immoral — and why could the novel not have begun at the point where it left off? In the same column of "Recent Fiction," it is, again, a Continental writer who is the more admired; Anatole France's *The Revolt of the Angels* was praised for the novelist's attitude toward the world, "so gently skeptical, so appreciatively ironical," even though some readers would find France's typical paragraphs mildly distasteful. In his final review of "Recent Fiction," Cary commented upon W. L. George's *The Second Blooming,* Compton Mackenzie's *Sinister Street,* and Nexö's *Pelle the Conqueror.* He praised all three: George's work, an example of a novel that could hardly have been written a generation ago, was excellent, and *Sinister Street* gave a more complete account of the mind of a young man of our day than had been written previously in English. But the superlatives of the review were reserved for a Continental artist: no living writer perhaps was more at home than was the Danish novelist Nexö in the description of peasant and working-class life. In sum, Cary's "Recent Fiction" dealt mostly with the lighter, more ephemeral fiction of the time, although, obviously, the reviewer responded to the serious naturalism of such an American novel as *The Titan* or such a European novel as *Pelle the Conqueror.* Apparently he found no American novels of ideas comparable to *Sinister Street* or *The Revolt of the Angels.* In the "Recent Fiction" of July 1, 1914, for example, Cary wrote that Robert Herrick never completely forgot that his obligations to his public included that of educating it; yet he criticized Herrick's *Clark's Field* as employing precisely the same formula as Herrick's earlier *One Woman's Life.* Perhaps the basic value of Cary's fiction reviewing for *The Dial* lay in his attempt to deal comparatively with European and American work and in so doing to educate his readers (and possibly the writers among them) to expect competence of performance and truth of portrayal.

In any case, because of its limitations, "Recent Fiction" was not an adequate vehicle to express what the new Editor had to say. That was ready at hand in the leading article of each issue. Lucian Cary healed the split in editorial policy that had become evident by early 1914, and he advocated the new poetry, the new theater, and the new art with the enthusiasm that Waldo Browne had reserved for the utopian and social aspects of the movement. Beginning with the fall of 1914, the leading articles in every number exemplified Cary's determination to align his magazine with *Poetry,* the "Friday Literary Review," *The Trimmed Lamp,* and other journals of the Chicago vanguard. The series started disappointingly with "Greenwich Village," in the issue of October 1; as an assessment of the American Bohemia, the "parallel of the Latin Quarter," the essay fails to amount to much, because it is too even-handed. The writer saw the strength and weakness of the Village as lying "in the very fact that it is a community banded together for mutual protection and mutual stimulation under a convention designed to establish kinship among its members" — at its best, "perhaps the pleasantest society in the world; but it is seldom stimulating. [A college community] offers play without responsibility; the other offers gossip without malice. Both of these are happy manifestations of the human spirit, but neither is a substitute for the intellectual intercourse of equals."

A much stronger piece in the same issue was contributed by Alice Corbin Henderson, the associate of Harriet Monroe on the staff of *Poetry,* who reviewed a group of volumes of "Recent Poetry," one of only two such reviews that Cary published: T. Sturge Moore's *The Sea Is Kind,* Robert Frost's *North of Boston,* Dora Sigerson Shorter's *Madge Lindsey and Other Poems,* Patrick MacGill's *Songs of the Dead End,* and James Oppenheim's *Songs for the New Age.* Of Frost's volume, the most significant of the group, Mrs. Henderson wrote that it "leaves such a strong impression of men and women in the mind that one is led to think of it as a new novel rather than as a book of verse." And on the strength of this second volume of poems, the reviewer compared Frost "with Mr. John Masefield, Mr. D. H. Lawrence, and Mr. W. W. Gibson, the three English poets who are most eager in the attempt to express the gesture and feeling of everyday life in something other than 'the grand style.' "

It was also in this issue that a future Editor of *The Dial* made his second appearance as a reviewer. George Bernard Donlin, a young Chicago journalist, who edited the magazine in 1917-18, had first appeared as the reviewer, in the issue of August 1, of a volume of plays by George Bernard Shaw; of *Misalliance, The Dark Lady of the Sonnets, and Fanny's First Play,* Donlin had remarked that Shaw had done more than any of his contemporaries to encourage a moralistic attitude, albeit an attitude at variance with that convenient substitute for earnest thought that is traditional morality, and he had praised Shaw's intellectual precision and his concern with the education of the child. In line with the new editorial policy of admitting as contributors the younger and, politically as well as aesthetically, more advanced writers, Cary printed a second review by Donlin, of Ellen Key's *The Younger Generation.* "Miss Ellen Key's Socialism" was a more personally revealing review than that of Shaw's plays, and an equally friendly yet more temperate analysis than Amelie Boguslawsky's essay, of what must at that day have seemed to some people a dangerous advocacy of the great movement for social reform among the workers. Donlin characterized Miss Key as a fastidious radical with a bias in favor of the individual, one who did not believe in the efficacy of easy nostrums. He thought it characteristic of Miss Key's idealism that she accepted the communistic ideal of socialist reform without a rigid examination of the underlying economic argument. She did not concern herself with the machinery that would create the new socialism, as her acceptance of this ideal was the result of a feminine and sentimental revolt against suffering she believed to be needless. Donlin characterized this document as both rebellious and sentimental rather than informed and rational. He approved even though all the while he preserved an emotional distance a bit removed from "The Younger Generation." In two years, however, Donlin had cast his lot with them and would be editing *The Dial* as one of them.

One interesting result of Donlin's review was the leading

article for the issue of November 1, entitled "The Younger Generation," which analyzed the young people placing themselves in
that group. It was not, began the argument, composed of persons
of an equable cynicism nor those making a last stand for the
judiciary, the home, and Victorian literature; nor was it made
up of "the young poets who imagine they have invented 'poly-
rhythmics,' nor the young idealists who believe that the Industrial Workers of the World are about to establish the only true
democracy." Robert Herrick, Edith Wharton, and Theodore
Dreiser were too old; Arthur Bullard, author of *A Man's World*
and *Comrade Yetta* was, however, of it, for "without being a
propagandist, he is thoroughly at home with the emotion and the
personalities of radicalism," and though not the son of foreign-
born parents, "he is able to envisage America as a country inhabited by others than New Englanders." Of the poets, no younger
ones had written very much. In journalism, Herbert Croly,
author of *The Promise of American Life,* and editor of *The New
Republic,* the founding of which had just been announced, was to
be grouped with Bullard, as also were Walter Lippmann and
Francis Hackett. The shortness of this list was due to the fact
that, "As one of the younger men put it the other day, 'It is not
that we have nothing to say, or that we do not know how to say
it. It is that we have no place in which to say it.'" The writer
found the spectacle of youth struggling to express itself
sometimes comic but always moving and significant. He concluded by pointing to *The Masses, The New Review,* and *The
International* as being regarded by the younger generation with
an interest out of all proportion to their achievement, and even
of *The New Republic,* he said that its first issues were being
awaited as impatiently as though its potential readers had not
been many times disappointed.

At least one reader responded to the message of "The
Younger Generation," though in a manner not perhaps altogether
intended by *The Dial.* Its issue of January 15, 1915, is distinguished chiefly by Ezra Pound's combative letter to the Editor,
headed in the "Communications" as "A Blast from London."
It was directed against the sentence in the leading article in

"The Younger Generation" that had coupled Pound with Lord Tennyson: "The poets are more controversial than the novelists; it really matters to them whether one believes in Tennyson or in Mr. Ezra Pound; but the younger ones have written very little so far." Pound answered that it didn't matter whether the younger generation believed in Tennyson or in himself but whether they believe that poetry "had traditions, even traditional freedoms before, say, 1876; whether poetry is good or bad according to some standard derivable from the full mass of poetry of Greece and China and France and the world generally, or whether poetry is good or bad according to the taste of American magazine editors of 1876." Pound ended by appealing for some understanding of the reasons that so many members of the younger generation had become exiles: "It is not that the younger generation has not tried to exist 'at home.' It is that after years of struggle, one by one, they come abroad, or send their manuscripts abroad for recognition; that they find themselves in the pages even of the 'stolid and pre-Victorian "Quarterly"' before hustling and modern America has arrived at tolerance for their modernity."

Pound's letter is as significant as the leading article that inspired it, as both pieces indicate the extent of the change in policy of *The Dial*. Despite the restrictions imposed by the format, the traditions, and the interests controlling *The Dial*, and despite his status as an employee rather than a stockholder, Lucian Cary was, in these months at the close of 1914, attempting to transform the magazine into the journal most fully voicing the aspirations and discontents of the younger generation. This much is obvious. What becomes equally obvious is that Cary also had to continue policies that were not congruent to his primary aim. In *The Dial* for November 1, in which "The Younger Generation" was the leading article, there was, of course, the usual fodder of the old *Dial*. Charles Leonard Moore, in the second article of the issue, "Some American Pictures in the Metropolitan Museum," concluded that "Inness, Fuller, Homer, Sargent, and Whistler, these seem to be the high notes in American painting, at least as revealed in this collection." Far more conservative than Edward Everett Hale's praise of Van Gogh, Moore's essay sounds as though the Armory Show had never transpired. More hopefully, Louis I. Bredvold reviewed Henry James's *Notes on Novelists;* but William Kilborne Stewart's review of Houston Stewart Chamberlain's *Immanuel Kant* is merely another in the long line of *Dial* reviews of biographies of eminences.

By September 1, *The Dial* was beginning to take note of the first World War. "Casual Comment," the regular column of editorial opinion and topical notices, thus included three items about the war out of a total of thirteen, in that issue: it commented on Norman Angell's *Arms and Industry,* which was also reviewed in the issue by Edward B. Krehbiel; it reprinted a sonnet on the opening of the war by Alfred Noyes, a "clear-toned message from one of the most earnest of pacifists" ("Thus only should it have come, if come it must,/Not with a riot of flags, or a mob-born cry, / But with a noble faith. . . . "); and it applied the lesson of Caesar's *Commentaries* to current events in Belgium: "when the Teutons of that day, together with the Cimbrians, wished to enter the Belgian territory in arms, in defiance of international law, the sturdy Belgians withheld their consent and gave the said Teutons and Cimbrians convincing proof of their determination not to be intimidated or overrun by any arrogantly assertive military power from beyond the Rhine." By the first of November, "Casual Comment" was noting the effect of the war on the great Leipzig book fair (the impressions of the ALA representative there made "somewhat melancholy reading," despite the glamor of the presidency of the King of Saxony and the zestful spirit of the colorful delegations from the German university student societies). The same "Casual Comment" made the first of many complaints *The Dial* printed about wartime censorship, and in two items, it yoked the subjects of poetry and war. In the first of these, the editorial writer upheld the cause of the oppressed and impoverished artists — "Keats, Burns, Heine, Leopardi, and indeed one might add Dante, Milton, and Shakespeare" — who are forced to see the seamy side of life in the midst of material prosperity, and the gratuitous question was asked rhetorically: "What poet or composer has been given to the world by the imperial Germany that was started on its prosperous course by Bismarck and Moltke?" The column proceeded to plumb some sort of nadir with its admiration of the "eloquent protest" of an antiwar poem by Mrs. Caroline Fletcher Dole, beginning: "War! In this year of ourLord / Too late for the barbarous sword. . . ." Editorially, *The Dial* was shaken out of its preoccupation with what Charles Leonard Moore in the leading article for the issue of August 16 listed as "Woman's rights, Socialism, the uplift of the masses, questions of education," all the matters that "furnish material for contemporary European literature" and that were still forbidden to American readers because of what Moore termed "the spinelessness, the timidity, the insipidity of American Literature"; "like the Queen of Spain the American woman has no legs, and our lords of finance control too many publications and churches and professional parasites to have their doings questioned," he fulminated. This is not to say that the topics Moore mentioned ceased to occupy the available editorial space, but it is true that Cary, from August 1914 on, not only had to cope with the ordinary restrictions imposed on him but also had to devote an increasing amount of effort and wordage to the vicissitudes of the war. Just how willingly he did so is a question; the rather simplistic attitude in favor of the Allies that certain reviews and editorial comments made in the early months of the war were not at all in harmony with the ideas and sentiments uttered in *The Dial* by either Lucian Cary or Waldo Browne. This is one of the paradoxes of Cary's editorship.

Another paradox was typical of *The Dial* in the fall and winter of 1914-15: the good gray reviews were juxtaposed to the younger generation's incendiary advocacies. For example, in the issue of October 16, the reviews were those by Percy F. Bicknell of François Cellier and Cunningham Bridgeman's *Gilbert and Sullivan, and Their Operas;* T. D. A. Cockrell on J. A. Cramb's *Germany and England;* W. W. Comfort on C. Gasquoine Hartley's *The Age of the Mother-Power;* Frederic Austin Ogg on William Milligan Sloane's *Party Government in the United States of America;* George Bernard Donlin on Georg Brandes' *Friedrich Nietzsche;* and the Editor, as usual, on "Recent Fic-

tion." Except for the reviews by Donlin and Cary, the dominant
tone here is academic — intelligent, informed, liberal and humane
in outlook, interestingly written, but nevertheless academic. And
while *The Dial* had built its reputation precisely on this sort of
reviewing, the new policy was, albeit tacitly, opposed to the
received, the established — the academic. In the same issue, as
an instance of the new editorial policy, there appeared, as the
leading article, the first extended praise *The Dial* had ever be-
stowed on an American poet of the vanguard. "Mr. Vachel Lindsay" was the title of the essay, which praised "The Congo" and
"General William Booth Enters into Heaven," and other poems
by Lindsay, and concluded that "He may cease to grow as a
poet. He may have gone as far as he will ever go. In that case he
will never be held to have expressed the emotion of the Middle
West. But we do not know a young man of any more promise
than Mr. Vachel Lindsay for the task which he seems to have set
himself."[7] The very appropriate second article was Amelia von
Ende's essay on "New Tendencies in French Poetry," with its
mention of Arthur Cravan ("the nephew of Oscar Wilde"; he
was also the husband of Mina Loy, whose poems were published
in *The Dial* during the 1920's), André Spire, and Albert Londres,
and, in particular, the group of poets in France and Germany
who, though dispersed by the circumstances of the war, consciously allied themselves as disciples of Walt Whitman. Aspects
of Amelia von Ende's remarks were elaborated by Edward J.
O'Brien in a letter to the Editor printed in the issue of November 16, and entitled "The Young French Poets." In an effort to
suggest certain tendencies of interest to American readers, O'Brien
pointed out that "Young France today is enrolling under the
standard of M. Paul Claudel or of M. Nicolas Beauduin, according as it inclines to passive or dynamic life," he cited as the
organs of the young French poets *La Vie des lettres and La
Nouvelle Revue Française,* and he added that translations of their
work were currently appearing in such magazines as *Poet Lore*
and William Stanley Braithwaite's *Poetry Journal.*

In contrast to such engaged and enlightened comment, the
leading article of the issue in which O'Brien's letter appeared

was one of the weakest of the group printed while Cary was with *The Dial*. It is also one of two strongly contrasting leading articles on the theater and is important chiefly as revealing Cary's interest in the Little Theatre movement of the time. Entitled "Le Theatre Manque," the article discusses the work of the Drama League of America, the amateur theater, and the need for American playwrights: "We shall never have a living art of the theatre until we have living dramatic authors." This is all very well, but like the leading article on "Greenwich Village," it fails to amount to much. Perhaps it is to be taken as an objection to the fare of Maurice Browne's Little Theatre, which consisted largely of classics and importations.

The Little Theatre movement in Chicago was largely supported by the well-to-do and the wealthy in Chicago and its suburbs; and elsewhere it was a bourgeois movement. Indeed the honorable exception was constituted by the productions in Jane Addams's Hull House, and even here the aesthetically inclined bourgeois mingled with social worker, proletarian, and bohemian. The chief homes of the Little Theatre, as a movement, were Maurice Browne's Chicago Little Theatre and the small private theater established by the poet and playwright Mary Aldis on the grounds of her estate in Lake Forest. The emphasis was not so much on a theater of realism as on an expressionist, symbolist drama; successful performances of plays by Euripides, Synge, and Claudel indicated the bias of the group, which also performed the socialist comedies of Bernard Shaw. But even Shaw, with his intellectuality and wit and occasional fantasy, was attuned to the art theater of the few rather than to the commercial successes advertised in the Chicago newspapers and performed in the theaters of the Loop, for the prosperous thousands unwilling or unable to support performances of *The Trojan Women*.

Instead of asking for "living" dramatic authors, the writer of "Le Theatre Manque" might well have asked some questions about the social function of the Little Theatre movement in the campaign to liberate the arts and their audience, as well as the creative artist, from conventions that were outworn. Precisely that campaign of rebellion was examined in a later and very

different leading article, "Democracy and the Theatre," published in the issue of January 1, 1915. The attack here was
against the restrictive practices of the commercial theater. The
audiences attending the theater and paying two dollars for a seat
were, alleged the article, too "special" — too prosperous, too
limited in their interests — to be "representative of America, of
a democracy in which the average head of a family enjoys an
income of perhaps $600 or $700 a year." Fortunately, the "case
for the democracy of prose fiction, or of music," was a good
deal stronger: a novel could be read by several people sharing
a single copy, and despite the restriction of grand opera to half
a dozen cities where only the most prosperous attended the performances, "music travels wherever a piano, or a gramophone, or
a flute may go."

Two other pieces further distinguish the issue as remarkable, given the context of *The Dial* in those years. For a second
time, the new poetry was reviewed. Another poet prominently
connected with *Poetry* and its group and indeed with many
among the Midwestern vanguard, Arthur Davison Ficke, reviewed
Arthur Stringer's *Open Water,* Amy Lowell's *Sword Blades
and Poppy Seed,* Harriet Monroe's *You and I,* and George Sterling's *Beyond the Breakers.* Entitled "Metrical Freedom and the
Contemporary Poet," Ficke's review was undoubtedly an oblique
response to the leading article of the preceding year, "New Lamps
for Old," with its attack on Carl Sandburg and *Poetry.* Although
Ficke discriminated among Miss Monroe's work — "her best
accomplishment is in the vein of less ambassadorial utterance"
than her poem about the Panama Canal, "Our Canal" — he
praised her "personal poems where she subdues a small world
more perfectly to the service of poetry." He caviled at the
"carelessness" of Amy Lowell's relatively untrammeled meters,
but he warmly responded to the metrical "Browning Centenary
Ode" of George Sterling — "It is interesting to speculate as to
how the devotee of *vers libre* would have gone about attaining
this lift and soar of flight. It may be doubted if he could possibly do so except by falling back upon that fairly regular
variety of free metre which Matthew Arnold and Milton some-

times employed." The trouble seemed to be that *"Vers libre* often comes perilously near to the less insistent rhythms of prose, and loses the characteristic power of poetry thereby." If the position taken was opposed to that held and put into practice by Sandburg, at least it was an arguable position and one taken discriminatingly and as it were within the family of the new poets, whereas Payne's condemnations obviated any discussion.

By comparison, the words of George Bernard Donlin about "Dostoeffsky," the second article for the issue, lack the fresh impact of Ficke's review, for *The Dial* had always been hospitable to European writers: "One comes from this great Russian writer with an uneasy realization of the superficiality of our average judgments, the thinness of our spiritual experiences. He increases our sense of wonder and our capacity for awe. And he adds immeasurably to our understanding of the pathetic dignity of the downtrodden and oppressed." Donlin's insight into the religious qualities that have attracted the readers of the mid-twentieth century to Dostoevsky's fiction reveals precisely what it was in the "great Russian writer" that, by and large, failed to attract the vanguard of 1912-14, who were engaged by issues more immediate and concrete than transcendental values, *pace* Waldo Browne and his views of socialism. Rather, it is Donlin's last sentence that aligns his essay so intimately with the views of the younger generation and that makes all the more understandable the admiration for Dostoevsky *The Dial* continued to hold into the 1920's, when it printed Charles K. Trueblood's review of *An Honest Thief and Other Stories* in June 1920 and reproduced Stuart Davis's drawing of the novelist in August 1920 (in company with Davis's drawings of Dreiser, Synge, and Ostrovsky).

Of all the leading articles published while Cary was Editor, the most forthright and least equivocal are two dealing with problems of censorship. That particular problem exacerbated both the vanguard and its opponents, the one because they were accused of writing about the unclean and abnormal, the other because they felt their opponents were spreading the contagion of immorality and decadence. These two articles, moreover, discuss for the first time a problem that increasingly engaged *The*

Dial and its contributors as the years went on, especially in the
period just after 1920, so crucial for *The Dial, The Little Review,*
and James Joyce. In the issue of December 16, 1914, *The Dial*
opened the long discussion with a leading article on "Our Hostility to Art," attacking a pamphlet *What Makes a Novel Immoral,* which had been written by a librarian, Corinne Bacon.
The stand of *The Dial* was now in pretty complete contrast to
its pronouncements when William Morton Payne had been the
dominant critical force in the affairs of the magazine. Miss
Bacon had said that such novels as *Jude the Obscure* and *The
Story of an African Farm* were untrue to "the normal life of
men and women." To which *The Dial* replied that the "only
answer to Miss Bacon's absurdities, which should not occupy us
for a moment if they were not so widely held as gospel, is to
repeat that a work of art, and none more obviously than the
novel, is a personal confession." As for Olive Schreiner, the
author of *The Story of an African Farm,* she assuredly was "an
abnormal woman, though we should prefer to put it less scientifically and call her an altogether exceptional woman." One wonders what William Morton Payne must have been thinking as
he read his copy of *The Dial!* Whatever his reaction, the essay
is important as a harbinger of the debate over censorship in which
The Dial of Scofield Thayer and James Sibley Watson, Jr., would
place itself during 1920-22 and even later, in 1927-28, when the
Editor and the Publisher of *The Dial* defended both the publication of *Ulysses* in Margaret Anderson's *Little Review* and the
importation, into the United States as a work of art, of Constantin Brancusi's *Bird in Flight.*

The second leading article on censorship, in the issue of
February 1, 1915, was the last *Dial* piece in which Lucian Cary
promoted the views of the younger generation. Reminiscent of
his review of Holbrook Jackson's *The Eighteen Nineties* in the
"Friday Literary Review," the *Dial* essay is a consideration of
the place of *The Yellow Book,* which seemed then that it would
be remembered as epitomizing the decadence of the years from
1891 to 1898, a periodical that was the "epitome of the exotic,
the bizarre, the wicked, of 'art for art's sake,' and the *fin de*

siècle." The article further suggested two matters of current importance: popular response to the little magazines in which the
new poetry, the new plays, the frankly naturalistic fiction were
appearing; and the freedom of publication necessary for survival
of the new art and literature. The vulgar legend about *The
Yellow Book* the article found absurd, and varying the arguments
used earlier against Miss Corinne Bacon, the writer held that *The
Yellow Book* was destroyed by the debacle of Oscar Wilde, itself
caused by the commonplace quality of the Victorian spirit, which,
whatever its faults, was not blind to its enemies. It saw Beardsley
in *The Yellow Book* and sensed, if it did not know, that Sir Frederick Leighton was no match for him. But although the criticism
of the period knew that such a poem as Ernest Dowson's "Non
sum qualis eram bonae sub regno Cynarae" was infinitely more
important in the consideration of Dowson than the morality of
his way of life, even while it was compelled, on the whole, to
sympathize with the art of these men, it paid its respect to public
opinion by emphasizing always their physical and moral weakness and never their artistic strength. It is no piece of rhetoric
that furnishes the refrain to Dowson's poem: "I have been faithful to thee, Cynara, in my fashion." It is, concluded the article,
the precise truth: "Dowson was faithful to an ideal of art. And so
was Beardsley. They literally died for it."

The rest of the issue was no match for that affirmation!
Arthur L. Salmon's essay on "The Poets of Belgium," with its
praise of Émile Verhaeren and Georges Rodenbach seems the
academic piece that it is, for all its enthusiasm for those poets
whose counterparts had been all too recently under violent attack
in *The Dial.* And Grant Showerman's review of some plays exem-
plifying "The Drama Movement" was, despite its awareness of
the popular Little Theatre movement in the Chicago area,
covertly an attack because in Richard Burton's *How to See a
Play* and Sheldon Cheney's *The New Movement in the Theatre*
and Archibald Henderson's *The Changing Drama* — the three
volumes under review — the authors allegedly counted all too
lightly "the classics, both ancient and less remote." During the
remainder of 1915 and on into 1916, Grant Showerman was one

of the chief hatchetmen used by Waldo R. Browne in his opposition to everything that Lucian Cary had all too briefly advocated in *The Dial* for those months of 1914 and 1915.

The comparatively minor place accorded poetry in Lucian Cary's scheme of editorial policy is exemplified by the secondary position in *The Dial* of February 1 of Salmon's essay on the Belgian poets of the Great War. In all the issues from June 1914 through the middle of February 1915, only one leading article was devoted to the cause of the new poetry, the essay on Vachel Lindsay. The two second articles on contemporary poetry were devoted, respectively, to young French poets and Belgian poets in time of war. Two reviews, by Alice Corbin Henderson and Arthur Davison Ficke, dealt with current publication in poetry; but it is obvious that these are minor in contrast to the eight reviews of "Recent Fiction" contributed by the Editor himself, or even to the two leading articles on the theater. And a letter by Ezra Pound was little enough to publish by way of publicizing the new poets. The main point is that Lucian Cary did attempt to spread the gospel of the younger generation and that its views of poetry occupied a minor place in that gospel as Cary understood it.

The most significant new writer to appear in *The Dial* in 1914 was George Bernard Donlin; during Cary's regime, Donlin contributed four long reviews and the second article on Dostoevsky. Undoubtedly his appearance as a contributor to *The Dial* in these months was one reason that when Martyn Johnson purchased the magazine, in 1916, Donlin returned as Editor of a *Dial* more fully attuned to his interests and point of view. Another contributor, Charles Leonard Moore, was represented by eight essays in the front pages; he may have been on the staff at this time, but as the magazine carried no masthead, his name does not appear except as an author. Two contributors continued to be published in *The Dial* during the editorship of Donlin and after — Horace M. Kallen and Carl Becker — and both were professors. The tone of Cary's *Dial* oddly wavers, indeed, between the comparative sobriety of the academic contributors — among whom were Edward Everett Hale, Jr., Archibald Henderson, Louis I. Bredvold, Norman Foerster, and Grant Showerman — and the polemic of the few members of the vanguard who appeared in the magazine. Of this younger, non-academic group, all were Midwestern; *The Dial* had not yet reached out to attract members of the New Movement in the East.

The appearance of the magazine remained as antiquated as ever despite the infiltration of the new spirit into its contents. Lucian Cary must have been greatly hampered by the format of *The Dial*. There was a much more considerable element of opposition as well. All this time, Herbert Browne was associated with the Henry O. Shepard Company and remained active on the business side of *The Dial*. His power in its affairs was decisive; by 1915 Cary was nearing the end of his editorship for the Shepard company, which was accustomed to publish periodicals such as *The Inland Printer* and *Business Equipment Journal* rather than the "Friday Literary Review," on which Cary had gained his training. Before Cary's final review of "Recent Fiction," in the issue of February 1, 1915, the publisher had persuaded Waldo Browne to resume his editorship, and Cary was out of a job. The forces traditionally dominating *The Dial* seemed once again securely in control, but the situation was the opposite of what it seemed. The transition of *The Dial* was an irreversible process, and the importance of Lucian Cary as its Editor is that in his brief period of editorship, he first aligned The Dial with the forces of the future.

III

The Brownes Sell THE DIAL *(1915-16)*

THE name of Waldo Browne first appeared as Editor of *The Dial* on the cover of the issue for April 1, 1915. He did not return to Chicago to live, however, and all in all, his notions of editorial procedure were not the most comfortable. He decided to work at his chores as Editor and to direct magazine policy from his farm in New York state, while his Associate, Alma Luise Olson, ran the office in Chicago.[1]

In addition to these editorial complications, the costs of paper and printing were rising steadily because of the inflation brought about by the war. As a result, *The Dial* immediately showed lessening profits and in a few months showed a loss for the first time in its history. Not unnaturally the Shepard company was anxious to rid itself of its latest acquisition, despite the cultural prestige of *The Dial*. Urged by the owners to buy back his family's old journal, Herbert Browne organized a company for that purpose, purchased *The Dial*, and thus became the President and chief owner of the new Dial Company. The first number to be printed by the Blakeley-Oswald Printing Company and issued by the new publisher was that of March 16, 1916. By the beginning of May 1916, other changes were in the offing. One, for the better, was accomplished with the removal of the Dial offices to larger quarters in the Transportation Building, at 608 South Dearborn Street. The other was the sale of *The Dial* by the Brownes in June 1916. It is from this not very encouraging background that the details of Waldo Browne's editorship emerge.

While he was Editor, *The Dial* continued to look much as it had in previous and quieter years. As for the contributors, one meets the names already encountered as reviewers and critics in the final period of Francis Browne's editorship and in the months of Lucian Cary's editorship. The younger men included Carl Becker, Hobart Chatfield-Taylor, Herbert Ellsworth Cory, Grant Showerman, Charles Leonard Moore, Raymond M. Alden, and Archibald Henderson. New contributors were few; among the more surprising were Mabel Loomis Todd and Arthur Davison Ficke, a holdover from Cary's regime. The appearance of J. C. Squire as a new contributor meant that *The Dial* under Waldo Browne did initiate one durable feature, the regular publication of literary letters from abroad, with gossip and reviews of current interest.

Perhaps most important of the contributors to *The Dial* of Francis F. Browne — indeed, he must have been considered indispensable to the purposes of Herbert and Waldo Browne in rescuing and recreating their father's journal after the aberrations of Lucian Cary — was William Morton Payne. Payne had sold his interest in the old Dial Publishing Company, but at Waldo Browne's persuasion he returned to *The Dial* early in 1915 as a reviewer and contributor of leading articles. He wrote the leading article for the issue of March 4, 1915, and thereafter contributed to every issue through October, except that of September 30, 1915. His resumed collaboration was short-lived. Editorial policy led in one direction, and Payne's tendentious literary journalism led in another. What brought about a permanent parting of *The Dial* from its leading contributor was a twofold disagreement over tendencies in the new schools of writing and the arts and in wartime politics. When the Shepard company had persuaded Waldo Browne to take up the editorial work of *The Dial* again, he had thereupon written Payne asking him, for the sum of twenty-five dollars per article, to contribute, as one of various writers, signed literary essays to be used to open each issue.[2] Despite Browne's qualification — which Payne ought to have interpreted as a warning to himself — that *The Dial* would keep more closely to purely literary interests than in the past, Payne apparently understood the invitation as meaning that his work would be accepted as freely by the son as it had been by the father. The former Associate Editor would soon learn his error.

Browne requested Payne to change the old policy of writing quarterly reviews of recent fiction to one of contributing weekly or at least monthly reviews of freshly issued novels, — "as is the custom with several of the English weeklies."[3] This kind of reviewing would of course be much more hasty and superficial than the considered criticism that Payne had previously been able to write; and for his labor amounting to a page and a half each issue Payne would receive the not very munificent sum, as Browne admitted it to be, of twenty-five dollars a month. Payne nevertheless took on the assignment, and between March 18, 1915, and October 28, 1915, he contributed eleven reviews of "Recent Fiction."

Before the latter date, however, he had quarreled with the Editor. Browne had warned Payne that the field of literature would be "wide enough to occupy all our space and energies, without straying off into the domains of education, art, politics, etc."[4] The older man proved temperamentally unable to heed this advice. Caught up in the excitement of the war years, this aging, gentle intellectual became a fierce partisan of the Allies against the Central Powers. Unaware that his opinions on art and education were outmoded and his politics repugnant to his editor, Payne asked Browne to accept an editorial on German war guilt; entitled "The Vision of Judgment," this would appear as the leading essay in *The Dial* for September 30, 1915. Browne refused: he was unhappy about the subject even before looking over the editorial; he was sick of all the debate about the war;

and in particular, he was opposed to "discussion from the violently partisan stand-point."⁵ On reading "The Vision of Judgment," Browne stood his ground, and saw to it that Payne no longer wrote any leading essays for *The Dial*. Instead of "The Vision of Judgment," Browne printed in its place in the issue of September 30, 1915, Grant Showerman's essay, "The Great Vocation." Payne's final contribution shortly appeared, a review of "Recent Fiction" in the issue of October 28, 1915.

Payne parted with *The Dial* because his opinions no longer represented fairly the general policy of the magazine. His reviews of the newer writers read more like arraignments of erring economists and moralists than like the uncontroversial, judicial analyses of works of art that Waldo Browne preferred. Of Galsworthy's *The Freelands* Payne wrote in *The Dial* for September 16, 1915, that it was, "as the name of the author almost inevitably implies, more of a humanitarian plea than a novel, or, at least, it [was] a novel so charged with a humanitarian message as to obscure its character as mere fiction." That a later age would only confirm Payne's assertion, as well as his adverse judgment, was of course no consolation in 1915. In the same issue and preceding the fiction reviews, Waldo Browne balanced Payne's attack on Galsworthy with Edward Everett Hale's tolerant defense: "It is a long time since we have had one who came so near the great satirist of an earlier day who gave us his view of partial evil and universal good" — an evaluation that now seems so overly generous as to be well-nigh indefensible. In the same review in which Payne had castigated Galsworthy for "in reality attacking the right of landed property," he admitted to a grudging admiration for Maugham's *Of Human Bondage* as "far from being, in the publishers' phrase, 'compellingly great,' but allowing once for all its inartistic method. . . . at least a noteworthy piece of creative composition." The trouble with Payne's critical bludgeoning was that it not only drove away paying customers but hit the wrong novelists, i. e., those in favor with the Editor.

Browne decided to make other arrangements for the reviews of fiction appearing in *The Dial*. In informing Payne of this decision, Browne admitted that his chief reason for changing reviewers lay in Payne's "ever-increasing bitterness of tone toward those who do not think as you do, — in particular, . . . toward the younger writers, such as Mr. Wells and Mr. Galsworthy, who are striving to rouse the social consciousness to some realization of the inequities and iniquities of our time." It would be fatal, the Editor concluded, "in the long run for any journal to stand sponsor for such a tone and such an attitude."⁶ One may surmise with what mixed emotions Payne severed his connection with *The Dial* and after three decades of service turned to other outlets for publication. At any rate, he did not long survive the break; he died in 1919, living to view an Allied triumph and a leftist *Dial*.

The quarrel between Waldo R. Browne and William Morton Payne dramatizes even more clearly than does the death of Francis Fisher Browne the crisis in the history of *The Dial*, a small crisis within that larger crisis changing the texture and the direction of American life. During his brief and unsettled period of editorship, from February 1915 to July 1916, Waldo Browne set *The Dial* off on a new trail, the end of which could not then have been foreseen. Deliberately he sacrificed something of the conservatism, the urbanity, the self-assurance of the genteel tradition for the aspirations of the liberal protest against the inequities of that day. This is not to indicate that *The Dial* followed the path pioneered by *Poetry*. Rather, Waldo Browne settled for the genteel tradition in the arts and letters and for the pacifist-liberal cosmopolitanism and the democratic socialist spirit in politics foreign and domestic. The ensuing problem thus has to do not with the loosening of the magazine's moorings that had held it in its hard-won haven but rather with the course it would steer through the uncharted war years.

Waldo Browne had been at once truthful and evasive when he had informed William Morton Payne that *The Dial* henceforth would be more exclusively literary in its interests than it had been in the past — presumably, under the editorship of the founder. Francis Browne's *Dial* had, of course, devoted its pages to literary criticism and bibliography, with an occasional foray by Payne into educational theory and practice. Waldo Browne's

Dial would gradually eschew the reviewing of most of the current publication in politics and history and politically oriented biography. After the beginning of 1916, for example, every one of the leading articles — which set the tone of the magazine — was expressly literary. Even such obliquely social and political essays as Benjamin Brawley's "The American Negro in Fiction" in the issue of May 11, 1916, or H. W. Boynton's "New Ways and the Old Person," which led the issue of February 17, 1916, were primarily literary, for all the authors' preoccupation with the social revolution proceeding about them. True, one comes upon an occasional political outcry, as in Benjamin M. Woodbridge's long review, in the issue of January 20, 1916, of eight books either about wartorn Belgium or by Belgians dealing with what Émile Verhaeren, in his book reviewed by Woodbridge and endowing the review with its own title, termed *Belgium's Agony*: "In M. Verhaeren's view, Germany has a barrack-bred culture but no civilization, for civilization means a sense of honor that outbalances egotistical interest, a spiritual force which is the negation of brute force." Yet Woodbridge felt constrained, in writing his review of Verhaeren's war poems, to quote his earlier words about the poet, written when he reviewed Stefan Zweig's *Émile Verhaeren* in *The Dial* for September 2, 1915: "This singer of force, of universal energy working with common interest toward cosmic progress, finds a higher ideal still — the union of humanity by universal love and admiration which joins men in their common purpose and musters individuals and nations into a common cause — the striving for the onward march of life. . . . " That is to say, in commenting on the Great War, *The Dial* through its editor and contributors repudiated the conflict. It turned away from the facts of brute force and nationalist hatred and instead advocated Waldo Browne's ideals of love and cosmic progress, which were compellingly set forth in works of literature and art.

The most forthright presentation of the position the Editor took toward the war he published in the form of a review, "Inter Armas Caritas," of Romain Rolland's *Above the Battle*. Printed toward the term of his editorship, in *The Dial* for March 16, 1916, the review had an importance for him that is gauged by its being the only one he signed fully while he was Editor (his previously printed review of *Jean-Christophe,* in the issue of March 1, 1914, was signed "W. R. B."). "If any remnants of human wisdom survive the era of murder and hysteria through which the world is now passing," Waldo Browne began, "it will be universally recognized that one great task must take precedence over all others, — the task of internationalism. Somehow, and soon, the ideal of human fraternity must be brought to prevail over the outworn creeds of nationalism and individualism." In the remote past of early 1914 — a reference to the leading article, "When Swords Become Plowshares," for April 1, 1914 — "we prided ourselves that progress had been made on that road, and that certain seemingly powerful influences — Christianity, Socialism, the comity of literature and art and science — were working on our side. What a ghastly jest now seems that belief!" With the call to arms, all the basic tenets of Christianity were flouted. International Socialism, "founded in the faith that the workers of all nations are comrades in a common cause," went down like a house of cards, "its adherents as ferocious as any in the work of mutual examination." The intellectuals of every country — "poets, novelists, philosophers, scientists, all who labor to keep alive those impartial fires that light and warm the spirit of man in its upward struggle" — consecrated their gifts to the fostering of hate and bitterness, "selling their intellectual birth-right for the pottage of a recruiting sergeant." For those who still held faithful to the vision of human brotherhood, the spectacle of war made the cup of tragedy run over "in these black days." But Waldo Browne refused to despair, for the cause of internationalism, he held, "though for the moment defeated, [was] far from being crushed." Of the "free and firm spirits of Europe," the followers of Jaurés and his work for unity, the foremost was Romain Rolland. Browne recommended Rolland's book under review because "No saner counsel has yet been heard above the turmoil of the conflict. Here is a book which proves that the tradition of Goethe and Carlyle is not yet dead, — that at least one man lives in the world who can speak out with something of their eloquence and their wisdom in behalf of the eternal claims of humanity."

These sentiments and Waldo Browne's advocacy of them in *The Dial* are important for several reasons. First and most obviously, by alluding to the vitality of the tradition of Goethe and Carlyle, Browne was appealing to the American Transcendentalist tradition, and its ideals of unity, cosmopolitanism, brotherhood, and progress through peaceful means. Second, Browne's review illustrates the vitality of that tradition in *The Dial* itself. Whatever other changes *The Dial* suffered, in one respect it was consistent, from its first issue of May 1880 to its last issue of July 1929: it advocated the ideals of the cosmopolitan spirit in literature and the arts.

Finally, the review is important as an extension of the quarrel between the Editor and William Morton Payne. Without doubt, the chief reason *The Dial* became increasingly "literary" was that the obsessive topical subject in 1915-16 was the first World War. As it was also a subject repugnant to the Editor, he turned to the more congenial field of literature and the arts; for works of art were, properly, vehicles of the gospel of universal love and cosmic progress. Viewed in such a light, the literary battles then raging were as reprehensible as the military conflict, and most probably Waldo Browne viewed the struggle between the defenders of the genteel tradition and the aggressive, younger vanguard of the New Movement in the arts and letters as strikingly analogous to the war between the Allies and the Central Powers. One recalls his letter to William Morton Payne and his opposition to Payne's violently partisan standpoint of discussion and ever-increasing bitterness of tone toward writers who did not think as he did. As the Editor wished as it were to be gathered into the artifice of eternity — away from all conflict, aesthetic as well as martial — *The Dial,* at any rate on the surface of events, did not so much participate in the literary wars of the time as it observed, reported, and opened to both sides its columns of "Communications" to the Editor.

What actually occurred beneath the surface of events was that Waldo Browne at best temporized with the spirit of the

New Movement, the same spirit to which in social affairs and politics he was so eagerly receptive; and usually, in matters literary and artistic, he rejected that spirit and its advocates outright. Thus in the very years, 1915-16, in which T. S. Eliot was revising the most basic concepts of poetry with the publication of his early poems in that other Chicago journal, *Poetry*, John L. Hervey, in "The 'Distinction' of Longfellow," his leading article for *The Dial* of January 20, 1916, was defending Henry Wadsworth Longfellow against an unnamed critic who had recently found Longfellow to be a poet "utterly destitute of 'distinction.'" Instead, concluded Hervey, "those of us who are so happy as to retain our youthfulness of spirit, our early sensitiveness and sympathy, to the 'grand climacteric' and beyond, will continue to cherish the poetry of Longfellow in our hearts, irrespective of the dicta of Olympian criticism." In sum, the controversial topic of the first World War was not to be faced directly in *The Dial*, and the adherents of the genteel tradition must not be angered but must, rather, be defended. The editorial attitude controlling *The Dial* in 1915-16 is suggested in Herbert Browne's remark to Fredric Mosher that *The Dial* of the 1920's was a magazine his father "would not have liked."

Granted the editorial bias, the reviews and critiques in the fields of philosophy, history, and political science nevertheless sustained the high quality of *The Dial* of Francis Fisher Browne; in this respect, *The Dial* of Waldo and Herbert Browne did not fall below the achievement of the journal of their father. Their *Dial* advocated their father's liberal, humane tenets, tenets of which they were avowedly proud. In at least two respects Waldo Browne carried on the traditions of Francis F. Browne's editorship. First, the father's open opposition to the Spanish-American War foreshadowed the son's pacifism and deep-seated mistrust of the opposing forces in the first World War. Second, Francis F. Browne's liberalism foreshadowed his son's. As Waldo Browne had written in his father's obituary sketch, when, at the time of the furore over the Haymarket Riots in 1886, "four innocent men were legally sacrificed to a public stampede of fear and revenge," Francis Browne had done "all that one man could do to prevent the wrong. When the American press was hounding Governor Altgeld to death, he prepared for one of the English reviews a detailed vindication of the man and his official acts, which, flouted as it was at the time of its appearance, now squares in nearly every statement with the generally accepted estimates." Waldo Browne retained his own strong personal interest in Altgeld, and in 1924 Macmillan published Browne's biography, *Altgeld of Illinois,* the first detailed study of its subject, and dedicated to "the Memory of My Father, Francis Fisher Browne." No doubt it was due to their sympathy with such views that *The Dial* continued to attract the historians, political scientists, and philosophers who had written for it in the past. Reviewing L. Cecil Jane's *Interpretation of History,* in the issue for September 2, 1915, Carl Becker insisted that the value of history is "not scientific but moral: by liberalizing the mind, by deepening the sympathies, by fortifying the will, it enables us to control not society, but ourselves — a much more important thing; it prepares us to live more humanely in the present and to meet rather than to foretell the future." One of the few writers who linked the old *Dial* of the founder with the ultimate *Dial* of the 1920's (his last signed piece was a long review essay of Bertrand Russell's *Philosophy* and *The Analysis of Matter* in the issue for August 1928), Horace M. Kallen wrote with ironic wit that philosophy maintains in its great tradition an essentially compensatory character: "The world is not one which was made for us. That slow reconstruction of it in fact, which we call civilization is too slow and too inadequate to satisfy the impatient mind," which leaps beyond to the heart's desire; such leaping beyond "has been predominantly the part of philosophy in its great tradition."[7]

The strongest contrast of Waldo Browne's editorship is that between his openness to new currents in philosophy and politics and his inhospitality to the new poetry. In this respect he was differing quite consciously from the policy initiated by Lucian Cary in 1914. Although for the first months of Cary's editorship there appeared no noteworthy contribution by an advocate of the new poetry — unless one wishes to suggest a letter sent in by Joel E. Spingarn and printed in *The Dial* for August 16,

1914, as a rebuttal to a leading article entitled "Grocer-Shop Criticism," which had appeared in the issue of July 1 — the "Recent Poetry" was reviewed at length, in *The Dial* for October 1, 1914, by one of its chief advocates, Alice Corbin Henderson; and the next issue, for October 16, had a leading article enthusiastically advocating the poetry of Vachel Lindsay. Now editorial policy changed radically.

When he returned as editor, Waldo Browne requested Payne to suggest "anyone for the poetry" and admitted to being at a loss for names of possible candidates for the work, as he so seldom read reviews of verse.[8] The result of his request was that Browne regularly printed reviews of "Recent Poetry" by Professor Raymond M. Alden of Leland Stanford University. Alden had been a founder of the Drama League of America in 1914, and at the time was only forty-one; he was thus a contemporary of Edwin Arlington Robinson and Sherwood Anderson, and might reasonably have been expected to share their enthusiasm for the new poetry. He had, to the contrary, no taste for *vers libre* or Imagism. His "Recent Poetry" for June 24, 1915, the first in his series of reviews, specifically castigated the Imagists, who when they spoke of their aesthetic principles, reverted to "obvious matters on which it is difficult to believe they have any peculiar claim"; Amy Lowell and John Gould Fletcher were two of the victims. Fletcher replied in a letter headed "An Imagist to the Defence," in the issue for August 15, protesting the reviewer's "dogmatic statements"; but in his appended reply, Alden gave back as good as he got: in answer to Fletcher's defence of the argument that the basic unit of the poem is the line representing a single breath, Alden asked, "if we assume that each line of verse does represent a breath, is not the art of *vers libre* alarmingly unhygienic, in tending to develop such irregular breathing as it implies?"

The chief victim of the review was Edgar Lee Masters; of "our group of modernists," the *Spoon River Anthology* "might be called the *reductio ad absurdum* of certain of the new methods, — such as the abandonment of conventional form and the fearless scrutiny of disagreeable realities." Alden held that all this formless blundering of Masters' poems, seriously purposed though it was, was, under whatever name it went, "of value to the thoughtful reader for inferential and negative rather than positive reasons." Like Imagist poetry, *Spoon River* exemplified the "deliberate abandonment of faith in a type, a law, an ideal . . . to which the fleeting momentary experiences caught up by the poet are referred." What is left is "a complete and instructive pathologic specimen of the process. What remains may be called poetry, but it is a poetry like that religion which has abandoned both religion's ritual and its faith." *Spoon River* was attacked and defended in the "Communications" column to the end of Waldo Browne's editorship.[10]

Despite his prophecies of doom, Alden was not as adamant in his opposition to new poetry as his fulminations against Miss Lowell, Fletcher, and Masters indicated. Mentioning Robert Frost's *North of Boston* in the "Recent Poetry" of September 30, 1915, Alden alluded to Alice Corbin Henderson's earlier *Dial* review and approved what he called Frost's "fresh line of experimentation in the new diction" (i.e., "the new development of a verse style which shall seem to be very nearly that of common speech"). What he always opposed was the abandonment of meter; the experiments of Frost and Edwin Arlington Robinson, which worked within the bounds of meter, Alden welcomed. Thus in his final review of "Recent Poetry" in *The Dial* for July 15, 1916, Alden found praise for Robinson's *The Man against the Sky* for the poet's "real creations in character" and his "interesting studies in the problem of making diction at once colloquial and poetical."

Through the winter of 1915-16, Amy Lowell remained the victim of *The Dial*'s animus against *vers libre* and Imagism. Perhaps two reasons account for the selection of Miss Lowell as a scapegoat; her accomplishment as a poet self-appointed to lead the vanguard combined with her eccentric personal habits — her cigar-smoking, her rising at late hours — to make her an easy mark; she was all the more vulnerable because she was a member of a great American family, the sister of the President of Harvard University. And her aggressiveness and high temper invited opposition. In the years since 1912, Amy Lowell had been trying to get herself into the good graces of Harriet Monroe and the group of *Poetry*; but her Chicago forays, while successful as readings of the new poetry, did not succeed in overcoming Miss Monroe's coolness to Miss Lowell's talent. Chicago gossip about the situation — which, in a letter to Harriet Monroe, Amy Lowell termed "a studied insult" — may well have affected the editorial attitude of *The Dial* toward the poet from Boston.[11] Of the Chicago literary magazines, not only *The Dial* and *Poetry* but Margaret Anderson's *Little Review* as well were all put off by Amy Lowell's well-intended patronage and by her advocacy of Imagism. They were not alone in the Midwest: although William Marion Reedy of *Reedy's Mirror*, in St. Louis, was more gallant in manner, he too permitted her opponents to attack her in his journal, and one contributor shared by *The Dial* and the *Mirror* was John L. Hervey, who followed Waldo Browne's editorial line in his letters and reviews for both magazines.

"Casual Comment" for November 25, 1915, devoted two items to attacks on two new poets, Amy Lowell and T. S. Eliot. William Stanley Braithwaite had just published in the *Boston Evening Transcript* his annual review and criticism of the publication in poetry for the year ending in September 1915; he selected as the best of 1500 poems by 530 writers he had read five, in the following order of merit: Amy Lowell's "Patterns"; Odell Shepard's "The Adventurer"; Margaret French Patton's "Needle Travel"; Robert Frost's "The Road Not Taken"; and Wallace Stevens's "Peter Quince at the Clavier." Many would take issue, asserted "Casual Comment," with Braithwaite "in his bestowal of highest honors upon the *vers libre* of the Imagist poet whose name stands first in the foregoing list; and, fortunately, everyone is at liberty to draw up a list to suit himself, an exercise as harmless and inconclusive as naming the ten or twenty or hundred best books." And, when Amy Lowell became a literary entrepreneur, *The Dial* noticed her no more favorably. In the issue for March 2, 1916, W. W. Comfort reviewed in scathing detail Miss Lowell's *Six French Poets*, studies of Émile Verhaeren, Albert Samain, Rémy de Gourmont, Henri de Regnier, Francis Jammes, and Paul Fort. Despite her claims for these poets — "now softly insinuating, now positively hysterical" — she left Comfort cold, "in no degree persuaded that we have been missing anything vital in the literary expression of French genius." He did not recall less judgment, "revealed in airy vaporings and in careless style," in any book of the sort; and he regretted that "such a new and attractive subject should have fallen to the lot of such unscientific and uncritical appreciation."

The distance between Braithwaite's sensitive percipience and Comfort's academic diatribe is one measure of the obtuseness and intransigence of *The Dial*, under Waldo Browne. Still another is its dislike of the work done by John Gould Fletcher, Amy Lowell, and Edgar Lee Masters — all, at that time, exponents of *vers libre,* Imagism, or both. Perhaps a final measure of the distance between *The Dial* and the forces then revivifying American cultural life is its attack on T. S. Eliot, made in the same column of "Casual Comment" in which the item about "Patterns" appeared.

"Casual Comment" began by again attacking Imagism as the enemy and pointed out that "Imagism and plagiarism" might be found "in rather surprising association" in *Poetry* for October 1915:

> The last piece in a group of what are described in the contents list of this issue as 'three poems by T. S. Eliot' consist of some dull data concerning one Miss Nancy Ellicott, evidently a person of extraordinary physical if not intellectual weight, who 'strode across the hills and broke them, . . . riding to hounds over the cow-pasture,' and who 'smoked and danced all the modern dances,' while 'her aunts were not quite sure how they felt about it, but they knew that it was modern.' (We like those aunts, by the way.) This stuff, with more of the same sort, is broken up into lines of irregular length, each of which begins with a capital letter. The old-fashioned reader to whom poetry is something more than capitalized lines of irregular length, if he finds sufficient entertainment in following this society

item to the end, will be struck at once by the closing
line, — a phrase whose genuine poetic quality stands out
in vivid contrast with the prose wish-wash that precedes
it. 'The army of unalterable law,' — there is a familiar
ring to that; and the old-fashioned reader will probably not be long in identifying it as the closing line, also,
of Meredith's fine sonnet, 'Lucifer in Starlight.' It
would be edifying to have Meredith's own comment
on this incident, and his opinion of the company into
which his fastidious muse had been forcibly introduced.
One can only agree with J. J. Healy when he remarks that "Free
verse was treated by *The Dial* [when Waldo Browne was Editor]
as a form of free living, in which advocates of the one supported
the other. Comment in *The Dial* on vers libre became at times
an exercise in derision."[12]

This particular exercise in derision was almost immediately
taken up. In the next issue, for December 9, John L. Hervey
used it as a weapon against Harriet Monroe in their drawn-out
epistolary feud over William Cullen Bryant.[13] Hervey, as one
of *The Dial*'s old-fashioned readers, castigated Miss Monroe for
her own castigation of Bryant's alleged dishonesty in allowing
his name to appear as "author" of a history of America when
at most he carefully had supervised the work as an editor. Then
Hervey tore into Miss Monroe:

> Speaking of proof-sheets reminds me, moreover, that
> Miss Monroe must herself be somewhat negligent in her
> inspection of those of the publication which she is be-
> lieved to edit. Else how could she ever have 'let past'
> that thrilling 'new' poem in a recent issue which, as has
> already been pointed out in THE DIAL, contains a sur-
> prisingly flagrant plagiarism from George Meredith?
> We are obliged, in the first place, to feel sure that
> Miss Monroe, as an experienced practitioner of the *ars
> poetica* not only, but one deeply versed in its repre-
> sentative exponents, must be familiar with a poem so
> celebrated as 'Lucifer in Starlight.'

Hervey added that Miss Monroe should have suspended publication rather than allow the offending line to appear — if her editorial sense were as rigorous as it seemed from her strictures on Bryant. Having scored that particular point, he was not content to rest but went on to suggest that if Miss Monroe had ever examined the proofs of the poem, she should have forwarded them to "the inspired (if somewhat at second-hand) author and requested a new, a truly 'new,' climacteric line." And at the same time, she should have pointed out "how grotesque was the marshalling, as the 'army of unalterable law' of 'Matthew' (Arnold) and 'Waldo' (Emerson). For she must be vividly aware of the fact that over a half-a-century ago the former gave to the world two of the finest poems in free verse that any language can boast; while the latter's influence (which was and still remains the most powerful ever exerted by an American writer) has ever been an incitement to revolt against 'art made tongue-tied by authority,' and life as well." Hervey's letter was of course disingenuous and was designed to score off *Poetry* and its editor. It is difficult to assume that he wrote the letter in good faith and out of honest indignation at Eliot's "plagiarism."

Precisely that notion had occurred to Arthur Davison Ficke, who wrote to the Editor from Davenport, Iowa, about the matter; his letter and Waldo Browne's reply, signed as the "Editor," concluded the "Communications" in which Hervey's polemic took up so much space:

Surely you do not mean to accuse Mr. T. S. Eliot of trying to 'put something over' when, in your issue of November 25, you use the unfortunate word 'plagiarism' in connection with your discussion of his recent contribution to 'Poetry.' I read the poem in question when it appeared; and, in common with you, I recognized the line, 'the army of unalterable law,' as the last line of Meredith's 'Lucifer' sonnet. It seemed to me then, and seems to me now, a rather neat transposition. The thought never entered my naive brain that Mr. Eliot (who is, by the way, entirely unknown to me personally) could have supposed that the line would be regarded as anything but a quotation. I could as easily

fancy a man trying to palm off as his own such phrases
as 'justify the ways of God to men,' 'I shall not look
upon his like again,' or 'To be, or not to be: that is the
question.' Plagiarism is the corrupt attempt to pass off
as one's own work the work of another writer; there is
no possible relation between it and Mr. Eliot's employ-
ment of a great and world-famous phrase in a position
where the reader's recognition of it *as* a quotation is precisely the effect aimed at.

Genuine plagiarism is a rare vice; it generally occurs
in regions where the reward for successful stealing is
considerably higher than any reward that the poet is
likely to get.

Waldo Browne refused to give an inch to the advocates of
the new way of writing poetry and made plain his attitude that
it has always been an elementary law of literary ethics that quotations must be enclosed in quotation marks, or otherwise plainly
acknowledged; and he said that the writer who fails to conform
to this law cannot justly escape the charge of plagiarism. "Of
course exception is commonly made in the case of such phrases
as those mentioned by Mr. Ficke, which have become counters of
our literary currency, worn thin by universal daily use." Eliot's
guilt lay in the fact that "Meredith's line is not of this class" — a
matter sufficiently proved, if proof were needed, by its absence
from the "ten or fifteen thousand 'familiar quotations' comprised
in the latest (1914) edition of Bartlett's standard reference book."

J. J. Healy writes that Waldo Browne's reply to Arthur
Davison Ficke "provided the spectacle of the editor rebuking one
of his own contributors." Actually, Ficke, a minor poet of some
distinction, had been a contributor to *The Dial* when Lucian
Cary was Editor and was known to be sympathetic to the forces
of renewal in poetry, but he did not sympathize with the poets
who used *vers libre*. Of Amy Lowell's *Sword Blades and Poppy
Seed*, Ficke held that its free verse poems only proved that "good
vers libre is absolutely not so expressive as good rhythmical verse."
The same review, in *The Dial* for January 1, 1915, concluded
that free verse often comes "perilously near to the less insistent

rhythms of prose, and loses the characteristic power of poetry thereby." This apparently traditionalist attitude undoubtedly opened the pages of Waldo Browne's *Dial* to Ficke on the one uneventful occasion on which, in the issue of October 14, 1915, he reviewed for Browne a volume of *Selections from the Symbolical Poems of William Blake*.[14] When Ficke's dispute with Waldo Browne arose, it was not concerned, really, with their differences over *vers libre* or Imagism but with the moral and legal problem of plagiarism. *The Dial* saw Eliot as another "bad" poet; he attempted to "put one over" both because he rejected meter and broke the stuff of his poem into lines of irregular length and because he plagiarized. Browne's answer to Ficke's letter thus failed to recognize the essential rightness of his stand, its combination of poetic insight and legal common sense that resulted from his own practice as poet and as lawyer. Instead, Browne's official sharpness — he signed his riposte as "Editor" — was designed to indicate to the readers of *The Dial* its shift in policy as regards the new poetry and the new poets. The ferocity of the attack on "Cousin Nancy" and its author may well have been due, also, as Healy suggests, to what Waldo Browne regarded as Eliot's impropriety in satirizing "the old figures" of the New England tradition, the chief representative of which was the second editor of the first *Dial*, the very man whose namesake Waldo R. Browne was.

No single poem engaged the energies of the old guard among readers, contributors, and staff of *The Dial* as did "Cousin Nancy," and for the remaining months of Waldo Browne's editorship, Raymond Alden was allowed to have his will with the modern poets. In the issue of January 16, 1916, one volume Alden reviewed was by Ficke, *The Man on the Hilltop*. Surprisingly, Professor Alden remarked that he counted himself among the admirers of Ficke's poems, though these kind words were offset by the rest of the review of a volume that the reviewer summed up as a "disappointment." Even here, the most "modern" of the poets commented upon were Ficke and G. K. Chesterton (whose "robust and whimsical personality" Alden responded to) .

For the rest, a good deal of sniping from both sides was to
be observed in the "Communications." Just when it seemed that
the new poetry would be lost amid the thickets of a protracted
correspondence about the identity of Shakespeare, one or another
of the guerrillas would pop up again and fire away. Thus in a
letter in the same issue in which Raymond Alden announced his
disappointment over *The Man on the Hilltop,* Harriet Monroe
— despite her wish not to strain the editorial hospitality by demanding further space "in the Bryant controversy" — made two
further points. First she quoted an unnamed young poet who
had asserted to her recently that "I now see that Bryant is a
symbol of everything that we moderns must sweep aside." Second, she insisted that she "was familiar with the Meredith sonnet
whose final line so neatly pointed Mr. Eliot's brief satire. As the
very point of its use was the fact that it was quoted, it never
occurred to me — and no doubt I speak also for the poet — to
risk a delicately humorous situation by attempting to intrude
therein anything so obvious as quotation marks." So that was
settled; what was not, what could not, be settled was the mis-
giving of the old guard about the writing of the vanguard.
John L. Hervey's defense of Longfellow, in his leading article
("The 'Distinction' of Longfellow") in the issue of January
20, 1916, was not enough to stem the opposing tide of correspondence. Nor was it enough that in the same issue W. H.
Johnson's letter to the Editor attacked the assertion of Harriet
Monroe's young poet about Bryant and in its turn asserted that
the "very idea of 'sweeping away' any of the old time classics
is puerile," and that the "militant with the broom on his shoul-
der" would never enter the profound depths of the human soul
plumbed by the classics.

     Bit by bit and step by backward step, the old guard had
to retreat, as is best revealed by the correspondence about the
Spoon River Anthology. After Raymond Alden's polemic review against the book had appeared, J. C. Squire, the new London Correspondent of *The Dial,* admitted in his "Literary Affairs in London" for February 3, 1916, that "Some people here
are enthusiastic about Mr. Masters' exposure of the human

race" in *Spoon River Anthology,* but that "others, amongst whom I count myself, think that the readableness of his book is largely accounted for by the originality of his idea of (I don't use the phrase in an offensive way) plying the muck-rake in a cemetery." A sane view, thought Squire, was to hold that Masters was "an American Masefield with more sense than Mr. Masefield, but a smaller poetic gift." Even this much merit was not allowed "that orgie of verse-prose," by Orvis B. Irwin in his letter printed in *The Dial* for March 30; *Spoon River* "contained none of the 'noble and profound application of ideas to life'" but was rather "a description of life as naked and analytic as we might find between the covers of a work on sexual psychology." An oblique attack on the form of *Spoon River* was made by Robert J. Shores in his letter printed in the issue of April 13, to the effect that "Free verse is verse which cannot be sold and which must, therefore, be given away." The only defense of Masters came from Urbana, in a letter by Professor R. S. Loomis, of the University of Illinois, who wrote, in the "Communications" for April 27, that *Spoon River* would be read in the more "constructive age" of the future "as a book that faithfully mirrored a microcosm palpitant with vitality, that did not blink the worms that grope through ordure, or dim the splendor of those energies that now seem groping too, but which, we may reasonably hope, if they are redirected, will evolve a new world." But, then, Professor Loomis did not review poetry for Waldo Browne's *Dial.* And Orvis C. Irwin, undaunted, returned to the battle in the "Communications" for May 25, to differ with Loomis and to conclude that while *Spoon River* "thoroughly analyzes and reflects a certain type of life; I seriously doubt that it meets the requirement of 'high seriousness' which makes poetry an art. As science, it needs no apologia; as poetry, it needs some chloride of lime." In the last issue of the Browne family's *Dial* (and the next-to-last issue that Waldo Browne edited), for June 22, 1916, Professor Loomis replied that "truth" was truth when it denoted a correspondence between idea and reality and that "poetic" truth seemed to denote a correspondence between idea and desire. He protested against all those poets and critics who demanded of all literature such a manipulation of life as assorted with their *a priori* theories and that would leave them "in much the same mood as a bottle of Burgundy." As for *Spoon River,* it was "a ringing challenge to the unreality, the hectic idealism, of much that passes for classical literature." Orvis Irwin was invited to bowdlerize Masters' volume if he would — "along with Chaucer, Shakespeare, the King James Bible, and several other reputable works" — but that done, "about nine-tenths of the book will still remain." To which Waldo Browne appended merely the editorial note that "We cannot devote further space to this discussion," a halt called because he had sold his *Dial.*[15]

Free verse was attacked, week after week. Raymond W. Pence ironically suggested in a letter published in the issue of February 3, that the reason the *vers libr*ists had not done away with the capitals at the beginning of the lines of their *vers libre* was their "lurking fear that their poetry may be mistaken for prose." In the next issue, for February 17, "Casual Comment" said that a vast storehouse of poetry, "in the 'new' manner, is contained in the country's commercial and journalistic records. Here is a field overflowing with unsuspected (and unsuspecting) bards, — a garden of poesy so boundless and luxuriant that the future anthologist may well despair when he comes to cull his bouquet of blossoms from its confines." Two examples were given:

I

Railroad stocks
More than held
Yesterday's gains
At the opening this morning,
3,000 shares of Pennsylvania, for example,
Appearing on the tape
At an advance
Of 1¼ points.

II

Children
Under five years of age
Will be carried free

When accompanied by parent
or guardian;
Five years of age and under twelve,
Half fare;
Twelve years of age
Or over,
Full fare.

And toward the end of Waldo Browne's editorship, when he must have known that the prospective purchasers of his *Dial* were advocates of the new poetry, he printed, in the issue of June 8, a letter from Alfred M. Brooks of Indiana University still holding out for — according to the heading given the letter — the "New 'Old' Poetry." Brooks realized, he said, that the old order changeth: "as many a soul dedicated to *vers libre* affirms," it had changed; nevertheless, whether "the change shall prove good, remains to be seen. The sole judge is Time. One thing, however, is certain. A wise man never accepts affirmation for proof." It was indeed most difficult to admit retreat.

In all the correspondence, only one note of hopeful compromise appeared, in a letter from the Reverend Nathan Haskell Dole, which Browne printed in *The Dial* for February 17 — when matters looked brighter for his future as Editor than they did in May and June. Alleging that he gained delight from the *vers libre* of the French poet Gustave Kahn as well as from Longfellow's "Psalm of Life," Dole was quite as evenly divided in his response to music; his pleasure in Mendelssohn's *Songs without Words* did not preclude him from "waxing enthusiastic over the splendid richness of Strauss and the frequently cacophonous originalities of Schoenberg and the high-colored magnificence of Debussy." "Let us ride Pegasus," the liberal clergyman concluded — "if we want to do so. If others choose a whirring motor aeroplane and stun us with its noise, perhaps they too will reach the top of Olympus even more quickly. It is a big little world, and there is room for all. So hail to Longfellow and Mendelssohn!" It was a rare tolerance of Dole's to which *The Dial* gave space, and it was unfortunate for Waldo Browne that he failed to share it. But perhaps, as old things are often said to do, the old *Dial* tradition was dying a hard death. In any case there is a glaring contrast between the Editor's poetical intransigence and his social and political liberalism, whatever caused the disparity.

And in any case, to the very end of his regime, and even beyond, in *The Dial* for July 15, 1916, an issue that he produced for the new owners before he left his post, Waldo R. Browne made it known that he disliked the new poetry; for in that issue he printed the last of Raymond M. Alden's reviews of "Recent Poetry." As unrepentant as his editor, Professor Alden concluded that "free verse, and the other more superficial elements of exaggerated romanticism, lend themselves rather too easily to the art of the parodist to make the results very highly worth while." In the very next issue of *The Dial,* free verse had its long awaited revenge: the only letter the new Editor printed was Amy Lowell's "In Defence of *Vers Libre.*"

The reviewing of fiction was in its way a more serious problem for Waldo Browne as Editor than was the reviewing of poetry, if only because — as he must have been made aware each day by the proximity of Herbert Browne's *Books of the Month* — of the disparity between the sales of novels and of books of poems. Also, there was the problematical connection between the social role of the novel and the social views of the Editor of *The Dial;* that too had to be considered. To the end of his editorship, Waldo Browne upheld such causes as the enfranchisement of the Negro, and the cosmopolitan ideals of what he termed "liberal culture." In the issue for May 11, Benjamin Brawley wrote a leading article on "The Negro in American Fiction," in which the conclusion was reached that "Some day our little children will not slave in mines and mills, but will have some chance at the glory of God's creation; and some day the Negro will cease to be a problem and become a human being. Then, in truth, we shall have the Promised Land. But until that day comes let those who mould our ideals and set the standards of our art in fiction at least be honest with themselves and independent" — a thrust at the stock portrayals of the Negro in the "novel as a vehicle for political propaganda" written by Thomas Nelson Page and Thomas Dixon. And the final column of "Casual Comment" that Waldo Browne wrote for his own *Dial,* that for June 22, 1916, protested the "periodical obsession" of the war years, in which even the "more serious monthly and quarterly current periodicals" gave "not far from one-half their contents" to subjects more or less closely related to the war: "Naturally the magazines of the belligerent countries give more space to the dominant theme than do those of neutral countries, though our own periodical literature is strongly enough tinctured with war. A query, futile and foolish enough, arises as to what imperishable literature might under less deplorable conditions have filled all those pages now showing only the panoply of war." Such attitudes were liberated and advanced. It took courage for *The Dial* to support the cause of philosophy, the cause of the Negro, the cause of international co-operation and peace in a decade of jingoism, race riots, and trench warfare.

At the same time, the Editor displayed a strange ambivalence. Responsive as he was to liberal, even radical developments in politics and society, Waldo Browne was at best temporizing in his attitude toward the contemporary developments in literature and the arts. Obviously, he was receptive to such "social" novelists as Galsworthy and Wells and in general to the writers seriously concerned with social problems. The leading article for the issue of March 16, 1916, was Edward E. Hale's fine obituary tribute to Henry James, however — a master very different from Bennett and Galsworthy and Wells: "Henry James moved on ahead, not following the ideas of his times, but aware of them and keeping well on in the lead. New notions and new fashions appeared and disappeared; he continued in his course. And in time people got back to his line, and then they found him well in advance. He had gone forward with other great minds of the time while we had been amusing ourselves." The next issue of *The Dial,* for March 30, 1916, had as its leading article William B. Cairns's "Meditation of a Jacobite," which defended the later work of James against "the ridicule and the more serious criticism of those who adhere to the *de facto* dynasty in fiction" with regard to the alleged lack of action in the novels, James's moral tone and purpose, and his later prose style. Cairns concluded that "there are many passages in the later prose which the younger man, even at his best, could not have equalled." The praise of Henry James — now safely dead — represents the extreme that the Editor allowed. Perhaps, with his father's death in mind, Waldo Browne was applying the adage *de mortuis nil nisi bonum.*

The regular reviewer for the column of "Recent Fiction" after Payne's departure was Edward Everett Hale, Jr., a contemporary of Payne, having been born in 1863. Like Payne, Hale was an advocate of the New England tradition usually summed up as the genteel tradition; he was the son of the famous preacher and author of "The Man Without a Country" and thus by heritage as well as education and livelihood — he was at this time, as for many years, a professor of English at Union College in Schenectady — shared Payne's predilections. But he was a mild and tolerant man. It was precisely the aggressiveness of Payne as reviewer of "Recent Fiction" that made Waldo Browne unhappy, and when Hale assumed the position of chief reviewer of fiction, with the issue of November 11, 1915, he did so because he had proven himself in years past as an appropriately conciliatory reviewer for the Brownes. Hale's reviewing represents the implicitly "official" attitude of *The Dial* under Waldo Browne's editorship, and his first column of "Recent Fiction" exemplifies the Editor's attempt to return *The Dial* to some mean of opinion at once critically respectable, gratifying to publishers and authors, and attractive to readers and subscribers. In the first sentence of "Recent Fiction," Hale announced, mollifyingly for Waldo Browne and his likeminded readers, that "Mr. H. G. Wells is the chief figure in English letters nowadays." Passing such rivals as Arnold Bennett, Bernard Shaw, and G. K. Chesterton, Wells "continues to think indefatigably, and to write almost as by instinct. He is, of course, deeply concerned with day-to-day anxieties of the war, like every other Englishman worth his salt; but he seems to be able to disregard that horror at least in his thinking." Wells was able to eschew the great horror of Armageddon and to focus his eye on "the limitations of the finer life," in *The Research Magnificent*. Mr. Theodore Dreiser did not hold Wells's "commanding position in letters," but his work was always worthwhile, "for he has certain fine possessions, one of which is a vast amount of knowledge of the thing he is writing about, which is joined to an unrestricted willingness and great ability to impart whatever he knows." On the other hand, the reviewer confessed to disappointment with Mrs. Humphrey Ward's *Eltham House,* and Judge Robert Grant's *The High Priestess* he considered as belonging, in so far as it is a particular story based on fact, to sociology or current history rather than to literature. One lack in all four novels under review, according to Hale, power of construction, "ability so to order one's material as to make the most telling effect on those who read," one of the great things of fiction preeminently possessed by Mr. James and Mrs. Wharton and others of their contemporaries. This final observation gives *The Dial* away: Hale's comfortable suavity had replaced Payne's elderly acerbities, but the aesthetic point of view, if not the temperament, had not changed. It was of course the point of view of the genteel tradition.

Other contributors to *The Dial* were less reticent than Hale. H. W. Boynton defended what Owen Wister in *The Atlantic Monthly* had attacked as the reigning school of genteel critics, who failed to influence the mass of Americans in their selection of popular reading. In doing so, in asserting that the best of the reviewers were almost painfully ready to welcome signs of promise in a new writer, Boynton must have realized that he was defending the critics and reviewers on *The Dial* — who did not attempt to influence the five million readers of Harold Bell Wright's books.[16] The positive directive criticism of current fiction that *The Dial* did attempt is illustrated by Boynton's leading article for November 25, 1915, "Just a Nice Story," in which he analyzed the meek virtues of "the-white-and-gold volume with the red-haired girl on the cover," the kind of fiction that its former devotees, now become addicts of the novels of sex, of crime, of sophistication, of the supernatured man and the denatured woman, pass on to one another as "just a nice story." Boynton defended this kind of commodity as having its proper function: "If we are going to look upon the world as it is not, we may quite as profitably see it the color of a rose-bank as the color of a dunghill. After all, daydreams are better medicine for tired hearts than nightmares are. We may safely let mother have her sweetmeat." In its condescension parading as tolerance and its cynicism posing as optimism, Boynton's concluding comment exemplifies the uneasy survival, passive and compromised, of the genteel tradition in *The Dial* during 1915-16.

The reviews and critiques in the field of the fine arts yielded no ground at all to the revolutionary forces of the New Movement. It is strange to read the few reviews dealing with the fine arts that Waldo Browne printed during his second editorship of *The Dial*. Perhaps his hostility toward the revolution in the arts was connected with his no doubt unhappy memory of the recent fiasco of Browne's Bookstore, which he had managed with his brother Herbert and which, despite its fame as the most beautiful bookstore in America in the last years of Francis Browne's life, had gone out of business with an indebtedness of $22,000. Whatever the cause, a gratuitous hostility by the Editor as well as by the reviewer is shown in the appearance of such a review as that on Willard Huntington Wright's *Modern Painting*, which was entitled "The New Painting," in *The Dial* for November 25, 1915. The reviewer, Grant Showerman, confessed to feelings of dismay, as a lover of art, when he contemplated the "history of painting as told in these pages." He denounced out of hand the schools he listed as the Impressionists, Pointillists, Divisionists, Chromo-luminarists, Neo-Impressionists, Cubists, Futurists, Intimists, Vorticists, Synchromists; there had been, he felt, endless theorizing, talking, and experimentation, "with a good deal of wild putting of things on canvas." And, he asserted, what Mr. Wright's criticism means "is that what the modern painters say of themselves is true because the modern painters say it is true." In sum, *Modern Painting* was seen to have a fundamental defect in its advocacy of "the doctrines of unrecognizability and the all-sufficiency of color." For readers who desired to regard the painter's art from a different angle from that of *Modern Painting,* the reviewer could not too strongly recommend the solid and spirited book of Kenyon Cox, who at this time was saying, "Detestable things are produced now, and they will be no more admirable if we learn to understand the minds that create them." For, held Cox, even if such works should prove to be "not the mere freaks of a diseased intellect," as they seemed to him, but instead "a necessary outgrowth of the conditions of the age and a true prophecy of 'the art of the future,'" they would not necessarily be the better thereby. "It is only that the future will be very unlucky in its art."[17] But as with poetry and the novel, the aesthetic message had been inscribed on the wall for all to see if for relatively few, at the time, to heed. Waldo Browne did not read the message; he was not interested in it anyway, as he reprehended any straying off by his contributors into art. *The Dial* soon would veer sharply away from this strictly negative policy.

Although the physical appearance of *The Dial* did not change essentially in the years following Francis Browne's demise, the numbers were irregular in periodicity. With the issue of March 4, 1915, *The Dial* became a fortnightly, appearing every other Thursday; there was a month's lapse between the issues for July 15 and August 15, 1915, as for each of those months there was but a single issue. A typical *Dial,* for February 3, 1916, began with a leading article, "On Reading for Enjoyment," by Charles Leonard Moore. J. C. Squire's special London correspondence, "Literary Affairs in London," followed, a monthly communication in the tradition of Charles Stearns Wheeler's German letter in Emerson's *Dial.* It is notable that, despite the ill feeling later to exist between Squire and *The Dial* of Thayer and Watson, this London letter would have its imitations in their magazine. After the London letter there followed several pages of "Casual Comment," consisting of random paragraphs on such topics as the fortieth anniversary of the *Harvard Lampoon* and the year's literary harvest in England. "Communications" to the Editor came next; such a scholar as the late Chauncey B. Tinker here might be found discussing "The 'Twelve Days of Christmas' Folk-song." But the heart of the journal was the department of "New Books," ten pages of reviews by Percy F. Bicknell, Norman Foerster, Alexander MacKendrick, H. M. Kallen, and others. These reviews were the contributions that, though not paid for, constituted the chief claim of *The Dial* to serious consideration as a literary review. The issue concluded with brief paragraphs in the departments of "Briefs on New Books" and "Notes" (" 'The Accolade' is a new novel by Miss Ethel Sidgwick scheduled for February publication by Messrs. Small, Maynard & Co."), and the bibliographical columns of "Topics in Leading Periodicals" and "List of New Books."

The Dial thus was not an expensive periodical to produce. The poetry once printed by Francis F. Browne no longer appeared; all the departments save the leading article, the letters to the Editor, and the reviews of new books were written by the staff; and of the matter regularly contributed by outsiders, only the leading articles were remunerated. The limitations of this editorial policy, with its enforced parsimony, were twofold. *The Dial,* though neat and precise and professional in appearance, was not interesting to look at and was indeed rather unprepossessing. Second, the contributors continued to be drawn from academic life, where they lived by teaching, rather than from Greenwich Village (or its counterparts), where a man must live off the proceeds of his writing; and in consequence the pages of *The Dial* still were more notable for staidness and for restatement of received opinions than for excitement and the statement of critical novelty.

The finances of *The Dial,* after 1913, were not in good shape. Businessmen that they were, the Brownes, Waldo and Herbert, kept up the custom of special holiday issues that their father had instituted. In 1915 these issues appeared on November 25 and December 9. At the rate of forty dollars per page for special advertising that still applied in this, the last holiday season in which members of the Browne family directed the *Dial* — though the Henry O. Shepard Company as yet had not sold out its ownership — the thirty pages of special advertising in *The Dial* for November 25, 1915, would have brought in a gross sum of $1,200, and the twenty-four pages of such advertising in *The Dial* for December 9, 1915, would have grossed $960. The circulation figures for *The Dial* probably were, as Herbert Browne said, about five thousand. With an annual subscription rate of $2.00, "Foreign postage fifty cents per year extra," the gross sum brought in by subscriptions would total only ten thousand dollars. Editorial costs were rising, even though leading articles such as those by William Morton Payne were paid for at the low rate of twenty-five dollars per month, with Payne's reviews of fiction included in the agreement, while reviewers were paid off in review copies of books.

A staff of four persons now earned their livelihood at least in part by working for *The Dial*. Waldo R. Browne was Editor. Alma Luise Olson was his Associate; there appeared in *The Dial* but one item signed by Miss Olson, a fervent letter to the Editor, headed "Once in a Blue Moon," in defense of women and women's rights, in the issue for December 9, 1915. Paul G. Smith was Secretary, and Herbert S. Browne was Business Manager.

Herbert Browne also continued to manage *Books of the Month,* which his father had founded as *Trade Book List.* Sold along with *The Dial* to the Shepard interests in 1914, the Brownes repurchased it with *The Dial* from the Shepard company, and it moved, with *The Dial,* to the new offices in the Transportation Building. According to a house advertisement, *Books of the Month* was an "attractive, accurate classified guide to the month's new books, compiled in the offices of the THE DIAL, America's leading literary periodical." When the Shepard company became publisher, it began to advertise *Books of the Month* more intensively in *The Dial* than had the Brownes, but they continued this apparently profitable policy, after the return of Waldo Browne. Yet, as owners once again of *The Dial* and *Books of the Month,* the Brownes never advertised the latter in *The Dial. Books of the Month* was, in fact, radically dissimilar from *The Dial.* It was a bookseller's throwaway, containing a concise, clear outline of the plot or general scope of each book listed, with no lengthy reviews or publishers' puffs. These outlines were intended to enable the reader to decide at once whether or not a particular book was within his range of interest. An advertisement stated that "leading booksellers in all parts of the country have it and are glad to supply it, free of charge. . . . If you can not obtain a copy from your local bookseller, send us his name and we will forward several copies direct to you, without cost." An ordinary issue of *Books of the Month* comprised about thirty-six pages, but the special holiday number for 1914 was an issue of sixty-eight pages — a "handy, compact, complete descriptive guide to the best Holiday and Juvenile Books of all American publishers for 1914." The covers of the issues were designed in the tradition established by *The Chap-Book* posters; some of these illustrated covers are of unusual charm, as attractive indeed as *The Dial* itself was nondescript.[18]   Herbert Browne kept the controlling interest in *Books of the Month* until 1920, when he sold it to the R. R. Bowker Company, owners of *Publishers' Weekly*.

To print *The Dial* and its ephemeral throwaway offspring, there were two printers, one of them brother to the deceased Editor, his assistant a man known to history only as Mr. Gillespie.[19] Even though the owner-publisher also printed *The Dial*, printing costs were increasing, as well as the office overhead. Clearly, then, in a wartime economy, the advertising pages in *The Dial* by 1915 had taken on a new importance for the ongoing publication of the magazine.

The effort to keep and to find readers was more intense than it had been since the mid-1890's. A *Dial* advertisement in the issue for November 25, 1915, asserted that "GOOD MEDIUMS are many. Efficient mediums for the publisher are few. Every reader of THE DIAL is a regular and habitual buyer of worthy books." The holiday issues of *The Dial* were aimed at the buyer of books, and not only would he read the rich offerings of the advertising pages, he would also be directed by the staff what to purchase in a three-part serialization of "Holiday Publications." Among the books admired in the section on "Art and Architecture" are Joseph Pennell's *Lithography and Lithographers* and *Joseph Pennell's Pictures in the Land of Temples*; Pennell, incidentally, was one of the few artists admired by both *The Dial* of 1915 and *The Dial* of 1924. Among the "Biography

THE DIAL

VOLUME LXV   NO. 771   AUGUST 15, 1918

CONTENTS

George Bernard Donlin, Editor   Harold E. Stearns, Associate

Contributing Editors

Conrad Aiken   Van Wyck Brooks   H. M. Kallen
Randolph Bourne   Padraic Colum   Clarence Britten
Robert Dell   Henry B. Fuller   Scofield Thayer

  The Dial (founded in 1880 by Francis F. Browne) is published weekly from the first week in
October to the last week in June inclusive; monthly in July and August; semi-monthly in
September. Yearly subscription $3.00 in advance, in the United States, Canada, and Mexico.
Foreign subscriptions $3.50 per year.
  Entered as Second-Class matter at the Post Office at New York, N. Y., August 3, 1918, under
the act of March 3, 1879. Copyright, 1918, by The Dial Publishing Company, Inc.
  Published by The Dial Publishing Company, Inc., Martyn Johnson, President; Willard C.
Kitchel, Secretary-Treasurer, at 152 West Thirteenth Street, New York City.

The End of the Chicago *Dial* (August 15, 1918)

THE  DIAL

JANUARY 1920

AN AUTOBIOGRAPHIC CHAPTER

BY RANDOLPH BOURNE

GILBERT was almost six years old when they all—Mother, Olga, and baby—went to live with Garna in her tall white house. And his expanding life leaped to meet the wide world, with its new excitements and pleasures. It was like a rescue, like getting air when one is smothering. Here was space and a new largeness to things. Gilbert was freed forever from the back-street.

Garna's house was ridiculous but it was not despicable. For your meals you went down into a dark basement dining-room, behind a blacker kitchen. And the outhouse, buried in Virginia creepers and trumpet-vine, was down a long path bordered by grape-vines, where you went fearfully at night. Gilbert was afraid of this dark, long after he was old enough to be ashamed that his mother must come with him and stand protectingly outside. In winter, the stars shone at him with icy brilliancy, and the vines made a thick menacing mass around him.

Back of the house was a pump, painted very bright and green, where the water came up cold and sparkling and ran suddenly out of its spout over your shoes unless you were careful. And when they had finished pumping, the well would give a long, deep sigh, whether of fatigue or satisfaction, Gilbert never knew. In the dark kitchen, which you entered down a flight of stone steps, there was another pump, but it brought forth, after long persuasion, only rain-water which to Gilbert tasted uninteresting, and which he was not allowed to drink, but which they carried in zinc pails up two long spidery flights, and for Aunt Nan's room, three, so that you could wash your face in the morning. Only on wash-day, was that pump

1

In Memoriam, Randolph Bourne (January 1920)

On Being Queer

Christopher Columbus was queer. He had queer ideas about the earth being round. He thought India could be reached by sailing westward when everybody knew that it lay to the east. He was a freak, an oddity to be shunned by everyone.

Benjamin Franklin was queer. He stood out in the rain on dark nights and flew kites. He had strange ideas about education and government.

Walt Whitman was queer. He would stand for hours on a street corner and gaze abstractedly at the passing throng. He consorted with bus drivers, Broadway hoodlums, and others outside the pale of respectable society.

THE DIAL

is queer—to all lovers of the commonplace. It contains queer pictures, odd verse, bizarre stories, subtle essays, erudite book reviews, and exasperating criticism of art, music, and the theatre. It doesn't like what everybody likes simply because everybody likes it—which is why discerning people like it. "The vivid and various Dial," as the New York *Evening Post* describes it, is queer—in the same way that all things of distinction are queer.

Queer things do differ from the divine average of mediocrity.

House Advertisement (May 1921)

William Gropper, *Editorial Conference*

E. E. Cummings, *S. T., S. W., G. S.*

Henri de Toulouse-Lautrec, *The Chap-Book*

Aubrey Beardsley, *The Savoy,* *"Contents" Page of the First Number*

Aubrey Beardsley, *Don Juan, Sganarelle, and the Beggar*

Aubrey Beardsley, *Black Coffee*

Aubrey Beardsley, *Alberich* (for Wagner's *Das Rheingold*)

Aubrey Beardsley, *Scene* from *The Scarlet Pastorale*

Aubrey Beardsley, *His Book-Plate*

Gaston Lachaise, *Three-Quarters Length Figure*

Gaston, Lachaise, *Caligari* (December 1925)

ston Lachaise, *Seated Nude with Upraised Arms* (Study for a Sculpture also in the
Dial Collection)

Claude Bragdon, *A Drawing* (October 1922)

and Memoirs," Maxim Gorki's *My Childhood* would delight all "who like Russian realism of an unflinching intensity"; Gorki, too, continued to delight the readers of *The Dial,* with his reminiscences of Leonid Andreyev and Leo Tolstoy, in 1924 and 1925.[20] The other books recommended to the readers of the Chicago *Dial* are rather different from these, however; an anthology of "dog poetry" entitled *To Your Dog and to My Dog,* J. Horace McFarland's *My Growing Garden,* and John Martin Hammond's *Quaint and Historic Forts of North America* fairly represent the level of editorial recommendation.

The special issues announcing spring and fall books in 1915 were unusually full. For years under Francis Browne *The Dial* had listed selectively, each spring and fall, the new books in the publishers' catalogues. "Announcements of Fall Books" in *The Dial* for September 16, 1915, was then no innovation, but it was much more elaborate than most of its predecessors had been. Presented "in accordance with a long-time annual custom of this journal," it was "as nearly complete as the exigencies of the publishing business and the necessary coöperation of the publishers in supplying the needed data" had permitted the compilers to make it.[21] This listing as well as the regular listings, "List of New Books" and "Topics in Leading Periodicals," were obviously directed at the custom of booksellers and librarians. Indeed, in the issue just preceding the special issue listing fall publications, the editors advertised that "THE FINANCIAL SUCCESS of many books depends wholly upon whether or not they are bought by Libraries. For reaching and impressing the Librarian there is no better medium than *The Dial.*"[22] The increasingly specialized character of the magazine is overtly indicated by still another advertisement, in the issue for September 16, 1915, stating that "THE PUBLISHER'S GREATEST PROBLEM is the problem of securing economical publicity for his books. At the cost of one page in THE DIAL the publisher secures more direct, efficient publicity than an expenditure of many times the amount will bring in mediums of general circulation." Such means of keeping *The Dial* going were wholly in keeping with the proven business procedures by which Francis F. Browne had established it as a sober and reputable literary journal as well as a modestly prospering family enterprise.

The Dial no longer prospered, however, and later in 1916 the ownership changed a third time. Herbert Browne's newly organized Dial Company no sooner had taken over the magazine than the difficulties became even greater than they already had been. Waldo Browne wanted to relinquish his editorial task, and indeed everybody realized that editing The Dial from Hillside Farm was unsatisfactory. Herbert Browne began looking around for a buyer, and the Brownes prepared to sell The Dial (but not Books of the Month, ownership of which Herbert Browne retained).

Ralph Fletcher Seymour's memoir has it that after Francis Fisher Browne's death, The Dial suspended publication and that the "printer Browne and the assistant Gillespie thereupon moved the typesetting plant into the Athenaeum Building across the alley, and kept on setting type for books, advertisements, and commercial items." In an evident allusion to the purchase of The Dial by the Henry O. Shepard Company, Seymour asserts that that firm "inherited the reliques of that magazine, and having no use for the publication rights sold them to a band of young literary dilettantes, who rechristened it 'The Trimmed Lamp' and issued several numbers."²³

Actually, The Trimmed Lamp began publication as Art; a Monthly Magazine in October 1912, being thus an exact contemporary of Harriet Monroe's Poetry. Its initial purpose was to comment upon painting in order "to keep the art world of Chicago and the West familiar with the contents of our galleries"; the galleries referred to were the O'Brien Galleries, of the family of the editor, Howard Vincent O'Brien, then just embarking on his career as a Chicago journalist.

A major change of policy was signalized with the issue of March 1914. When Art changed its title to The Trimmed Lamp: A Periodical of Life and Art, about the only aspect of the magazine that failed to alter was its price of a dime per copy. Art had begun publication as a house organ, but Howard Vincent O'Brien, Yale '10 and aflame with the missionary ardor of

Fabian socialism, soon turned his magazine into an organ expressing the aspirations of the political, if not the aesthetic, vanguard.
The importance O'Brien attached to such views is attested to
by the place in the contents of each issue of *The Trimmed Lamp*
(as, earlier, of *Art)* he accorded the pages of editorial paragraphs: they came first in every monthly number. In March 1914,
the contents began with the admission that the new title of "THE
TRIMMED LAMP, at first glance, means nothing. But at second
and successive glances, it means a very great deal. At worst, it
is exclusive of nothing which might be read into it: at best,
it is inclusive of all the ideals of life and art it holds. The
change — like all changes — is a cause for fear and trembling,
for auguries most dismal; and it springs from necessity rather
than from choice. Hence . . . salutamur." That is to say, Martin
O'Brien, proprietor of the O'Brien Galleries and the youthful
editor's father, had disowned this changeling, and Howard Vincent O'Brien was on his own. The editorial explained that
Art as the title had been dropped because to the "timorous and
elusive individual [it] is more repellent than attractive." From
now on the social and political tenets of *The Trimmed Lamp*
were almost indistinguishable from those of Waldo Browne's
Dial.

A harbinger of the future of *The Dial* was an article that
appeared in the next issue of *The Trimmed Lamp,* that for
April 1914. The future Publisher and proprietor of *The Dial,*
Martyn Johnson, made his first appearance with "Impressions
of an American Returned," in which he said that he had gone
to London for three years in order to get a better perspective on
America. Johnson criticized American complacency and materialism: "We have our wealth, how are we going to use it? Is
the mere making of money enough to satisfy us?" In the same
issue appeared an advertisement for *The Masses,* and the cover
was a drawing by John Sloan reprinted from *The Masses;* O'Bri-
en's editorial bias was now obvious to all his readers. In *The
Trimmed Lamp* for May 1914, the editorials were admittedly
Fabian and economic in orientation, and a house advertisement
announced that there was no connection between the magazine

and the firm of M. O'Brien & Son: "Responsibility for whatever appears in THE TRIMMED LAMP is limited to the editor,
except when otherwise specified." Accordingly, each number
listed Howard Vincent O'Brien as sole owner and publisher.

Like Waldo Browne, O'Brien expressed his total dismay at
the start of the first World War, in the lead editorial in the
issue of August 1914: "As this is written, some forty million men
are awaiting the order to set about killing one another. Before
it is read, it is likely that the teachings of Christianity will have
been discarded with a completeness to make the devil weep with
joy. . . . War, of this sort, is but the product of a monstrously
perverted convention. And that convention is the wisdom of
bureaucrats and kings . . . . Some day the Man in the Street and
the Man with the Hoe will wake up and take matters into their
own amply capable hands. Until then, for Kaiser and Czar and
King — rulers by divine right — God save the jest! . . . Christ's
prayer on the cross for his murderers." (Yet when the United
States entered the war, O'Brien enlisted and served as a lieuten-
ant in the artillery, foregoing his views of 1914-16.) Increasingly
the editorials and the contents generally came to express disil-
lusionment with institutional Christianity and with the Wilson
administration; instead the new religion of "Democracy . . . an
end in itself" was advocated along with socialism. By the end of
1914, O'Brien's advocacy of what, in the final issue of *Art* (February 1914), he had called the Red Flag of Socialism and had
praised as really signifying "the common brotherhood of man,"
caused the death of *The Trimmed Lamp* as his own organ.

After the final issue of his *Trimmed Lamp,* for November-
December 1914, the flame was revived only with the issue of
March 1915. The editorial pages, now entitled "Gleams," explained that the periodical had had "an interesting and instructive career." It had begun, "under the succinct but inclusive
title of 'Art,' as a primer in aesthetics. It was informative, attractive and innocuous; therefore it prospered greatly." But, continued the editorial, the editor had had a conviction that art
was not a mere means of delectation to the Persians of the tea-
table, and gradually he had given expression to that conviction.

"He lent a sympathetic ear to heterodoxy, was impertinent with regard to wealth and the established church, and generally pleased himself more than cloistered conservatism. His punishment was prompt and all but thorough." His subscribers vanished, as did his advertisers. "At this point beginneth Chapter III." A few people had found O'Brien's experiment in "free journalism . . . an interesting and valuable one to them," and they invited "others of like mind . . . to join in the task of salvage." The result was "the formation of a body which is, we believe, unique in the publishing world. Composed of conservatives and radicals, men with wealth and men without it, artists, writers, lawyers, architects, and plain 'business men,' it is committed to no color of opinion." This body would, asserted the editorial, carry on *The Trimmed Lamp* "co-operatively, without intent of profit, and without formulated policy, other than to be *free*, to be *true*, and to be *interesting*." The heterogeneous construction of the editorial board would "unquestionably develop friction. But the concomitant of friction is heat: and heat, carried far enough, is *light*." No one person would dominate the freshly glowing *Trimmed Lamp*: "The founder and editor hitherto of the magazine relinquishes all control, financial and editorial. From now on it will be owned and published by the new association." Finally, promised the editorial, the magazine would not be "precious or intellectually snobbish. It wants as large a circulation as it can get." This eclecticism adumbrated the policy of *The Dial* of Thayer and Watson, a curiously coincidental parallel.

Howard Vincent O'Brien continued, until the end, as a member of the editorial board. There were various changes in the personnel of the board and in the format of the magazine; but it does seem really to have kept to the policy of a cooperative editorship. In the final issue, that for May 1916, the "Statement of Ownership" stated that the Editors were the "Same as Owners" listed as "all residents of Chicago": Joseph Husband, Howard V. O'Brien, Martyn Johnson, Richard E. Danielson, Chauncey McCormick, Cecil Barnes, Walter B. Wolf, Kenneth S. Goodman, Samuel M. Rinaker, Willard C. Kitchel, Ralph F. Seymour, Carl Sandburg, Ernest Ballard, Laird Bell, and Wallace Hughes.

Johnson was named as Managing Editor, Chauncey McCormick as
Business Manager, and Willard C. Kitchel as Treasurer. It was
a roster of Chicago's wealth and family distinction.

The editorial line of *The Trimmed Lamp* in its final phase
was still liberal, if not socialist; it opposed the war, it opposed
the Wilson administration, it opposed the exploitation of working people. The editorials and political articles, especially those
by Richard Ely Danielson, were trenchant and forthright. Martyn Johnson contributed to most issues; his poems and essays
themselves are of no essential significance, but they constitute
evidence of his attitudes and predilections and are portents of his
policy as the Publisher of *The Dial*. Perhaps the most noteworthy
is his brief evaluation of the sculpture of Alfeo Faggi, accompanied by a cut of a Faggi drawing of a nude; Faggi was one of
the artists sponsored by Scofield Thayer in his *Dial* in the
1920's. The editorial board continued Howard Vincent O'Brien's
policy of reproducing pictures by contemporary artists, and if
anything their joint policy resulted in the publication of better
pictures than had appeared in *Art*. The last seven or eight issues
of *The Trimmed Lamp* carried handsome cover illustrations,
drawings by Ralph Fletcher Seymour, John Norton, and J. O.
Smith. Smith it was who designed, also, the covers for some of
the issues of the Brownes' *Books of the Month*; yet otherwise there
is almost no resemblance between their periodicals and *The
Trimmed Lamp*, for Waldo Browne's literary tastes lagged behind the orientation of *The Trimmed Lamp*. The editorial
board established a poetry contest — judged by Harriet Monroe,
Mary Aldis, and Arthur Davison Ficke — and poems in the Imagist manner regularly appeared in every issue, contributed by
such writers as Vachel Lindsay, Mary Aldis, Helen Hoyt (whose
contribution, "Come to Me Out of the Dark," won one prize
in the contest), Margaret Widdemer (her poem, "The Faun's
Sweetheart," won the other prize), Arthur Davison Ficke, and
Amy Lowell. John Gould Fletcher contributed both poems and
criticism. Clinton Joseph Masseck, editor of Martyn Johnson's
Dial for one issue in August 1916, contributed a sketch, "My

Encounter with the Hun," to the *Trimmed Lamp* for February
1916.

The names, the policy are important to recount, for they
constitute the nucleus of the contributors and indicate the drift
of the editorial policy that would be *The Dial*'s in a short time,
when *The Dial* had been purchased by the interests controlling
The Trimmed Lamp.

During the final phase of publication, says Seymour, "This
outfit undertook to produce an issue each month. Editorial rooms
were established in an old loft building which stood at the foot
of Wabash Avenue, No. 426 River Street, a location now [i. e.,
in 1945] as much a memory as the magazine. Every week some
or all of these editors came together for dinner in their quarters
and for the materializing of each issue. Uniformed waiters borrowed from the University Club" — then as now near the Fine
Arts Building but not at all convenient to 426 River Street —
"served them food and drink. The columns of 'The Trimmed
Lamp' would have improved had the table conversation been
featured. As it was, the editors had too good times to permit
of very profound editing, little of literary merit appeared in the
magazine, the trimmed flame grew dim, flickered, and expired.
Willard Kitchel bought the remains and transported them to
New York, where they again flared into the literary sky," over
the "restored name" of *The Dial*.

Seymour's statement that *The Trimmed Lamp* inherited
the "traditions" of *The Dial* is the opposite of what happened.
In June 1916, Herbert Browne found his buyer in Martyn Johnson, a "Chicago decorator" (the connection with O'Brien may
well have confused Browne). Herbert Browne, many years later,
recalled that nothing came of his early negotiations with Johnson and a group of "young Chicago men." Then Martyn Johnson formed the Dial Publishing Company, with the aid of Willard C. Kitchel, and bought *The Dial*. *The Dial* thus absorbed
The Trimmed Lamp but in the process was transformed.

Not the least interesting aspect of these events was the reticence of the older journal, which never mentioned in its pages
its absorption of *The Trimmed Lamp*. It was a silence quite

dissimilar from the publicity *The Dial* gave its absorption of *The Chap-Book*. On the other hand, *The Dial* had not publicized either the first sale by the Brownes or their repurchase of it. And it may have been the desire of the new owners that the change be accomplished without publicity.

Among the editorial board of *The Trimmed Lamp* were three men who purchased the stock of the Brownes' Dial Company: Martyn Johnson, Willard C. Kitchel, and Laird Bell. Martyn Johnson became Managing Editor and Business Manager under the new regime, and Willard C. Kitchel became the Secretary-Treasurer. Laird Bell was at the start of a most distinguished career that combined the practice of law and public service with an interest in higher education, and he was never active in the affairs of *The Dial*. One contributor to *The Trimmed Lamp,* Mary Aldis, also became a stockholder in the Dial Publishing Company. Mrs. Aldis was the wife of the prominent real estate broker and owner of the famous Monadnock Block, Arthur Taylor Aldis, of Chicago and Lake Forest. A leading figure in the amateur theater movement in Chicago, she was a playwright and poet, and she had been from its early days a contributor to *Poetry*. Like Laird Bell, Mrs. Aldis was not active except as a financial backer of Martyn Johnson's *Dial*. To the issue of December 28, 1916, her son Graham Aldis contributed a review, "The New Spirit," of Ralph Barton Perry's book of essays, *The Free Man and the Soldier,* interesting because it echoes something of Waldo Browne's mistrust of the arguments for American participation in the war. In the issue of May 17, 1917, Homer E. Woodridge reviewed Mary Aldis's *Plays for Small Stages* as one of five volumes in an omnibus review of "Some Experiments in American Drama" (also reviewed was Theodore Dreiser's *Plays of the Natural and Supernatural*; that it was reviewed with sympathy exemplifies the extent to which *The Dial* changed within a year of Waldo Browne's departure as Editor). One surmises that Mrs. Aldis's interest in the Little Theatre movement — her plays had been written for "one of the most successful of our small amateur theatres, 'The Playhouse' at Lake Forest, Illinois, and acted there by an amateur company" —

drew her into the circle of Martyn Johnson's *Dial,* as Johnson and his first Editor, Clinton Masseck, were both active in the Little Theatre movement. The only other stockholder to invest in the newly organized Dial Publishing Company was Mary L. Snow of Dearborn, Michigan. While not all of the five new owners were young (Mrs. Aldis had been married in 1892), they were sympathetically interested in the art and the literature of the New Movement; at least four of them were persons of considerable means. Mary Aldis and Laird Bell were deeply involved in the civic affairs of Chicago, and a measure of civic pride as well as their own more personal interest in the poetry and theater of the New Movement probably prompted them to finance Martyn Johnson's purchase of *The Dial.* In sum, the new owners took over *The Dial* and, for that reason, ended the publication of *The Trimmed Lamp.*

Perhaps a second reason for the reticence of *The Dial* about the change was its very nature. For the new owners brought with them such contributors to *The Trimmed Lamp* as Amy Lowell, Carl Sandburg, John Gould Fletcher, and Margaret Widdemer. Herbert and Waldo Browne had, admittedly, little understanding of the new poetry that *The Dial* would henceforth be committed to advocating; they disliked the new art as well. As long as the Brownes controlled *The Dial,* they did not allow it to advocate the opinions and the works of the artistic vanguard; beyond the letters to the Editor printed in the column of "Communications" — and, of course, printed only because they were deemed pertinent to previously printed critiques and reviews — *The Dial* of Waldo and Herbert Browne guarded its old aesthetic traditions. Obviously, once the Brownes departed, major changes would be made. It was *The Dial* that would inherit the "traditions," such as they were, of *The Trimmed Lamp,* that organ of the New Movement. So *The Dial* printed no announcement of its sale while Waldo R. Browne remained the Editor.[24]

The final number published by the Dial Company was dated as June 22, 1916. Waldo Browne edited one more number, that for July 15, 1916, for the new owners of the Dial Publishing Company, and then the last Browne left the magazine that his father had founded and conducted for so many years. Waldo Browne had begun to work for Francis Fisher Browne as a printer's devil and ended as Editor of *The Dial*. After he left the magazine, Browne continued his career of writing and editing; in 1919 he served *The Nation* as literary editor. His chief book was his biography of Altgeld, but his active work as an editor continued on into old age, when from 1935 to 1939 he was a member of the central editorial staff of the Federal Writers' Project in the latter stage of the New Deal. In 1954, having outlived *The Dial* itself, Waldo R. Browne died in Wyoming, New York, at the age of seventy-eight. His life was long, his career honorable, and the years after his editorship of *The Dial* were not anticlimactic. Is it justifiable to regard the Brownes' sale of *The Dial* as in some sense a defeat of the intentions of their father and of their own aspirations as his children? Whatever the truth of the matter for Herbert and Waldo Browne, with the passing of the family journal from their control, the forces of the genteel tradition once and for all were routed from their dominance of *The Dial*.

IV

Martyn Johnson's DIAL *(1916-18)*

WITHIN five months of the announcement that Martyn Johnson had become President of the Dial Publishing Company — printed in the issue of August 15, 1916 — the magazine underwent a remarkable change.

Martyn Johnson not only made the change decisive and overt, he set *The Dial* on a recognizable course. Evidently he felt that his *Dial* must do its best "to carry on a fruitful tradition," and he voiced a tribute to what he rather undiscriminatingly if understandably termed the "wise guidance of the late Francis F. Browne and his son, Mr. Waldo R. Browne," in one of the Announcements that *The Dial* was addicted to in those years.[1] The new publisher thus paid his respects to the past and the Brownes.

Like the Browne brothers, Johnson was a Midwesterner, born in Hudson, Wisconsin.[2] Graduated from the University of Michigan in 1905, he went into journalism in Chicago. His obituary in the *New York Times* states that for several years he was on the editorial staff of the Chicago *Inter-Ocean,* a manifest impossibility, as the *Inter Ocean Curiosity Shop* seems to have been published only from 1876 to 1892, in Johnson's early childhood. The Publisher's announcement that Johnson had become Business Manager of *The Dial*, made in "Notes and News" in the issue for August 15, 1916, asserts that "Mr. Martyn Johnson, the new business manager, has been associated with 'The New Republic' during the past year and a half. He has contributed articles and stories to English and American magazines." What his connection with *The New Republic* may have been remains unknown, as his name does not appear among those of the staff and contributors of that period, the first two years of that weekly's publication. It is likely that Johnson was employed in some capacity by *The New Republic,* as the connection would plausibly explain his acquaintance with Randolph Bourne and others on its staff and their consequent coming to *The Dial* as contributors and staff members.

Similarly, his British publications remain unidentifiable. He wrote six articles between 1909 and 1916 for *Putnam's Magazine, Everybody's Magazine, The World To-Day,* and *System: The Magazine of Business.* In 1916 he purchased the controlling interest in the Dial Publishing Company; but after his experience as owner of the magazine, he seems never to have undertaken a similar venture. In 1920, Johnson was secretary to Nelson Morris, United States Minister to Norway. Shortly after that service, he went to Los Angeles, where — according to the *New York Times* — for a number of years he was engaged in business. In 1922, the *Drama* magazine of Chicago published his one-act play, *Mr. and Mrs. P. Roe,* in its December issue, and the publishers of the magazine, the Drama League of America, reprinted the play in pamphlet form; it had first been played at the Chicago Little Theatre in 1913.

The same year, there is a last elusive glimpse of Johnson at work, reviewing D. H. Lawrence's novel, *Aaron's Rod,* for the *Los Angeles Sunday Times.* Citing Johnson as "formerly editor of *The Dial,*" the New York publishing firm of Thomas Seltzer quoted from his review in an advertisement of *Aaron's Rod* in *The Dial* for July 1922. Writing about a novelist who was a chief ornament of the refurbished *Dial* that Scofield Thayer and James Sibley Watson, Jr., had purchased from him, the former Publisher of *The Dial* said that "D. H. Lawrence is the most significant figure in English letters today, probably one of the most important in the entire range of literature." Martyn Johnson died late in January 1934, according to the *Times* obituary of January 26, 1934. His prime significance is as the link between *The Dial* of the Browne family and *The Dial* of Thayer and Watson — and as owner of *The Dial* in its most tumultuous if hardly its most attractive phase.

For all his tribute to the Brownes and to the tradition of their *Dial,* Johnson was more actively engaged by the challenge of the new movements in politics and letters. Less than two months after becoming the principal stockholder of the Dial Publishing Company, he announced in a house advertisement in the issue of September 21, 1916, that "It is the purpose of the Publisher to bring to the service of THE DIAL the best critical talent in America" and that "It is his desire that THE DIAL shall be a source of inspiration as well as information." By specifying the best critical talent that would furnish the desired inspiration, the new owner indicated the variety of inspiration he referred to. Some of the names are of men who had been contributing to *The Dial* for a number of years: Norman Foerster, Percy F. Bicknell, Theodore Stanton, Edward E. Hale, Jr., Joseph Jastrow, J. C. (later, Sir John) Squire, Henry Seidel Canby, Arthur Davison Ficke, Edward B. Krehbiel. Others, however, are of figures controversial then as in the future: Van Wyck Brooks, Edward Garnett, Harold J. Laski, Amy Lowell. Johnson also listed the names of Edward Eyre Hunt, John J. Lowes (John *L.* Lowes?), William Lyon Phelps, Oliver N. Sayler, and Barnett Wendell (Barrett Wendell?) as being among the contributors secured for *The Dial*. Decidedly the owner leaned to the left; what is significant is not the remainder of old contributors but the addition of new ones. In the context of Johnson's effort, such names as Harold Laski and Amy Lowell patently were representing the vanguard respectively in politics and in poetry. Among the

Americans in this group, only Barrett Wendell was known as an opponent of the new trends.[3]

An indication of Johnson's interests had already been given in the "Notes and News" announcing his appointment as Business Manager and identifying him as having been "associated with 'The New Republic' during the past year and a half." Founded in late 1914, *The New Republic* was by 1916 the country's leading journal of the young liberals of New York — Herbert Croly, Randolph Bourne, Walter Lippmann, and others. The Morgan partner Willard Straight financed the weekly but steered clear of dictating its policy, basically an advocacy of the democratic socialism toward which *The Dial* was leaning. The allusion to *The New Republic* suggested, no doubt, that it would be a model for *The Dial* in an attempt by the new owner to attract many of *The New Republic's* readers and contributors.

Martyn Johnson's determination to set *The Dial* on an openly liberal course of publication seems to have been one of his more stable qualities as publisher. In the number for August 15, 1916, he announced that Dr. Clinton J. Masseck had been appointed Editor; "Notes and News" stated that "Dr. Masseck is a graduate of Tufts College, with an A.M. from Harvard University, and bears in addition the degree of *Docteur de l'université de Paris*. He is an instructor in English at Washington University, St. Louis. Dr. Masseck is perhaps best known for his association with modern drama and poetry through his connection with the little theatre movement and as sometime lecturer at Butler College, Indianapolis, and elsewhere." The association of the new Editor, as well as the new owner, with "modern drama and poetry" had an immediate consequence in the response of *The Dial* to poetry influenced by Imagism and *vers libre*. Another result was that, briefly, there were published from Chicago three of the leading journals advocating and printing the work of the literary vanguard. "Notes and News" also announced that Travis Hoke would be the Associate for Masseck; Hoke was said to be "identified with various newspapers of the Middle West; with the Greater St. Louis Committee as Secretary; with the Civic League of St. Louis as its Assistant Secretary; and as contributor to various magazines."

The new Editor stayed with *The Dial* about a month. The very next issue, that for September 21, 1916, announced in "Notes and News" that, "owing to the pressure of his duties at Washington University, Dr. C. J. Masseck has resigned his editorship of THE DIAL." And "Notes and News" went on to specify other changes in policy. On January 1, 1917, the subscription price of *The Dial* would be increased to three dollars for the year. To palliate the rise in subscription rates, the size of the regular issue would be increased from thirty-two to forty pages, and the "best critical writers in this country and England" would become "frequent contributors." The increase in the subscription rate, "Notes and News" explained, had been made necessary by "the increased cost of paper"; the increasing cost of paper stock during the war years and after would eventually become an insoluble problem for Martyn Johnson. Its solution would come only with the purchase by Thayer and Watson of his holdings in the Dial Publishing Company.

The flurry of changes announced in Johnson's first two issues of *The Dial* resulted in the irregular publication of the magazine during the next three months of his regime. Apparently there ensued an editorial interregnum lasting from September 1916 into January 1917, during which Johnson, Travis Hoke, and the Secretary-Treasurer, Willard C. Kitchel, carried on, somehow, the business of editing and publishing. The legally required statement of ownership and management lists Martyn Johnson as both Managing Editor and Business Manager in the issue for October 5, 1916; he must have been, in these weeks, an extremely busy man.

The new year would not inaugurate another period of drifting. 1917-18 would be crucial in the history of *The Dial*, and not only because the magazine now was set, albeit erratically, on the course along which it had formerly drifted; also the first five months of 1917 brought to *The Dial* the group of young American writers who changed it radically and essentially. Three of these men would write for and would be on the staff of *The*

Dial of the Twenties: Gilbert Seldes as Associate Editor and editor-contributor of the monthly article on "The Theatre"; James Sibley Watson as Publisher, editorial writer of the monthly "Comment," reviewer and translator, and above all as one of the two men centrally concerned with molding *The Dial* and supporting it against all enemies and hazards; and Paul Rosenfeld, editor-contributor of the monthly "Musical Chronicle," essayist, and reviewer. Two other names also appear in 1917-18, those of Randolph Bourne and Scofield Thayer. Bourne is central to any history of *The Dial* in its transitional years, as it was on his account that Scofield Thayer so fatefully entered into a relationship with the magazine and its staff; but Bourne died before *The Dial* of Thayer and Watson came into being in January 1920. As for Scofield Thayer, despite his essential importance to this account of *The Dial,* he was the last of its future staff to enter into a connection with the Chicago *Dial* after its purchase by Martyn Johnson. The entry of Seldes, Bourne, Watson, and Rosenfeld into the history of *The Dial* signalizes its metamorphosis from a journal that had had renown primarily as a critical review in the genteel tradition to a leading organ for the advancement of the New Movement in ideas and arts.

The first issue of *The Dial* in 1917, that for January 11, was, fittingly enough, its first issue ever to be devoted to the plastic arts, especially painting. The leading article, "The Secret of Far Eastern Painting," was by John Gould Fletcher. Fletcher had been attacked in *The Dial* during Waldo Browne's editorship; and he had become a contributor through his work with the group backing *The Trimmed Lamp* and now reforming *The Dial.* His essay fittingly initiates the change in editorial policy. In it he not only dealt pointedly and informatively with the contrasts between Western and Oriental art in "their ideas of composition, perspective, and color," he also applied the lessons that Western artists might learn from the artists of the Orient. The reason for the astonishing diversity between the two bodies of production is, held Fletcher, "less a divergence of conception than a divergence of technical means." But the Western artist must not imitate the aesthetic practices and ideology of the

Oriental artist slavishly. Rather, for the new development of Western art that was coming, the Western artist — above all, the American artist — must join in the revolt against the shallow pseudoscientific training, the stifling realism and superculture of the nineteenth century.

Fletcher in the same breath decried the European developments of cubism and futurism as producing work devoid of anything but surface sensation. Because of the war such experiments had ceased, but the future development of European art would be, after the war, a reversion to the sterile academic formulas of the Salon schools and the Royal Academies. America, more fortunate than Europe, was escaping the war at a period when it was more necessary than ever before for Americans to cease taking in elements from without and begin to create something like a homogeneous national development. "Paris has nothing more to teach our artists," Fletcher announced. Then, inconsistently, he continued: "But China and Japan can teach us these great lessons: Natural form is necessary to a picture, but natural form that is not felt is unnecessary. Realism is bad art, but reality that is interpreted and made lofty and dignified by its interpretation, is great art. . . . Finally we must understand style but never degrade it, for style is the universal morality of art."

Fletcher's peculiarly literary usage of the terms of art — a usage that confounded ethics with technical problems — followed the tradition that Margaret Fuller instituted in the first number of *The Dial* back in July 1840, with her essay on Washington Allston. Fletcher's adulation of Far Eastern models also followed the tradition popularized, if not actually initiated, by Emerson with his series of Ethnical Scriptures published in the first *Dial.* Fletcher's conversance with technical terms and painterly problems was more sophisticated and easy than was Margaret Fuller's or Emerson's, because with the passage of three-quarters of a century some Americans had availed themselves of hitherto unknown opportunities to extend their aesthetic and ideological vision. Even so, Fletcher wrote not as a critic of art objects but rather as a critic of literature. His essay marks a transitional

phase between the literary-ethical evaluations of the nineteenth
century aestheticians adhering to the school of content or idea
and the critics active in the Twenties and favored by Thayer and
Watson — Henry McBride, Thomas Craven, Paul Rosenfeld,
Walter Pach, Roger Fry, Clive Bell — who were developing a
formalist aesthetic.[4]

This New Year's issue of *The Dial* still remains an astonishing performance. Following Fletcher's article, which is as much
manifesto as it is art criticism, came Richard Aldington's "Poet
and Painter: A Renaissance Fancy," in which the author showed
how the imitations of Cicero, Horace, and Vergil by the Italian
poets of the Renaissance constituted means by which the more
original painters came into contact with that part of the spirit
of antiquity that remains enshrined in literature. The "Communications" column consisted of a letter by Alfred Emerson,
"Warning the Amateur," in which the correspondent dealt with
art prices then current and current sales: ". . . come to New York
and watch the way money passes from hand to hand at a good
metropolitan art sale. Pricing ermine and sables at Altman's,
or a little venture in diamonds at Tiffany's, will open your
praire-bred eyes no wider." One notes Emerson's assumption
of superiority to the prairie-bred readers and staff of *The Dial*,
and his supercilious invitation to come to the center of things,
as a hint perhaps barely noticeable but prophetic of the further
change soon to come.

Of the longer reviews that followed Emerson's letter, four
dealt with volumes about the fine arts: Frank Jewett Mather's
"The Artist as Superman," a review of Willard Huntington
Wright's *The Creative Will,* and a much more judicious and
even-tempered critique of Wright's work than was Grant Showerman's, a year earlier; Claude Bragdon's "Our Architecture — an
Optimistic View," a review of Talbot Faulkner Hamlin's *The
Enjoyment of Architecture;* Helen Gardner's "Reconstruction of
a Master," a review of Frederick Mortimer Clapp's *Jacopo Carucci
da Pontormo;* and Edward E. Hale's "A Painter of the Forest,"
a review of Eliot Clark's *Alexander Wyant.* In other aesthetic
fields Russell Ramsey reviewed Carl Van Vechten's *Music and*

Bad Manners, and Arthur Davison Ficke returned to *The Dial* to review Lafcadio Hearn's *Appreciations of Poetry.* The column "Briefs on New Books" pursued the theme of the issue, with its brief paragraphs on William Aspenwall Bradley's *French Etchers of the Second Empire,* Alexander Benois's *The Russian School of Painting,* John Thomas Smith's *Nollekens and His Times,* George Wharton Edwards's *Vanished Towers and Chimes of Flanders,* Carl H. P. Thurston's *The Art of Looking at Pictures,* and A. D. F. Hamlin's *A History of Ornament Ancient and Modern.* The contribution by Claude Bragdon has a special interest: he had been a contributor to *The Chap-Book,* and he contributed not only to Martyn Johnson's *Dial* but to *The Dial* of Thayer and Watson. According to Dr. Watson, it was Claude Bragdon who introduced him to Martyn Johnson's Editor, George Bernard Donlin; Bragdon thus was a fateful link in the chain of circumstances culminating in the eventual purchase of *The Dial* by Scofield Thayer and James Sibley Watson, Jr. Not all of the notices in this issue are as significant or as well-written as Bragdon's, but taken as a whole they make a relatively strong contrast to the reviews dealing with books of and about the arts previously published in *The Dial.* To generalize further is helpful only when one has read these reviews in the specific context of the similar reviews *The Dial* later published; in that context, they are a hopeful sign. The art admired and advocated by the publisher, the editors and contributors, and at least some of the readers of the new *Dial* was not the art of any one aesthetic school, but if their taste seems amorphous, if it professed mistrust of cubism and futurism, it was open to experience and to assimilating the experiments, still novel to most Americans, of Cézanne, Gauguin, and Van Gogh.

The next number of the new *Dial* for January 25, 1917, announced in a full-page advertisement that it appealed to book readers, book sellers, book collectors, and book writers. The two classes of clientele added — book collectors and book writers — would buy *The Dial* because of the new column "Notes for Bibliophiles" and because the magazine would now stimulate all who were thinking and working along literary lines or were interested in knowing what other writers were doing.

Two pages after this announcement, and beginning the body of the magazine for the issue, the publisher made "An Announcement" on two matters. Johnson announced the appointment of George Bernard Donlin as Editor, and "Notes and News" carried the information that "Mr. George Bernard Donlin who with this issue assumes the editorship of *The Dial* was educated at the University of Chicago. He has been a contributor to various American journals and for several years was an editorial writer on the 'Chicago Record Herald.' He has contributed frequently to *The Dial*." Opportunely, Johnson also made a statement of the principles of *The Dial*. Its *annus mirabilis* had begun.

First, Johnson briefly sketched the historical background of *The Dial*. Unlike Francis F. Browne, he paid his overt respects to the original *Dial*; although an essay in the first issue of the Chicago *Dial*, for May 1880, constituted one of the early attempts to give an historical account of the Concord *Dial*, the only explicit connection between that *Dial* and Browne's lay in the title of the essay, "The Original 'Dial.'" Johnson echoed the phrase of his predecessor: the original *Dial*, he wrote, with Emerson among its contributors, reflected the best American radicalism of its day — a radicalism long since absorbed into a respectable tradition. The statement, of course, is Johnson's recognition that the tradition of the Transcendentalists and the Come-Outers had gradually hardened into the mold of the genteel tradition, which was that of the Chicago *Dial*. He quoted from the Concord *Dial* the assertion that it was founded to express "freer views than the conservative journals are ready to welcome," and from the Chicago *Dial* the brief and modest announcement of its editor that "THE DIAL has no desire to be classed with the destructive school of criticism." Johnson then mentioned the service the Chicago *Dial* had been able to render under the wise guidance of Francis Browne and his son Waldo, which "is a part of the literary history of America."

Second, the publisher announced the principles inspiring the policy of his *Dial*. The present management would endeavor to carry on a fruitful tradition. *The Dial* would remain a journal of criticism, but in doing so it would try to meet the challenge of the new time by reflecting and interpreting its spirit, "a spirit freely experimental, skeptical of inherited values, ready to examine old dogmas and to submit afresh its sanctions to the test of experience." The spirit alluded to was in some measure the spirit of Waldo Browne, but the courage was solely the courage of Martyn Johnson; essentially this is the difference between the new management and the old. Johnson moreover stressed the peculiar need for criticism, since criticism, "with its sharply intellectual values, its free curiosity, and its necessary concreteness, can share almost equally with creative writing the privilege of revealing us to ourselves." In a democracy "such as ours no task is more worth while." *The Dial's* criticism would be sympathetic, for without sympathy understanding would be impossible; it would be addressed to all who find in books an enhancement and an interpretation of life; and it would try to interest those who cared for ideas and believed that "in the free and vigorous circulation of opinion lies our best hope for the future." The danger of the times was that criticism, "which strikes such deep roots in the past, may become a morbid growth, nourishing a few mouldy leaves on a monstrous underground network of memories, timidities, and conformities." The new *Dial* recognized no gap between past and present, had no divided allegiance, but it would serve its purpose best by indicating drifts and tendencies and by seeking just values of living men or suggesting new valuations of the dead rather than by repeating the familiar estimates of the textbook.

Obviously Johnson's *Dial* would be what Margaret Fuller's *Dial* had been for 1840 — the organ of the Free, used against the dominant powers. It would attack the genteel tradition and its adherents, and Johnson's assurance to readers that his journal was committed to no propaganda and supporting no cliques, schools, or movements is disingenuous. *The Dial* of Francis F. Browne also had believed just as much as did Johnson's *Dial* that it encouraged talent by — to use Johnson's words — "helping to create a community in which talent will feel more at home and in which it may be sure at least of the reward of intelligent appreciation." Many persons believed that the old Chicago *Dial* had lifted the level and broadened the base of American culture. There is, for example, the testimony of Harold Stearns that the Browne family's *Dial*, of which Chicagoans were still inordinately proud in 1917-18, "was almost like a civic accomplishment, a living refutation to the Eastern ill-wishers who said that Chicago cared only about meat-packing and making money." An astonishing number of people Stearns met in Chicago, who seldom if ever even looked at *The Dial*, could nevertheless tell its history and string off the names of some of its early famous contributors.[5] This was the magazine that Johnson and his Editors, George Bernard Donlin and Robert Morss Lovett, and their Associate Editors, Harold Stearns and Clarence Britten, would transform according to the principles of the new owner's announcement. This was the magazine that stood in important basic ways for — to quote again Martyn Johnson's editorial phrases — the monstrous underground network of memories, timidities, and conformities that *The Dial* in future would seek to destroy.

George Bernard Donlin carried out the owner's wishes, with valor and speed. Robert Morss Lovett, Donlin's successor as Editor, wrote in a brief memoir of Donlin, published in *The Dial* for August 1920, that during the year before his failing health forced him to give up his active service, he with Martyn Johnson wrought "an extraordinary metamorphosis in the journal. In place of the conservative, laboured, academic criticism familiar to its readers, THE DIAL opened its columns to the free winds of new faiths and doctrines." The change Donlin thus brought about seems all the more remarkable in view of Lovett's statement that with "the movement which carried THE DIAL distinctly into the field of political and social discussion Donlin was not in entire sympathy." Lovett suggests that Donlin nevertheless accepted the change as inevitable. The removal of the magazine to New York "must have cost him some regrets. His own work had been so closely associated with the Middle West, and his view of the importance of such a journal as THE DIAL to that environment was so clear that he must have felt a sense of defeat when the field was abandoned, even for a larger opportunity." But he continued to serve on the editorial board of *The Dial* until May 1919.

Of Donlin's personal characteristics, Lovett admired chiefly his courage: "Hampered by deafness and ill health, he faced life steadily, and made his place in it." For Lovett, the most conspicuous quality of Donlin's editorship was "the skill with which he chose his contributors, and the happy certainty with which he suggested to each the task for which his talent and training fitted him." Lovett also praised Donlin's "wide knowledge of books and men, and extraordinary patience and tact which brought about the successful achievement of his plan for a literary journal. Hampered by lack of funds, Donlin was compelled to do a large part of the routine work of the editorial office himself and undoubtedly he laboured beyond his strength." Lovett here is indicating that the political aspect of the new policy of *The Dial*, though a continuation of policy inaugurated by Waldo Browne, was largely influenced by Martyn Johnson, whereas the literary aspect of that policy, so markedly in contrast to the editorial policy of Waldo Browne, was a continuation of policy inaugurated by Lucian Cary, during whose editorship Donlin first contributed to *The Dial*. Yet Waldo Browne, like Donlin, had wanted *The Dial* to become more literary and less political and social in its orientation. Both editors were prescient, for it was because of its politics that Martyn Johnson's *Dial* foundered at last.

The more easily apparent of Donlin's two major changes in *The Dial* had to do with its physical appearance and with ordering its contents. Before the advent of the new Editor, Johnson had announced, in "Notes and News" for September 21, 1916, that with the issue of January 1, 1917, the annual subscription rate would rise to three dollars and that the number of pages per issue would be increased from thirty-two to forty. The size of the magazine did not vary until it became a monthly in January 1920; however, the paper stock changed with the issue for October 11, 1917, from the smooth cream stock that had been used since 1880 to a white mat stock, like that of *The New Republic.*

During 1917 occurred changes in makeup consonant with the changes in tone and purpose of *The Dial.* The earliest of these is minor — a new column compiled by John E. Robinson and entitled "Notes for Bibliophiles," which ran regularly through 1917. It was primarily bibliographical and statistical: "A Sale of Americana by Charles F. Heartman, 36 Lexington Avenue, New York, on November 30, brought a total of $3136.25. The highest price, $305, was paid by J. Goldsmith for a manuscript of two pages, folio, New York, May, 1822, by Philip Freneau, about a new, correct and elegant edition of his 'Poems and Miscellanies,' three octavo volumes, at three dollars."[6] "Notes for Bibliophiles" contrasts curiously to the growing preoccupation of the publisher and the Editor with political, social, and economic problems.

Only occasionally appearing in Johnson's *Dial,* "Notes for Bibliophiles" represents not so much an interest of the owner as his attempt to attract certain readers; to this extent it is a link with the Browne family's *Dial* and anticipates *The Dial* of Thayer and Watson. It was one of the inherited compendious features of Francis Browne's journal, serving the booksellers, librarians, and rare-book collectors who constituted the substantial readership of his *Dial.* These readers were professionally interested in prices of books, lists of books just published, and brief review-notices, and reliance on that readership enabled Francis Browne to build a viable business enterprise.

Thayer and Watson continued, in a sporadic way, to publish items attractive to the rare book trade. In the advertising pages of their *Dial* there occasionally appeared an anonymous column, "The Bibliophile," as, for example, in the issue for September 1923. Its effectiveness was somewhat obviated by its being relegated to the advertising pages, which were distinguished from the text proper by pagination, complete separation of advertising copy from text, and paper stock used. To be sure, the Brownes and Johnson did not integrate the text of *The Dial* with its advertising, though they did not distinguish advertising except by separating it from the text of the issues. The point is that Francis Browne's *Dial* was centrally interested in such a continuing endeavor, while *The Dial* of Thayer and Watson was not; therefore "The Bibliophile" appears to be a less professional job, indeed a sop to the advertisers. Similarly "Notes for Bibliophiles" is not a column that was integral to Johnson's *Dial;* it would, of itself, hardly suffice to keep or attract the readership of the old *Dial*. The changes in basic policy — from a journal of reviews and critical essays to a journal of advanced social and political opinion and then to a review of the arts — caused *The Dial* to lose its sustaining core of readers, and it never recovered any similarly adequate body of loyal subscribers.

Editor and publisher soon brought about other and more significant changes in the contents. The column of "Casual Comment" was transferred, with the issue of May 17, 1917, from the rear pages to the front of the journal, where the Editor used it as his weekly editorial comment. (Again *The Dial* was imitating *The New Republic*. And again its feature, though undergoing major change, would be retained after 1920, in the editorial "Comment" in the rear of the monthly *Dial*.) The signed leading article that customarily followed was set in type of the same size as that of "Casual Comment" but more widely spaced, and the title of this article was set in large type and run as a banner across the page. The new treatment of the leading article is a harbinger of later changes; the "Casual Comment" was returned to the rear of the magazine, and the leading article, with its new appearance, came first in the issue for June 26, 1917, and later issues. With this same issue, the first in the sixty-third volume of *The Dial*, a special contents page was inserted, and thus was brought to a close the tradition of printing the contents of each issue in the left column of the first page of printed matter. *The Dial* was represented by a journalistic emblem, a sundial with a quill for gnomon; below this, occupying most of the contents page, was a list of the contents of the issue with their contributors; and the bottom of the page was occupied by a colophon listing the staff and other pertinent data.

For the first time since the turn of the century, verse received

the compliment of fairly regular publication in *The Dial.* The
inaugural issue was that for September 27, 1917. The inaugural
poem was Richard Aldington's splendidly modernist, *vers libre,*
Imagist lyric, "Fatigues":

> The weariness of this dirt and labour, of this dirty,
>   melting sky!
> For hours we have carried great bundles of hay from
>   barge to truck, and from truck to train. . .
> The weariness of this dirt and labour!
> But look! Last June those heavy dried bales waved and
>   glittered on the fields of England! . . .
> Dear crushed flowers! and you, yet fragrant grasses,
>   I stoop and kiss you furtively. No one sees.
> Dear gentle perished sisters, speak, whisper and move,
>   tell me you will dance and whisper in the wind next
>   June, upon my grave.

It was followed by H. M. Kallen's polemic review, "The Mind of
Germany," of two ferociously anti-German books, *Hurrah and
Hallelujah: The Teaching of Germany's Poets, Prophets, and
Preachers* and William Archer's collection entitled *Gems (?) of
German Thought* — however fitly attuned to the spirit of the war, a
far less appropriate companion to Aldington's poem than Henry
Blake Fuller's review, in the same issue, of *Some Imagist Poets,
1917,* with its sympathy for the new spirit of the arts and its
praise of Aldington's work. Fuller had been one of the chief
figures of the Chicago Renascence of the 1890's and had been
also one of the chief figures associated with Francis F. Browne's
Dial, and his acceptance and understanding of the poetry beginning
to appear in Johnson's *Dial* must have been most welcome if only
as a contrast to the diatribes of the reviewers in *The Dial* before
William Morton Payne's departure.

During the remainder of 1917, Aldington appeared again
with "In the Trenches," in the issue of December 6; and in the
next issue, that for December 20, Rose Henderson replied with
"To One in the Trenches." Accompanying the Henderson poem
was Edward Shanks's "Special Correspondence of THE DIAL,"
one of Shanks's letters from London, usually entitled "Literary

Affairs in London," which appeared occasionally in *The Dial* from 1917 through August 1920; Shanks discussed Edward Thomas and A. E. Housman. John Gould Fletcher's "Night on the Beach" was published in the issue for November 22, and Margaret Widdemer's "Garden Dream" appeared in that for November 8. All in all, Martyn Johnson's new program for his magazine was getting off to an auspicious start at least poetically.

The next volume of *The Dial*, its sixty-fourth, was the first to set aside a special category for poetry in its index. The year began, in the issue for January 3, 1918, with Leslie Nelson Jennings's sonnet "After One Evening" ("Surely we have not come so far to stand / Dumb in the presence of our hearts' desire!"), a poem more memorable for sentiment than for excellence. Jennings's verse was published more often than any other poet's, at first; but the ensuing six months saw publication in the magazine of poems by Babette Deutsch, Edward Sapir, Padraic Colum (whose "The Swallows" is decidedly the outstanding lyric of the lot), James Oppenheim, Maxwell Bodenheim, and Amy Lowell. In time the range, variety, and excellence of the verse in *The Dial* would far surpass the encouraging beginnings of 1917-18, with the brief lyric poems that served as fillers in the pages of those years.

Even though *The Dial* now placed itself with the vanguard of the New Movement, there was less controversy about poetry in its pages during Martyn Johnson's regime than there had been earlier. The first issue published by the new owners, for August 15, 1916, contained a letter by H. E. Warner, who, apparently under the impression that he was writing for the sympathetic eye of Waldo Browne, said that he could not "believe that free verse is to become a permanent literary form. It is . . . a hybrid whose sterility we may pretty certainly reckon." It was a very long letter, and it occasioned a long controversy in the "Communications" section of the magazine. Amy Lowell answered it in the next issue, that for September 7, with a letter "In Defence of *Vers Libre*," holding that it was "undoubtedly the case" that *vers libre* had "come to stay." The following issue, for September 21, printed letters by Lewis Worthington Smith and E. W.

Dolch, Jr., adding their bit to the fray, and in the issue for October 5, John Gould Fletcher attacked "Mr. Warner's feeble attempt to analyze the substance of certain *vers libre* poets." For five issues, no correspondent took up the challenge; but the year closed, with H. E. Warner's riposte, "Verse — Free or Confined?" in *The Dial* for December 28, a wholly defensive reply. The particular controversy was rounded out by Amy Lowell's leading article in the issue for January 25, 1917, on "Poetry as a Spoken Art," which followed the publisher's important announcement of changes in editorial policy. Miss Lowell energetically disposed of her opponents' question "whether *vers libre* is poetry or prose" by assuring them that it "can be treated quite summarily. It is assuredly poetry. That it may dispense with rhyme, and must dispense with metre, does not affect its substance in the least. For no matter with what it dispenses, it retains that essential to all poetry: Rhythm." Both the placement of Amy Lowell's essay in such an important issue of *The Dial* and her self-confident tone of laying down the law gave her leading article the stamp of editorial policy: *The Dial* would henceforth advocate the new poetry.

Between August 1916 and December 1919, the effective period of Martyn Johnson's direction of *The Dial,* the magazine published reviews of recent poetry by such men as Witter Bynner, Odell Shepard, John Gould Fletcher, William Aspenwall Bradley, Conrad Aiken, and Louis Untermeyer. Two of them, Aiken and Bradley, were contributing editors on Johnson's staff; all were, of course, partisans of the New Movement.

Conrad Aiken, by virtue of his post on the staff of *The Dial,* may also have played a part in the uncovering by the magazine of the Spectra hoax.[7] In 1916, Witter Bynner and Arthur Davison Ficke, as, respectively, Emanuel Morgan and Anne Knish, published in various little magazines, and chiefly in a volume entitled *Spectra: New Poems,* the verse of a new school, the Spectrists, rivals of the Imagists. What had begun as parody of Imagism and *vers libre* gradually became taken seriously by some poets and critics, and even the two perpetrators began to take half-seriously the situation that they had created.

The perpetrators of the hoax, moreover, abetted its spread; they could do so because their pen names were signed to the poetry (and to some correspondence), while their real names were signed to reviews and criticisms puffing the alleged new Spectrist school. A hitherto unremarked example of this dual means of publicizing the Spectra hoax is Witter Bynner's review of Robert W. Service's volume of verses, *Rhymes of a Red Cross Man,* which appeared in *The Dial* for December 14, 1916. Entitled "Poetry from the Trenches," the review began by implicitly contrasting the popularity of Service's book, *The Spell of the Yukon,* with its "staggering sale of five hundred thousand copies" to the lack of sales of volumes of the new poetry. While *The Spell of the Yukon* was accumulating its tremendous volume of sales "and while the wells of Kipling have been growing muddy or dry, the professors of poetry and the dilettanti have been paying attention to Imagists and Spectrists, leaving Service — they thought — to school-boys." One discerns already that the review would be a joke within a joke; by pretending to take Service seriously, Bynner satirized what he conceived to be the artiness of the new poetry as well as the sentimentalism of Service's false emotion:

> It happens that I had just read and reviewed "Spectra," the latest expression of "the new verse," and been struck with it as a strange phosphorescent crest of impressionism, when there came into my hands the volume by Service, "Rhymes of a Red Cross Man," two hundred pages of sturdy sentimental realism. And I started up with a gasp. Here was "the old verse." Here was something actual, intimate, human, alive.
>
> I will grant at the outset, to such as incline to disagree with my estimate, an occasional familiar crudeness in the book, and the mawkishness of poems like "Our Hero," "Son," and "The Convalescent." But the crudeness is the kind you grasp hands with heartily and the mawkishness is the kind you look away from respectfully, and what's left, by far the greater part, you thrill and laugh over like a boy. . . . We have been inquir-

ing for the poetry of the War. In my judgment, here
it is.

Bynner's disgust with the thinblooded excesses of Imagism,
the commercial mawkishness of Service's versifying, and the
patriotic attitudes of those advocating war went unremarked.
The readers of the new poetry accepted *Spectra* as a seriously
intended, even exciting volume. The little magazine *Others*
printed a special Spectrist issue in 1917. There were, of course,
doubters, such as Amy Lowell, who thought Emanuel Morgan
and Anne Knish were charlatans, but William Carlos Williams
took them seriously, as did others. At long last, "Casual Comment" in *The Dial* for April 25, 1918, exposed the hoax, the
first occasion on which it was described in print for what it was.
"The history of our so-called poetic renaissance will contain no
sprightlier chapter than the tale of the Spectrist school." After
summarizing the situation of the new poetry, "Casual Comment"
went on to relate the circumstances of the publication of *Spectra*
by Mitchell Kennerley, in 1916. The "public smiled, winked, and
swallowed"; and among the discerning, the reception of the
Spectrist poems was eager. "Casual Comment" concluded: "One
wonders whether the genesis and course of Spectrism is not the
most illuminating criticism of much that is most pretentious in
the new arts. It seems that Mr. Bynner, while watching a performance by the Russian Ballet, announced a sudden determination to found a new school in poetry. What to call it: His
programme lay open at 'La Spectre de la Rose.' Followed two
weeks of indefatigable composition in collaboration with 'Miss
Knish,' then publication and fame. Probably neither of the
authors was prepared for so gratifying a success. Indeed, there is
no telling how far the 'movement' might have gone but for
the interruption of the war, which gave 'Miss Knish' a commission as Captain Arthur Davison Ficke." Max Putzel says of the
exposé in *The Dial* that Bynner "must have asked" either Laird
Bell (in whose company at the Russian Ballet Bynner had originally been inspired and who was at the time a stockholder in the
Dial Publishing Company) or Conrad Aiken (then a contributing
editor) "to divulge the identity of the Spectrists. The exposé

appeared in *The Dial,* but so unobtrusively as to escape the notice
of the daily papers." Bynner then saw to it that the *Detroit
Daily News* — he was in Detroit at the time, lecturing — more
widely publicized the hoax. S. Foster Damon was probably
truer to the details of the exposé when he said that it was Martyn
Johnson who let the secret out in *The Dial,* rather than Aiken
or Bell, as "Casual Comment" was an editorial expression; of
course Bell or Aiken or both may have given Johnson the information about the identities of Emanuel Morgan and Anne
Knish. Whoever leaked the news to *The Dial* was well known
to the staff; and such informal gossip was far removed from the
sobriety and the factual emphasis of Francis Browne's "Notes"
and "Briefs on New Books" in the old *Dial.*

As fundamental as was the change in what *The Dial* published was its change in whom it published. Thus the major
change in *The Dial* wrought by Donlin and Johnson had to do
with the selection of contributors as well as what would be published. Four of the contributors to the second number for 1917,
that of January 25, moved in the more advanced artistic and
intellectual groups of the war years: Amy Lowell contributed
the leading article, "Poetry as a Spoken Art," just after the
announcement made by the new owner; and among the reviewers
were Harold Laski with "The Justification of History," H. M.
Kallen with "The Zionist Hope," and Gilbert Seldes with "A
New Literature for Peace." Three of these four writers would
be more or less closely associated with *The Dial* from 1917 until
it ceased publication, but Harold Laski was to prove to be too
politically oriented for Scofield Thayer's taste. Laski's review
was an omen of the drift of Johnson's *Dial* away from its usual
literary preoccupations toward involvement in the engrossing
events of the war. Perhaps Johnson was not, after all, as deeply
interested in the arts as he had averred; more probably the mood
of the war years was too pervasive and overwhelming not to
affect his direction of *The Dial.*

Certainly Johnson's statement of intentions in the next issue,
for February 8, 1917, ran counter to the contents that had appeared in the January numbers of *The Dial* and to his own

"Announcement" made just prior to this manifesto. Now, asserted the publisher, *The Dial* stood by President Wilson, and changing its policy, it would publish "articles and discussions inspired by the trend of events." In the event, it did not stand by President Wilson with conspicuous steadfastness, but increasingly its emphasis was on the topical rather than the belletristic.

As a means of securing the services of writers he liked, Johnson formulated the device of the board of contributing editors. Such a board added prestige when it appeared on the masthead, and as its members were active on *The Dial* in widely varying degrees, they occasioned relatively little expense and trouble. Later the device of the board of contributing editors got out of hand when, as the editors were selected for their politics, they feuded with each other. But until Johnson moved *The Dial* to New York in July 1918, this device seems to have worked fairly well as a means of providing articles and reviews of critical excellence; indeed, it seems to have been one of the more stable aspects of the magazine during its latter days in Chicago.

With the issue of March 22, 1917, Johnson announced the first of his groups of contributing editors: Percy F. Bicknell, Randolph Bourne, William Aspenwall Bradley, Padraic Colum, Henry B. Fuller (who, at the same period, was also on the Advisory Committee of *Poetry*), H. M. Kallen, J. E. Robinson, J. C. Squire, and Theodore Stanton. Most of these men had written for *The Dial* when the Brownes had controlled it, and Colum and Kallen were to preserve their association through the changes of the next few years and throughout the Twenties. Randolph Bourne died at the close of 1918, but he would play a significant part in the transformation of *The Dial* into a monthly devoted to the arts. Percy F. Bicknell left the staff with the issue of May 3, 1917, and was replaced by John Macy and Conrad Aiken, with the issue for June 14, 1917. Theodore Stanton was dropped from this group, and Van Wyck Brooks was added to it with *The Dial* for October 11, 1917. Mary Carlock briefly replaced Travis Hoke as Associate Editor on the masthead from August 16 to December 6, 1917. As announced in "Notes and News" for April 11, 1918, William Aspenwall Bradley resigned as contributing editor to enlist in "the Sanitary Corps of the United States Army," and Robert Dell, a foreign correspondent for *The Dial* and *The Manchester Guardian*, replaced Bradley. Dell published his despatches regularly through the issue of June 6, 1918, when *The Dial* announced in its column of "Casual Comment" that Dell had been asked to leave France because he had purportedly sent some war news annoying to the French government. Thereafter there were no "French Letters" while the war lasted. With these changes, the contributing editors remained with *The Dial* until the reorganization of the magazine after Johnson removed it to New York at the beginning of July 1918.

In about a year and a half, Martyn Johnson and George Donlin between them secured for *The Dial* as contributors many of the young writers then just making their appearances in American literature and journalism, writers whose poetry, fiction, reviews, and criticism transformed American culture, directed it up a new and different path, and endowed it with a vitality widely admired and yet inimitable. A significant number of these young men and women formed the staff of *The Dial* of the 1920's, constituted its core of contributors, and made it the leading journal of arts and letters in America in its decade and after.

The first of the future *Dial* editors to write for Johnson's *Dial* was Gilbert Seldes, who made his initial appearance, as Gilbert Vivian Seldes, with a long review, "A New Literature of Peace," in the issue for January 25, 1917, two years and a half after his graduation from Harvard. Seldes wrote on C. R. Buxton's edition of a group of papers entitled *Toward a Lasting Settlement*, on R. W. Seton-Watson's *The War and Democracy*, and on J. A. Hobson's *Toward International Government*. This review essay on international trends and the politics of the war years does not, however, display Seldes's writing as he typically wrote for *The Dial* of Thayer and Watson, and except for the fact itself of his appearance at this juncture in the fortunes of the magazine, the review is worth noting only as an expression of the cosmopolitan attitude shared by the writers central to the formulation of *The Dial* in which Seldes figured prominently in the early 1920's.

Seldes contributed two other reviews to Johnson's *Dial*, both during 1917. "Rediscovery and Romance" — in the issue for July 19 — dealt with two books by Thomas Burke, *Limehouse Nights* and *Nights in Town*. Both were English publications; just why an American journal would ordinarily review them is perhaps more easily understood by reference to "Notes and News" for the issue with its statement that "Gilbert Vivian Seldes, who has been studying social conditions in England since the beginning of the war, is a Philadelphia journalist and critic. He is a graduate of Harvard." In the issue for October 25 appeared Seldes's last review, of the series for Johnson. "A Parnassian Romance," in which he discussed James Elroy Flecker's *The King of Alsander,* another English publication. Seldes was again identified in "Notes and News" for the issue as "a young American critic and journalist, who has been living abroad, chiefly in England, since the beginning of the war." The emphasis on Seldes's English exile and his connection with Harvard is more consequential than the substance of his two reviews. While the work of neither Thomas Burke nor James Elroy Flecker was representative of the writing Scofield Thayer published as Editor of *The Dial,* like Seldes he had studied in England — philosophy rather than social conditions, however — after graduation from Harvard; and Thayer and Seldes had been friends as undergraduates at Harvard. That Seldes did not appear again in *The Dial* until 1920 may be explained by his enlistment in the Army in 1918 and by his job as an associate editor with *Collier's* in 1919.

The second member of the future editorial staff of *The Dial* to contribute to Martyn Johnson's *Dial* was James Sibley Watson, Jr., who at the end of 1919 became Publisher of the magazine and President of the Dial Publishing Company. In the number for May 3, 1917, Watson published his first signed piece in *The Dial,* "The Author of 'Erewhon,' " a review of Gilbert Cannan's *Samuel Butler: A Critical Study* and John F. Harris's *Samuel Butler; Author of Erewhon: The Man and His Work.* At this time, the young reviewer, who called himself Sibley Watson, "after studying at Harvard," according to the "Notes and News" for the issue, and spending some time abroad, was "now devoting himself to writing."

In the autumn of 1916 Sibley Watson began a half year's residence in Chicago, hoping among other things to write for publication. He arrived in Chicago by way of Rochester, N.Y., where he was born in 1894, Groton, which he had attended for six years, and Harvard, from which, although he was of the class of 1917, he was graduated with the A. B. in 1916. According to William Wasserstrom, at Groton preparatory school, "during lulls of the strenuous life, curiosity about periodicals and books was not discouraged." Moreover, at Groton Watson was greatly influenced by a speech given by John Jay Chapman, at the Lenten service in the school chapel on February 27, 1913; although Dr. Watson, writes Wasserstrom, "no longer remembers what Chapman said, he refers to this as the occasion when, hearing a man fired by modern ideas, his own thought crystallized." One would like to know just what it was that fired Watson so in his senior year at Groton; for there seems to be little enough that he has, later, held in common with Chapman, that interesting and most individual but quite reactionary writer. At Harvard Watson was active on *The Harvard Monthly* and earned his undergraduate degree in three years. Graduating at the age of twenty-two, he married Hildegarde Lasell and moved to Chicago, then the most exciting American city for writers and journalists. Watson had been reading *The Dial* off and on since his schooldays, finding its book reviews helpful, and also the publishers' advertisements. It was thus pretty much in the nature of things that he should gravitate to *The Dial* as an outlet for his writing.

What was perhaps not altogether in the nature of things was that Watson wanted to become a writer. His conventional metier would have been finance and industry, for he was the son of a banker listed in *Who's Who in America* as president of the Security Trust Company and the Rochester Savings Bank and as a director of the Eastman Kodak Company. The distinguished architect and theatrical designer, Claude Bragdon, had known "Sibley" as a child in Rochester and opined that he was quietly rebelling against his life and environment there. Bragdon's memoir *More Lives than One* suggests the atmosphere of material plenty in which Sibley Watson was reared: the extensive home with its stables, greenhouses, and garden; and the ocean-going yacht, *Genesee,* which was, to Bragdon's eye, "the last word in that order of marine architecture."[8]

In 1915 Claude Bragdon was invited to deliver two lectures at the Art Institute of Chicago under the Scammon Foundation; he was well known in the city through his many connections there both architectural and literary, going back to the 1890's and ranging from Herbert Stone to Louis Sullivan, men whose work Bragdon admired. For several years, too, Bragdon's own Manas Press — its title derived from the Sanskrit word signifying the mental principle — had advertised its publications, chiefly Bragdon's own architectural and theosophical writings (among them, *Projective Ornament* and *Episodes from an Unwritten History*), in *The Dial.* On a visit to Chicago, Bragdon introduced Watson to George Bernard Donlin and suggested that Watson review some of the work of his friend, Francis Grierson. Dr. Watson recalls that he submitted such a review in late 1916 or early 1917, as well as some of the "Briefs on New Books" that were, of course, printed unsigned; the Grierson review was never printed.

Dr. Watson also recalls having dinner late in 1916 with Scofield Thayer at the old Blackstone, on Thayer's return East from a honeymoon trip to the West Coast. The two men had met only once at Cambridge when they were undergraduates, although both had been active on *The Harvard Monthly;* but Thayer was in the Harvard class of 1914 and thus had made friends more nearly his contemporaries than was Watson, in the usual way of undergraduates. The dinner engagement at the Blackstone Hotel came about, therefore, not because Thayer and Watson were at that time well acquainted but because Hildegarde Watson was an old friend of Thayer's, from Worcester days. Dr. Watson cannot recall that anyone mentioned *The Dial* that evening.

Scofield Thayer only recently had come to know Chicago, and at the time, as he has expressly stated, he did not know Martyn Johnson, though, as Dr. Watson has suggested, he may have made some friends among the group backing *The Dial*. This possibility is suggested also by the appearance of Mary Aldis's story, "The Mosque of the Empress," in the issue for October 1922. (Ignoring Mrs. Aldis's intimate connection with *The Dial* in 1916, "Notes on Contributors" merely stated that Mary Reynolds Aldis "was born and lives in Chicago. Her published work includes *Plays for Small Stages, The Princess Jack, Flashlights,* and *Drift.*") Thayer had first come to Chicago in 1915 or 1916, probably the latter year, because of a wager. He had been told that he could not support himself, and to prove the falsity of the allegation, he had put himself aboard a train bound for Chicago, a town completely strange to him, and had taken with him only five dollars. Finding himself a job as a salesman of the Britannica (according to Hermann Riccius) or some sort of directories (according to Dr. Watson's recollection), Scofield Thayer not only supported himself but also made the friends in Chicago whom Watson was aware of.

Sibley Watson did not stay long in Chicago. In 1917 he entered the Medical School of New York University, from which he received the degree of M.D. in 1921. In his memoir, Claude Bragdon described Watson in those years as living in Greenwich Village with his wife Hildegarde, while he studied medicine. Bragdon agreed with Llewelyn Powys, who came to know Watson a few years later, that he drifted through life with the adaptability of a long, drooping straw caught in the middle of a lively trout stream. Watson, said Powys, was enormously rich and yet liked to appear poor; he was extremely wise, yet preferred to be thought foolish. "With a small black bag, he was to be encountered in a perpetual drooping peregrination through the sidestreets of Greenwich Village. He made one think of those silent, evasive eels one hears about, eels that find their way to the ocean from remote ponds, sliding their sinuous bodies through night-dusky, dew-drenched pastures. He possessed a subtle, cynical mind, which he did all in his power to conceal." But one cannot agree with Bragdon's approval of Powys' assertion that Watson was "an extremely able doctor, who never practised, an extremely clever writer, who never wrote." Write he did for

The Dial, as W. C. Blum or anonymously — as well as in his own name. Powys was of the opinion that Watson "ever remained aloof and uncommitted," whether one met him "in the French pastry-shop, or in the hall of his house, with its mullioned window and noble stone chimney-piece." Powys further asserted that even his wife's resplendent presence at their lighted dinner table was never sufficient to overcome Watson's embarrassed diffidence, "a diffidence that seemed to cover the most inconvenient reticences. . . . he was capable of interjecting some whispered comment that would completely destroy one's confidence and would keep recurring to one's mind for days afterwards, because of its teasing ambiguity." To Powys, Scofield Thayer was an imperious Roman emperor, and Watson a supersubtle Nicodemus.

Bragdon also contrasted Thayer to Watson. He saw Thayer as "an Oxford-Harvard product, and something of a dandy, well-spoken, well-mannered, and well-dressed" — much more conventional as an image of the *beau idéal* than Sibley Watson "in his shabby clothes and with his deprecating, apologetic air." And Watson himself was in contrast to his wife Hildegarde, aristocratic in dress and bearing, receiving visitors as the butler ushered them into her lofty manorial music room overlooked by a gallery.

During his years as a medical student, Watson did not lose interest in *The Dial.* It thus happened that he wrote a second review for Martyn Johnson, of George Moore's collection *A Story-Teller's Holiday,* printed in the issue for December 14, 1918, at a time when his friend Scofield Thayer, after having lent some money to Johnson, was having difficulties with Johnson over finances and editorial policy. It was Watson who suggested that Thayer purchase the controlling interest in the Dial Publishing Company, along with himself, in order to rebuild the magazine according to their shared vision of its possibilities.

Like Thayer, Watson had a background of wealth and cultivated leisure; unlike Thayer, Watson had an absorbing vocation beyond the life of literature and the arts, a vocation in which he achieved distinction, and in which he was able to combine a professional knowledge of medicine, skill in photographic and cinematic techniques, and that feeling for the arts he already displayed in 1917-18. With Thayer, he became a leader and patron of the young men attracted to *The Dial* in 1917. Watson brought to *The Dial* an invaluable stability and calm, and he shared Thayer's selflessness in their support of the magazine. Not only did he introduce Thayer to the notion of actively directing *The Dial* by owning it, he it was who saw *The Dial* through to the final page of the last issue in July 1929.

Because of his future role as Publisher of *The Dial* Watson's two early reviews are significant. As regards their content, moreover, both reviews anticipate certain issues of *The Dial*, especially of the early 1920's. In the first review, "The Author of 'Erewhon,'" Sibley Watson applauded Samuel Butler for having "tried to be himself and himself only. He never worried about his soul's salvation, had no desire to soar in unearthly realms or to swim in sentiment, never wanted to be like Shakespeare or anyone else whom he did not resemble. He resisted all attempts to make either himself or others conform to ways of believing which were not natural and reasonable to them, and he attacked hypocrisy wherever he found it." As for Butler's twin "obsessions," Watson held that it might almost be said "that the church was the first cause of his writing, the central object of his satire," and that Butler's animosity toward Darwin was due to his defense of a theory different from Darwin's, "defending free will in the natural order against a determinism as stupidly and superstitiously guarded by its high priests, the Darwinists, as religious dogma had ever been." Rather obliquely, Watson added that "In his unwearied opposition to his age Butler might have been compared to a man who refuses to join his country's army at a time when joining the army is considered the thing to do," an uncomfortable remark to make in a nation that had gone to war against the Central Powers less than a month before Watson's review appeared.

Although most of the review occupied itself with John F. Harris's views of Butler, as the more recently published of the two volumes under discussion, Watson's generally complimentary attitude toward Cannan's book is important to note; it adumbrates a more detailed consideration of Gilbert Cannan in *The Dial* for February 1920. This second number of the reconstituted, monthly *Dial* published two caricatures of Cannan by Ivan Opffer: "Gilbert Cannan," a profile portrait dated 1920; and "Gilbert Cannan after Reading the Following Article," a half-length caricature. The essay in question was Evelyn Scott's critique, "Gilbert Cannan: Inquisitor." The leading book review, "The Authoress of the Way of All Flesh," of Henry Festing Jones's *Samuel Butler: A Memoir,* was written by Cannan himself, of whom "Notes on Contributors" said, in allusion to Watson's review of 1917, that "Gilbert Cannan's critical study of Samuel Butler has unfortunately not yet been published in this country."[9]

Watson's second review appeared just over a month after the Armistice, in *The Dial* for December 14, 1918. It is in the nature of a general consideration of Moore's work, despite the noncommittal title, which is also the title of the book under review, *A Story-Teller's Holiday.* Watson did not take Moore, whom he called "our friend of deathless middle-age," very seriously, and the treatment of Moore's work is facetious and ironic: Moore's interest in "incident, scenery and character . . . is as beautiful morally as the enthusiasm of an old gentleman at work in his garden; but moral consolation is not the precise thing we are looking for in a A Story-Teller's Holiday." And when "we think of Moore we always think of the feminine temperament — passive, swayed by every impulse, yet parasitic, ungrateful, hard toward the world's opinion, proud to be 'ashamed of nothing but to be ashamed.' So he had described himself, and so he is to be known."

Watson's attitude toward Moore is as uncomfortable in its way as his earlier remark about the man who refused to join the army, for he made it soon after Moore had become a contributor to *The Dial.* Martyn Johnson wrote Scofield Thayer on July 30, 1918, that Thayer would be "interested in knowing that a manuscript from George Moore has been submitted to us. It is a series of imaginary conversations between himself and Edmund Gosse, in which he supplies new endings for old masters in English literature. I am rather inclined to accept it, since its publication in THE DIAL would attract a certain new public who would take this as evidence of THE DIAL's being the official literary journal in America, all of which, of course, is desirable."

The first "Imaginary Conversation: Gosse and Moore, I," appeared in the issue for October 5, 1918, and was continued in the next two issues. Martyn Johnson's payment to Moore for it eventually caused *The Dial* much trouble, as the sum paid was exorbitant from the point of view of Thayer and Watson and besides was well known to various writers in London who shared Watson's ambivalence about Moore and his writing. This payment caused, in part, the series of disagreements and delays that made publication of *The Waste Land* such an unhappy affair. When Moore's "Conversations" were incorporated in his *Conversations in Ebury Street,* nevertheless *The Dial* printed Marianne Moore's ironic and amusing review of the book, published in the issue for March 1925 as "Histrionic Seclusion." That George Moore continued to be published and reviewed in *The Dial* despite the very mixed emotions with which Thayer and Watson regarded him is still another instance of the continuity of *The Dial* from 1917 on — though undoubtedly they never viewed their publication of work by him and about him as constituting substantiating evidence of *The Dial's* being the official literary journal in America. Watson's strongly individual view of the first World War (an attitude that he shared with Thayer) and his preference for Samuel Butler's iconoclasm as against George Moore's suggest certain qualities basic to *The Dial* during the 1920's: its gusto, its willingness to take an unpopular stand, its search for a criticism somehow more satisfactorily premised than the religion of *l'art pour l'art*.[10]

A third name is almost equally portentous for *The Dial,* that of Paul Rosenfeld, who first appeared in *The Dial* with an essay on Rimsky-Korsakov in the issue of March 28, 1918. Rosenfeld had begun to make a name for himself in 1916 and 1917 with his pieces appearing in *The Seven Arts* and *The New Republic.* Whether his views on the war agreed with those of the group in charge of *The Seven Arts* is problematical, as he published even more frequently in *The New Republic,* the new weekly that voiced the opinions of the liberals who supported American participation in the struggle, than he did in *The Seven Arts,* which opposed American entry and advocated, instead, both a national emphasis on the settling of domestic problems and American support for world-wide revolution, peaceful or otherwise. At the time Rosenfeld's "Rimsky-Korsakov" was published, *The Dial* had taken over the subscription list of *The Seven Arts,* which had been forced to suspend publication because of its advocacy of an American policy of peaceful abstention from the first World War. It may well be that what attracted Rosenfeld to *The Dial* was not so much its political policy as a hospitality, shared with *The New Republic* (for all their divergence in politics), to the New Movement in art and music and letters. Paul Rosenfeld's first essay for *The Dial* thus constitutes an appropriate inaugural piece for the man who would write the monthly musical column for *The Dial,* from November 1920 to June 1927.

With its texture as rich as marzipan and its colorful images, the prose of Rosenfeld's impressionistic method has fallen into disfavor, and the more astringent prose of a more rigorously formalist critical method has displaced it. Yet this prose, which entertains and charms more than it informs through technical analysis, retains the freshness of its enthusiasm. Rosenfeld wrote of Rimsky-Korsakov's music as "the loveliest of picture-books," but "nothing more": "It is as if Rimsky-Korsakov had ignored the other and larger functions of his art, and been content to have his music only picturesque and colorful." There is patent in Rimsky-Korsakov's work a vast love of erudition and a vast faith in its efficacy. Even Tchaikowsky, a good deal of an intellectualist himself, complained that Rimsky-Korsakov "worshipped technique" and that his work was "full of contrapuntal tricks and all the signs of a sterile pedantry." Rosenfeld contrasted the superficiality of Rimsky-Korsakov's work to "the living virtue that informs even a single page" of *Boris Godunov;* he even paid homage to the nineteenth century by extolling the "nobly human stature" of Moussorgsky and Borodin's "rich and vivid sense of the past."

If the superficial technical discussion, moral judgments, and impressionistic imagery all hang together successfully, they manage a pleasant unity because Rosenfeld used these tools to reveal his attitude toward a related series of musical compositions rather than to give his readers much specifically musical information about Rimsky-Korsakov's work. As a personality, Paul Rosenfeld may have charmed the readers of "Rimsky-Korsakov" into believing they knew more about Rimsky-Korsakov's music than was perhaps the case, if their knowledge depended on the contents of the essay. Rosenfeld here conveyed the impression that he was familiar with music in a musicianly sense (as indeed he was), but the information actually given was not specifically musicianly. The tone here is that of an easy familiarity with languages and letters and the fine arts in an atmosphere redolent of good cigars and vintage sherry.

To judge by this and his later criticism in *The Dial*, Paul Rosenfeld was interested in revealing an attitude toward life, in ascertaining the comparable and comparative qualities of the arts — qualities readily observable to the practised and cultivated connoisseur — rather than in a close analysis of any given work of art. The critic of "Rimsky-Korsakov" presented himself as a gentleman who worshipped the Graces that made life bearable rather than as the professional who analyzed the craftsmanship in a work of art.

In a *Dial* increasingly obsessed with the politics of native liberalism and with the Great War, Paul Rosenfeld recaptured something of that old cosmopolitan breadth with which Francis Browne and William Morton Payne had endowed the magazine in the Nineties. Rosenfeld did not feel that he was cut off from the mainstream of American life by virtue of his interests in the arts and aesthetic criticism. He neither repined nor searched for what Gilbert Seldes has termed the great audience. As a critic, Rosenfeld took for granted that he kept his audience with him, that an intimate group distinguished for its intelligence and coherence of tastes remained eager to share the critic's discoveries.[11] Like John Gould Fletcher's essay, Rosenfeld's appreciation represents a transitional stage between the nineteenth-century aesthetic of content or idea and the formalist aesthetic toward which American criticism of the arts has evolved; and like Fletcher's essay, it exemplifies the advanced critical work published in the decade 1910-20.

"Rimsky-Korsakov" also exemplifies the widening artistic interests of *The Dial*. Almost exclusively belletristic as the American aesthetic tradition had always been, in keeping with the limitations of this tradition, *The Dial* had always interested itself in the criticism and the history of literature. Not until the beginning of 1918 did the subtitle of *The Dial* change from its long-used phrase "A Fortnightly Journal of Literary Criticism, Discussion, and Information" to "A Fortnightly Journal of Criticism and Discussion of Literature and the Arts." Thus recently had the magazine come to express formally the major interest in painting, sculpture, and architecture that since early 1917 it had evinced through the content of its pages; now with the publication of Rosenfeld's essay, it achieved a certain fullblown sophistication in the field of music criticism as well. Though, to be sure, Rosenfeld's suave aestheticism contrasted ever more strangely, as month succeeded month, to the outcries of the reformers of political and social wrongs — a divergence of interests that developed into an open conflict between the aesthetes and the activists and that finally wrecked Martyn Johnson's *Dial*. But in the early months of 1918, politics of the liberal-pacifist kind and the art of the New Movement seemed mutually compatible. The events of 1918 and the death of Randolph Bourne militated against any warm compatibility — at least against its being displayed in the pages of Martyn Johnson's *Dial*.

For all his devotion to Randolph Bourne as close friend and as intellectual force, Paul Rosenfeld contributed only one more musical essay to *The Dial,* written before October 1918 — before he was demobilized from the Army and helped nurse Bourne in the illness from which he died. Not until the issue for February 8, 1919, did Rosenfeld's "Pélleas et Mélisande" appear. Perhaps his own illness as a soldier inspired the conclusion of the essay, with its veiled expression of personal unease: Debussy's "death robbed us of no fair development we might reasonably have anticipated. Indeed, in his very last works, the gold is spread more thinly, the emotion is less warm. He had completely fulfilled himself. His age had demanded of him an art that it might hold far from the glare and tumult, an art into which it could retreat, an art which could compensate it for a life become too cruel and demanding. And this he gave it, in perhaps imperishable form." It was an unintended elegy for Bourne; but Paul Rosenfeld's tribute to his dead friend was not printed until his essay on "Randolph Bourne" appeared in Scofield Thayer's *Dial* for December 1923.

By all odds Randolph Bourne furnishes the prime example of the possibilities open to Martyn Johnson as owner of *The Dial* and of the blighting of those possibilities. They opened to Johnson through the participation of Bourne both as contributor and as influence. As a contributor, Randolph Bourne first appeared in *The Dial* during the early months of Johnson's regime, when he wrote the leading article, "Seeing It Through," a review of H. G. Wells's patriotic novel of the petty bourgeois in wartime England, *Mr. Britling Sees It Through,* for the issue of December 28, 1916.

By December 1916, Bourne's stand against American participation in the war was limiting his usefulness to the editors of *The New Republic,* and he told Elizabeth Shepley Sergeant in a letter of December 6 that they had suggested that he become their authority on prohibition, "a doleful subject." If Bourne thus needed *The Dial* as a substitute for *The New Republic,* he refused to compromise his Fabian, pacifist, and cosmopolitan principles, for the review of Wells's novel was openly hostile. As John Dewey soon would do in the United States, so in England Wells — the most influential novelist in his country and one with an almost equally great influence in America — dumped his cargo of Fabian notions and plumped for jingoism and what Bourne sardonically termed the "quick flop into religion," as "the cosmification of his own despairing struggle." Bourne reacted to such a *bouleversement* as to a sort of wilful bankruptcy of intellect.

Wells's "plunge into the rubbish of Captains of Mankind, World-Republics, Religion as the first and last thing, will steel our hearts against such cheap and easy consolations for calamities against which there can be no consolation," opined the reviewer; he countered that "past religion into creative intelligence, such effort should lead all who will resolutely seek such consolation. Nothing else is a seeing it through." As would be expected, several letters to the Editor took sides about Bourne's review. In the issue for January 25, 1917, John Cotton Dana applauded such "sound and solid stuff"; but three other correspondents suspected it. M. H. Hedges and Harry B. Kennon, sharing the "Communications" column with Dana, were uneasy about Bourne's criticism as too subjective, even though Kennon thought the novel too hastily written and Hedges thought Bourne's purpose sound in exposing Wells's dangerous leadership. But like a fourth correspondent, Erving Winslow (in *The Dial* for March 8, 1917), they deplored, in varying degrees of sternness, what Winslow called Bourne's "propaganda of atheism."

Bourne came to *The Dial*, it is clear, as a controversial figure; nevertheless on March 22, 1917, Johnson announced Bourne as one of his group of nine "contributing editors" to *The Dial*. From this start, Bourne was significant for *The Dial* not only as a contributor but also as an influence. His name on the masthead suggested presumably that the pages of the magazine were open to advocacy of certain policies, and his many reviews and essays seemed, at first, to confirm the inference.

When Bourne came to *The Dial*, war had not been declared; in one respect, he was at the peak of his productivity and popularity, writing not only for *The Seven Arts* and *The New Republic* but also for such well-established magazines as *The Atlantic Monthly*. In fact, he had first contributed to the *Atlantic* in April 1911, while he was a student at Columbia, and for its issue for July 1916 he wrote his most characteristic essay, "Trans-national America," one that at least for the future of *The Dial* was also his most influential piece of writing. The theme of Bourne's paper was closely related to one of the basic and enduring attitudes of Francis Browne's *Dial*: liberal cosmopolitanism.

It was an attitude overtly and directly opposed to the regional and nationalist concerns of most Americans of the times, distant as they were from foreign countries and foreign tongues; it was also an attitude that was most often associated with the anti-imperialist, socialist, pacifist hopes and aspirations of many intellectuals in the Western world as well as in the Russian Empire, then in some ways closer in feeling to the West than later in the century. Bourne called it transnationalism, and he defined it as "not a nationality but a trans-nationality, a weaving back and forth, with the other lands, of many threads of all sizes and colors." America, he asserted, was "already the work-federation in miniature, the continent where for the first time in history has been achieved that miracle of hope, the peaceful living side by side, with character substantially preserved of the most heterogeneous peoples under the sun. . . . Here, notwithstanding our tragic failures of adjustment, the outlines are already too clear not to give us a new vision and a new orientation of the American mind in the world." And again, Bourne held that "the contribution of America will be an intellectual internationalism which goes far beyond the mere exchange of scientific ideas and discoveries and the cold recordings of facts. It will be an intellectual sympathy which is not satisfied until it has got at the heart of the different cultural expressions, and felt as they feel. . . . Against the thinly disguised panic which calls itself 'patriotism' and the thinly disguised militarism which calls itself 'preparedness' the cosmopolitan ideal is set."

Bourne even proposed dual citizenship for those naturalized Americans who wished to keep their cultural ties with the lands of their birth. Only America, he held, by reason of the unique liberty of opportunity and traditional isolation for which she seems to stand, can lead in this "cosmopolitan enterprise," and for precisely the reason that she is already a world-federation in miniature.[12]

Such writing and Randolph Bourne's charm of character overcame the pathetic deficiencies of his broken body; hunchbacked either from a fall in infancy or from the effects of tuberculosis of the spine, he was grotesquely deformed, with a stunted body, large head, and heavy features misshapen from a clumsy forceps delivery at birth. Born in Bloomfield, New Jersey, in what had been a country town but had become part of the burgeoning Northeastern urban-industrial complex, he felt estranged from his family in their old, dull, and very uncomfortable house. He seemed queer to them; his sister was almost a passionate vulgarian; yet after his graduation from high school, Bourne had to eke out seven years of work, mostly in a factory that produced paper rolls for player pianos. It was an experience that confirmed his mistrust of employers and of capitalism.

At the age of twenty-three he entered Columbia University on a scholarship and proceeded to obtain not only a bachelor's degree but the M. A.; he wrote for the undergraduate newspaper, the *Spectator,* and edited the *Columbia Monthly.* In 1913 Bourne published his first book, *Youth and Life,* and received his master's degree. Columbia then awarded him the Richard W. Gilder Fellowship for the study of political and social conditions in the United States or abroad, and Bourne sailed for Europe in July 1913. The major result of his *wanderjahr,* which he entitled "Impressions of Europe, 1913-14," was duly presented to Columbia on his return to the United States. By this time, Bourne was a seasoned journalist — after all, he had first contributed to the *Atlantic* in April 1911 — and when Herbert Croly and his associates founded *The New Republic* in 1914, Bourne joined the staff. For the rest of 1914 and throughout 1915-16, the bulk of his writing was published in the weekly issues of *The New Republic.*

1917, that year of crisis for most Americans, brought a crisis in Bourne's affairs. At the beginning of the year, he had found two important outlets for his journalism to supplement *The New Republic.* He became a contributing editor to *The Dial,* and in April 1917 appeared his first piece, "The Puritan's Will to Power," in the new avant-garde monthly, *The Seven Arts.* At the same time, in *The New Republic* for March 10, Bourne and others published an advertisement, "DO THE PEOPLE WANT WAR," in which he published his stand against the entry of the United States into the first World War. Good Friday of

1917 made that particular announcement and the attitude behind it seem, to many, no longer merely dubious but actually
treasonable.

In all, in the twenty-four months of December 1916 through
December 1918, Bourne contributed a total of thirty pieces to
The Dial; his thirty-first contribution was published posthumously in the issue for January 1920. As he came to write more
frequently for *The Dial,* he wrote less frequently for *The New
Republic.* Like Croly's weekly, *The Dial* was avowedly liberal
and cosmopolitan in its international outlook, indeed it had
been avowedly so since the turn of the century. The particular
attraction of Martyn Johnson's *Dial* was that since about 1915,
in the last days of Waldo Browne's ownership, it had seemed
to advocate a policy of peace as well as liberalism and cosmopolitanism, whereas *The New Republic* in 1917 opted for a liberalism that went to war in support of the British Empire. In
large measure the interest of Randolph Bourne's life at its end
lies in the story of his gradual disillusion with the editorial policy
of *The Dial,* which veered toward advocacy of American participation in the war.

It is misleading, however, to treat Bourne's writing for *The
Dial* as specifically political and social in its purpose. Of his
thirty-one contributions, eighteen were literary. There are two
essays, "The Art of Theodore Dreiser," published in the issue
of June 14, 1917, and "Traps for the Unwary," published in
the issue of March 28, 1918. There is a final appearance, a posthumously published fragment entitled "An Autobiographical
Chapter" which appeared — obviously both a challenge and
memorial tribute — as the piece opening the first issue of the
refurbished *Dial* of Thayer and Watson, in January 1920; the
same year it was included in Bourne's collection, edited by Van
Wyck Brooks, *The History of a Literary Radical,* as "Fragment
of a Novel." All the rest of Bourne's signed writing on *belles lettres*
for *The Dial,* which is to say, all such writing that Michael True
has attributed to Bourne in his bibliography of Bourne's work,
consists of book reviews.[13] Eleven reviews deal with fiction, ranging from Dostoevsky's *The Eternal Husband* (entitled "The Im-

manence of Dostoevsky" in *The Dial* for June 28, 1917) to a double review of William Allen White's *In the Heart of a Fool* and Willa Cather's *My Ántonia* (entitled "Morals and Art from the West" and posthumously published in *The Dial* for December 14, 1918). Bourne also contributed a double review of two collections, Robert Cortes Holliday's *Walking Stick Papers* and Carl Van Vechten's *The Merry-Go-Round* (entitled "The Light Essay" in *The Dial* for November 16, 1918). He reviewed two very dissimilar volumes of biography — Brander Matthews's autobiographical *These Many Years* (entitled "A Vanishing World of Gentility" in *The Dial* for March 14, 1918) and Lytton Strachey's *Eminent Victorians* (entitled "An Examination of Eminences" in *The Dial* for December 28, 1918 — another posthumously published review, and the last of those written by Bourne for *The Dial*).

Bourne contributed thirteen political and social pieces to *The Dial*, only two of which were articles. The first of these, "Conscience and Intelligence in War," was published in the issue of September 13, 1917; the other article was "The Idea of a University," published in the issue of October 22, 1917. There were eleven reviews relating to education, women's rights, labor, and, chiefly, the war in its military, revolutionary, moral, and philosophical aspects.

The statistical account of Bourne's contributions to *The Dial* leads to the surprising conclusion that his importance to the magazine was primarily as a reviewer, not as an editorial writer. His last leading article for Martyn Johnson was a literary essay, but a polemic all the same, on the dangers encountered by "bold modern writers" who broke the genteel tradition only to be smothered in the embrace of that same gentility in disguise: "The literary artist needs protection from the liberal audience that will accept him though he shock them, but that subtly tame him even while they appreciate." The occasion was the spring book issue of 1918, and the second article was Paul Rosenfeld's "Rimsky-Korsakov." Of Bourne's fourteen contributions published in *The Dial* later in 1918, all were reviews.

Although he undoubtedly preferred to write about the

higher politics of the Great War, it is obvious that Bourne was usually given the assignment of reviewing, instead, such diverse volumes as the translation of a novel by Dostoevsky, a treatise on American secondary education, a late novel by Henry Blake Fuller, and the memoirs of the Columbia professor Brander Matthews, whom he disliked because Matthews's mind "moved submerged far beneath the significant literary currents of the time." The versatility of Randolph Bourne is itself the most remarkable aspect of his intuitive and widely ranging, if not closely analytical, mind.

That mind was peculiarly at home in the disorder of the war years, and Bourne was never so much at ease as when he recited a litany of the new social dogmas as a means to bring order, a speculative order, to supplant the chaos swamping Europe and threatening America: "the need of liberating the creative rather than the possessive impulses, the principle of growth, the value of reverence towards individuality, the obsolescence of a society based on property and power, the inadequacy of security and liberty as sole political ideals, the need of autonomy within the state for subordinate groups, the hope for gild socialism, and the organization of an international order that shall harmonize with the true community of sentiments among mankind — these are the ideas which have been made familiar in 'Justice in Wartime' and in 'Why Men Fight,'" wrote Bourne in his review in *The Dial* of January 17, 1918, of Bertrand Russell's *Political Ideas*. What an irony it was, he cried, that it should be Bertrand Russell "who comes from the chill and remote regions of mathematics with this liberating idealism!" The admiration characterizes the cast of Bourne's mind in the last two years of his life; Russell and George Bernard Shaw became increasingly influential upon Bourne's thinking, not only because both were Fabian socialists but also because, in wartime England, both men dared unpopularity (and in Russell's case, dismissal from his post at Cambridge University and detention from travel to the United States) by advocating a policy of peace and by professing respect for aspects of German culture. Bourne's admiration for Russell was shared by Scofield Thayer; when Thayer became

Editor of *The Dial*, Bertrand Russell was, with Thayer's Harvard
mentor George Santayana, active as one of the two leading contemporary philosphers regularly to contribute to *The Dial* of the
1920's. Such friendships and such admirations were personal, of
course, but they were based, also, on the cosmopolitan attitude
toward culture, itself a dangerously unpopular attitude in 1917-
18. Only after the war could *The Dial* safely and openly advocate
an international order in harmony with the true community of
sentiments among mankind.

Besides Bourne's cosmopolitanism — or, to use his own
term, transnationalism — there exists another link with *The Dial*
of the 1920's that is equally fundamental, and that is Bourne's concern as a literary critic with problems of aesthetic form. Bourne's
concern sprang from his acquaintance with the nineteenth-century tradition of the novel; the critic contributing to *The Dial*
with whom Bourne shared a concern for literary form was not one
of the younger writers but was the older Chicago novelist Henry
Blake Fuller. Reviewing Fuller's short novel *On the Stairs*,
Bourne utilized as a point of departure two recent leading articles
by Fuller — "A Plea for Shorter Novels" and "New Forms of
Short Fiction," published in the issues for, respectively, August
30 and March 8, 1917 — in a piece entitled "The Brevity School
of Fiction." Here Bourne praised Fuller's short novel precisely
for its formal distinction: " 'On the Stairs' is thus a variety of
good and delightful things, summing up into a delightful piece of
literary art. But its chief significance ought to be the liberation
of those embryo American novelists who have been writing their
stories in free verse. Here is a brilliant and sound working model
of the 'novel within narrower limits.' " Bourne's concern with
form and his insistence upon the autonomy of art (as demonstrated in his *Dial* article "Traps for the Unwary") thus display
his affinity, as Michael True has asserted, to the critical writing
"of the most influential critics of the century, to T. S. Eliot's,
for example, which appeared, as Bourne's had appeared before it,
in the *Dial*" throughout the 1920's.

The fact remains that for all the frequency of Bourne's
appearances in *The Dial*, he was mostly a reviewer and thus was

implementing rather than helping to set policy. The situation was not what one would expect of a contributing editor of Bourne's talent and force. It was due, rather, to the conflicting attitudes toward the war that swiftly evolved in the community of American intellectuals in 1917 — attitudes that divided a minority of intellectuals from the larger community of the nation actively engaged in waging war — and to the consequent difficulties some of them encountered in seeking publishing outlets that were both congenial and solvent.

Along with his close friend Van Wyck Brooks, Bourne was another of the contributing editors to *The Dial* who also wrote for the new and ill-fated *Seven Arts* of 1916-17. The magazine was established on the advice of the analyst who treated James Oppenheim and Mrs. A. K. Rankine — one its chief editorialist, the other its president and financial support. *The Seven Arts* published its first monthly number — there were only twelve issues in all — in November 1916; for the first time the New Movement was sustained by a journal that achieved a synthesis of its liberating effects socially, aesthetically, culturally. In an advertisement in *The Dial* for April 19, 1917, *The Seven Arts* asserted that among its contributors were Robert Frost, Theodore Dreiser, Louis Untermeyer, Willard Huntington Wright, James Oppenheim (the editor), Van Wyck Brooks (by March 1917, he had succeeded Waldo Frank as associate editor), J. D. Beresford, Romain Rolland, Kahlil Gibran, Sherwood Anderson, Edgar Lee Masters, Amy Lowell, Wilbur Daniel Steele, and D. H. Lawrence. Most of these names were by now familiar to the readers of the Chicago *Dial*.

There was also another name that appeared in *The Seven Arts* that spring of 1917, a name familiar in Chicago especially: John Dewey had gained his early fame as a teacher at the University of Chicago under George Rainey Harper. He had gone East, like many another figure of what was even then being termed the Chicago Renaissance, to Columbia University and to the apogee of his influence as the voice of instrumentalist, pragmatic philosophy and progressive education. Soon after war had been declared, Dewey appeared in *The Seven Arts* for May, with a temporizing essay, "In a Time of National Hesitation." The editorial for the issue, by James Oppenheim, was equally temporizing and, really, gave no indication of the sort of policy toward the war that the magazine would follow. Oppenheim expressed dismay and doubt but was not forthrightly antiwar; instead, he quoted Whitman on the Civil War and concluded that "like those before us, we must go into the great fires, learning what was learned before, in the hope of the peace to be."

The editorial for the next month, June, was stronger but offered no positive suggestion. "Peace failed in Europe," it began, "now peace fails in America." More accusingly, the editorial said that "We too must know war because we could not volunteer and meet together as human beings to create great peace and great persons." The most important essay for the issue uttered no such laments. It was Randolph Bourne's "War and the Intellectuals," and it marked a turning point, a turning point that was also a rallying place for the members of the vanguard who, like Waldo Browne, were vocally despairing because a century's hopes for peace had been proved illusory. Bourne began, like Oppenheim, by accusing American intellectuals for not having prepared American public opinion for the events that brought about the declaration of war in 1917, and he went on to decry "the coalescence of the intellectual classes in support of the military programme." In the event, their socialism was shown to be a thin veneer. Moreover, this war was no more just than any other: "Are not our intellectuals equally fatuous when they tell us that our war of all wars is stainless and thrillingly achieving for good?"

Bourne had no use for the intellectuals who, by their acceptance of war, "put themselves into a terrifyingly strategic position"; by attempting to guide the ruling powers, these intellectuals were leading their country "to disaster and the frustration of national life": "is their guiding any more than a preference whether they shall go over the right-hand or the left-hand side of the precipice?" Instead of accepting such temporizing counsels, in reality counsels of despair, American intellectuals must recall "that the real enemy is War rather than imperial Germany."

Bourne advised his comrades to be irreconcilable in their opposition to the waging of the war as the propagandists were waging it. But the "irreconcilable" need not be disloyal, he need not even be "impossibilist": "His apathy towards war should take the form of a heightened energy and enthusiasm for the education, the art, the interpretations that make for life in the midst of the world of death." Bourne concluded ringingly that the intellectual must forge new ideals even as the old ideals crumbled; his mind should continue to roam widely and ceaselessly. His time would come. If the American intellectual class riveted itself to a "liberal" philosophy that perpetuated the old errors — i. e., by supporting a peace that would leave "all the old inflammable materials of armament lying about the world" — there would then be "need for 'democrats' whose task will be to divide, confuse, disturb, keep the intellectual waters constantly in motion to prevent any such ice from ever forming."

The target was of course John Dewey. Dewey contributed only one further piece to *The Seven Arts,* some comments on H. G. Wells's polemic *God, the Invisible King,* printed in the issue for July 1917. He then turned to intensively propagandizing for America's participation in the war as one of the Allies; his chief outlet at first was *The New Republic,* which, as it had been founded with Morgan money (the backer, Willard Straight, was a Morgan partner and had close British connections), was by August 1917 as vociferously prowar as *The Seven Arts* had gradually become antiwar. The August issue of *The Seven Arts* included John Reed's "This Unpopular War," Bourne's "The Collapse of American Strategy," and Hendrik Willem Van Loon's "Friday, June 22, 1917," this last an amazing performance if only as an angry humanist and anti-Christian manifesto decrying "The dire inheritance of revealed authority" and, as then only a Dutch neutralist could, preaching the liberal, pacifist gospel.

As may be imagined, John Dewey was not idle in defense of the position that he had taken — as he outlined it in the earliest of his prowar pieces, "Conscience and Compulsion" in *The New Republic* for July 14, 1917 — against "moral futility." That is to say, if "at a critical juncture the moving force of events is always too much for conscience, the remedy is not to deplore the wickedness of those who manipulate events. Such a conscience is largely self-conceit. The remedy is to connect conscience with the forces that are moving in another direction. Then will conscience itself have compulsive power instead of being forever the martyred and the coerced." Two issues later, Dewey discussed "The Future of Pacifism," or, as he put the matter, "the failure of the pacifist propaganda to determine finally the course of a nation which was converted to pacifism in advance." He found the "pacifist literature of the months preceding our entrance into war" breathlessly and frantically "opportunistic." And he had little patience with those who were so anxious to save their influence for some important crisis that they never risked its use in any present emergency. On the contrary, he continued, in the third of these pieces (in *The New Republic* for August 18, 1917), "What America Will Fight for," he found generally that the mistrustful "pacifists" were isolated. Instead in America there "is the sense of a job to be undertaken in a businesslike way, and there is a vague but genuine vision of a world somehow made permanently different by our participation in a task which taken by itself is intensely disliked." Moreover, there was a positively transcendental aspect to the general American attitude, for this "sense of a job to be accomplished cannot be segregated from an underlying national idealism." A task must be accomplished "to abate an international nuisance, but in the accomplishing there is the prospect of a world organization and the beginning of a public control which crosses nationalistic boundaries and interests." Indeed it was "ridiculous to say that they are mere idealistic glosses, sugar-coatings of the bitter pill of war." Rather, they "present genuine possibilities, objects of a fair adventure."

Bourne of course heatedly and publicly disagreed. He had already adopted the posture of the vanguard intellectual, who, in his restless search for new ideals to replace crumbled idols, was irreconcilably opposed to any pragmatic accommodation to the demands of conscience. Dewey's Machiavellian advice that intellectuals should "connect conscience with the forces that are moving in another direction" was thus the subject of Bourne's leading article, "Conscience and Intelligence in War," in *The Dial* for September 13, 1917. By that date, the future of *The Seven Arts* had been decided: the backer and president, Mrs. A. K. Rankine, had withdrawn her support because of the pacifism of the group writing for the magazine, and in the October issue the editor announced the cessation of publication to "the friends of the The Seven Arts." The "subsidy has been withdrawn," he confessed, because "the idea of combining financial backing with full editorial freedom has broken down." He went on to ask his supporters each to send in ten dollars to keep *The Seven Arts* alive; it stood for "the spirit of the new world," and to "these spirits, the Great War is a mere prelude to the Revolution, which, here bloodily, there peaceably, and beginning with Russia, shall sweep the Earth. For we demand that life be something richer, quicker, more human than it has been." All the same, that proved to be the end of *The Seven Arts*.

Waldo Frank recalled, many years later, that after Mrs. Rankine withdrew her support from the review, a second financial backer appeared: Scofield Thayer. Thayer persuaded others, including Sibley Watson, to help him salvage *The Seven Arts*; a difficulty arose because Thayer's group favored an editorial board rather than an editor-in-chief like Oppenheim. Waldo Frank and Van Wyck Brooks approved and wanted Randolph Bourne as a fourth member of a board of editors, but Oppenheim felt that good editing, just like good art, was a one-man job. At the same time, Bourne refused to be an editor unless Brooks, Frank, and Oppenheim served on the board with him. Because of these opposing views, the project collapsed, and Martyn Johnson's *Dial* inherited the remnants of *The Seven Arts*.[15] Waldo Frank's recollection rings true; Thayer's insistence on an editorial board was no doubt a result of his work on *The Harvard Monthly* in 1912-13, an early experience invalidated by his later service on Martyn Johnson's editorial board. The fact is that Scofield Thayer allowed no coeditor when he conducted his own *Dial*.

It was no coincidence that except for Robert Frost, Willard

Huntington Wright, Theodore Dreiser, and J. D. Beresford, all the group *The Seven Arts* cited in its house advertisement in *The Dial* in the issue of April 19, 1917, also were among the most prominent contributors to *The Dial* after Martyn Johnson became the publisher. Except for Edgar Lee Masters and Wilbur Daniel Steele, the same group continued to write for *The Dial* after Scofield Thayer and Sibley Watson assumed control. In fact, Sherwood Anderson and Van Wyck Brooks were given Dial Awards during the 1920's. It is clear that these writers and their companions came to *The Dial* because of its changed orientation under Johnson and Donlin — an orientation changed geographically as well as politically. The editor of *The Seven Arts,* Waldo Frank, had originally been identified with Chicago, as had been Dreiser, Anderson, and Masters, but its editorial offices were on Madison Avenue in Manhattan; the majority of the contributors either lived in New York or used it as a convenient base.[14]

The Dial nevertheless attempted to do more than attract to its pages the writers who, through *The Seven Arts,* were giving new directions to American arts and letters. Just as in 1898 *The Dial* had absorbed the first American "little" magazine *The Chapbook,* so in 1917 *The Dial* absorbed *The Seven Arts*: *The Dial* absorbed the more creative, and more controversial, journal ceasing publication. "Casual Comment" for the issue of October 11, 1917, ran a concluding paragraph worth quoting as evidence of the relation of *The Dial* to *The Seven Arts*:

> Those who are interested in the cause of literature and in America will regret that "The Seven Arts," which made so valiant a start under the direction of a group of vigorous young New York writers, has been obliged to suspend publication. Its loss is one of the upsets caused by the war. When the editors were faced with the alternative of modifying the policy of free discussion they had announced or of losing financial support, they very properly declined to submit to dictation, feeling that without complete independence they could do little to further either critical taste or sound sense. By arrange-

ment with the editors, THE DIAL has undertaken to fill
the unexpired subscriptions, and since readers of "The
Seven Arts" will find some of their friends among the
regular contributors to THE DIAL, we hope that they
will not feel they have been thrown among strangers.
The expression of solidarity with *The Seven Arts* and the final
sentence expressing the hope that readers of *The Seven Arts*
would not find themselves among strangers at *The Dial* seem
strongly to indicate that in the fall of 1917 *The Dial* shared the
pacifist view of the war that had put a stop to *The Seven Arts*.
That was not the case; Martyn Johnson had an ulterior motive
in assuming the responsibility for the unexpired subscriptions
to *The Seven Arts*. He wanted the réclame of *The Seven Arts*,
and he sought it by attracting its readers and contributors, without in the least changing his own policy of support of President
Wilson. He intended, also, to move *The Dial* from Chicago
to New York. A postcard postmarked October 20, 1917, from
"The Editors" of *The Seven Arts* advised their subscribers that
the magazine was obliged to suspend publication during the
period of the war. Until the war would end and thus enable
The Seven Arts to resume publication, its editors would make
arrangements whereby *The Dial* would take up and fill out
all unexpired subscriptions to *The Seven Arts* in the correct amounts; the editors felt that as *The Dial* was a cultural
and artistic fortnightly of exceptional quality, no better medium
could have been found for their purpose. In gaining the readers of *The Seven Arts* for *The Dial*, Martyn Johnson was changing the character of the public that read the older magazine by
leavening this public with the presumably younger and certainly
more radical readers of a journal that, whatever its admitted artistic and literary virtues, was notoriously pacifist in its views of
the war, that had opposed the entry of the United States into
that war, that indeed had had its subsidy withdrawn by its patron-
ess and president, Mrs. Rankine, precisely on account of its un-
compromisingly pacifist stand.

In attracting to *The Dial* the new writers identified with
The Seven Arts and the readers who identified themselves with

those writers, Johnson was changing the nature of *The Dial*
more overtly than Waldo Browne had attempted to do. In
bringing about this change, the new publisher also brought about
another, which went with the transformation of *The Dial* from
a journal of literary opinion and information to a journal actively advocating the cultural views of the liberals. Martyn Johnson turned away from Chicago, just as those of the new writers
who had once worked there had already turned away from it; and
in turning away from the critical and creative talents still living
in the Midwest, Johnson turned to New York. Thus, even before
The Dial obtained a financial backer from the East, it was edited
by a group largely Eastern in orientation — only Donlin, Britten, and Henry Blake Fuller were then identified with the Midwest — and it largely was written by people who either had always
lived in the East or had gone there to better their fortunes.

V

THE DIAL *Moves to New York (1918-20)*

THE probability that New York would become the home of *The Dial* increased early in 1918 because of an event that proved, immediately, a misfortune. George Donlin had to go West on account of his tuberculosis, and Martyn Johnson was forced to search for still another editor.[1] Donlin's name appeared as Editor on the masthead through the issue for September 19, 1918, after which it appeared without any specific title along with the names of Clarence Britten and Harold Stearns. Donlin's merely nominal connection must have accelerated the movement that carried *The Dial* distinctly into the field of political and social discussion as a left-liberal organ, a movement with which he perhaps was not in entire sympathy.[2] The "Contributors" column in the issue of January 11, 1919, announced the appointment as Editor of *The Dial* of Robert Morss Lovett and stated that the change in editors had been enforced by the continued ill health of Donlin, who "though necessarily absent from the offices, will remain on the staff of THE DIAL as an associate editor and will contribute as his health permits."[3] After the issue

for May 3, 1919, Donlin's name no longer appeared on the masthead.

At the beginning of 1918, when *The Dial* lacked an editor,
Harold Stearns came to it. Stearns, from his own account, was
living in a state of semihysteria in those days "when it seemed as
if the war would never, *never* end, as if it were going on for an
eternity with madness and death and unreality."[4] Having traveled
to New York to look for his editor, Johnson met Stearns through
somebody's recommendation, and the two men had several con-
ferences at Ike's Bar on Sixth Avenue, the chief question between
them being not so much that of Stearns's professional qualifica-
tions for the post as his prospective immunity from the draft. At
last, Johnson hired Stearns, who later confessed he had not had a
regular job since his days on the *New York Press* in 1914. The
inducements Johnson offered were a good job as an editor with a
well-known periodical; the prospect of moving with *The Dial* to
New York soon; a weekly salary of fifty dollars, part of which
Stearns might send home to his mother in Boston; a favorable
status in the draft, because he would be supporting his mother;
and the rather stimulating idea of going to Chicago for a while.
With the issue of January 3, 1918, Harold Stearns began his official duties as Associate Editor.

Needing somebody to assist him in getting out *The Dial,*
Stearns persuaded Clarence Britten to throw up teaching in the
Department of English at the University of Wisconsin for a
working literary life as an assistant on *The Dial*. Britten, urbane
and understanding, acted as anchor man in the editors' office.
His appointment to *The Dial* took effect at the same time as did
Stearns's.

At the time Stearns came, the editorial offices of *The Dial*
were in the Transportation Building, 608 South Dearborn Street,
in Chicago — according to Stearns, "a conventional business office
building, not far from the La Salle Street Railroad Station —
about as unlikely a spot for the home of an essentially literary
magazine as could well be imagined." It had moved to that
office from 632 South Sherman Street at the beginning of May
1916, when Waldo R. Browne was still Editor — into, as a house

advertisement in the issue of May 25, 1916, stated, "larger quarters." As Stearns describes the *Dial* quarters, the two rooms were, though "relatively small, . . . adequate for our needs. In the larger room, Clarence and I had an enormous double flat-top desk, with our chairs facing each other" — incidentally, the same editorial arrangement that obtained in the New York offices of *The Dial* through the 1920's — "and plenty of dictionaries, reference books, and the books under consideration for review piled up between us. There were, too, several of the old-fashioned sliding glass-door bookcases, usually crammed with books that were to be sent out to the different reviewers we had on our list — and it was a long list — or to be kept for shorter notices, since we actually tried to 'cover' all the books published by the more important houses. I had a small typewriter desk beside me, because, as usual, I never wrote anything by hand, but directly on the machine." Britten still wrote out his copy, rapidly if necessary but, in the cases of longer, more pretentious reviews or articles, rather slowly, two or three days in advance, conscientious, in Stearns's view, to the point of absurdity.

Morning mail was heavy, because the contributors, "with the exception of less than half a dozen in Chicago itself," were in New York, Paris, London, "or Madison, Wisconsin, or even Dublin. . . . Some of these contributors, of course, were almost traditional with the paper," and Stearns tried to send them for review the types of books they had been in the habit of reviewing before his advent to *The Dial*. Of contributors whom Stearns had attracted to the journal, he mentioned Alfred B. Kuttner, for two pieces on "A Study of American Intolerance," John Dewey — whose first piece for *The Dial* was "Current Tendencies in Education," the lead article for the issue of April 3, 1917 — and H. M. Kallen. Stearns confessedly sought out among his acquaintance in New York "the many liberal writers known at that time by their pieces in the *New Republic*," and generally he tried to compensate through letters and friendly editorial interest for the low rates of remuneration the magazine had to give. Edward Shanks wrote occasional letters from London, a practice continued by Thayer and Watson until the end of their *Dial*. Usually

Stearns reviewed one or two more important books in each issue, and there was also a longish column or two of general editorial comment, "of which I should say now, Clarence [Britten] did about a third and I did the rest."⁵

During the months in Chicago, Stearns met Robert Morss Lovett, who in less than a year would come to *The Dial* as Editor; Stearns also met Waldo Frank and Janet Fairbank and others of the more advanced artistic and academic sets there. Late in the spring of 1918, Harold Stearns again met Scofield Thayer, who had come to Chicago for a fortnight or so. They had been casual acquaintances as Harvard undergraduates. At this time, according to Stearns, Thayer did not suspect himself of any intention of buying *The Dial;* in reality he had already become interested in backing Johnson. Thayer just did not bother to inform his old college acquaintance.

Early in the spring of 1918 Johnson informed Stearns that he had accomplished the purpose he had set for himself, of bringing *The Dial* to New York "bag, baggage, and traditions of 40 years, on the first of July." Stearns could not abide the flatness of Chicago and always remained a Bostonian *malgré lui;* and the aim of transplanting the magazine from its native Midwestern prairie to a city with hills by a big river had been one of the inducements the publisher had offered Harold Stearns the evening at Ike's when he was hired as an Associate Editor. Now the publisher had made his preparations to move to New York and had even acquired a charming office in Greenwich Village at 152 West Thirteenth Street, the offices of *The Dial* for the remainder of its publication. With his new backing Johnson had formulated a much more ambitious program for "the new 'Reconstruction' *Dial*," as he liked to call it, than had been the "purely literary and rather thin one of the later Chicago years." Johnson wrote Stearns that he had "hooked up" Thorstein Veblen, John Dewey, and Helen Marot among others, and at that Stearns "feared that we might be put in the position of merely trying to imitate either the *New Republic* or the *Nation*." But Johnson also assured Stearns that "we were to continue our rather unusual schedule of bi-monthly publication. We were not to become 'just another Liberal weekly.' "[6] Was periodicity to be the only distinction between the reconstructed *Dial* and the two liberal weeklies?

Scofield Thayer, the cause of all this optimism, was to be as deeply affected by the decision he had made to support *The Dial* as was Johnson himself. His arrival at the magazine was indeed fortuitous but would not have been hard to predict. Born in Worcester, Massachusetts, in 1889, Scofield Thayer was the only child of wealthy parents.[7] His father had prospered in the woolen trade in those decades of general prosperity in New England after the Civil War, and his mother was a sponsor of worthy cultural causes in the community; his uncle Ernest was also famous in Worcester, for having composed "Casey at the Bat." Scofield Thayer was especially close to his mother, whose influence is discernible in his mature tastes and leanings. The family fortune was sufficient to support a large establishment in Worcester (now demolished, after ending its days as the Worcester Elks Club), another in Newton Center, and a large shingle "cottage" in Edgartown fronting the ocean. There was also a splendid steam yacht, for cruises in the summers along the Atlantic coast.

Young Thayer attended the approved schools. First there was Milton Academy, where he was a slightly younger contemporary of T. S. Eliot. Summers, he traveled in Europe, with his tutor, Major D'Estrées. Then came Harvard, from 1909 to 1912 as an undergraduate with another year as a graduate student — though he did not receive his A.B. until 1913. At Harvard Thayer met many of the men who later became his associates on *The Dial* as contributors or members of the staff. His major interest in studies was philosophy; he took a course or two with George Santayana and thereby initiated a friendly relationship that eventually brought Santayana to *The Dial* as a major contributor and, reputedly, Thayer to the pages of American literature as one of the models for Oliver Alden, the main figure of Santayana's single novel, *The Last Puritan*. Thayer was also active on the editorial board of *The Harvard Monthly;* this literary and philosophical magazine was established in 1886 by the Laodicean Club, which had numbered among its undergraduate members Santayana himself when the *Monthly* had been founded. By 1913, Thayer was Secretary to the editorial board of the *Monthly* and thus had a chief part in preparing its special issue of April 1913, devoted to criticism of George Santayana's newly published *Winds of Doctrine*.

The special issue of *The Harvard Monthly* is an essential document to an understanding of the history of *The Dial* from about 1917 until it ceased. Not only is it evidence that Scofield Thayer had a strong interest even in his university days in the work of an editor, but it also indicates the kind and quality of work he would commission as Editor of *The Dial*. Of the seventeen names comprising the roster of names on the editorial board of the *Monthly* — the masthead page lists an Editor-in-Chief, Secretary, nine Editors, a Business Manager, and five Assistant Business Managers — six later figured in *The Dial*. There was of course the Secretary, Thayer; and five of the Editors of the *Monthly* were important to *The Dial* in their various ways. J. Donald Adams became a contributor, a minor one to be sure, with a poem or two; but Cuthbert Wright, E. Estlin Cummings, and Gilbert V. Seldes were indispensable to *The Dial* in its heyday, the early 1920's. Wright published some poetry in *The Dial*, and he was a favored reviewer, especially of works dealing with the history of religion. Gilbert Seldes, by appearing in Martyn Johnson's *Dial* for January 25, 1917, actually preceded Thayer to the magazine; he is one of the four or five persons most intimately associated with *The Dial* as Associate Editor, writer of the monthly column "The Theatre," and contributor, not only as a major reviewer but also as author of *The Seven Lively Arts*, much of which was published in *The Dial* in the course of 1923. Like Georgia O'Keeffe, E. E. Cummings was an artist whose work was first published in *The Dial* and thus brought to the attention of an international audience; Cummings appeared a a poet and cartoonist in the very first issue of the "renovated" *Dial* (the adjective is Thayer's) of January 1920 and contributed more caricatures and poems, reviews, theater criticism, and a portion of his comedy *Him* throughout the 1920's. He was also given the Dial Award for 1926; along with

T. S. Eliot, Marianne Moore, Wallace Stevens, Ezra Pound, and Hart Crane, Cummings is one of the poets usually associated with the distinctive achievement of *The Dial* of Thayer and Watson. Of the Editors of *The Harvard Monthly* in this group, the final name is that of Merrill C. Rogers; not a contributor to *The Dial* of the 1920's, Rogers nevertheless has a unique importance in its history. It was at his home in New York in the early winter of 1917-18 that Scofield Thayer met Martyn Johnson and first became interested in backing *The Dial,* also, through meeting Randolph Bourne there.

The contents of *The Harvard Monthly* for the issue are equally revealing. The entire issue was planned around *Winds of Doctrine,* and accordingly, the editorial "Announcement" explained that each of the six essays composing Santayana's book was treated in a separate paper in the special issue, with an additional "exposition of the philosopher's metaphysics by one of his former students." The entire number was presented as "some small tribute" to Santayana's genius. The essays, in order, were "The Intellectual Temper of the Age," by Andrew J. Onderdonk, Jr.; "Modernism and Christianity," by Cuthbert Wright; "The Philosophy of M. Henri Bergson," by Gilbert Seldes; "The Philosophy of Mr. Bertrand Russell," by Lincoln MacVeagh; "Shelley: or the Poetic Value of Revolutionary Principles," by Scofield Thayer; "The Genteel Tradition in American Philosophy," by Henry R. Carey; and "George Santayana — the Metaphysician," by C. Gouverneur Hoffman. Such an array of topics and authors would have done credit to *The Dial* of the 1920's — and indeed, did grace many an issue.

Four of the seven authors of these essays were connected with *The Dial* from 1917 on. Wright, Seldes, and Thayer were also on the editorial board of the *Monthly*; the additional name is that of Lincoln MacVeagh. MacVeagh's first connection with Thayer's magazine was as the reviewer in the issue for June 1920 of Clement C. J. Webb's Gifford Lectures, *God and Personality.* According to "Notes on Contributors" in that number, MacVeagh had "studied philosophy under Josiah Royce at Harvard and the history of religions under the Abbé Loisy in Paris. He is now

connected with one of the leading New York publishing houses."
The connection would be important for Thayer and *The Dial*,
indeed of greater importance than MacVeagh's excellent reviews.
As an old friend of the Editor, MacVeagh served as Secretary-
Treasurer of the Dial Publishing Company from the end of
1923 until *The Dial* ended publication in July 1929. He also
became the director of the Dial Press in January 1924, a firm
financed and founded by Scofield Thayer and occupying the
same brownstone building that his magazine did but not cor-
porately connected with *The Dial*. Thayer's contribution to
the Santayana number of *The Harvard Monthly* suggested the
incisiveness of his later writing and the direction of his literary
and political thought. And the very topics themselves of the
seven essays foreshadow much of the writing in Thayer's *Dial*,
for the two thinkers most often and substantially represented
there were George Santayana and Bertrand Russell, and each
philosopher often reviewed the writings of the other. All in all,
The Harvard Monthly for April 1913 crowned the Harvard years
of Scofield Thayer with considerable distinction and with great
promise for the future — promise that was amply fulfilled.

After graduating *cum laude* in 1913, Scofield Thayer went
to Oxford, for further study in classics and philosophy at Mag-
dalen College. The beginning of the first World War, however,
brought an end to Thayer's academic life abroad, and he returned to the United States without any definitely formulated
plans. Hermann Riccius recalled that the Army draft rejected
Thayer because of flat feet; Merrill Rogers said that, on the
contrary, Thayer was nervous that he might be drafted into the
army but thought that if he were identified as an editor or sub-
editor of an established publication, he might be able to claim
exemption (it apparently worked in those days). At any rate,
by 1918 Thayer was casting about for a congenial occupation.
He presented himself — to the not entirely sympathetic observation of Harold Stearns — as "of an almost psychopathic nervous-
ness, the outward characteristics of which were a high, shrill
voice and an almost hysterical laugh. . . . he led me a merry pace
for a few days, though it was a relief to talk with him just the

same, for, oddly enough, he appeared to know little and didn't hesitate to say that he cared less, about the war." That he did not serve in the armed forces "was just as well, for he might have wrecked the discipline of any company to which he was assigned."⁸

Thayer's visit to Chicago just prior to June 1918 was no sociable fortnight but was a business trip to look over a property he was interested in. The financial aspect of Thayer's new venture is important to emphasize at this point. He met both Johnson and Bourne at the home, in New York, of Merrill Rogers, the friend and coworker of Thayer's days on the staff of *The Harvard Monthly*. In a few years, Rogers had traveled quite a distance from the academic staidness of that journal. After graduation from Harvard in the class following Thayer's, Merrill Rogers came to a new Socialist magazine, *The Masses*, edited by Max Eastman in New York; John Reed, a friend of Rogers' elder brother, was a guiding influence on the staff and attracted Rogers to it. Rogers served *The Masses* as its business manager from the middle of 1916 through most of 1917. That November, he was indicted, along with six other members of the staff, by the federal government under the provisions of the wartime espionage act, for obstructing the war effort. Like Bourne, the staff of *The Masses* were not only Socialist but, more dangerously, pacifist, and the consequences of their stand on the latter issue proved serious for themselves and rapidly achieved notoriety among their following and indeed among American liberals generally. The magazine was of course liquidated, and its business manager was jobless. Martyn Johnson then approached Rogers about a position on the staff of *The Dial*, and about February 1918, he became Johnson's business manager.

Thus it was that, prompted by his new employer's pressing need for additional backing to move *The Dial* to New York, Rogers approached Thayer. Two circumstances were propitious for Johnson's plans: under the circumstances, Thayer was disposed to accept a reasonable approach from *The Dial*; and though they had not yet met, Thayer greatly admired an important contributor to *The Dial* — Randolph Bourne. Merrill Rogers' new bride, who had been Joy Young, was a good friend of

Bourne's, and so, to Thayer's excitement and pleasure, the Rogerses invited Thayer and Bourne to dinner. The result of that hopeful, fatal evening was all that Rogers and Johnson could have wished for. Johnson informed Thayer that, after the reorganization of *The Dial* and its move to New York, Bourne would be named to the "board of directors." Thayer used that phrase himself in 1920, reporting the history of his transactions with Johnson; an obvious reference to the group "In Charge of Reconstruction," the words reflect Thayer's experience at *The Harvard Monthly* and his recent plan for a salvaged *Seven Arts*. In these preliminaries, the appointment of an editor-in-chief was left undetermined; Harold Stearns would continue as managing editor. In consequence of Johnson's suggestions, Thayer became interested in *The Dial*. At the end of the winter of 1917-18, he purchased from Johnson some stock in the Dial Publishing Company and entered on a series of transactions to ensure financial support for *The Dial*. Specifically, as Thayer later admitted to Randolph Bourne, his interest in *The Dial* was aroused because of the prospect that Bourne would participate in its affairs.

Martyn Johnson outlined to the new backer an idea for a reorganized Dial according to which it was to be a magazine that would be primarily critical — critical in the literary, the scientific, and the political spheres. While such a review would not actively engage in politics, obviously its attitude would reflect the advanced views of the principal backer and his closest friend among the group of contributing editors. Admittedly Scofield Thayer's friends were Socialists, and he always voted the Socialist ticket. Thus even before he left for Chicago in the spring of 1918, Thayer was a part owner of *The Dial* and was already subsidizing it. His understanding was that the Dial stock he bought from Johnson and the money he was lending *The Dial* constituted practically a gift, and he believed Johnson also held this understanding.⁹ Thayer further assumed he would share control of policy with Johnson, an assumption that caused insuperable difficulty and that no doubt accounted for Randolph Bourne's statement to his mother that Johnson was very much

afraid of Thayer and himself, afraid that they would have much
to say about editorial policy.

Concerning these preliminaries to Thayer's trip, his new
acquaintance and future partner James Sibley Watson, Jr., recalled many years later that "Thayer said he would either start
a magazine or set up a fund for artists [— and in the event, he did
both, editing *The Dial* and initiating and, with Watson, financing
the annual Dial Awards for writers]. If he started a magazine,
would I come in with him? The answer was 'yes.' Then came
the question — should we start a new magazine or get hold of
an old one? Because I had written for the fortnightly *Dial* I
suggested we get hold of it."[10] Watson had contributed to the
journal as early as the issue of May 3, 1917, about six months
before Thayer's meeting with Johnson and a year or more
before Thayer's first appearance in its pages, but it was Thayer
who took the first overt step toward subsidizing *The Dial*.

By the late spring of 1918, not only did Scofield Thayer
think he would secure the future of *The Dial*; also he would
help the publisher direct that future and would contribute reviews and critical essays to the magazine. Just as importantly,
through such a course of action Thayer's good friend Randolph
Bourne would now have a journal in which to express, with the
assurance of the chief backer's support, his views on the war and
on American life. Such a journal and such assurances were essential to one who had contributed to *The Seven Arts* with such
articles as "The Collapse of American Strategy" in the issue for
August 1917, and who had seen the collapse as well of *The Seven
Arts* by October 1917, because of popular opposition to its advocacy of a national policy of peaceful isolation from the European
war. That is to say, such assurances were essential to Bourne
if he should continue to write and propagandize — in the words
of the editorial valedictory addressed "To the Friends of The
Seven Arts," in *The Seven Arts* of October 1917 — for those supporting "the spirit of the new world," to whom "The Great War
is a mere prelude to the Revolution, which, here bloodily, there
peaceably, and beginning with Russia, shall sweep the Earth."

The fresh energy gained by Thayer's purchase of Dial stock

rapidly achieved tangible results. *The Dial* announced in its "Notes and News" for June 20, 1918, that in accordance with its custom since becoming a fortnightly it would issue only one number in July and one in August — July 18 and August 20 respectively — and would resume fortnightly publication with the Fall Educational Number of September 5 and the Fall Announcement Number of September 19, 1918. At the beginning of this summer lull, on July 1, 1918, its publication offices would be moved to New York, and with the first "Reconstruction" issue — October 5, 1918, was the actual date, although "Notes and News" here announced it for October 3 — *The Dial* would begin publication as a weekly.

Read in the light of such an announcement, Thayer's reviews and brief critiques for *The Dial* in the latter seven months of 1918 are significant for two reasons. First, they came at a time in which the magazine was abandoning its old and widely honored "purely literary" policy, inaugurated by Francis F. Browne in 1880 and prosperously adhered to until 1913, a time moreover when that change was signalized by the move from Chicago to New York. Thayer's writing in these months went counter to the increasing activity in politics and social affairs of Martyn Johnson's editorship, a course taken despite Johnson's assurances to Thayer. However different Thayer's attitude toward art and letters from Francis Browne's, both men profoundly respected the life of literature; they organized their own lives in its service. One discovers a continuity of response here, which would wholly characterize *The Dial* in its last phase.

Second, Thayer's early writing for *The Dial is* important because it adumbrated his editorial direction of his journal from 1920 onward. Excellent in itself, admittedly it is minor criticism, minor in scope, minor in quantity. These reviews and essays merit detailed examination for their major importance for the later history of *The Dial*; and because of the place of *The Dial* in American literature, these contributions have, therefore, a place in the attempt to narrate some portion of the history of the modern development of the arts in America. The American milieu of the Twenties and after was affected, to a discernible degree, by the attitude expressed in the papers by Scofield Thayer that appeared in Martyn Johnson's *Dial* in 1918.

Besides his lengthier, signed contributions, Thayer sometimes wrote anonymously for "Notes on New War Books" and other occasional columns in *The Dial*. In the issue of June 20, 1918, he wrote the portion of "Notes on New War Books" that deals with Georges Lafond's *Covered with Mud and Glory*, Ferdinand Belmont's *A Crusader of France*, Jean Giraudoux's *Campaigns and Intervals*, and John Masefield's *The Old Front Line*. In contrast to the reviewer's strictures about the first two of these volumes, he wrote that Giraudoux's book "even in translation retains the delicate aroma of Gallic wit and fancy" and that having read it, "we understand still better why France must not die and indeed how absurd it is to fear that such a people as the French ever could die."[11] And of Masefield's book Thayer wrote with qualified enthusiasm, wishing that the author had devoted the time such a book must have absorbed to the evocation in verse of the essential reality of No Man's Land. To the issue of July 18, 1918, Thayer contributed, besides his signed review of Francis Hackett's *Horizons*, reviews to the column "Briefs on New Books" of Edward Eyre Hunt's *Tales from a Famished Land* and of Hugo von Hofmannsthal's *Lyrical Poems* as translated by Charles Wharton Stork. Von Hofmannsthal was to become a personal friend of Thayer after the war and would also be one of the chief ornaments of *The Dial* of the Twenties; in 1918 it took courage for a reviewer to praise an "enemy" artist as the most distinguished poet of the German language writing in this generation.[12]

After the war, in 1921, Thayer moved to Vienna, for psychoanalysis by Sigmund Freud — whom, not without irony, he called the Great Magician. There, as Editor of *The Dial*, Thayer knew von Hofmannsthal socially and as the correspondent of *The Dial* in Vienna. For the amusement of a friend, Thayer one day drew a verbal caricature of the famous poet, who was depicted as "now small and yellow like a Siamese. He says he is always so in the spring and that it is the natural course of nature. In the autumn he energizes and glitters and writes comedies for

Pallenberg, comedies which make money and are awful. When I lunched with him the other day he stopped in the middle to take aspirin to quiet his nerves, but now in the usual March in April weather he is setting out on an automobile tour to quiet his nerves. I thought he was crazy when he told me and presumably showed it in my eyes, so he called my attention to the fact that he never drove more than five hours in the day. Baroque creature!"

The last of these unsigned paragraphs in "Briefs on New Books" are two reviews in the issue of September 5, 1918, the first number of the New York *Dial*; one mentions Arthur Symon's *Colour Studies in Paris,* the other Florence Leftwich Ravenel's *Women in the French Tradition.*[13]

In these notices Thayer commented on the aesthetic aspects of the books, resolutely turning away from the ghastliness of the war to consider the arts from an aesthetic, not a moral or ideological standpoint. In the three French war memoirs, he praised Giraudoux as a conscious artist and condemned what he regarded as the faulty theology of Belmont, who sought consolation in his Catholicism for the terrors of the war. Even here, when Thayer attacked as a critic, he attacked the, to him, evident illogicality of a religious and social attitude. That Ferdinand Belmont believed God used war as one great means of teaching a lesson — in short, to chasten sinful men — furnished Thayer the opportunity to comment that Belmont, believing as he did, ought to have fought in the ranks of those to whose initiative mankind owes a blessing so immense, i. e., the ranks of the Germans. Of *Women and the French Tradition* Thayer wrote that "Any one of the distinguished women whom Mrs. Ravenel deals with — 'deals with' is the only possible way of putting it — would turn in her grave at these repetitious, formless vaporings." His attention, again, focused on form, brilliance of style, consistency at, it may be, the expense of profundity, content, sincerity of emotion. The point is one to emphasize, because the attitude expressed was to be a controlling attitude for *The Dial* of the Twenties.

Equally resolutely and much more elaborately, Thayer propounded his aestheticism in the six long reviews and critical essays he contributed to *The Dial* in 1918. The first of these, entitled "Lords of Language," a review of Frank Harris's *Oscar Wilde: His Life and Confessions,* appeared in the issue for June 6. In it Thayer objected to the impertinent paraphernalia of tragedy dragged into the biography by the author as well as to a not less impertinent, if less Greek, moral bias. The book indeed was almost as bad as a play by Sophocles. Were it not for such romantic touches as the thrice repeated phrase "strange sins" and for the stimulating atmosphere of *The Police Gazette,* Thayer feared, "some of us moderns could not have survived this bio-graphy of the purest modern of us all." More seriously, Thayer found it provoking to have Wilde, that deft master of the quirk and cigarette, silhouetted against a not less disturbedly fumy heaven than that behind the Dresden Rubens of Christ on the Cross.[14]

Especially apposite are Thayer's remarks, in his review of Harris's book, about Aubrey Beardsley. After asserting that a more virile character than Wilde would have put up a fight at his trials, Thayer continued: "Reading Wilde's life we can well believe his assertions of distaste at the animalism of Trinity and Oxford and his friends' witness that he always shrank from any gross or crude expression. The same idiosyncrasy of tempera-ment comes out in his inability to comprehend Aubrey Beardsley, even when illustrating his own 'Salome.' He was not sufficiently downright to savor the falcon-like intensity of him who so sheerly pounces to the sanguine heart of his subject. It would have been better to have kept complete silence than to have spoken of that divine guttersnipe as an 'orchid-like personality.'"

These remarks are Thayer's only published critical comment on an artist whom he admired so intensely that the walls of his living room were hung with Beardsley drawings, a collection housed today in the Fogg Museum of Art. One drawing in Thayer's collection of thirty-three vividly recalls *The Dial* and the young men who directed it, an illustration Beardsley drew for Molière's *Dom Juan ou le Festin de Pierre,* III, ii, and that he first published in the rival to *The Yellow Book, The Savoy* for

December 1896. In this scene, Dom Juan, accompanied by his man servant Sganarelle (a figure from the popular *commedia dell' arte* that had intrenched itself in the Parisian theatres of Molière's day), accosts a beggar to learn the proper road to the nearby town. The beggar directs the pair and asks for some alms. In the ensuing dialogue, Dom Juan tells the beggar — who rewards almsgivers by praying to Heaven for their welfare — that he should instead beseech Heaven to give him a coat and should not bother himself about the needs of others. Sganarelle thereupon explains that his master believes only that two and two make four and that four and four are eight. The brief scene concludes with Dom Juan's attempt to bribe the beggar, who will receive a *Louis d' or* as alms only by swearing to the literal truth that more often than not he lacks a morsel of bread to put between his teeth. Dom Juan cannot make the beggar swear to the truth of his exaggeration and, in disgust at the beggar's refusal thus to jeopardize his soul, exclaims: "je te le donne pour l' amour de l'humanité." The illustration depicts Sganarelle, in his costume of the *commedia dell' arte,* as actually dispensing alms to the genuflecting beggar, while the proud Dom Juan wraps himself in his black cloak and smiles scornfully.

Beardsley's drawing today constitutes at once a commentary and an association piece, whatever the artist's original intention. Dom Juan may be read as Scofield Thayer, Sganarelle as Gilbert Seldes, and the beggar as the type of the artist or intellectual befriended and patronized by the owners of *The Dial.* Seldes used Sganarelle as a *nom de plume* for his early writing in *The Dial;* the issue for April 1920, for example, contains Sganarelle's review, breathing *saeva indignatio,* of John Maynard Keynes's *The Economic Consequences of the Peace.* Adolf Dehn caricatured Scofield Thayer, quill in hand, as *Le Byron de Nos Jours* in *The Dial* for June 1926 — composing no doubt a sequel to Byron's mock-heroic masterpiece, *Don Juan.* And Thayer's predilection for beggars was notorious. One as close to and as admiring of Scofield Thayer as was Alyse Gregory said of him that he "administered his wealth largely as a trust, supporting or helping to support many young writers and artists." Others, like Harold Stearns, viewed Thayer's generosity as a weakness: "He had plenty of money and was not loath to spend it, either — a fact which, I was told later on, was mercilessly exploited by all kinds of quacks and charlatans." This admirable weakness was shared by his partner at *The Dial*. If anything, Sibley Watson's generosity to impoverished artists is better known than Thayer's, for it was specified in Margaret Anderson's memoir, *My Thirty Years' War*. In her bookshop in Greenwich Village, Miss Anderson sold Watson a copy of Eliot's *Prufrock and Other Observations* and was given in return a bill that she mistook for a dollar bill. She ran after Watson to tell him of his error: "Oh, no, he said . . . I brought it for the *Little Review*. It's good, I assure you." Watson came back several times "with his salutary hundred-dollar bill which kept the magazine alive when otherwise it would have succumbed."

Thayer's admiration for Beardsley undoubtedly was connected with a penchant they both shared for satire and with what a *Dial* advertisement for April 1920 termed "care for the graphic arts." Thayer learned much from Beardsley's work for *The Savoy* and *The Yellow Book* and utilized what he learned when Watson and he selected drawings and paintings for reproduction in their *Dial*. The connection was noted by Llewelyn Powys in 1927 in his memoir *The Verdict of Bridlegoose,* in his remark that *The Dial* was a journal "the most distinguished of its kind to appear in the English language since the publication of the *Yellow Book*." And just over two decades later his widow, Alyse Gregory, attempting to categorize the peculiar place *The Dial* held in American letters said that perhaps "it could best be compared with the *Yellow Book* of the Nineties." What nobody has seemed to remark, however, is that there was also a continuity of tradition in the realm of American literary periodicals, specifically with *The Chap-Book*.[15]

The critique of Beardsley displays Thayer's concern with a formalist criticism and his rejection of a criticism of content or idea, the moralizing criticism of a Thackeray or in our own day of an Edmund Wilson. Thayer may indeed be termed a formalist if by the epithet one can adequately describe his fascination with surfaces, forms, manner, style; fortunately he eschewed the technical apparatus of the formalist critics and aestheticians who later came to dominate criticism in America. When Scofield Thayer read and admired a work because of content rather than form, he did not display so surely the astuteness he evinced in assaying problems of form. Frank Swinnerton's novel *Nocturne* was a "tragic masterpiece" in which, so the reviewer emotionally assured his readers, the "genius of the author bites his subject hard and shakes it with so exhaustive an intensity that in these short 250 pages we feel that every nook and corner of its life has been searched out," and the style had "the invisibility of perfect glass, and unaware of it we see only the figures of these passionate puppets, outlined so deathly black against the crude gray of an unconscious universe."[16] As with most criticism of this kind, the reviewer unwarily exposed his own assumptions about the universe and ended by transmitting only his enthusiasm for the work in hand. Outside the unlit room of one scene of the novel, wrote Thayer, we fancy the dead revolving moon, so hideously alien to the human heart, so hideously at one with the unmeaning revolutions of the city's life in death. With his appreciation of Swinnerton's naturalism, one wonders whether Thayer distinguished it from the profoundly more disturbing attitude in *The Waste Land,* toward which, incidentally, he was not nearly so receptive as he was toward *Nocturne.*

Just one of Thayer's six review essays in *The Dial* in 1918 deals with another critic, and it is valuable if only because Thayer here comes to grips with one of the most popular reviewers of the day, Francis Hackett, whose *Horizons: A Book of Criticism* was under review.[17] Thayer's mixed reaction was not due to his objections to Hackett's intelligence as a critic, for "to every book and writer considered there is an appropriate and stinging reaction." The trouble lay rather with Hackett's lack of discrimination in dealing his "knockout" blows all round; "if we try to discover some method or even madness in these comebacks, we grasp only air." Hackett was not preoccupied with the culture of the past. "If, however, his eyes do not, like those of Mr. [Paul Elmer], More, regard the crumbly mosaic of more cultured centuries, he is also occupied with ideas, ideas that in his case appear to have been scratched before breakfast in the thin dirt of a suburban street," and thus he seldom judged a book from its immediate aesthetic quality, but rather with his eye rolling over a dozen disparate theories. This bias, in fact, put Hackett "outside of unchurched romantic criticism and, however protest-ingly, in the same steepled tradition with the [Stuart] Shermans, the [Irving] Babbitts, and the [Paul Elmer] Mores." After mak-ing this judgment, Thayer moved in for the kill: the same bias in favor of ideas rather than aesthetic effects was decidedly to Hackett's disadvantage as a critic of poetry. Still, there were good things as well as bad in *Horizons.* In a country where the critics were professors and where they so often exhibited the fatuous pomposity of the nincompoop, it was well there should be some-one running about, pockets crammed with rockets, and letting them off on all possible occasions and at all conceivable angles.

The reaction at *The Dial* to Thayer's frankness was mixed. Harold Stearns did not dare to change much — just one sen-tence, "largely by leaving out a phrase (two phrases come to think of it)." He was aware that Thayer was sensitive about those things, "and the change may make you a bit mad at first, yet I'm sure it won't when you look over the sentence a few times." As for Hackett's reaction, Stearns opined that he would probably "'come back' with a fearful wallop of some sort or other (he's fearfully egotistical about his writing)," and he should not have been given an obvious chance to do so. "It would have been bad for you, which of course I know you don't care about, but also bad for THE DIAL." The Publisher of *The Dial* reacted more positively. July 30, 1918, found Martyn Johnson congratu-lating Thayer on the review, which was arousing no end of amuse-ment; Johnson, moreover, thought it exceedingly well done. Not only was it sound, but it had real style and showed vast improve-ment over the review of Frank Harris's *Oscar Wilde.* The cor-respondence shows that the staff were already moving to New York, as Stearns's letter bears a New York postmark of July 9, 1918. The verbal changes Stearns made with so much trepidation are piffling, involving as they do a minor phrasal shift near the conclusion of the first paragraph of Thayer's review. Johnson's letter is rather vulgar in its condescension to a far better writer. Thayer, in contrast, would only deplore a judgment he no doubt would have placed in a part of the American intellectual landscape — "the great desert of earnest purpose which is American thought."

Thayer's review of *South Wind* in *The Dial* for August 15, 1918, displays his usual elegance of manner and has the additional advantage of dealing comfortably with a novel as hedonistic if not as unremittingly aesthetic in its basic assumptions as were the reviewer's own values.[18] Thayer did not wholly like Douglas's spirit of materialism, the well-nigh grim realism of the opening scene of *South Wind,* with its depiction of seasickness first sounding the bare physical note, unsoftened by any overtone of romance, and insisted on throughout the work. Brilliant as it was, this book had the added fault of being indubitably if divinely middle-aged — a characteristic to be seen in the delineation of the bad effects of poverty, as also of the essential lie in the conventional self-sufficiency of the genteel. Only the strong of heart would accept this universe in which the role of the stomach pump was neither unimportant nor wholly indecorous. Such was the definite philosophy Thayer found in *South Wind,* a philosophy he did not disagree with but preferred to soften with "romance."

The grimness of such a world as the Nepenthe of Norman Douglas was usually concealed by its more obvious hedonism; no such disguise softened the grimness of James Joyce's Dublin, "a long shot from the land of legend and of poetry; for Joyce, despite his own verses, is persistently occupied with such muddy raptures as in this life we do attain."[19] After considering his work, "we come uncomfortably near feeling that human life itself may be insolvent." Again, Thayer deals much more confidently with a mind so akin to his own in its assumptions and predilections, for Joyce was as great an aesthete and nihilist — though from a different philosophical approach — as Thayer. Agreeing perhaps that human life was insolvent, both men could be exu-

Jean de Bosschère, *"Où Irai-Je?"* (May 1921)

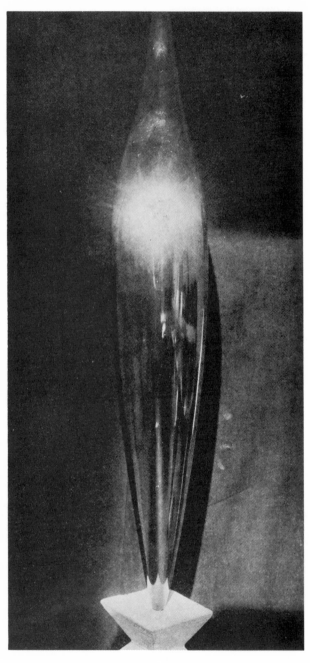

Constantin Brancusi, *The Golden Bird* (as photographed in *The Dial,* Nov. 1922)

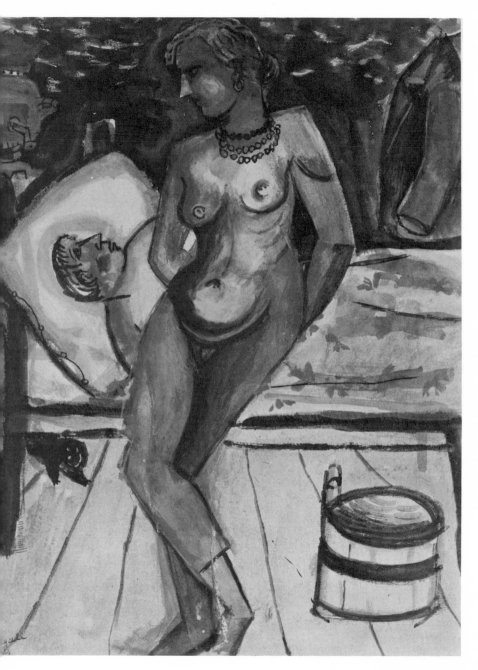

Marc Chagall, *Man and Woman*

Marc Chagall, *The Market Place* (February 1924)

Marc Chagall, *The Idiot* (November 1924)

Ivan Opffer, *Gilbert Cannan* (February 1920)

Hildegarde Watson, *A Drawing* (March 1928)

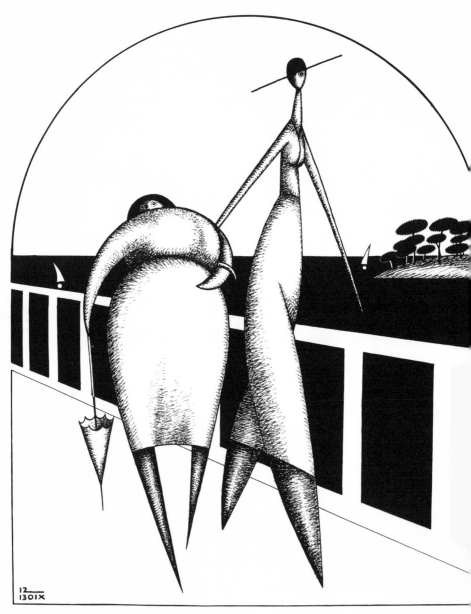

Richard Boix, *Walking Architecture* (July 1921)

William Gropper, *Second-Hand Romance* (November 1920)

Adolf Dehn, *The Violinist* (August 1924)

William Gropper, *Fox Trot* (May 1922)

E. E. Cummings, *Dancers* (August 1922)

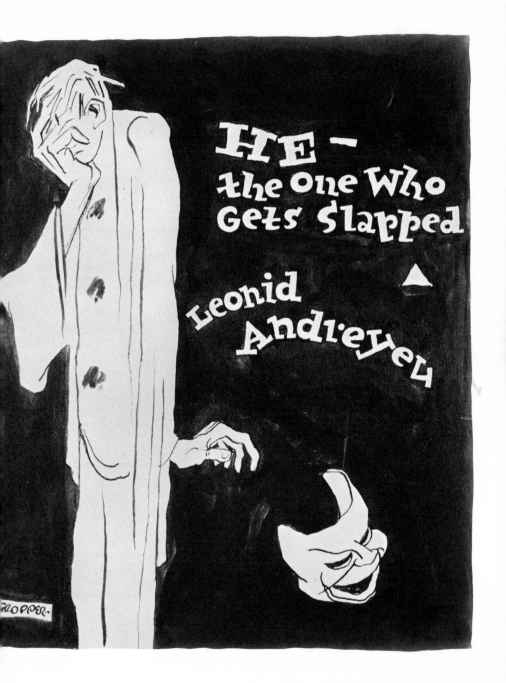

William Gropper, *He — The One Who Gets Slapped*

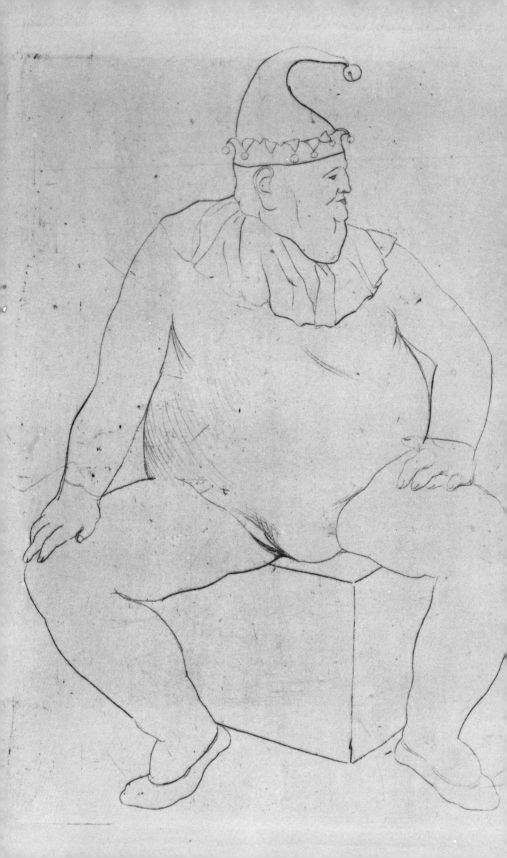

Henri de Toulouse-Lautrec, *Seated Clowness*

blo Picasso, *Clown Resting*

E. E. Cummings, *National Winter Garden Burlesque I* (January 1920)

berant about their nihilism and could find a common cause in art and therein some solace for *lachrymae rerum*. A master of prose himself, Thayer rejoiced in the "good old pitchfork rhetoric Mr. Joyce can on occasion throw." In his prose style the intelligent Irishman was not less protean than in his flittings among literary genres; and the critic praised that singular, spare, athletic phraseology which was perhaps the most distinguished achievement of this author. These remarks are acute in themselves, and their added importance is that Thayer's "James Joyce" in *The Dial* for September 19 is important as the earliest American critical survey of Joyce's work: *A Portrait of the Artist, Dubliners, Exiles,* and *Chamber Music.*

Thayer's generosity extended beyond one of such valiant early praise to the more solid and mundane sphere of financial aid.[20] Padraic Colum, a contributing editor to *The Dial* during its earlier Johnsonian phase, approached Thayer as a result of this essay in *The Dial* for September 19, 1918, laid the matter of Joyce's poverty and integrity before Thayer, and in June 1919 received a check for $700, with a half-promise that a friend probably would send a contribution of $300. Such at any rate is the outline of the story; in fact, Sibley Watson was the unnamed friend.

Actually there are two versions: the one that can be dated accurately is in a letter from the New York publisher B. W. Huebsch to James Joyce, dated June 10, 1919; the other, less accurate as to dating but more personal, occurs in Mary Colum's *Life and the Dream* and in *Our Friend James Joyce,* by both the Colums. According to Huebsch, Padraic Colum, with his fine enthusiasm, determined to lay the matter of Joyce's financial distresses before a wealthy young man, whose soul had not been crushed by his money, with the result represented by the check Huebsch sent Joyce with his letter, a personal check for a sum equivalent to $700. The donor desired Joyce to use the money as he saw fit, either for the payment of the writer's deficit or for other uses: "The idea is that you are to be freed of the difficulties that interfere with your health and work. The man's name is Scofield Thayer. . . . I suppose that you will want to write to him. Mr. Thayer tells me that a friend of his will probably make a contribution of $300, but I decided not to wait but to send that when it comes. (Please don't imagine that America is full of rich young men of that kind!) "

Mrs. Colum placed the incident at an indefinite time between 1920, after the first issue of the monthly *Dial* and the middle of 1921, when Scofield Thayer went abroad. She related the circumstances of Joyce's appeal to Benjamin Huebsch, who had published *A Portrait of the Artist,* the volume that had brought Joyce to Thayer's notice. Huebsch had collected a couple of hundred dollars for Joyce, but the Colums had no talent for asking for money. After hard thinking, one day as Mary Colum came home from her work of tutoring, she had a brain wave. She decided to telephone Scofield Thayer, whom she knew as Editor of *The Dial* and as the writer, in his editorial "Comment," of pieces about the parts of *Ulysses* that had appeared in the confiscated *Little Review.* Although she was brave at the start of her call, as Thayer's voice answered, she weakened and could not put over the request and simply said: "I have something to talk to you about." The Editor of *The Dial* promptly assured Mrs. Colum that he would be at her apartment in twenty minutes. When he arrived, his appearance, his interesting face as he sat in the sitting room up four flights of stairs, gave Mary Colum courage, and her husband began to tell Thayer about Joyce's case. At Padraic Colum's request, his wife began to read aloud Joyce's letter, rather nervously. Scofield Thayer's sympathy she would never forget. "Don't try to collect anything yourselves," he told the Colums. "It will only harass you. I will give what is necessary." He had kept a taxi waiting outside, for, as Mrs. Colum heard long afterward, he had come to their apartment as a friend, thinking she and her husband might be in some difficulties themselves. Mary Colum found herself weeping as Scofield Thayer left, not only because of his generosity, but because she knew that very few people undertsood what he was trying to do for art and literature and what a rare spirit he was. Mrs. Joyce later spoke to Mary Colum of the great lift the money sent the Joyces in Zurich by Scofield Thayer had given them. "It was a godsend," said Nora Joyce; and Joyce said very earnestly that the gift had saved him at the moment.

This, then, though earlier than Mrs. Colum placed it in her two memoirs, marked the start of the relationship between James Joyce and the owners of *The Dial* of the 1920's. Fear of American censorship obviated publication by *The Dial* of Joyce's major work, even though the review editorially and critically always championed it. As Editor of *The Dial,* Scofield Thayer told Joyce, in late October 1920, that he regretted deeply not being able to say he would print whatever the author of *Ulysses* sent: "As I have just written to remind Pound, we in America live & move and have our being in the sinister shadow of an appallingly Presbyterian post office. Miss Heap tells me *The Little Review* has been again denied the mails. *The Dial*'s truly enormous monthly deficit will not permit me any such honourable martyrisation."

In 1921, Scofield Thayer called on the Joyces when he went to Paris. Of their encounter he wrote that "James Joyce is much more Padraic Colum than reading Pound and Eliot one would have thought. The man is much more obviously ailing. His wife is blousy and blonde and most deplorable as can be judged at first blush. His daughter appears to be cross-eyed, and aware of the fact. Some English woman of means is subsidizing Joyce these years not too lavishly. But a Paris apothecary recently gave him inadvertently some acid for his eyes, the result being that he is mostly blind and strikes me as the most unhappy man I have ever seen. One is again aware how outrageously de trop refinement in this universe is." But from the meeting nothing more tangible emerged than this informal editorial reminiscence. *The Dial* published almost nothing by Joyce. Because of Thayer's fear of the censorship of the early 1920's, he published only Joyce's short lyric, "A Memory of the Players in a Mirror at Midnight," which appeared in the issue for July 1920 at the height of the furore over the serialization of *Ulysses* in Margaret Anderson's *Little Review.* One suggests that the poem appeared in *The Dial* as an oblique protest against the censorship that confiscated several issues of *The Little Review* and that brought Margaret Anderson and her coproprietor, Jane Heap, to trial.

The last essay that Scofield Thayer wrote in the series of reviews and critiques he contributed to *The Dial* in the course of 1918 was "Compton Mackenzie," in the issue for November 30. Not so significant as the essay on James Joyce, that on Compton Mackenzie is the result of an early infatuation with *Sinister Street,* outlived and regretted. It was, also, the longest essay Thayer ever wrote for *The Dial* excepting his serialized eulogy on the occasion of the Dial Award for 1924 to Marianne Moore, which occupied "Comment" for January, February, March, and April of 1925. For seven double-column pages, he praised in detail "the yet sprouting body of this world of Compton Mackenzie . . . so indubitably alive." Thayer especially admired *Carnival, Sylvia Scarlett, Plashers Mead,* and *Sinister Street,* the last for its mastery "of a style at once grave and fluid." There are reservations about *Sylvia Scarlett* with its disclosure of "the wires by which are jigged across the scene these agitated marionettes" (one is reminded of the "passionate puppets" of Thayer's review of Frank Swinnerton's *Nocturne*). But Thayer concluded with high praise for Mackenzie's view of existence, presented to the reader so that upon his apprehension "there obtrudes no object vulgarly real: in the past there is no vulgar and in the past there is no real. As we muse upon the ornate litter of a recessive world, that sea haze which is almost poetry absorbs and obliterates all."[21]

Eighteen months later, the tone of Gilbert Seldes' review of Mackenzie's *Poor Relations,* was far different from Thayer's encomium. Writing in the reconstituted, monthly *Dial* for May 1920, Seldes was not amused by what he entitled "Mr. Mackenzie's Jest" and concluded that "It would be easier to think lightly of Mr. Mackenzie's failure if one did not have to remember what Henry James said of him. Remembering that, . . . the brief story of Mr. Mackenzie's career takes on some of the proportions of tragedy." Still later, in the issue for January 1921, one of the unsigned short reviews in the regular section of such pieces entitled "Briefer Mention" gave the *coup de grace* to *The Dial's* fondness for Compton Mackenzie's novels. Probably written by Thayer himself — the style is his, certainly — the reviewer remarked of *The Vanity Girl* that it is "not meretricious only because it is not quite so pretentious as the novels which followed *Sinister Street*. What was gracious in Mr Mackenzie has yielded to what is smart, and his new novel is as utterly captivating as the Gaiety Girl he writes about can be on the stage. Unfortunately, in reading a book, one is not protected by the footlights and one has the sensation of being asked to chop down the trees in the second-act backdrop."[22]

Most obviously, Thayer's contributions to *The Dial* in 1918 display his aestheticism, both in the longer and more detailed essays and reviews and in the unsigned briefer, more ephemeral reviews and notices. In one sense such work was an extension into the world of professional journalism of his experience on the editorial board of *The Harvard Monthly,* but it was also a foreshadowing of things to come in his own *Dial.* For example, the attention to style — to style in one's own writing, to the style of one's own mode of living exemplified in this writing, as well as to the style of writing of one's contemporaries and to their style of living — is an especially striking element of Thayer's early contributions. Thayer's fascination with style largely explains his admiration of James Joyce and Compton Mackenzie, two writers otherwise so antithetical not to say antipathetic. His concern with another formal element, that of visual imagery, of plastic metaphor, constitutes both a major instrument of his own style and a basic aspect of his appreciation of such a poet and dramatist as Hugo von Hofmannsthal. That love of the visual and tactile image also helps to explain Scofield Thayer as a great collector of the art produced in his own time. The appreciations of Arthur Symons and Aubrey Beardsley provide an insight into Thayer's feeling for literature — the writing of the 1890's, "that perfumed time" (as he termed it), with its Symbolist fascination with the sensuous — and also suggest the response of this collector to pictures and sculptures by Edvard Munch, Pablo Picasso, Gaston Lachaise, and Elie Nadelman and, perhaps rather unexpectedly, to the line drawings and caricatures of E. E.

Cummings, Adolf Dehn, William Gropper, and Richard Boix, and the varied kinds of prints by many artists — all of which work was purchased by Scofield Thayer and James Sibley Watson for reproduction, by means of copperplate engravings in black and white on mat paper or by half-tone engravings on coated paper, in their *Dial* of the 1920's.

As with his partner Dr. Watson, Thayer's reviews in 1918 suggest both specific writers whom he would publish during the 1920's as well as the kind of writing that he would then seek to publish. Norman Douglas, Hugo von Hofmannsthal, Jean Giraudoux, even James Joyce contributed to *The Dial,* though von Hofmannsthal as Vienna correspondent was the only one among this group who contributed consistently throughout the 1920's and with whom Thayer was on terms of friendship. Perhaps more significantly, these reviews and essays suggest Thayer's preoccupation with language, style, sophistication of utterance, polish, the fully articulated and glossily formulated work of art; it was a preoccupation of Marianne Moore as well as of Thayer and Watson, and because of it — as expressed in the work *The Dial* published — their magazine became notorious and detested and derided as well as famous and adulated and taken seriously. As the review of Francis Hackett's *Horizons* attests, Thayer was quite willing to engage in controversy, indeed enjoyed it; as the relationship with James Joyce attests, Thayer could at the same time be very cautious in picking his opponents and about printing (or not printing) work so controversial that the circulation of *The Dial* might be endangered.

The emphasis in these reviews and essays of 1918 is on the response to art and letters of the isolated person. Scofield Thayer was not active — save as voter and patron-philanthropist — in politics and social welfare. He was not a leader of the socialist movement of his day, though to be sure he sought to make possible the leadership of his friend Randolph Bourne. He enjoyed controversy, because he himself held strong minority views, as the letters to Harold Evans attest. Yet the entrance by Thayer into controversy is almost never forthrightly political or social; his politics cannot be assessed, for example, from examination of his editorial "Comment" in *The Dial* after 1920, nor even from his writing for *The Dial* in 1918, when the journal was vocally liberal.

Thayer apparently did not resent being in a minority. His entire response to art and letters was conditioned by his willing acceptance of this comparative isolation, his feeling of comradeship with the few other isolated, "marooned" individuals who recognized him as, like themselves, "imaginative" — those who shared his views and whom he sought to attract to *The Dial.* Thayer nevertheless must also be recognized as not seeking to proselytize: he sought to attract the like-minded.

Thayer's responses to certain writers and artists as well as to certain literary and artistic *genres* suggest wider, perhaps more basic attitudes. The paradox of devotion to a collective political and social cause and the constant assertion of an extreme, even exacerbated individualism is commonly met with in American society, and it is consistently encountered in Thayer's *Dial,* as an extension of the editorial personality. On the one hand Thayer happily associated with liberals such as Randolph Bourne and Bertrand Russell. He advised the Philadelphia lawyer, Harold Evans, on Christmas Eve in 1920, when apprised by Evans of the rumor he had untimely ended the career of *The Dial* because it was a liberal publication, that "As to my desiring to cut short the existence of a liberal magazine, that is the greatest rot I have ever heard. I gave bail for one of the staff of The Masses during the war and most of my friends are socialists. I have always voted the socialist ticket." On the other hand, Thayer considered the "Imaginative Individual" always to be the "Marooned Individual," as he announced in his eulogy of Marianne Moore in January 1925.

These attitudes of Scofield Thayer, discerned in his early writing for *The Dial,* are among the controlling assumptions, often never directly voiced, of *The Dial* of the 1920's. To say that they dominated *The Dial* and that *The Dial* dominated the decade is of course an exaggeration. There were other influential editors in the journalism of art and literature, editors as various, in their dedication to the arts, as Harriet Monroe, Margaret Anderson, Henry Seidel Canby, and Frank Crowninshield. There were other magazines of the vanguard — *Poetry, The Little Review, Broom, The Fugitive*. It is essential, all the same, to understand *The Dial* and its Editor, in the two decades of the years 1912-1929, if one is to arrive at an understanding of American culture in its most exciting and fruitful years: Thayer is important as an influential editor, the publisher of certain writers, the collector of the works of certain artists, and the molder, through his advocacy in *The Dial*, of specific critical attitudes that have become central to the aesthetic life in twentieth-century America.

Thayer's writing for Martyn Johnson's *Dial* clearly indicates his distaste for politics and public affairs, his cosmopolitan humanism, his aestheticism, and his willed involvement with the life of art and letters. Superficially, these concerns would seem to argue for the continuation of a fruitful relationship between Johnson and his Associate Editor. That the two men disagreed so emphatically as to prompt Thayer's public break with Johnson is a measure of the strains of those months during which the first World War ended and the October Revolution began.

During the course of 1918, not only did Thayer's difficulties with Martyn Johnson increase, so did Randolph Bourne's. As one who had publicly announced his support of President Wilson's declaration of war, Johnson clearly was siding with John Dewey as the war drew to its close. The position of Bourne as a contributing editor on the board of *The Dial* thus became increasingly ambiguous. The chief advocate for a pacifist attitude and the chief advocate, among American liberals, for them to immerse themselves in the "business" of getting the war over and done with, these two men could not exist easily on the same editorial board. Yet Bourne needed *The Dial* as Dewey did not: Bourne's was a directly financial need to support himself through his journalism as well as a need to express himself freely in a sympathetic review when, under the circumstances, most doors were closed to him. He thus turned to Scofield Thayer and to *The Dial*. In *The Dial*, he opposed his own conscience to his former mentor's intelligence and discovered that Dewey's article on "Conscience and Compulsion" had applied "pragmatic philosophy in its least convincing form." War, said Bourne, provided its own end, war had made Europe a realm of the absolute: "In wartime, there is literally no other end but war, and the objector, therefore, lives no longer with choice of alternatives. The pacifist conscience attaches itself to no end because no end exists which connects with its desires." Peace would come through victory or exhaustion, and not through "creative intelligence" — a thrust at Dewey's favorite and famous phrase. The appeal to force removed everything automatically to a nonintelligent sphere of thinking and acting. But perhaps at "the back of Mr. Dewey's mind was . . . the hope that the pacifist conscience, though hating war and everything connected with it, might aid this war because of the radical social reforms it was sure to bring." That conscience should disabuse itself. Through war these reforms were frustrated, education was impoverished, national demoralization rather than integration was taking place. The realistic pacifists had foreseen these evils; once one accepts war, there is no choice but to be shoved along the line of inevitables with which war is organically bound up. In wartime, the forces moving in another direction, "to which Mr. Dewey invites the objecting conscience to attach itself," were illusory. War was just that absolute situation which was its own end and its own means. If one remained out of war, events remained to some degree malleable. Admittedly no social machinery existed to make dissent effective; nevertheless, alternative ends were illusory. One must protest: it might not be noble to concentrate on his own integrity, but it was perhaps better than to be a hypocrite or a martyr. Even the pragmatist had the right to choose what seemed inevitable to him. And what if one were skeptical that the present inevitable forces were the only ones to choose from? What if "a federalism of sovereign nations will only mean more competitive wars"? Bourne concluded that to the dissenter, the final choices were "resistance or apathy," and that he must "wait and hope for wisdom when the world becomes pragmatic and flexible again."

Faced with the spectacle of such a struggle — the romantic courage that walked alone to choose principle over the canny chance of mere survival, opposed by the cool and muted manipulations of the will to power — one needs no special grace of prophecy to know the outcome. John Dewey kept on writing for *The New Republic*; he quickly assumed the power of leadership in *The Dial*, especially after Martyn Johnson moved the magazine to New York; and he served the war effort by writing a confidential report on a minority, in this case the Poles in the United States. He rapidly became an authority on the Poles, at least to the satisfaction of the staff of *The Dial*. Dewey's collaborator in the Polish research was the eccentric art collector and manufacturer of Argyrol, Dr. Albert C. Barnes, who contributed an article, "Democracy, Watch Your Step!," to *The Dial* of December 28, 1918; it was about the "free Poland" automatically created by the Armistice of 1918. Barnes advocated the cause of General Joseph Pilsudski: "At a meeting in Poland at which all of the many political parties were represented, General Joseph Pilsudski, released by the armistice from a German prison, was selected to choose their Government and act as its first President. That was self-determination, prompt, pure and simple; it was Wilsonian democracy triumphant." Barnes was opposed to American support of Paderewski's group of Polish nationalists. Both the article and Barnes's tone — a combination of knowledge without firm foundation in fact, and brutal *realpolitik* — are typical of the writer. According to the "Contributors" column, "Mr. Barnes and John Dewey are probably the leading authorities on the Polish Movement in America." Barnes was also cited as "a manufacturer who is especially interested in the application of psychological theory to the problems of business and politics"; and he was a friend of Dewey's of long standing. In the 1920's he caused *The Dial* much grief.

Except for a sharp exchange of correspondence with Bourne over his review of the first American edition of Frederick Matthias Alexander's *Man's Supreme Inheritance*, for which Dewey had written the "Introductory Word," there was not the shadow of recrimination from the older man. Bourne reviewed the book in *The New Republic* for May 4, 1918; Dewey replied in the issue of May 11, and Bourne's rejoinder was published in that for May 25. In *The Dial* itself, there occurred no such exchange.[23]

Throughout 1918 Bourne's reviews were published by Martyn Johnson, but Johnson commissioned no further political pieces, and Bourne's final political leading article remained the answer to Dewey, "Conscience and Intelligence in War." Of Bourne's two later leading articles, one, "The Idea of a University," in *The Dial* for November 22, 1917, touched only tangentially on the issues of the war; it was more directly concerned with a current *cause célèbre* involving academic freedom — Charles A. Beard had resigned from the faculty of Columbia University in protest against the dismissal, by the university's trustees, of Professors Cattell and Dana.

The other leading article, "Traps for the Unwary," has been termed one of Bourne's two most important general essays in criticism, along with "The History of a Literary Radical."[24] It is in part an obvious attack on certain of John Dewey's positions, but, less obviously, it suggests the new force making itself felt in the affairs of *The Dial,* and complicating the struggle with Dewey. By the spring of 1918, Bourne had become a good friend of Scofield Thayer, who expressed a profound admiration for Bourne's qualities of mind by supporting his unpopular public attitudes. In these same months in which Bourne was differing with Dewey over the war, Martyn Johnson was seeking support for his magazine. Johnson found what he sought, in Scofield Thayer, the admirer of Randolph Bourne, who already was a contributing editor on the staff of *The Dial.* "Traps for the Unwary" thus possesses interest and meaning for itself and also for its place in the increasingly involved affairs of Martyn Johnson's *Dial.*

As the leading article for the Spring Books issue of March 28, 1918, "Traps for the Unwary" had nothing to do with the war. It was a battle cry nonetheless, if of a different struggle from that of the Allies and the Central Powers, and by sounding his ideas in some detail, Bourne undoubtedly was attacking obliquely Dewey's expressions in support of the war effort, as well as his many references to "democracy" as a criterion. Perhaps the nearest that Bourne came to any direct challenge was his appeal for "minds with a touch of the apostolic about them and a certain edge — a little surly, but not embittered — with an intellectual as well as artistic conscience, with a certain tentative superciliousness towards Demos and an appalling hatred for everything which savors of the bourgeois or the sentimental." Bourne also took exception to the current state of criticism, caught as it was between the rebellious vulgarity of H. L. Mencken, who represented "a moralism imperfectly transcended," and Stuart Sherman, an "arrant philistine," who defended the life lived through the conventions and was dangerous because he made philistinism sound like *belles lettres*. Responsible criticism of the new writers was practically nonexistent. The confused reviews of Amy Lowell's book on the Imagists disclosed, asserted Bourne, "how very novel is an intelligent attempt to place our current literary art not merely against the spiritual background of tradition, but in the terms and in the spirit of the contemporary imagination itself." Miss Lowell's very tone was "revolutionary"; she was neither sentimental nor apologetic. And then came the passage that adumbrated the entire critical effort of *The Dial* after 1920, a passage suggesting the direction taken in *The Dial* of Thayer and Watson toward the realization of a socially and aesthetically relevant criticism:

> Poetry appears for the first time on our critical horizon as neither a refined dessert to be consumed when the day's work is done, nor as a private hobby which the business man will deride if he hears about it, but as a sound and important activity of contemporary American life. . . . The problem of the literary artist is how to obtain more of this intelligent, pertinent, absolutely contemporaneous criticism, which shall be both severe and encouraging. It will be obtained when the artist himself has turned critic and set to work to discover and interpret in others the motives and values and efforts he feels in himself.

Just after Randolph Bourne, T. S. Eliot was writing at about the same time that the two directions of sensibility — creative and critical — are complementary; "and as sensibility is rare, unpopular, desirable, it is to be expected that the critic and the creative artist should frequently be the same person."

The attitude shared by Bourne and Eliot was opposed by no less a personage than Harriet Monroe. In her *Poetry* for May 1918, she rebutted Bourne in an editorial, "Mr. Bourne on Traps," minimizing the artist's dependence upon the literary critic for guidance. "To the artist," she wrote, "the critic is not very important, especially the professional critic who would soundly and sanely guide him past all manner of traps." What *was* important, she held, to the artist is his chance to be seen or heard, his chance of a frugal living while he is doing his work, his chance of admission to the company of his peers among the dead or the living. The most well-meaning and highly intellectualized criticism cannot give the artist one of these three things. To Miss Monroe, the little theaters and the little magazines were doing more to supply the essential needs of the poet and the playwright than any amount of "the new criticism" could. She concluded by advising Bourne that if the ideal artist did arrive on the scene, this "prodigy, once achieved, will not worry his mind about getting 'intelligent, pertinent, absolutely contemporaneous criticism, which shall be both severe and encouraging' " — here she was quoting Bourne back at himself — "He will have more important things to do. His problem will be, as it has always been, to get himself expressed in his art, and to get his art before his public. And the only aid which he will recognize is that which forwards these ends." What Miss Monroe failed to see — at any rate, one misses this point in her editorial — is that Bourne called for greater critical self-awareness on the part of the poet. She insisted, to the detriment of her argument, on establishing an absolute dichotomy between critic and artist, going so far as to suggest by the tenor of her presentation that editors and theatrical producers were not themselves practicing critics.

That weakness in Miss Monroe's editorial was what occupied Randolph Bourne and Van Wyck Brooks in their joint reply to "Mr. Bourne's Traps," a letter to *Poetry* entitled "The Retort Courteous" and published in its September 1918 issue.

Bourne and Brooks began by pointing out that Bourne had had
no intention of condemning "little theatres and little magazines,
which, by providing a medium of publicity and experimentation,
have done so much . . . to stimulate the artistic imagination of
the younger writers." What was objectionable was treating poetry
"entirely in terms of itself . . . the surest way to drive it into
futility and empty verbalism." Poetry would go to seed "unless
it is understood as an expression of life pregnant with possibilities. This is the kind of criticism we were asking for." Amy
Lowell's book, *Tendencies in Modern American Poetry*, praised
in Bourne's "Traps for the Unwary," was again praised as the
sort of criticism called for because it attempted to place the six
poets she discussed "with reference to the American intellectual
soil, and to the changing American attitudes toward beauty and
the joy of life." Amy Lowell moreover abandoned "the indis-
criminate note of propaganda" and handled "her six poets un-
sparingly, separating the false in their work from the true, and
placing them in relation to a larger intellectual and artistic
whole." That was what "was meant by criticism." Bourne and
Brooks cited Vachel Lindsay as an example of the uneven poet
who needs such criticism. "If criticism confines itself to a purely
aesthetic standard," they added, "then this verse is certainly
doomed," that is to say, verse that is emptily verbal in its experimentation or that is sentimental.

The Editor appended a note to "The Retort Courteous"
promising to reply to it in her next issue; " 'Aesthetic and Social
Criticism' " was her rejoinder in *Poetry* for October 1918. Her
text was the statement made by Bourne and Brooks that the
public of the new poetry, "enthusiastic and hospitable, seems to
be still moving hazily in a mist of values and interpretations, for
it still gets aesthetic instead of social criticism." Her reply constitutes a veritable credo: "The artist is born to express the
beauty of life. The first essential in this, his business, is that he
should feel this beauty — feel it perhaps more keenly, more profoundly than his fellow-creatures; the second, that he should be
able to express this feeling." Each artist has an "inalienable right"
to express his own notions of beauty, whether apprehended "in

strikes, or war, or pacificism, or settlements, or the Bolsheviki," or, "like Whistler, in the fall of a rocket or the turn of a girl's figure. The artist, of course, can express only himself." Her objection to "social criticism" in the arts is that it "is probably more befogging to the critic and his public than to the artist. The artist, big or little, is in his degree a seer; and it may be that he sees deeper than the critic who is obsessed by 'the movements of his time.'" For "Movements pass, but beauty endures." Miss Monroe concluded that her own age would endure in the beauty that it created; in that beauty "its essential movement will be expressed. It may be — as indeed I believe — "she affirmed, "that certain of our living poets will be remembered in that ultimate record; but if they fail it will be through lack of power to feel or express, or both, and not through lack of social criticism."

That remark was not answered by Bourne and Brooks. It was an especially appropriate remark, under the circumstances of the debate, for it indicated the direction in which the dominant school of American literary criticism would move during the succeeding half-century. Perhaps the phrase "social criticism" was an unfortunate choice; it reflects Brooks's cast of mind rather than Bourne's. Like Eliot, Bourne called for a criticism that was relevant to society as a whole, a criticism that was based on first principles, a criticism the product of practice rather than of academic reflection. For Brooks, criticism must be social; he did not accept Bourne's feeling of alienation from the effort of the war and felt, instead, "that to oppose the war was scarcely less futile than opposing an earthquake." If more passive than Dewey's intellectual position about the question, Brooks's attitude was basically the same pragmatic way of looking at the war. His outlook opposed T. S. Eliot's entire view as a critic; ignoring that aspect of Bourne's criticism that agreed with Eliot's, Brooks saw only what he termed the *Encyclopédiste* in Bourne — the optimism, the skepticism about established religion — and took it for the whole. Harriet Monroe's demand for an "aesthetic criticism" may appear to foreshadow, rather more closely than Bourne's demand for a more comprehensively relevant criticism, the avowedly nonpolitical stand of *The Dial* of Thayer and Watson. What is nearer the truth of the situation is that Thayer would have disavowed Harriet Monroe's theories about poetry and criticism as neither rigorous nor comprehensive enough to furnish an adequate *raison d' être* for his *Dial*. All the same, he tacitly approved her defense of the organs publishing the literature of the new movement and thus providing recognition of the new artists; his *Dial* was just such a magazine, the chief of its decade.

The time of the composition of "Traps for the Unwary" has a further interest, for the essay was, with the many editorials of the indefatigable Harriet Monroe and the early criticism of Eliot and Pound, one of those pronouncements that went to mold attitudes toward art and letters in the 1920's. It was almost certainly written in the spring of 1918, when Martyn Johnson was persuading Scofield Thayer to finance *The Dial*; and Johnson could succeed mainly because Thayer wished to convert *The Dial* into the critical journal that expressed his and Randolph Bourne's ideas and ideals. Randolph Bourne died before Scofield Thayer could bring to fruition his plans for a new journal of the arts different from Martyn Johnson's *Dial* not merely in degree but in the kind of magazine it was. To give voice to the attitudes and feelings of the younger generation about the life of art, in 1920 there was, instead of Bourne, the most influential critic of the century, Eliot.

Johnson permitted the publication of a nonpolitical essay by Bourne, and Thayer perhaps was mollified for the time being. As the year went on, however, his hopes for Bourne were frustrated. Not only was Bourne not allowed a controlling hand in policy, gradually he lost his position of power on the board of contributing editors on which Johnson had asked him to serve in the winter of 1916-17.

A new friendship — of great consequence for *The Dial* — brightened these months of tension. Alyse Gregory met Scofield Thayer through Randolph Bourne's introduction.[25] She was then living in Greenwich Village, running a tea and flower shop with her friend Linda. It was Linda who had thought up the scheme for a shop that would be unique of its kind and that also would soon make its proprietors rich enough to retire for the rest of their days. Alyse Gregory had saved a hundred dollars, and Linda, who knew the second-hand shops and auction rooms all over New York, set out to furnish the shop, which occupied the ground floor and basement of a little old two-storey house on the corner of Seventh Avenue and Eleventh Street. The new quarters were soon filled with a remarkable assortment of copper trays, teapots of every size and shape, odd cups and saucers, and six tables and sets of chairs, most of which were delivered on handbarrows by the sellers. The gas stove and the food safe needed for serving teas were located in the basement below the tearoom; the upper floor was the preserve of the Spanish couple who rented out the shop.

One pictures Scofield Thayer, "that embodiment of the aesthete" to Alyse Gregory, sauntering imperiously into her tearoom as he chatted with the small humped figure draped in a long black student's cape and topped by a black felt hat, picking its way sparrowlike through the doorway. Although Bourne was by this date a familiar sight in Greenwich Village, people "would turn to stare after him with the expression that any deviation from the normal seems inevitably to evoke among the vulgar." But Thayer told Miss Gregory that he thought his friend very distinguished in appearance and was always proud to be seen with him.

That Bourne and Thayer became close friends so soon was due to their affinities aesthetic as well as political. Bourne was an amateur of the piano, who played Brahms and Chopin by the hour, charming his audience of young women into forgetfulness of his ugliness. He had an ear for the melody of prose rhythms, for the "feel" of words as well as their meaning. In his own way, Randolph Bourne responded to the hue and form that most people take for granted in daily life; the anecdote is related in several accounts that when dying, he asked that an eggnog be made for him to drink, but before sipping it, he exclaimed with pleasure over its gorgeous saffron color. Thayer hated noise — including the noise of musicians' daily practice. His strength lay in his responsiveness to color, volume, design in

painting, sculpture, and drawings; yet as keenly as Bourne, Scofield Thayer attended to the subtleties of prose and poetry, to the
glancing play of paradox and epigram, to the sounds of words
juxtaposed one against another. Despite the very different paths
and motives that led Bourne and Thayer to the jostle of competitive journalism in New York, both men were superb practical
journalists, a third affinity as essential to their relationship as their
love of the arts and their Fabian socialism.

When Bourne first mentioned Scofield Thayer to Alyse
Gregory, he did so with warnings that she must curb any irrele-
vant witticisms. She came later to believe that Thayer was
"one of those men the key to whose nature is so obscurely hid-
den that they alienate people because they remain outside their
understanding." She also later found that she had met Scofield
Thayer when they had been children, one summer at the seashore
cottage of the New York publisher Nathaniel Trowbridge. Her
"Uncle" Nat, as she affectionately called him, and Thayer's
father had been classmates at Harvard.

In Alyse Gregory's memoir, *The Day Is Gone*, Thayer makes
a figure almost unrecognizably different from that depicted by
Harold Stearns. He was slender of build, swift of movement,
always strikingly pale, with coal-black hair, black eyes veiled and
flashing, and lips that curved like those of Lord Byron — the
model for Gaston Lachaise's head commissioned a few years
after the war. He pursued art and letters "with a purpose so
elevated and so impassioned that he remained insulated from
the ironical comments about him," made by those who saw him
as merely an aesthete with "overrefined tastes and sensibilities."
What some viewed as affectations were "mannerisms indigenous
to his character." In contrast to the gullible multimillionaire
caricatured by Stearns, Alyse Gregory saw Thayer as suspecting
the whole world; she thought that perhaps his general distrust,
as betrayed by the carriage of his head and the timbre of his voice,
created about him an attitude of strain. But he had, as Freud
confirmed to her in speaking of Scofield Thayer much later, "a
most gentle heart." In Miss Gregory's eyes, her new friend admin-

istered his wealth largely as a trust, supporting or helping to support many young writers and artists.

Thayer habitually dressed "with a considered simplicity, pleased to be seen in a suit of clothes he had worn since his university days." His abode on the top floor of an apartment house on Washington Square was luxury itself, however. The bookshelves were filled with rare first editions and folios of prints — what the Germans call *Mappen,* the models for Thayer's great folio of 1924, *Living Art.* His collection of drawings by Aubrey Beardsley adorned the walls. Opposite an antique Chinese cabinet in his living room was a high, narrow window seat, covered with shabby leather, on which a guest would perch as on one of those benches provided for lepers in medieval cathedrals. Here "monk and aesthete joined hands."

Hours the two friends spent together were never dull for Alyse Gregory, though she might find them nervous. "Like most people of distinction, he was often egocentric, though not egotistical; his courtesy could be exquisite and he was touchingly susceptible to the words of the people he valued." Scofield Thayer's chief verbal weapons were irony and wit. His irony, though as swift as Randolph Bourne's, was to Miss Gregory seldom as light. Thayer "was ice on the surface and molten lava underneath." In keeping with that paradox, his mind was "inflammable and satirical, and it was at the same time sober and sad. He defended himself with his wit, the best way of banishing fear. Like Diderot, he would rather be impatient than bored, and he alternated between the tempest and the frozen lake."

In her character of Scofield Thayer, Alyse Gregory concludes that he never felt wholly at ease in America and that with few exceptions, he preferred his English friends. It is true that Thayer returned to Europe in 1921; from his letters one gathers he found a way of life, especially in Central Europe, that he preferred to the noise and hubbub of New York City. Yet it was in New York that he befriended Randolph Bourne and thereby came to *The Dial* and met the woman who became, as he acknowledged, his closest American friend, an intimate ranking in his affections with his English friend Raymond Mortimer and his

German friend Robert von Erdberg. In 1923 Alyse Gregory was invited by Scofield Thayer and Sibley Watson to assume the post that Gilbert Seldes had just left, and she worked at *The Dial* as its Associate Editor; the posthumous influence of Randolph Bourne was indeed enduring.

Beyond this three-sided relationship, the situation at *The Dial* continued to develop to the detriment of Bourne and Thayer. For example, before Martyn Johnson decided to move the journal to New York, only two of the new board of three editors "In Charge of Reconstruction" — John Dewey, Helen Marot, and Thorstein Veblen — had contributed to *The Dial*. In 1917, Dewey contributed two articles; "Current Tendencies in Education" appeared in the issue of April 5, and "The Case of the Professor and the Public Interest" — by way of unintended prelude to Bourne's piece on the Beard case, published two weeks later — was printed in the issue of November 8. As Bourne's star dimmed, Dewey's brightened. During 1918, he appeared five times in *The Dial*. Such statistics alone are significant, although Dewey's first article of the year, "Education and Social Direction," did not of itself indicate the drift of Johnson's policy. Between the publication of Dewey's article in April 1918 and his next appearance in *The Dial* occurred the crucial event: in July Johnson moved *The Dial* to New York and decided to express a firmer editorial attitude toward the war. At that time, Dewey learned the membership of the proposed editorial board and refused to have anything to do with a project with which Bourne was associated. As Martyn Johnson considered Dewey's name more important than Bourne's for the planned editorial window-dressing, Johnson submitted to Dewey's objection and withdrew Bourne from nomination. Although — according to Merrill Rogers — Scofield Thayer was very angry, he apparently accepted the decision to restrict Bourne's participation in the affairs of *The Dial* to the duties of a weekly reviewer. Bourne was not yet aware of the intrigue against him. As late as July 1918, after *The Dial* had made the move to New York, Randolph Bourne told Alyse Gregory (in a letter written from Sound Beach, Connecticut, that month) that he was busy trying to satisfy Harold

Stearns's demand for reviews, and he wondered whether he was missing much in not being around for the debut of *The Dial*. He would have, Bourne added, six weeks before the gates of Martyn Johnson closed about his his soul, and he foresaw nothing ahead of him but work. He expected, it is clear, to go to work in September 1918 — when *The Dial* resumed publication after a hiatus because of its resettlement in New York — as a member of the *Dial* staff. These hopes were confounded. The masthead page of *The Dial* for September 19, 1918, was the last to carry Bourne's name as a contributing editor. The same issue carried a leading article by Henri Barbusse, "Poilu, What Are You Fighting For?" After advising the *poilu* to "love France as you do your mother," Barbusse informed him that he fought for "a magnificent booty": "you are fighting for justice, goodness, and beauty, and — in fine — for labor and the happiness and prosperity of all. . . . It is a holy task for the writers to tell you what you are fighting for." Obviously, Bourne's was a lost cause.

The next issue of *The Dial*, for October 5, made his defeat an accomplished fact. For the old board of contributing editors, Martyn Johnson substituted a new editorial triumvirate "In Charge of the Reconstruction Program," as the new heading in the masthead announced: John Dewey, Thorstein Veblen, and Helen Marot. It is interesting that, despite his connection with Bourne, Scofield Thayer allowed himself to be named as one of the regular editorial staff, along with Clarence Britten, George Donlin (by this time no longer very active), and Harold Stearns. Not only did Johnson thus rid himself of a troublesome contributing editor, he undoubtedly would have liked to rid himself of an equally troublesome backer; Thayer, however, was indispensable.

The tension of those weeks is vivid in Bourne's correspondence. By the middle of September 1918, Bourne had subleased Paul Rosenfeld's comfortable New York home. Paul Rosenfeld, an unhappy enlisted man in Virginia, wrote to Bourne on October 7, that Martyn Johnson had "shown himself a cowardly and contemptible brute — if I thought he would last in the field of letters I would hate him. But as I know him for the ephemerida

he is, I only hope his going will be soon. He really is the mess
I originally gave him credit for being." These were rare words
from the usually charitably inclined Rosenfeld, who shrewdly
continued: "In the light of the present political situation, and
the prospect of the return of peace, he must realize his pussy-
footing has done him nothing but harm." After a passing reference to "the slippery Harold" Stearns — another shrewd insight,
in view of Stearns's later relations with Thayer and Watson —
Rosenfeld asked: "As for the 'Dial,' do you give it a long life?
Is Thayer still as well disposed with his money? I do hope he
prefers a Belles-Lettres magazine . . . to the present false and
vaudeville elephant [?]." The strange situation is given firmer
outlines in a letter Bourne wrote to his mother on October 12,
1918, a few days after the publication of the rearranged staff
positions and roster of names. He had, he informed her, been
relieved of his duties on *The Dial* but would continue to
receive his salary just the same and would continue to write
for the magazine. Indeed, Bourne asserted that he preferred it
"this way," as it left him much freer. "The rich young man who
put up the money to back the *Dial* this year is a very good
friend of mine, and we are both in the same boat. He has strong
tastes and I have strong convictions, and the man who runs the
paper is very much afraid of us both, afraid we will have too
much to say about the policy."

Apparently Thayer was as helpless as Bourne. On November
4, Bourne again wrote his mother about *The Dial*. There had
been some fuss on the magazine about his being an editor, owing
to his "radical views," but he was paid just the same as though
he remained a contributing editor — and he had to write only
two articles (i. e., reviews) a month. He again wrote of Scofield
Thayer: "I seem to be in very strong with the young man who is
giving most of the money to back *The Dial* this year. He says he
gave his $25,000 largely on the strength of my contributions, and
he was very angry at their not wanting me as a regular associate
editor." But, Bourne added with a son's candor, he did not
"need to worry apparently, as long as the money lasts." It was
the last full month of his life. He was frustrated, his back was

to the wall, and only Scofield Thayer's financial aid to Martyn Johnson was sufficient threat to force Johnson to treat Bourne as a member of the *Dial* staff. Yet even here Thayer could not force a change in editorial policy, and in reality Bourne's was a kind of charity case.

Randolph Bourne — idealistic as Shelley, doomed as Keats — struggled against the overwhelming opposition to his pacifist transnationalism, struggled to earn a living, poured out his hack reviews for the magazine that he had once hoped to control; before 1918 ended he died in a borrowed bed. Falling ill from pneumonia (according to Alyse Gregory) or from influenza (according to Van Wyck Brooks), he was moved from his rooms newly taken above the old Country and City School, at 18 West 8th Street, to the apartment of Mrs. Agnes de Lima and Miss Esther Cornell. Alyse Gregory recalled Agnes de Lima as "the noblest woman I have known"; "with her dark eyes, her infectious laugh, Spanish vivacity, and heart as deep as the sea," she shed about the last three years of Bourne's life the feeling of security he had always hoped for. Esther Cornell was a Bryn Mawr girl, related to Ezra Cornell, the founder of Cornell University, and had been, in Van Wyck Brooks's account, on the stage in *Kismet* and *The Silent Voice.* "She was extremely pretty, imaginative, gay, resilient, with eyes a greenish blue and copper-gold hair. She had an uncanny perception and insight into character." Bourne courted Miss Cornell for over two years, and he could have afforded to marry her, despite the doors closed to him at such journals as *The Atlantic Monthly* and *The New Republic.* There was, of course, the *Dial* subsidy insisted upon and furnished by Scofield Thayer. Actually, Bourne, driven to the wall as he was, still had at the time of his death $800 in savings and twenty-seven dollars in his checking account in the Bloomfield (N.J.) National Bank, plus a sum of money in his pockets; and, when Esther Cornell promised to marry him, "he was looking forward happily."

Bourne used to remain with Mrs. de Lima and Miss Cornell for long periods both in the country and in the city. (The three went on a walking trip from New York to Cape Cod and across to Martha's Vineyard in September 1918.) It thus was fitting that these two attractive young women should share his last days, as among his few steadfast friends throughout the previous two years. Of the great flu epidemic of 1918-19, he had remarked to Agnes de Lima, "One in every three persons gets it, — so one of us three must die." He fell ill on December 17. To Alyse Gregory, Bourne looked strangely pitiful in bed. "I don't want to die," he said, speaking with difficulty; but the words were imbued with his wonted irony, and so deeply involved was she in her own affairs that she could not realize how serious was the threat to his life.

Randolph Bourne died on December 22 as Agnes de Lima raised him up in her arms; Paul Rosenfeld was there to help, kind, devoted, and watchful. Three days later a funeral service was conducted for him by Norman Thomas in the Spring Street Presbyterian Church in New York, with burial in Bloomfield. To Alyse Gregory Bourne had been her dearest friend. She thought it well within his scope to have become America's Jean Jacques Rousseau: "He was for his generation in America, in the matter of war, what Bertrand Russell was for his in England and Romain Rolland for his in France." Dying, Randolph Bourne left two precious monuments: the vicarious immortality of his friends' memories of him, a much richer monument than his mostly topical writing; and the inspiration for *The Dial* of the 1920's.[26]

In the context of such a tragedy — a small one perhaps, in the worldwide context of the Russian Revolution, the end of the first World War, and the devastating influenza epidemic, but nonetheless a most poignant tragedy for Bourne's friends and followers among the young American liberals — not the least interesting aspect of publication of Thayer's final essay for Johnson's *Dial*, "Compton Mackenzie," is its timing. It appeared as the major literary essay in the issue of November 30, 1918; the next issue of the fortnightly *Dial*, dated December 14, 1918, published the review by J. S. Watson, Jr., "A Story-Teller's Holiday," of George Moore's book of that title, and the last piece Randolph Bourne saw published in his friend Thayer's *Dial*, "Morals and

Art from the West," a double review of William Allen White's novel *In the Heart of a Fool* and Willa Cather's *My Ántonia.* Although Bourne wrote one other piece submitted to *The Dial* during his lifetime, it was published posthumously in the issue for December 28, 1918, "An Examination of Eminences," a review of Lytton Strachey's *Eminent Victorians,* along with a notice in the back pages under "Contributors" that "Randolph Bourne, for two years a member of the contributing staff of THE DIAL, died December 22 in New York after only a few days' illness. The exigencies of publication make it necessary to postpone until the next number editorial comment on this loss to liberalism." What might have been added except that in the circumstances to do so would have been tactless and worse was that Scofield Thayer's resignation — announced in one short sentence in the preceding issue, under "Contributors": "THE DIAL announces the resignation of Mr. Scofield Thayer as Associate Editor" — meant also the death of any hope that Randolph Bourne would have exercised a decisive influence in the affairs of *The Dial* had he lived, for Thayer had become the financial power behind *The Dial* and had backed it because of his friend Bourne's connection. And with the death of Bourne and the resignation of Thayer, Martyn Johnson would ultimately fail as publisher of the fortnightly *Dial,* indeed, would fail in less than a year.

VI

The End of the Fortnightly DIAL *(1919)*

A LAST reminder in Martyn Johnson's *Dial* of the deceased contributing editor was James Oppenheim's memorial poem, "Randolph Bourne," featured in the issue for January 11, 1919. A northwest wind, wrote Oppenheim, would "sing his requiem,"

Who was
Our Age,
And who becomes
An imperishable symbol of our ongoing,
For in himself
He rose above his body and came among us
Prophetic of the race,
The great hater
Of the dark human deformity
Which is our dying world,
The great lover
Of the spirit of youth
Which is our future's seed. . . .

Back among the editorials, the staff printed its eulogy. Like

Oppenheim's poem, it is a key document in the evolution of the myth of Randolph Bourne; one suggests Robert Morss Lovett as the writer. Perhaps the memory that would live most vividly of Randolph Bourne, began the memorial paragraph, would be that of his quick perception of sham and pretense. "Pompous gentility and ritualism, whether encrusted convention or mere tradition, aroused his power of biting irony; for graceful and engaging as was his satire, it never lacked the edge which gave it a peculiar distinction." Bourne's fine and alert intelligence was coupled with an extraordinary ability as a craftsman in writing. He could easily have won more substantial recognition by employing his gifts in the service of the accepted and the acknowledged, but he never once played false to his spontaneous sympathies and his personal bias. His sympathies and that bias demanded "of life richer esthetic experiences, the companionship of fuller intellectual straightforwardness, more emotional range and flexibility than his American environment could possibly yield without radical transformation"; Bourne gave his best efforts and ability to that transformation. The next sentence strikes one as a rather disingenuous allusion to the perhaps awkward fact that *The Dial* published Bourne as a reviewer mostly rather than as an editorial commentator: "In all of his work, whether in the book reviews that were themselves pieces of creative writing or in his books or articles on education or even politics, he was always sharply insistent upon the contributions which our immigrants could make to our national life, mockingly contemptuous of the timidity and surviving Puritan shyness which rejected them." The eulogist went on to mention Bourne's welcome and understanding of the more untoward forms that flaring rebellion might take even while he refused to be beguiled by "new formulas which were the mere fashionable radical escape from the old." That Bourne's "influence was a constant invigoration and challenge" could be admitted — with a sigh of relief as it were — once he was out of the way. But such praise was gilding this particular commemorative lily out of resemblance to poor quarrelsome Nature. The *Dial* staff would not have been so generous to Bourne living. The next bit of analysis strikes one as altogether accurate, however: Bourne "examined in a merciless Socratic spirit" the shibboleths and fine words of the day; it "was hardly in the way of systematic intellectual achievement that either his ability or his temperament led him: he was rather a watchman and questioner of the intellectual achievements of others — a challenger whom even the greatest could not afford to ignore." And then the peroration, which again strikes one (is it unkind to glance at the notion?) as a self-salving of the consciences of the *Dial* staff:

> Time would have matured his judgment and perhaps mellowed a wit as urbane as any in our tradition. But it would scarcely have changed the fundamental quality of his contribution to our intellectual life. The loss of that contribution is irremediable. All of us are the poorer for his going.

These graceful words were of course an attempt to cover the wound that had cleft the magazine. Or did the writer even then dimly realize that well within the year *The Dial* would come round to Bourne's point of view, sharing it if imperfectly and partially? The words of peroration are slight harbingers of Paul Rosenfeld's concluding praise in "Randolph Bourne," the memoir of his dead friend that Scofield Thayer published in *The Dial* for December 1923, five years after Bourne's death. Asserted Rosenfeld: "To-day, already, we know him for one of the rarest, freest, sweetest spirits that have ever come out of this land. . . . He was a humanist; and the men left us are sociologists, political thinkers, professors, and critics. . . . In his person, therefore, he has lent the world another image, another symbol and banner whereby the unborn thing which filled him, wherever and in whomsoever it grows, can come to greater consciousness, and therefore greater courage of itself, and be pressed onward toward birth. And, some day, the spring will come again to men." By the end of 1923, the aesthetic and moral revolution of the New Movement had won its struggle. Oppenheim's imperishable symbol of our ongoing had also become for Paul Rosenfeld another image, symbol, banner of the hopeful potential of the

American future; Randolph Bourne was a portion of the grand myth of a hardwon liberation.

In contrast to Oppenheim's poem and to the conclusion of the editorial paragraph commemorating Randolph Bourne was Edward Sapir's letter, also in *The Dial* for January 11, 1919. To Sapir, Bourne was one of those rare and extraordinarily fine-grained men whom it is always an exceptional privilege to know. Bourne's "occasional 'bitterness' was in reality but the keen edge of a remorseless sincerity"; his "extraordinary combination of the will to see things as they are with a warmth of idealism (not the phrase-making kind)" was particularly inspiring, but what Sapir liked most about Bourne was "his exquisite sensibility to the esthetic in literature, to the nuances of thought and feeling and expression," phrased in a well-nigh perfect style. Often clever, Bourne was "too sensitive ever to be merely clever," and he shrank from vulgarity of any kind as one shrinks from a disgusting bug. His loss would be keenly felt not only by *The Dial* "but by all who know how to appreciate a soul at once sensitive and remorselessly strong." Sapir's comments are imbued with the scholar's sense of fact, a quality that makes his tribute to Bourne all the more convincing, in contrast to those that glorified Bourne as a symbol rather than as a man. Thus from the very time of Bourne's death, the hagiographers contradicted the historians.

There was a new Editor for *The Dial* in 1919. Had Bourne lived, he would not have been Editor; instead Johnson picked Robert Morss Lovett, of the University of Chicago, to come to New York and to join the staff of *The Dial*. A distinguished scholar and professor of English, Lovett had contributed to the Chicago *Dial* and was well known for his espousal of liberal causes. When Johnson asked Lovett in the autumn of 1918 to take the editorship, he looked forward to his first assignment, "to make it possible for both John Dewey and Randolph Bourne to remain with the magazine."[1] It would have been a difficult task, as Lovett realized that Bourne's article on "The Intellectuals and the War" in *The Seven Arts* had been the death of that journal, and he well knew that Bourne would not compromise principles when it came to the conduct of the war; yet he admired Bourne and considered himself indebted to Dewey in philosophy. Lovett also knew, on the brighter side of *Dial* affairs, that Johnson had large plans for his magazine and wished to model *The Dial* after the London *Athenaeum*, to become a political as well as a literary journal. Fortunately Lovett was enabled by the flexible quarter system then in effect at the University of Chicago to obtain a leave of absence for the winter and spring of 1919. In its "Contributors" column for January 11, 1919, *The Dial* announced the change in staff: "with this issue Robert Morss Lovett, long a contributor to [these] columns, becomes [the] editor. In addition to his collaboration with William Vaughan Moody — A History of English Literature (1902) and A First View of English Literature (1905) — Mr. Lovett is the author of Cowards, a play produced in 1914, and of Winged Victory (1907). He comes to THE DIAL from the University of Chicago, where he has been a member of the Department of English since 1893 and a dean since 1903." The announcement went on to say that the "change in editors is enforced by the continued ill health of George Donlin, who, though necessarily absent from the offices, will remain on the staff of THE DIAL as an associate editor and will contribute as his health permits."

Immediately on arriving in New York to take over his editorial duties, Lovett learned of Bourne's death; there could be no reconciliation such as he had hoped for. He was disheartened at losing the most important contributor to the literary function of *The Dial*, and, it may well have been, he was even more disheartened by a close look at the disintegrating situation in the *Dial* office. Prudently he collected his half-year's editorial salary in advance, but with the consequent disadvantage that he became "banker of the office" when a contributor or staff member needed a loan for a drink.

The trouble was easy to spot. As Harold Stearns said, in the "old New York *Dial* office others and myself must have rearranged the whole map of Europe at least two or three dozen times — and at least a hundred different ways." Martyn Johnson was ready, the new Editor learned, to commit the future of *The*

Dial — under the persuasion of a liberal Protestant clergyman, Percy Stickney Grant — by turning it into the organ of the Forum Movement. Lovett himself went around making speeches in favor of the toleration of the Bolsheviks. Back at the office there were not enough working journalists getting out *The Dial* itself; Lovett found the "little magazine was top-heavy, overstaffed, and underfinanced." Johnson, moreover, had contracted for articles to which was mortgaged the limited space of the issues. Yet despite the "overstaffing," there was only one person on the staff who saw to the actual business of publication. She was Miss Florence Haxton, who put together and got out each fortnightly issue. The extent of disorganization is revealed in Lovett's reminiscence that when once in Miss Haxton's absence, he got out the issue, the "compositors saw to it that nearly every page opened with a 'widow' — i. e., an incomplete line closing a paragraph" — a dereliction "seriously regarded by my colleagues."

The truth was that most of the editorial staff was window dressing, put on the masthead page to make an impression. Although George Donlin, Harold Stearns, and Clarence Britten remained on the staff, Donlin and Stearns at any rate were not much help. Poor Donlin was dying of consumption in South Pasadena, California. The erratic Stearns was lent to Mrs. Willard Straight's office force backing "the Co-operative Movement, which assumed pretentious form in Charles Phillips' plan of organizing communities by blocks, to supply consumers' commodities." A lavish suite of rooms in the Metropolitan Tower housed the propaganda department of the enterprise, "under the able direction of Dorothy Thompson," to which *The Dial* contributed Stearns's services.

As for the fourth member of the staff to which Lovett came, Scofield Thayer resigned from *The Dial* in December 1918. Thayer was, of course, unhappy about the anomaly of his and Bourne's positions on the staff. Because of Dewey's opposition, Bourne's name had not been placed with the names of the editors in charge of Reconstruction, and that meant the exclusion of Bourne from editorial meetings. True to his word, however, Thayer remained a stockholder in *The Dial,* even though he did not remain quiet in his disapproval of the way things were going. That the chronology of all that happened in these months is as disorderly as was the state of the magazine itself, becomes obvious from Lovett's allegation that Thayer on one occasion threatened a law suit "to protect his name," when *The Dial* "published the constitution of the Union of Soviet Socialist Republics simultaneously with its publication by the *Nation*." The chief problem raised by this statement is that the Soviet constitution was not promulgated until July 1923; perhaps Lovett meant to refer to the publication by *The Dial* of the Original Decrees of the Soviet government in its "Foreign Comment" column in the issue of December 14, 1918. Such a date would accord with Thayer's resignation early in December 1918 from Johnson's staff, and he may well have used the incident of the publication of the Original Decrees both to emphasize his disapproval of Johnson's policy and to serve as an excuse for resigning — instead of presenting Johnson with the ultimatum to put Bourne back on the staff as an editor or to look for another backer. Although Lovett related the anecdote as though he had participated in it, he may well have been using the editorial *we* in writing that "Thayer disapproved our attitude and threatened a law suit to 'protect his name.'" Again, Johnson may well have consulted Lovett in the matter shortly before he left Chicago for his new post on *The Dial;* such is the probability, as Lovett by his own account arrived in New York only after Bourne's death on December 22, 1918.

During the course of 1919, there were several new staff members added to the masthead at one time or another.

The new poetry pressed upon the Editor until Conrad Aiken was made "arbiter" of it. It is curious, all the same, that Aiken, who had been one of the numerous contributing editors in 1917 and a colleague of Randolph Bourne and Henry Blake Fuller among others, was not to have his name on the masthead in 1919. Had it appeared there, it would have been as the sole representative of the New Movement in literature and the arts in a group of names associated with social, economic, and political matters. Aiken was one of the more frequent contributors to *The Dial* in 1919, with a total of seven articles, from January through October, and in the issue of May 31 he received the compliment of John Gould Fletcher's essay, "Conrad Aiken — Metaphysical Poet."

The first of two new staff members who became, for a few weeks, Associates on the staff appeared one morning, "a tall handsome youth in khaki . . . Lewis Mumford, in fact, just discharged from the Army. He qualified at once as a reviewer," and contributed, in all, nine articles and review essays to *The Dial* in 1919. In contrast to his later, more aesthetic orientation, Mumford's writing for *The Dial* in 1919 dealt with social and political problems, from his first piece, "International Angling," in the issue for March 22, to "An Evangelist of Civilization," in the issue for November 29, the first number with Scofield Thayer as Editor and the last issue of the fortnightly *Dial*. The "Contributors" column for March 22 introduced Lewis Mumford as "a resident of New York City" and the contributor of "numerous articles to technical and general magazines. He has been an investigator in the dress and waist industry, a laboratory worker in the Bureau of Standards, and a radio operator in the United States Navy." Robert Morss Lovett's memory was inaccurate when he recalled that Lewis Mumford succeeded him "as editor"; Mumford's tasks may have been similar to Lovett's, but for the last six months of Johnson's proprietorship, there was no single Editor of *The Dial*. Moreover, Lovett's name remained on the masthead with those of Johnson, Oswald Knauth, Veblen, and Miss Marot until the end as an "editor," while from the issue of September 6 through that of November 15 — the final number of Johnson's *Dial* — three Associates replaced John Dewey: Mumford, Clarence Britten, and Geroid Robinson. Mumford later married Sophia Wittenberg, the "extremely competent and attractive stenographer" for the staff, and she continued to work for *The Dial* for several years after Scofield Thayer became Editor. Lewis Mumford remained a contributor to the monthly *Dial*, though he contributed seldom and irregularly and was not a member of the inner staff gathered by Thayer and Watson.

The third Associate of the last weeks of the fortnightly *Dial*, Geroid Robinson, was another arrival at about the same time as Mumford. Martyn Johnson, "with the aplomb of the captain of a sinking ship, who thinks that one or two more victims will make no difference, engaged" Robinson as well as Mumford. Robinson's first appearance was with the leading article in the issue for July 12, "Trade Unionism and the Control of Industry." He predicted that labor unions would soon gain control of entire industries and that accordingly there would be greater local autonomy in such unions, a movement that was already shaking the foundations of the craft system; but "in every instance, if control is to be more than an irresponsible dictatorship, the organization exercising the directive power must be coterminous with the field of operation it controls, capable of assuming the duties as well as the rights of industrial democracy." The column of notes on new "Contributors" for the issue introduced Robinson as "a Western newspaper man" who had been "engaged in an industrial survey on the Pacific Coast during the early months of the war. After a half-year's service as a Personnel Officer in France, he has recently joined the staff of THE DIAL." Robinson's stay at *The Dial* was brief. He contributed two other articles, "Collective Bargaining in Politics" and "Military Paternalism and Industrial Unrest," to the issues for July 26 and August 23 respectively. With the issue of September 20, these had been collected and were advertised in the magazine as "An Important New Dial Reprint," under the title *Collective Bargaining — or Control,* a pamphlet of twenty-four pages selling for a dime per single copy, with special rates for copies bought in quantities up to 1,000. By that time Robinson had left the sinking ship of Johnson's *Dial* for the firm ground of Columbia University.

When Mumford and Robinson were announced as Associates, Oswald W. Knauth was also announced as a staff member. For one issue he was Secretary-Treasurer; the next issue, for September 20, listed him in the editorial box as an editor, and an editor he stayed until the end. At the same time, Knauth became a stockholder in the Dial Publishing Company and remained one with the change in majority ownership of Dial stock. He also contributed an article to Johnson's *Dial,* "Can Real Wages be Raised," published in the issue for September 6.

That Lovett may have suffered a lapse of memory about just who did help him edit *The Dial* is understandable. Nobody could possibly remember with complete accuracy the complicated and seemingly haphazard changes in staff during the fifteen months from September 1918 through November 1919. The fact that in these months twelve issues out of thirty-one announce changes, important or minor, in the lists of editors, publisher's staff, and Dial Publishing Company stockholders, suffices to exemplify the instability of *The Dial* before Martyn Johnson relinquished his control to Scofield Thayer and James Sibley Watson, Jr.[2]

The unique feature of the staff was its triumvirate of editors "In Charge of the Reconstruction Program." Johnson appointed them — Helen Marot, Thorstein Veblen, and John Dewey — to *The Dial* when it moved to New York, and they were published on the masthead of the issue for October 5, 1918. There they stayed through the issue for June 28, 1919; the next issue reorganized the staff, but Dewey, Veblen, and Miss Marot remained on it, though the Reconstruction Program vanished. A paragraph in the "Casual Comment" for September 6 announced with "regret" the resignation of John Dewey from the editorial board of *The Dial*; Miss Marot and Thorstein Veblen remained as editors until the new owners took over *The Dial*. Beyond the writing they contributed to *The Dial,* the three editors in charge of its Reconstruction Program gave the magazine its tone, an avowedly liberal tone. Generally their contributions followed and commented upon the Peace Conference held at Versailles, the Russian Revolution, the international labor movement, the progress of the liberal movement throughout the world, and the economic situation of postwar Europe, Asia, and the United States.

The least of the three "Reconstruction" editors, Miss Helen Marot, was nevertheless a formidable expert on laboring conditions, especially the conditions of American working women and children. Her first contribution to *The Dial* was "The Creative and Efficiency Concepts of Education," published in the issue for April 11, 1918, and later used as a portion of her best-known work, *Creative Impulse in Industry: A Proposition for Educators*, published later that year. "Notes and News" for the issue said that "Helen Marot, who discusses industrial education in this issue, was a member of the Committee on Industrial Relations and was for seven years Secretary of the New York Woman's Trade Union League. She is the author of a book entitled 'American Labor Unions' and of several magazine articles dealing with industry and education." Born in Philadelphia in 1875, Miss Marot began her career as a librarian in the Wilmington, Delaware, public library. By 1899 she had compiled *A Handbook of Labor Literature* for the Philadelphia Free Library of Economics and Political Science, and from then on she was active as an investigator, committee member, and writer in the American labor movement. Shortly before she became a contributor and staff member at *The Dial*, she was a member of the editorial board, in 1916, of *The Masses*. Her *Creative Impulse in Industry* was, according to her obituary in the *New York Times* of June 4, 1940, a textbook widely used in sociology and economics courses in colleges. Her point of view is suggested not so much by her association with *The Masses* as by her words — taken from "Why Reform Is Futile," in *The Dial* for March 22, 1919 — that the movement for labor reform in the United States had failed and that any progress would be made, "not through any instinct or passion of a people for the abstraction of justice or democracy, but through the failure of the established institution to function." The present American industrial infirmity was "due to the failure of the institutional order to secure the co-operation of labor in the enterprise of wealth production." What organized labor should do would be to enter into agreements with employers to deliver "the greater output which results from its own saving in workshop energy" and to stipulate "that on delivery its own saving of its own energy shall not be appropriated by others." It was an interesting combination of Fabianism, Marxism, and Deweyan pragmatism that Miss Marot had evolved, and she acknowledged, in her introduction to *Creative Impulse in Industry,* her debt to John Dewey for the notion that "the educative process is the process of growth," and also to her other colleague in charge of the Reconstruction Program, Thorstein Veblen, who in his *Imperial Germany and the Industrial Revolution* explained that "the psychology of the German people was still feudal when the modern system of industry . . . was imposed, ready-made, upon them."³

John Dewey returned the compliment in a house advertisement of *The Dial* appearing in the issues for March 8 and 22, 1919. *The Dial* announced that it had become nonreturnable at the newsstands and that for new subscribers only it was making a special offer good only until the first of April: with each full year's subscription, at three dollars, the editors would send free a copy of Helen Marot's *Creative Impulse in Industry*. Franklin Giddings, Charles F. Taylor, and John Dewey were quoted in praise of the book, with Dewey asserting that "The reader will find in Miss Marot's book the most sincere and courageous attempt yet made to face the problem of an education adapted to modern society which must be industrial and which would like to be democratic."

Besides "Why Reform Is Futile," Miss Marot contributed only an occasional signed article to *The Dial* in 1919. "Labor at the Crossways" appeared in the issue for February 22; "Labor Control of Government," in that of April 19; and "Responsible Unionism," in that of August 23. While she was not so active a writer as her two cohorts, Veblen and Dewey, she did give direction and did help to establish a certain tone through her writing for Martyn Johnson.

In still other ways, Helen Marot was of essential service to Johnson. It was she who brought Thorstein Veblen to *The Dial* as an editor. In *Thorstein Veblen and His America*, Joseph Dorfman says that "Helen Marot, who owned some stock in *The Dial*, became interested in Veblen's views and persuaded him to prepare some articles for that magazine."⁴ More specifically, Dorfman says that "Helen Marot thought that *The Dial* should begin emphasising the importance of organising economic activity in times of peace with the unified machinery that the war had brought into action." Horace M. Kallen of the University of Wisconsin, and another prominent contributor to *The Dial* — of the Brownes, of Martyn Johnson, and of Thayer and Watson — "suggested that Veblen's services be obtained. Miss Marot found that Dewey and Veblen were ready to lend their support to a reconstruction policy based on the realities of productive capacity. A board was to be formed and Veblen was to settle in New York." Whether these are the facts as Miss Marot saw them or as Martyn Johnson may have seen them must remain a moot question, but at any rate Dorfman's account is the only circumstantial relation of the establishment of the triumvirate in charge of the Reconstruction Program, and it does not conflict with the role that Scofield Thayer played in bringing *The Dial* to New York. The only ascertainable inaccuracy has to do with Helen Marot's ownership of any Dial Publishing Company stock. According to the record she never owned any stock in *The Dial*, but in the issue of October 18, 1919, the "Statement of the Ownership, Management, Circulation, Etc ," regularly published in each volume of the magazine, does reveal that in the latter six months of 1919 the "known bondholders, mortgagees, and other security holders owning or holding 1 per cent or more of total bonds, mortgages, or other securities" of the Dial Publishing Company were Scofield Thayer, Martyn Johnson, Edward F. Sanderson (of the People's Institute on Fifth Avenue; he otherwise does not enter this history), Willard C. Kitchel, and Helen Marot. In sum, Miss Marot, like Scofield Thayer, lent Johnson money in order to keep *The Dial* going, and she therefore was able to influence Johnson's policy. (One nevertheless wonders about the People's Institute: could it also have been instrumental in financing Veblen while he was at *The Dial?*

Besides her support of Veblen and her loan to Johnson, Miss Marot used *The Dial* for her, and its, good causes. In the number for March 22, 1919, the editors ran an editorial about the conscientious objectors who had been imprisoned at the Leavenworth penitentiary. They were the special cases, different from the majority of objectors who were willing to serve in some noncombatant capacity. The "absolutists," in the editorial terminology, refused to serve in any capacity and so received a federal sentence of one to twenty years. *The Dial* reported that the absolutists "whose consciences revolted at every direct or indirect form of conscription for war are left, presumably, to serve out their sentences. In other words, the War Department offers the temptation to these men to deny their consciences and impeach their own sincerity." Of the 101 men thus imprisoned, all but thirty-seven finally made their separate peace with the federal government, denied their consciences, and went free. Then, in April 1919, the thirty-seven who refused to bow to such temptation were granted the right of appeal from their sentences. Perhaps Helen Marot was author of the editorial in *The Dial* of March 22, because a closely related item appeared in the "Contributors" column for April 19 stating that arrangements had been made at the *Dial* office "for Helen Marot to receive real-estate or other bonds to be used as bail for the thirty-seven men at Leavenworth who have just been granted the right of appeal from their sentence. . . . Some of these men are seriously ill and most of them have families. The granting of the appeal implies a reasonable doubt and is the first sign that the prejudice against these men is giving way. Everyone who can help in giving them liberty with [*sic*] help break through that prejudice." In sum, Miss Marot's financial support of Martyn Johnson was essential, and it surely did not undercut her influence — as is clear from the support the magazine gave her espousal of the cause of the thirty-seven conscientious objectors in a year dangerous for such causes and their backers. Of the three "Reconstruction" editors, Helen Marot was the only one who, on the evidence, supported *The Dial* by deed as well as by word.

On April 25, 1918, *The Dial* published an article by Thorstein Veblen that occasioned editorial comment. "Notes and News" for the issue said that "Thorstein Veblen, author of the famous 'Nature of Peace,' has previously contributed to THE DIAL, and needs little introduction to our readers. [He had contributed a review of Eduard Meyer's *England* to the issue of April 19, 1917.] 'The Passing of National Frontiers,' which is the leading article for the current issue, is the first of a series of papers on internationalism that Professor Veblen will contribute from time to time. For the present, Professor Veblen has given up academic duties for work connected with the United States Food Administration." The wording of the item suggests that Martyn Johnson and Helen Marot may have approached Veblen with some plan for joining the *Dial* staff early in the spring of 1918. By May *The Dial* was confident enough to quote both Veblen and Dewey in a house advertisement. The issue for May 23 used for that purpose Veblen's statement that "There is insistent need of such a publication as THE DIAL, to speak without fear or favor or respect of persons, and with a clear vision of the shifting forces that are now beginning to make the New Order, — to speak sanely and soberly and without undue bias of outworn preconceptions." And Dewey was quoted as saying that "THE DIAL is a journal to be reckoned with by those who think, especially because of its combination of honest informed book reviews with humane and progressive social policies — and, not least, good writing, hard hitting, tolerant, straightforward writing proceeding from an imaginative vision." Johnson's confidence was soon justified.

On June 6, *The Dial* announced that on July 1 its publication offices would be moved to New York and that on October 3, 1918, it would begin weekly publication, a step never actually taken. In this lengthy "Announcement" Martyn Johnson made the statement that in New York the editors would be John Dewey, Thorstein Veblen, Helen Marot, and — as Editor-in-Chief — George Donlin. "Thorstein Veblen, who will contribute articles dealing with economic and industrial reconstruction, is perhaps best known through his volume 'An Inquiry Into the Nature of Peace.' Mr. Veblen combines with an accurate knowledge of facts a ruthless power of analysis and a brilliant irony which makes his style an intellectual adventure." Joseph Dorfman says that the magazine "was referred to as the 'Veblenian *Dial*.' "⁵ Despite the lavish praise of Johnson's announcement, however, that particular epithet does not occur in it; perhaps Veblen's pupils used it among themselves.

With its issue of October 5, 1918, *The Dial* began to implement its "Reconstruction" policy. The leading article, by Harold Stearns, was "Why Reconstruction?" Reconstruction, Stearns explained, was not something to follow after the war; it was part of the war itself. Americans were beginning to realize that mere geographical readjustments — was this a reference to the map of the world hung on the wall of the *Dial* office, and re-arranged daily by such staff members as Stearns and, in 1919, Geroid Robinson, with Veblen looking on as an interested party? — are not fundamental. They must create a new world indus-trially, financially, economically, just as certainly as a new world politically. But the liberals must not, Stearns continued, allow the planning for the future to be done entirely by the interested classes, nor would they. And he concluded by calling on the idealism and the protest against exploitation to struggle against the franker and bolder imperialists. Future generations might be grateful that the present generation had so generously given of its lives, but the future would profit from it only if "today we give as generously of our intelligence." The masthead of the editorial page carried, besides the names of the working staff, the names of the triumvirate "In Charge of the Reconstruction Program"; and for the next fourteen turbulent months of its declining fortunes, *The Dial* was the tool of John Dewey and Thorstein Veblen. Two less likely confreres it would be hard to discover outside the environment of a large university.

In the fall of 1918 Veblen and his family arrived in New York from Washington, where he had refused a $4,800 job with the War Labor Board. Not long ago after Veblen's arrival in New York, his wife began having delusions that he was being persecuted. She suffered a nervous breakdown and had to be removed to a sanitarium. The two step-daughters, Becky and Anne, were sent to stay with the Walter Stewarts in Amherst, where Veblen had taught that spring. Veblen thus was alone, and he may well have realized that there was no hope of his wife's recovery; she died in 1920. He shared an apartment with his friend, Leon Ardzrooni, who was teaching at Columbia Univer-sity and who became, in Joseph Dorfman's phrase, the *fidus Achates* to the master's Aeneas. During the "spiritual debacle of 1919," said Lewis Mumford in a memorial essay, "Thorstein Veblen," printed in *The New Republic* of August 5, 1931, Veblen also suffered a severe attack of influenza, and this completed his enfeeblement; for he had long been an invalid, and he was then past sixty. These unsettling and debilitating circumstances and the spectacle of an equally tragic international disorder go far to account for the increasingly polemic and at times even despairing tone and language of Veblen's writing for *The Dial*. Robert Morss Lovett recalled the arrival of Thorstein Veblen as adding to the already acute problem of the lack of space in *The Dial* to accommodate all the writing that Martyn Johnson had commissioned: "The problem of space continued to haunt me, especially after Veblen arrived from California to take up four or five pages in each issue." The statement itself raises another problem as Lovett was not yet Editor in the autumn of 1918 and was still in Chicago — nor, of course, did the Veblens arrive in New York from California.[6]

Leon Ardzrooni settled the arrangements with *The Dial* for Veblen's services, and it was agreed that he would receive $2500 for one year and would write when and how much he chose. Although he was present at the meeting, Veblen did not say a word, but after it was ended, he turned to Ardzrooni and remarked that he did not think he was "really worth twenty-five cents." As a result of that agreement, the first of Veblen's difficulties with *The Dial* arose. Dorfman ironically remarks that the "interest of *The Dial* editors in advanced social philosophy did not diminish their belief in the ordinary canons of literary style and journalism." They asked Veblen to limit his articles to 1,000 words, but Veblen told them that it took him that much space to get started. His characteristic literary style — with its leisurely gait and understated ironies — exasperated the editors. According to Helen Marot, Veblen "gave meticulous care to every article he wrote" and charged her "with the pleasant task of seeing that no punctuation mark was ever omitted after it had left his hands." She always enjoyed the tussles that ensued in the office with the literary editors, who considered these articles of Veblen impossible journalism. Lovett tried to edit the articles until the proof came back with cuts restored and a note of admonition to let them run. "As Veblen's contributions were paid for outside the office by admirers," Lovett recalled, "he was independent of editorial authority." Helen Marot said that only once did the editors of *The Dial* ever have the opportunity to delete and change the text. "It was a first and last time. Veblen would not stand for it."

Dorfman thought that the incident referred to by Miss Marot was the one described by Lewis Mumford in his essay, "Thorstein Veblen." In the essay, "Peace," printed in *The Dial* for May 17, 1919, Veblen had written that in the peace covenant arrived at by the Allies, the vested interests wielded power through — as he ironically put it — a Soviet of the Elder Statesmen; there were no Soldiers' and Workmen's Deputies to represent the mass of the people involved, those who had done the necessary fighting at the front and the necessary work at home. The conference was a conclave made up of the spokesmen of commercialized nationalism, in effect a conclave of the political lieutenants of the vested interests. By and large, neither the wishes nor the welfare of the soldiers, the workmen, or the industrial system as a going concern was visibly consulted in the drafting of a covenant. Although the American workmen might be alleged "to have been represented at this court of elder statesmen, informally, unofficially, and irresponsibly, by the sexton beetle of the A. F. of L.," that qualification made no serious inroad on the broader statement. Such thinly veiled savagery is the reason that Joseph Dorfman has said that on the face of it, "Peace" is perhaps Veblen's most seriously written article.

Unfortunately one of the editors at *The Dial* did not take the writing as seriously as did the author and in preparing the manuscript for the printer, changed "sexton beetle" to read "sexton beadle," in order to make sense. When Veblen saw the article in print, wrote Lewis Mumford, he "was furious: his white ashen face was more ashen than ever with anger — such anger as seemed especially terrible in the mild and reticent person that Veblen always was. He wanted to know if the unknown dunderhead who had mutilated his copy did not realize that a sexton beetle was an insect that spent its life in storing up and covering over dead things? Besides, there was an overtone in the allu-

sion: [Samuel] Gompers looked more like a beetle." Mumford
added that Veblen was right: "I never saw Gompers after that
without recalling the insect."

Thorstein Velben nevertheless continued to write for *The
Dial,* though his association was profitable neither to the magazine nor to his reputation — at any rate, so thought one of his
former students, highly placed in the government, who wrote
the master that his *Dial* articles were giving people the misleading
idea that he was a radical. His old students and sympathizers
generally held that Veblen was not at his best in the compass
of a magazine piece and that the agitator and phrase maker was
taking precedence over the thinker. As so often happened in
his checkered career, Veblen's marvelous irony and invective were
incompletely understood. It may be, also, that Veblen's former
students were discomfited by his writing for *The Dial* because
they did catch the drift of his intention and disapproved of it.
In "Thorstein Veblen," Lewis Mumford suggested that Veblen
discarded his customary irony and declared himself plainly in
favor of a revolution in 1919: "During the Reconstruction Period,
when revolution was sweeping rapidly over Europe and seemed
ready to descend on America, Veblen occasionally forgot the
Olympian ironist and showed where his hopes and sympathies
lay. For a time, he looked toward an immediate revolution which
would wipe out the kept classes, as he called them so punctili-
ously: he was in favor of turning the productive machinery over
into the hands of disinterested technicians, who would serve the
common weal."

One critic who might be expected to have shown just that
understanding and empathy called for in 1919 was H. L. Mencken. He was at the height of his early success astounding,
shocking, or amusing a much wider public than the one that read
Veblen's writing in *The Dial.* Mencken's magazine, the *Smart
Set,* had George Jean Nathan as coeditor, and together Mencken
and Nathan were in the struggle on the side of *The Dial* in its
campaign of liberation of American taste from outgrown prejudice, although *The Dial* was liberal and Mencken was a kind
of idiosyncratic Nietzschean anarchist-reactionary. Still, as out-

siders by choice, Mencken and Veblen had in common a profound mistrust of the Elder Statesmen who were arranging the postwar world. But Mencken disliked what he termed the learned gentleman's long, tortuous, and intolerably flapdoodlish phrases, and said so in a long critique, "Prof. Veblen and the Cow," published in the *Smart Set* of May 1919. Despite Veblen's popularity, "on the majestic level of the old *Nation,* among the white and lavender peaks of professorial ratiocination," beginning in 1917 — it seemed Veblen "was all over the *Nation,* the *Dial,* the *New Republic,* and the rest of them, and his books and pamphlets began to pour from the presses, and the newspapers reported his every wink and whisper, and everybody who was anybody began gabbing about him" — Mencken thought Veblen's works singularly laborious and muggy, incomparably tangled and unintelligible. Mencken, never at a loss when it came to slanging, called this Prof. Dr. Thorstein Veblen "head Great Thinker to the parlor radicals, Socrates of the intellectual Greenwich Village, chief star (at least transiently) of the American *Athenaeums.*" His ideas were often almost idiotic, simply Socialism and water; his prose was without grace or distinction. One special point of ridicule was Veblen's theory of conspicuous consumption. Mencken adverted to the passage in *The Theory of the Leisure Class* in which Veblen explained that cows were not used to keep the lawns clipped around our country houses and that cheap foreign labor was imported instead to work at such gardening for the leisure class because "to the average popular apprehension a herd of cattle so pointedly suggests thrift and usefulness that their presence . . . would be intolerably cheap." Plow as he might through a bad book, from end to end, Mencken could find nothing sillier than that example of conspicuous waste. "Has the genial professor," he asked rhetorically, "pondering his great problems, ever taken a walk in the country? And has he, in the course of that walk, ever crossed a pasture inhabited by a cow *(Bos taurus)?* And has he, making that crossing, ever passed astern of the cow herself? And has he, thus passing astern, ever stepped carelessly, and —"; but Mencken could not bring himself to conclude that particular period. In

1949, Mencken wrote that he had heard from some of Veblen's friends that the onslaught greatly upset Veblen, and, in fact, made him despair of the Republic. But Dorfman reported merely that after the essay appeared in the *Smart Set,* Veblen remarked to Isador Lubin — successor to Leon Ardzrooni as *fidus Achates* — "Now I am an agricultural economist." The piece made, asserted Mencken, a considerable pother.[7]

Veblen's supporters at *The Dial* indeed had to recognize the concrete and immediate difficulty caused by Veblen's writing for the magazine. Helen Marot said that the difficulty had been, in fact, predicted by the office staff at *The Dial.* The "public would not stand for Veblen to the extent of supporting a magazine weighted with such portentous material. The point of difference was clear — should *The Dial* continue or should Veblen be published while we had the chance. The continuation of *The Dial* was to me unimportant in comparison to the publication of his articles, charged as they were for those few who read them with creative and revolutionary import." That is to say, the group backing Veblen was quite willing to kill off *The Dial* by using it as his organ. What is surprising is that *The Dial,* under such circumstances, lasted long enough to be rescued again by Scofield Thayer, aided this time by Sibley Watson. Still, Veblen did have his supporters outside *The Dial* and his own circle of friends and disciples. In the "Communications" column of November 2, 1918, appeared a letter by Maxwell Anderson, then still teaching English in college, about the influence wielded by a writer on others. "I once asked a friend if he had read The Theory of the Leisure Class. 'Why, no,' he retorted; 'why should I? All my friends have read it. It permeates the atmosphere in which I live.' Perhaps professors are, in a vague way, makers of atmosphere. . . . Who knows by what devious and shadowy trails civilization and culture are advanced?" That enthusiasm could have been only cold comfort to the staff of a magazine struggling against public opinion and financial odds to survive.

Writing for *The Dial* changed Veblen as a craftsman just as his contributions changed *The Dial* itself. He was by far the most prolific of the "Reconstruction" editors, contributing not only a number of unsigned editorials (not all of them as yet fully identified) but also sixteen signed essays in the period from October 19, 1918, to November 1, 1919. The majority of Veblen's *Dial* pieces were components of two series later published as books, and he thus accomodated his discursive talent to a periodical by the device of serialization. On the other hand, his editorial writing and his single essays indicate a real modification of technique and presentation, and he mastered the art of composing a brief, trenchant, and topical editorial.

Veblen began his editorship on *The Dial* with the series entitled "The Modern Point of View and the New Order." The "Contributors" column for the issue noted that "Thorstein Veblen's article in this number is the first of a series of discussions of the psychology of reconstruction which will appear in successive issues under the general title The Modern Point of View and the New Order. This series resumes the argument of a group of lectures which Mr. Veblen delivered before students in Amherst College in May 1918." Like many scholars, Veblen used and reused his materials, and he expanded and rewrote his college lectures as a series serialized in eight parts in *The Dial* in consecutive numbers from October 19, 1918, through January 25, 1919. The topic of the series was an inquiry into "the nature and uses of the vested interests," and as with so much of his work, it was concerned with the uses of modern capital by the businessmen who control large corporations. The chapters of the series as they appeared in *The Dial* were entitled "The Instability of Knowledge and Belief," "The Stability of Law and Custom," "The State of the Industrial Arts," "Free Income," "The Vested Interests," "The Divine Right of Nations," "Live and Let Live," and "The Vested Interests and the Common Man." In 1919, he used his materials a third time and published the *Dial* series as *The Vested Interests and the State of the Industrial Arts*. Some of the chapters of the book were elaborated by the introduction of new material, but the book was substantially what had been published in *The Dial*. Dorfman criticized *The Vested Interests* as somewhat careless in its use of language and thought the weakness betrayed a new tone in keeping with a literary journal rather than with a professional periodical; it indicated, he said, that Veblen was attempting to break away from the involved apparatus which had become the master of his style and thought instead of his creature.

Before "The Modern Point of View and the New Order" had completed three parts of its eight, the Armistice was signed and the protracted negotiations for peace, coupled with those establishing a league of nations, were begun. Heretofore *The Dial,* whatever its reservations, had supported the policy of President Wilson. Martyn Johnson and John Dewey had undoubtedly been more forceful in establishing that major aspect of *Dial* policy than had Veblen. Now, with the swift disillusion of liberal opinion with the negotiations toward the peace covenant, Veblen's influence became much stronger than that of Dewey; one reason he was heeded was that Dewey was away in the Orient and consequently had no voice in the editorial meetings. Veblen, moreover, spoke with the authority of a man who had been consulted by the administration. At the end of 1917 and the beginning of 1918, before President Wilson gave his famous "fourteen points" speech of January 8, 1918, setting forth an outline of the terms of a desirable peace, his aide Colonel House had been charged to prepare a memorandum to guide the President in his peace maneuvers. House had set up a committee headed by President Sidney Mezes of the College of the City of New York and with Walter Lippmann as secretary. Veblen had prepared some memoranda touching the working program of the committee of inquiry; but the events of early 1919 showed him that his suggestions had been ignored. There was still left his freedom to criticize.

The new events of the peace conference and the hardening attitude of Lloyd George and Clemenceau, as well as the civil war in Russia, furnished new terms of contrast for Veblen. In Dorfman's view, Veblen changed his mind about Bolshevism, and began now to use that, as he had machine technology, as a term of contrast to the prevailing control by corporate magnates and corporate capital. Veblen's writing for *The Dial* in most of the signed pieces did not change materially from his familiar academic style, lit by paradox and acerbity; however, the un-signed editorials and all his signed *Dial* essays of 1919 are openly polemic — even violent and angry on occasion. Veblen's increas-ing bitterness about what he regarded as Wilson's "panic-stricken policy" and betrayal of the best interests of the American "common man" to the advantage of the "vested interests" of cor-porate capital — this emotion is tellingly conveyed by the compa-ratively unadorned style and vivid images of the editorials and such an essay as "Peace."

Even before the republication of his series on the new order as *The Vested Interests,* Veblen restated his theme in an article in *The Dial* for February 22, 1919, "Bolshevism Is a Menace — to Whom?" Bolshevism by this time had become used in Veblen's thinking as a special epithet, jargon as it were. In the Veblenian usage, it was another name for the industrial republic; it aimed to carry democracy and majority rule into the domain of indus-try and was therefore a menace to property and business, to the "vested interests" in contrast to the "common man." Along with the peace settlement and the new League of Nations, Amer-icans generally were interested in Bolshevism in 1919, and it is not surprising that Veblen should have attended to such matters on the staff of a journal passionately occupied with them. Dorf-man wrote that Veblen anxiously read the newspaper accounts of the Bolshevik revolution and even began learning Russian. During the summer he followed with interest the military move-ments against the rightist leaders Denikin and Kolchak; Geroid Robinson recorded the Russian civil war daily, with pins, on a map in the *Dial* office. Veblen frequently attended editorial con-ferences, and he was interested in the *Dial* "workers' soviet" formed that summer, apparently an attempt by the staff to bring about "Bolshevism," i. e., industrial democracy, in the workings of the magazine. But he never participated in the discussions, except to ask an occasional question.

One of Veblen's disciples, Robert L. Duffus, was given the assignment of reviewing *The Vested Interests.* Duffus — in his memoir of the Veblenian circle, *The Innocents at Cedro* — recalled that *The Dial* had been brought to New York from

Chicago, had indeed "been polished up . . . to serve as a vehicle for some of the Veblenian ideas." He came to New York in March 1919 and was asked to join the staff and did so on a part-time basis and for "some months . . . contributed editorials and reviews and saw a little of Veblen."⁸ His signed pieces besides the review of *The Vested Interests* are two — in the issue for August 9, a review of Glenn Frank's *The Politics of Industry* entitled "A Handy Guide for Business Men," and in the issue for September 20, a satirical sketch, "When Good Fellows Get Together," about the postwar reunion of some college classmates now become middleaged. The "Contributors" column noted that "Robert L. Duffus, who has had some years' experience as a newspaper editorial writer, now holds this position on the staff of the New York Globe. He has contributed to various liberal journals a number of articles on political and economic subjects."

In his memoir, Duffus recalled the distinguished personalities that floated around the *Dial* office; "hopes of success rose high." Those hopes — "which Veblen may or may not have shared" — seemed to have a certain pathos to Duffus in 1944. "Veblen and his associates believed that the first World War had set in motion economic and social forces which could not be arrested. It had demonstrated the enormous productivity of modern industry. Had not this country, for instance, carried on a prodigiously costly military venture abroad and at the same time raised rather than lowered its civilian standard of living? Indeed, it had. Did not this prove the old moral of the mud-hole parable — that productivity was in normal times artificially restricted? Had not the time come for that sort of nonsense to stop? And wouldn't people in general understand all this and do something?" It is difficult to believe that Veblen shared the hopes of the *Dial* group in 1919, but it is clear that he did share their indignation at what they conceived as the betrayal of the American cause.

Duffus' review, in *The Dial* of July 26, shed light on the effect that the protest of *The Dial* and its staff and contributors was having, when he only half-jokingly prophesied that "If Mr. Veblen escapes the clutches of the several leagues and committees which are now engaged in eliminating Bolshevism from the United States he will be accused of the slightly less heinous crime of preaching a variety of Socialism." Duffus went on to explain that, in fact, Veblen was "as far from the dogmatism of Lenin or Marx" as he was from that of Adam Smith or J. S. Mill: "He is an observer, not a Utopian." But ordinary people could not be expected to draw cool rationalizations in the heat of the public scare over Bolshevism, and *The Dial* continued to be suspect and to lose readers. In his review, Duffus also explained why it was that Veblen's writing had not won him popular acclaim: "In a less dangerous field of inquiry work comparable with that of Thorstein Veblen would win recognition as the beginning of an important new school. It is only because most of us are too deeply a part of our own institutions to be able to consider them scientifically that the exquisite irony of The Theory of the Leisure Class, the penetrating analysis of The Theory of Business Enterprise, and the dazzling conceptions which underlie the somewhat formidable Instinct of Workmanship have not won Mr. Veblen a formal place in the front rank of contemporary thinkers and prophets. The so-called difficulty of Veblen's style has nothing to do with the scant recognition that the Brahmins have accorded him. He is as easy to read as any man with as much to say." But that particular apology was made by one of the converted!

Perhaps the most notorious article Veblen wrote for *The Dial* was "On the Nature and Uses of Sabotage," for its issue of April 5. The title of the article is sensational enough, but even more sensational were Veblen's charges that the federal government itself was engaged in sabotage, in the sense of "going slow . . . any maneuver of slowing-down, inefficiency, bungling, obstruction." His pungent example was the current attempt by the Wilson administration to interfere with subversive activities — ranging from Bolshevist arson to the serialization of *Ulysses* in Margaret Anderson's *Little Review* — by disallowing, to "speak after the analogy of private business," "such use of the mail facilities as does not inure to the benefit of the administration in the way of good will and vested rights of usufruct." Veblen con-

cluded the essay by proving himself an able political prognosti-
cator, when he said that such "peremptory measures of disallow-
ance" would doubtless be of a salutary nature, because "an
unguarded dissemination of information and opinions or an
unduly frank canvassing of the relevant facts by these outsiders,
will be a handicap on the Administration's work, and may even
defeat the Administration's aims." The Democrats were defeated
in 1920; and in the long run the "censorship, somewhat rigorous," and the "selective refusal of mail facilities" have proved
unviable for the nation. So popular was "On the Nature and
Uses of Sabotage" that the Dial Publishing Company reprinted it,
along with *A Voice out of Russia,* a forty-eight page pamphlet
compiled from the writing for *The Dial* of several contributors.
In the issue of May 17, a house advertisement announced both
pamphlets, and of *Sabotage* it said that "We have had so many
requests for Mr. Veblen's article on the Nature and Uses of
Sabotage that we have made a twelve-page reprint of it to facili-
tate its wider distribution." It was one of several such pamphlets
that Martyn Johnson issued in the latter days of his regime, all
reprints of contributions to his *Dial.*

It was also at about this time, according to Joseph Dorfman,
that Veblen began writing his unsigned editorials for *The Dial.*
While Dorfman was uncertain about the authorship of several
items that he analyzed in *Thorstein Veblen and His America,*
he attributed certainly to Veblen a total of nine anonymously
published *Dial* editorials and said that Veblen "is supposed to
have suggested" changing the title of the editorial section to
"The Old Order and the New." That title all the issues of the
sixty-seventh volume (July 12 through November 20, 1919)
bore (in the list of contents on the cover, if not always in the
text of the magazine), save the final issue, edited by Scofield
Thayer. The nine editorials all evince Veblen's preoccupations
of 1919, Wilson's betrayal of the peace for the "vested interests,"
the peculiar Veblenian notion of Bolshevism, and the opposing
interests of the "common man" and the "Elder Statesmen" who
settled the terms of the peace covenant. Seven of these brief pieces
have never been collected (though Dorfman has analyzed them

in scholarly detail) : "Bolshevism Is a Menace to the Vested Interests," the lead editorial for the issue of April 5, 1919; also "Sabotage" and "Congressional Sabotage" in the same number; "Immanuel Kant and Perpetual Peace," May 3; *"Panem et Circenses,"* June 14; "The Red Terror — At Last It Has Come to America," September 6; and "The Twilight Peace of the Armistice," a view of the "the comfortless state of things" twelve months after the end of the war, in *The Dial* for November 15. Two of Veblen's unsigned editorials were posthumously collected in his *Essays in Our Changing Order* (1934): "Open Covenants Openly Arrived at" and "A World Safe for the Vested Interests," both published in *The Dial* for July 12, 1919. All these editorials express Veblen's deepening pessimism about the durability of the peace settlement at Versailles and about the fairness of the treaties to the common people on both sides of the recent conflict. Their only hope lay in Veblen's vision of a future based on an order created by the industrialized working people working with the "engineers" — an order that is frankly apolitical and that would seem to have much in common with anarchist syndicalism.

After the essay on "Peace" in *The Dial* for May 17, there appeared two articles that seem to be single, independent pieces but that were components of Veblen's book of 1921, *The Engineers and the Price System*: "Industry and the Captains of Industry" in the issue of May 31, and "The Captains of Finance and the Engineers" in the issue of June 14. Veblen's writing for *The Dial* was rounded off with a second series of essays, these also incorporated in *The Engineers and the Price System*. They were written at the peak of hysteria, in America, over the Reds, and Joseph Dorfman termed them "conspicuous for their recklessness and their savage use of inverted meaning." The general title of the series as it appeared in *The Dial*, "Bolshevism and the Vested Interests in America," bore the unique imprint of Veblen's special language, a kind of Red-baiting in reverse. Its parts were entitled "On the Danger of a Revolutionary Overturn," published in the issue of October 4, 1919; "On the Circumstances Which Make for a Change," October 18; and "A

Memorandum on a Practical Soviet of Technicians," November 1.
By that date Veblen and his associates had succeeded in
rendering *The Dial* useless to anyone unable to rescue it through
complete refinancing and a completely reoriented editorial policy.
Having helped to sabotage *The Dial* by the autumn of 1919,
Veblen fortunately found a timely refuge, in the New School for
Social Research then just coming into being. A full-page advertisement in *The Dial* of September 20 stated that the New
School for Social Research "will open October first for the study
of current economic and governmental problems" and that "the
work will be conducted by a group of well-known writers and
teachers." Among the group were such *Dial* contributors as
James Harvey Robinson, Harold Laski, and Horace M. Kallen,
besides Veblen. So Veblen was rescued; and in another month
there occurred a comparable rescue operation for *The Dial*.

The third member of the "Reconstruction" triumvirate
must have found *The Dial* a more harmonious journal, with Randolph Bourne out of the way. Like Veblen, John Dewey proceeded to consolidate his position on being appointed an editor,
and he did so in the same fashion in November 1918, with a
series of four articles: "The Approach to a League of Nations,"
in the issue of November 2; "The League of Nations and the
New Diplomacy," November 17; "The Fourteen Points and the
League of Nations," November 30; and, the final part of the
series, "A League of Nations and Economic Freedom" in *The
Dial* of December 14.

By that date he had already left New York for California,
where he was teaching at the University, in Berkeley, before
going on to Japan. In Japan, he gave a series of lectures at the
University of Tokyo and met and encouraged the Japanese liberals, already heartened as they were by the Allied victory.[9] Still
represented on the masthead of *The Dial*, Dewey contributed
two pieces from Japan early in 1919: in the issue of February
8, an obituary sketch of Theodore Roosevelt, whom Dewey had
once supported with mixed feelings and whose demise he noted in
a tribute equally mixed (by dying, Roosevelt was "forever saved
from any danger of becoming the figurehead and leader of re-

actionaries"); and, the first result for *The Dial* of the months in Japan, an article, "Japan and America," in *The Dial* for May 17. Despite his long absence in the Orient, or perhaps because he was too distant to protest, Dewey's name headed the list of the editorial staff, in the editorial box among the editorials, in the issues from July 12 through August 23; then the "Casual Comment" for September 6 announced with "regret . . . the resignation of John Dewey from the editorial board of THE DIAL; Mr. Dewey's plans for an extended absence in the Far East make it impossible for him to continue his editorial connection with the magazine." The chief fruit for *The Dial* of Dewey's lectures in Japan appeared after he had severed his official connection with the journal and had gone to China for two years, to lecture at the National University in Peking. Under the general title of "Liberalism in Japan," he contributed a series of three articles to the issues of October 4 and 18 and November 1, with the respective titles of "The Intellectual Preparation," "The Economic Factor," and "The Chief Foe." He thus remained a dominating influence into the final month of the publication of Martyn Johnson's *Dial*. Unlike Randolph Bourne, John Dewey wrote no book reviews for *The Dial*, as he was not reduced to the necessity of turning out hack work in order to earn his living. Nor was he reduced to recrimination; his single exchange with Bourne, in *The New Republic,* was sharp but merely defensive. The importance with which Dewey regarded his writing in *The Dial* may be gauged by the fact that he reprinted six of the nine pieces he wrote for it in his years of association. He did not republish the two contributions he made in 1917; but all the pieces he contributed in 1918 and 1919, with the exception of "Japan and America," eventually found their way into two later volumes, the essay on "Education and Social Direction" (published in *The Dial* for April 11, 1918) in *Education Today* (1940), the other seven in the two volumes of *Characters and Events* (1929) .

Aside from the specific policies influenced by the "Reconstruction" triumvirate of editors, what of the other interests of Martyn Johnson's *Dial* when Robert Morss Lovett edited it in

1919? Like Stearns, Lovett recalled the year as one of yeastlike fermentation. The makers of the new world — a kinder phrase for them than Stearns had — were as busy in New York as in Paris. The great name of "Reconstruction" covered a multitude of movements and enterprises to which *The Dial* was editorially committed. There were the Youth Movement, the Labor Movement, the World for Christ Movement, this last occupying a huge department store building on Sixth Avenue, where Lovett could see many of his young radical friends solemnly pounding typewriters. There was the Forum Movement, for which the popular Reverend Percy Stickney Grant's Sunday evening forum at the Episcopal Church of the Ascension furnished the model. Under Grant's persuasion, Martyn Johnson was ready to commit the future of *The Dial* by turning it into an organ of a national organization to establish clubs for the popular discussion of public questions. There was also Mrs. Willard Straight's Co-operative Movement, to which *The Dial* lent Harold Stearns.

The political interest of *The Dial* centered about the peace conference in Paris, where President Wilson was struggling — honestly struggling, in Lovett's recollection — to redeem his promises of the Fourteen Points, on which Germany had explicitly surrendered and which Great Britain and France were no less committed to as the basis of the armistice. *The Dial* welcomed Wilson's first triumph in gaining the acceptance of the Covenant of the League of Nations, but after his return to Paris it was difficult to keep a note of skepticism out of the leading articles.

The change in the attitude on the part of the *Dial* staff toward the general problem of peace and a league to prevent future wars began at least as early as the issue of November 30, 1918. Lovett demurred to a cautious editorial by Harold Stearns on "Reasons Why Wilson May Fail," but Martyn Johnson, less optimistic and probably influenced more directly and strongly by Thorstein Veblen, was for abandoning the leaking vessel of American hopes (which were the hopes of *The Dial* too) before it sank. Almost undoubtedly the article Lovett referred to in his memoir was the leading article for November 30, 1918, by "A European

Liberal," a person invented by the new Editor to supplant the signature of Harold Stearns, all too recognizably a member of the staff. Indeed a first cold premonitory chill of the dying, defeated idealism was wafted from the forthright forecast of the pseudonymous liberal that the "liberal policy" of a "League of Nations, broadly democratic in type, based upon the self-determination and democratic representation of peoples, and equality of economic rights and opportunity as between great states and small" would fail. "The American policy of a League of Nations will demand for its success profound faith in its practicality and need," but its execution would in the early stages "be in the hands mainly of the most conservative elements in Europe, who quite frankly have but the faintest faith in it." The article concluded by warning that only a political miracle could give success to American policy in such conditions: "Perhaps it may happen — political miracles have happened under President Wilson."

The leading editorial of December 14, 1918, moved in doubt well beyond the warning of the European liberal: "The high hopes which the world has entertained for a peace settlement that will make future wars impossible do not seem likely to be realized." And it foresaw the coming League of Nations as "a league of the strong nations against the weak." Issue after issue, *The Dial* pounded away at its contention that the great coalition of the victorious powers was promoting a vengeful, sordid peace of the strong, the kind of peace that would not last because it was based on an outmoded concept of sovereignty. An editorial in the issue of February 8, 1919, said that nations were no longer sufficient unto themselves: "No matter how adequate and flexible a system of representation is devised for individual countries within the framework of a League of Nations, what will really determine decisions of world polity will be the interplay of economic and industrial forces bigger than national boundaries. The groupings will be of a type necessarily different from that in the old days when nations were self-sufficient and self-supporting blocs, with a numerical weight of men who could take up arms. What we are witnessing is the passing of the old order of national irresponsible sovereignty." What, then, was a wise course of action for a president responsible to the electorate through popular suffrage, in a nation committed to both a just peace and the concept of national sovereignty?

Precisely that problem occurred to Robert Morss Lovett, and he dealt with it in his leading article of March 8, 1919, "The Covenant — and After." Lovett foresaw trouble with the Senate about the constitution of the League of Nations that the President brought back from Paris early in 1919. The Senate would ratify only if the country answered. Lovett went on to specify the cause of popular suspicions of the proposed League. The League covenant was a blank check, no true League of Nations but a perpetuation of the victorious Alliance. The rights of the weaker, smaller nations must be beyond any peradventure safeguarded; and the mandates over undeveloped peoples must be carried out in conspicuous good faith. There were other matters, too, that the covenant was obviously vague about: disarmament; the commercial intercourse of nations; the freedom of movement among peoples; and, finally, the treatment of labor in the several nations. Potentially the League covenant was a great thing, much greater than even President Wilson realized. But, really, the covenant mattered only as a "promise to be redeemed in full in the terms of international settlement repeatedly laid down by President Wilson and endorsed by all the Allies." It was that, or nothing, and in that sense *The Dial* called on liberals to accept the covenant — only a beginning, "the first dawn of the morning" with the "burden and heat of the day . . . all before us." Lovett was thus in favor of maintaining faith in Wilson in spite of evidence that he was buckling, but he failed to convince even his own colleagues.

Influenced instead by Veblen's skepticism, the newest member of the staff, young Lewis Mumford, wrote a review of Professor William Herbert Hobbs's *The World War and Its Consequences,* that would have appropriately fitted in an issue of *The Seven Arts.* In the issue of April 19, in "Patriotism and Its Consequences," Mumford acknowledged that Randolph Bourne had been right in suspecting the motives of the "patriots" who led America into the war: "the war animus revealed in

Professor Hobbs' work was one of the most important psychological by-products of the war, and to those who accept the liberal
point of view it appears at long last the most dangerous. The
virulence of this animus was not sufficiently accounted for in
the liberal prospectuses" — a palpable thrust at John Dewey's
recent propaganda for American participation in the war — "and
the difficulty of handling it proved so great that within the
executive department itself the spirit of the President's first
exhortation to fight without rancor was broken within a few
weeks of the declaration. Perhaps the only writer who gauged
this imponderable element at its full worth was the late Randolph
Bourne." Mumford's remark is all the more worthy of note, as
he had never shared what he justly termed Bourne's absolute
pacifism. The accusation that the liberal prospectuses had not
been sufficiently prescient is a specific echo of Randolph Bourne's
warning in his notorious essay for *The Seven Arts* of June 1917,
the piece that, so ran the gossip of the times, had "killed" that
magazine. Bourne commented there on what he termed the sterile results of an intellectual policy that had failed to prepare
American public opinion for the impact of British propaganda
(and, to a secondary extent, German propaganda) about the
war, from 1914 onward. The results were inevitable, he warned.
They were the victimization of personal opinions by propaganda
for the war. "During the war the American intellectual class
has produced almost nothing in the way of original and illuminating interpretation. Veblen's 'Imperial Germany'; Patten's 'Culture and War,' and addresses; Dewey's 'German Philosophy and
Politics'; a chapter or two in Weyl's 'American Foreign Policies';
— is there much else of creative value in the intellectual reper-
cussion of the war?" The editorial policy of *The Dial* thus was
coming round full circle to the position Randolph Bourne had
placed himself in, of the intellectual leader who accepted without rancor the opposition of the majority in order to stand by
his principles and thus really to lead — even at the expense of
social solidarity. By May 1919 that circle was completed.

The issue of May 17 showed a realization that the vessel
of American hopes, and of the liberals' hopes, had sunk, split

assunder on the twin rocks of the League covenant and American policy toward Russia. *The Dial* opposed the peace settlement and the institution of the covenant; and it opposed the Wilson administration in its duplicity toward the new government of Russia, talking with Lenin's representatives while sending an expeditionary force to Far Eastern Siberia and aiding the Whites led by Denikin and Kolchak. Thorstein Veblen wrote in "Peace," the leading article, that the defect of the covenant was not that it fell short but rather that it was quite beside the point. The point was the avoidance of war, at all costs: "the war arose unavoidably out of the political status quo; the Covenant reestablishes the status quo, with some additional political apparatus supplied from the same shop." Veblen opposed the obstructionist nationalist intrigue that chiefly hampered the everyday work of industrial production, with its irresponsible control of production by the vested interests of commerce and finance, seeking each their own profit at the cost of the underlying population. He opposed also the many covert agreements that were covertly arrived at in the four or five months of diplomatic twilight of early 1919. And he opposed the suppression, as he called it, of Soviet Russia for the profit of the vested interests identified with the Allied powers. Indeed he saw the League covenant as an instrument of commercialized nationalism.

To its last member, the *Dial* staff were in favor of the Russian Revolution. *The Dial* published articles by Albert Rhys Williams, George V. Lomonossoff, and other firsthand observers of the Russian Revolution. Its editorials, articles, and house advertisements argued for the recognition of the Soviet diplomatic representative, L. A. Martens, and the dismissal of Bakhmetev, representative of the Kerensky government. *The Dial* for June 14 ran a full-page advertisement headed "Against the Betrayal of Russia": "At a dinner given by THE DIAL, May 22, in honor of Professor George V. Lomonossoff and Mr. L. A. Martens, at which five hundred guests were present, a resolution was passed 'reaffirming our faith in the Russian people, our sympathy with their effort to establish democratic institutions of their own choosing, and our protest against all forms of military intervention and economic blockade designed to modify such institutions and exploit the country in the interest of foreign powers'; also pledging 'our best efforts to persuade our government to recognize the government of the Russian Soviet Republic.' " The advertisement concluded with a protest calling on Congress "to bring about the abolition of the blockade against the Russian Soviet Republic." Interested parties were advised: "Affix your name to this plea and send it immediately to your representatives and senators, with as many additional signatures as you can get." Like most of the causes supported by Johnson's *Dial* in 1919, this one too was lost.

Under Lovett's editorship, *The Dial* also espoused the cause of the Friends of Freedom for India. In 1917, according to Lovett's account, the day after the American declaration of war against the Central Powers, a number of Indian revolutionists, refugees in this country from the British Raj, were arrested and held for trial in San Francisco on the charge of conspiring to ship arms to India. The charges were sensational, involving as they did German espionage and search without warrant of the apartment of Taraknath Das — an American citizen and a former fellow in political science at the University of Washington — by Sir George Denham, head of the British police in Calcutta. The trial of the Indians was equally sensational and ended with the conviction of Dr. Das and others. Lovett and his acquaintances, under the leadership of Rose Strunsky, Norman Thomas, Roger Baldwin, and Agnes Smedley, formed the Friends of Freedom for India.

In the issue for February 22, 1919, there appeared one of the numerous appeals made by the editors that year, signed by John Dewey, Mrs. Ernest Poole, Clarence Darrow, Mary K. Simkhovitch, Robert Morss Lovett, and several more, protesting the indictment, under the Espionage Act, of the Hindu nationalists and asserting their right to political asylum in this country. The appeal referred to the apprehension of Taraknath Das and his associates, and it asked for contributions to defray the expenses necessary to insure legal aid and protection to the unfortunate Hindus. They were indeed most unfortunate. Lovett

in his memoir reported the case of Sailendra nath Ghose, held
for months in the Tombs in New York under an impossibly heavy
bail, on the charge of writing to the Secretary of State without
the authorization of a foreign power. Someone in the district
attorney's office, wrote Lovett, gave as the true reason for the
imprisonment a suspicion that Ghose meant to marry Agnes
Smedley. When the case was brought before Judge Learned
Hand, he pointed out to the district attorney that such honorable
intention was no crime, and Ghose was soon released on reduced
bail. Whatever the facts of that case, Ghose was one poor Indian
whom *The Dial* materially helped. Toward the end of Lovett's
editorship, in the issue of June 14, Ghose furthered the case
of India with his detailed analysis, "India's Revolution," dealing
with the struggle toward Indian independence, led by Mohandas
K. Gandhi, "that great passive resistance advocate," a struggle
often lapsing into bloody riots.

As with the Russians and the Indians, *The Dial* looked
kindly upon the Irish, the Italians, and, in fact, all "oppressed
peoples" when it came to internecine strife between vested interests and common men. Ernest Boyd's letter, "Dublin, March 6,"
in the issue of April 5, protested the unavailability of the publications of the "mere Irish" and contrasted the censorship of
Irish poetry (admittedly glorifying the Rising of Easter Week
1916) to the desecration wrought by Queen Victoria and Albert
the Good on their famous visit toward the end of the Famine,
when the Queen and her husband scrawled their names in ink
upon an illuminated page of the priceless Book of Kells. Less
literary were Arthur Livingston's articles, "Turmoils in Spain,"
in the issue of June 14, and "Maximalists and Minimalists in
Italy," in that for November 15. Flavio Venanzi, an Italian
journalist associated with *Il Proletario*, contributed a hopeful
piece on "The Impending Revolution in Italy" to the issue of
May 3. And even after Martyn Johnson had closed his books,
Scofield Thayer printed a last article about uprisings, "The
Labor Movement in Barcelona," by Fernando de los Rios; he was,
according to the "Contributors" column, one of six Socialist deputies in the Spanish Cortes, elected after his exposure of "the La

Chicas, father and son, who were the caciques, or bosses of Granada." The final month of Martyn Johnson's *Dial* was initiated with a full-page advertisement in the issue of November 1, appealing for "self-determination for all peoples." It was made by the League of Oppressed Peoples, of which Dudley Field Malone was Chairman; Martyn Johnson, Helen Marot, and Robert Morss Lovett were on the list of sponsors. The League opposed "certain politicians, generals, and financiers abroad," who "without the proper warrant or consent of their own peoples" were "making a mockery of the principles which were so recently sanctified by American blood." "Armies of coercion, defying common law, resorting to extreme violence and cruelty are being maintained in IRELAND, EGYPT, INDIA, and KOREA. CHINA's rights have been shamefully abused; PERSIA's sovereignty compromised by intrigue and force majeur, preventable massacres of JEWS continue in various places, while by an illegal starvation blockade hundreds of thousands of innocent women and children in RUSSIA have been brought to agonizing death." The appeal concluded with the usual reference to money — the oppressions noted were being done with money borrowed from freedom-loving America, who had poured out her blood for freedom. *"Shall she now pour out her dollars for oppression?"* The curious and the outraged could find out the truth and make their protest really effective by sending in the filled-in blank at the bottom of the advertisement together with one dollar for membership and whatever additional sum they preferred "as a subscription." The more encompassing its aims became, the nearer Johnson's *Dial* moved toward its end.

The Dial protested Red-baiting here at home. One of its advertisements, in the issue of July 26, presented in the name of a New York City alderman, Algernon Lee, the case of the Rand School of Social Science, which had "been unlawfully raided by the Lusk Investigating Committee [created by the New York state legislature to deal with seditious elements] and its agents, its property damaged, garbled quotations from its correspondence published broadcast, to the great detriment of the school in the minds of the public who know nothing of its well-established educational work in Socialism and allied subjects now in existence for thirteen years." The advertisement contended that the school and its officers and teachers had "been denied any hearing to present their side of the case and therefore are obliged to appeal to the people of the United States for the simplest right of self-defense." Contributions for the cause were invited from all public-spirited citizens.

As *The Dial* waned in the autumn of 1919, its demands on the attention of the American public waxed more imperative. The climax of its militancy was a special "Industrial Section," issued "by Sanction of N. Y. Printing Trades Unions" as Section II of the issue for November 1 and comprising a brief editorial, "The Labor Crisis," perhaps written by Thorstein Veblen (though not mentioned in Joseph Dorfman's biography); a long essay with charts and statistics, "Coal: A Mismanaged Industry," by Walter N. Polakov, whom the "Contributors" section identified as "a consulting engineer of note"; another article, "The Coal Issue in Great Britain," by W. N. Ewer, the Foreign Editor of the Socialist London *Daily Herald*; and a printing of the recently introduced British coal nationalization bill. The editorial for the supplement advocated transferring "the administration of the coal resources to an organization of men competent to mine coal, together with technicians expert in problems of industrial engineering, chartered for the purpose of operating the mines in the interest of the present and future generations." In a house advertisement appended to the supplement, *The Dial* announced: "This supplement is the first of a series under the direction of Mr. Thorstein Veblen, aided by a group of economists and industrial engineers, dealing with fundamental conditions in the industries around which the great questions of the day are centered."

Because the venture came at the end of Johnson's regime — only two later issues of the fortnightly *Dial* were published, the latter being Scofield Thayer's first number as Editor — the series was abortive. Although Dorfman did not mention it in *Thorstein Veblen and His America,* it may have grown out of Veblen's ambition to guide a group of able students in an investigation of the economic order. In July 1919, a representative of the Federal Council of Churches discussed with Veblen and some friends, spending a weekend at Amherst, the idea of collecting a staff to make a thorough analysis of economic conditions, and the Inter-Church World Movement — another of those movements *The Dial* attached itself to! — had a large amount of money available for the project. Although nothing came of the plan, because the Inter-Church World Movement thought it too radical, F. Ernest Johnson, executive secretary of the Department of Research and Education of the Federal Council of Churches, did have a conference with Veblen and Helen Marot. Veblen was interested in the credit system, and the Council instead turned to an investigation of the great steel strike of the day. Yet someone must have furnished Martyn Johnson, Helen Marot, and Thorstein Veblen with the money to commission the special supplement to *The Dial* of November 1, 1919; Johnson could not have afforded even the two lengthy articles, much less their elaborate apparatus of charts and statistics. Undoubtedly this section was a last desperate device to avoid closing his *Dial* or selling it to Thayer and Watson.

The flirtation with elements of liberal Protestantism at this time is especially interesting, for the group closely associated with *The Dial* during Martyn Johnson's regime were characteristically agnostic, when they were not skeptical or hostile toward institutional religion. From time to time books dealing with some aspect of religion were reviewed — for example, Edward S. Drown's *God's Responsibility for the War* in *The Dial* for February 22, 1919, and a collection by members of Yale's Faculty of Religion, entitled *Religion and the War*, in the issue of March 8, 1919 — but the tone of the reviews usually was one of ill-concealed if tolerant contempt for religion. "Religion" was equated with "Protestantism," of course; though Jews and their ways were more interesting than were the Catholics, who were usually ignored. Mont Schuyler, a civil engineer and a member of the Industrial Department of the Inter-Church World Movement, contributed the only significant article dealing with religion *The Dial* printed in 1919. Entitled "The

World's Challenge to the Church," it appeared in the issue of
September 6. According to Schuyler, the dilemma disturbing
church organizations was: "by what means are we to retain the
salutary struggle of industry, but still do away with the devasta-
tion of the present method of production and distribution? How
are we to retain competition, but place it on a higher plane?"
The task of the Church was to interpret the teachings of Christ
"in terms of this day — setting aside special pleading in favor
of scientific exposition." "The churches alone can do this
work," held Schuyler, and do it they must or face "the extinction
of the Christian Church as an institution." Except for Schuyler's warning appeal and some brief, unsigned reviews, *The
Dial* gave scant space to religion.

It was a curious situation in which the Editor of *The
Dial*, a prominent man of letters, gave most of the space in each
number to politics and sociology. For the months of his editorship, Lovett did much of the reviewing of current fiction and
abandoned the device of the regular column of "Recent Fiction."
In all, Lovett signed his name to nine articles and review essays
while he was Editor. One was an editorial, "The Covenant —
and After." The rest were the kind of literary exercise that Francis Browne preferred to print; they explored such writing as
Mrs. Humphrey Ward's memoirs, *A Writer's Recollections* (in
the issue of May 3), Sem Benelli's play *The Jest,* in which John
and Lionel Barrymore were then acting on Broadway (in that
of May 31), and Booth Tarkington's novel *The Magnificent
Ambersons* (in that of January 25). The most important novels
reviewed by Lovett were Louis Couperus' *The Book of Small
Souls* and *Old People and Things That Pass* (in the issue of
February 22) and Johan Bojer's *The Great Hunger* (in that of
March 22); work by Couperus and Bojer was favorably reviewed
in Scofield Thayer's *Dial,* and Bojer's *The Prisoner Who Sang*
was serialized in *The Dial* of May and June 1921. Although he
published not a single signed article or review in Johnson's *Dial*
in its final six months, Lovett remained a *Dial* favorite when
Scofield Thayer and Marianne Moore were Editors, and his

reviews and reminiscences were printed in the magazine all through the 1920's.

The poetry and criticism of poetry in 1919 were undistinguished, in contrast to the poetry and critiques of poetry that appeared in *The Dial* during the 1920's, especially in the first six years of the decade. The indifferent quality of most of the poems printed in the magazine in 1919 is surprising, for according to Lovett, Conrad Aiken was made arbiter of the new poetry. For its historical relevance, James Oppenheim's "Randolph Bourne" remains notable, perhaps the most interesting poem of the year. The poets flocked to the *Dial* office in the afternoon, Maxwell Bodenheim always among the first, until in despair Lovett would lead the party to the saloon opposite the office, on the corner of Seventh Avenue: "Thirst among editors and contributors was flagrant." Bodenheim published occasionally in *The Dial* that year; for example, in the issue of September 6 appeared his "Youth's Ending":

> Only when youth flings his last kiss at us —
> A mist-bud that dies upon our lips —
> Only then so we plant the remembrance of his kiss
> In our hearts . . .

Babette Deutsch, then Veblen's secretary, appeared in the issue of July 26 with a sonnet, "July 4, 1919," in which

> Grim darkness broods above the stricken earth,
> Still as old terror swooping from the sky;
> The nets of death are wrenched apart and lie
> Across the meadows, barbed with savage mirth.

A good deal of the poetry published in book form was reviewed, and several poets were complimented with review essays. In the issue of May 31, John Gould Fletcher wrote on "Conrad Aiken — Metaphysical Poet" and praised *Senlin* as "a kind of poetry profoundly unsettling of our cherished conventions and prejudices," and "The Charnel Rose" as profoundly disturbing and intoxicatingly daemonic in its insight. "Conrad Aiken has shaped this world for us, has striven to make tangible to us the intangible substance of our lives, and we cannot with-

hold from him a meed of praise as great as that of any poet living
and writing in America today."

That issue of May 31 was largely devoted to poetic matters — an anomaly in Johnson's *Dial*. The essay following Fletcher's was Martin Schütze's "Rainer Maria Rilke," surely one of
the earliest pieces of criticism published on Rilke in this country.
Schütze wrote that Rilke was chief among the lyrical gem
makers of Germany at the time: "He makes little perfect things
after the patterns of old great things. Taking an intimate, poignant, but minute impress of a great emotion of intimation, he
gives out an attenuated copy of it wrought in exquisite miniature
workmanship." The chief shortcomings of Rilke's poetry lay in
the poverty of its inner life, an astonishing remark: "What remains is an intense but impoverished gesture of creativeness. . . .
However, with all its shortcomings of externalism and inner
sterility, this poetry has a claim on our attention as an expression
of a type of individuality developed by modern civilization and
as a conspicuous feature of the literary life of this century."

A third poet reviewed in that issue was John Crowe Ransom. Louis Untermeyer wrote of Ransom's *Poems about God*
that the whole volume bristled with acerbity, a pungence often
carried to an unusually bitter climax: "Small though the range
may be, Mr. Ransom's manner is varied enough." Even the
editorial pages carried a paragraph on poetry — "Why should
nearly everybody indulge a conviction that he can write poetry?"
By all odds, this issue was more distinguished for the poems it
published than any single issue of *The Dial* before that of January 1920, which introduced E. E. Cummings and printed poems
by Edwin Arlington Robinson, Evelyn Scott, and Carl Sandburg. In the issue of May 31, were Amy Lowell's "Coq d'Or,"
Maxwell Bodenheim's "Mood," Carl Sandburg's "Steamboat
Nights," Lola Ridge's "Reveille," Eden Philpotts' "On the Hill"
(so that the Georgians were represented) , and Hazel Hall's "Sun
Glamour." Yet the critiques — in this issue or another — generally
were uneven. Of Gerard Manley Hopkins' *Poems* an anonymous
reviewer wrote that the "chief interest in these posthumous poems
lies in their metrical eccentricities. . . . The subject matter of

Father Hopkins' poetry is too prevailingly theological to gain a wide reading. . . . These poems . . . express a strange talent, but will claim few readers." And this was in the literary review that later printed *The Waste Land* as well as I. A. Richards' pioneering essay on Hopkins; Thayer's hand was badly needed.

One major change in editorial policy is to be inferred from a casual statement made by Lovett. Speaking of the excitement of his months in Greenwich Village in 1919, when the AEF was being demobilized, he recalled a young reviewer, just back from Europe and one of the most engaging of the lot. Malcolm Cowley "sometimes appeared early in the day to collect no fewer than three volumes for review. At noon the reviews were on hand, the pay-check issued, the volumes exposed for sale at Frank Shay's bookshop — and Malcolm was lunching." The vignette is pleasant for itself, and what Lovett said about editorial policy reveals that for the first time in the history of *The Dial*, reviewers were being paid in cash as well as in reviewers' copies.

Another aspect of *Dial* policy gave difficulty to Lovett. Francis Fisher Browne had edited a journal designed for a clientele of booksellers, publishers, and serious readers and collectors. In contrast, during 1919, Lovett confessed, "It was with difficulty that we kept even with the book market, which I continued to think was the chief reason for our existence." That is to say, Lovett realized that to exist, *The Dial* must rely on the subscription list built up over a third of a century by Francis Browne; his opposition came from the publisher, who wished to attract a readership comparable with that of *The New Republic*. Such an aim did not give Lovett the free hand he thought he needed; he came, as he said, to a magazine with its space already heavily committed to certain articles, a commitment disastrous not only to an independent editorial policy but also to the economic vitality of *The Dial*. Two of the examples cited by Lovett to show Johnson's rashness are writing by George Moore and John Gould Fletcher, men of letters rather than economists or sociologists or political scientists. George Moore gave trouble because his typescript was in such a wretched state. Communication with London was slow, and it seemed doubtful that corrected manuscript or proof would ever be returned. Moore's "A Second Imaginary Conversation: Gosse and Moore" dragged through the issues of March 22 and April 5 and 19, 1919; it always remained on Lovett's editorial conscience that he "had not the wit to change the name of an etcher typed as Frank Hall to Frans Hals" in the installment printed in the issue of April 19 (as "Rembrandt and Frank Hall"; but Lovett failed to mention two other howlers in the same installment, in which Madame Récamier was transformed into "Madame Rec'cannier" and Madame de Warens into "Madame de Wareus"). John Gould Fletcher sent another manuscript from London, explaining free verse — a topic on which he had previously commented in *The Dial.* Fletcher's essay, "A Rational Explanation of Vers Libre," had its examples so carefully marked that Lovett could follow the text exactly. He did not intend to send proof to London, but according to office routine, it was sent. Weeks later it was returned with the system of accents and caesuras so changed that Lovett "became skeptical of any theory underlying free verse." The essay was printed anyway, changed accent marks and all, in Lovett's first issue as Editor, that of January 11, 1919.

For all his difficulty in keeping up with the book market, Lovett adhered to the tradition of *The Dial* in presenting many long, signed reviews and brief, unsigned notices of recent books. These latter were grouped under the heading "Notes on New Books" and closely resembled the short reviews grouped under "Briefer Mention" in *The Dial* of Thayer and Watson. On March 22, 1919, appeared the "Spring Announcement Number," marked by its "Spring Announcement List" with its categories of fiction; books of verse; drama and the stage; essays and general literature; travel and description; biography and reminiscences; history; the war; politics, reconstruction, economics, and sociology; and the arts. A month later there came the "Spring Educational Number," with its "Spring Educational List" of noteworthy books. On June 28 came the "Summer Reading Number," with a selected list of fiction, distinguished by such titles as Joseph Conrad's *The Arrow of Gold,* Joseph Hergesheimer's *Java Head,* John Galsworthy's *Saint's Progress,* Theodore Dreiser's *Twelve*

Men, and Sherwood Anderson's *Winesburg, Ohio.* The list also cited such translated novels as Johan Bojer's *The Great Hunger,* Vicente Blasco Ibañez's *Blood and Sand,* and Pio Baroja's *Caesar or Nothing.* Then on September 20 came the "Fall Educational Number," with a list similar in scope to the list of its counterpart of the spring. The final number of Martyn Johnson's *Dial* was the "Fall Announcement Number" with its "Fall Announcement List" and "A List of Books for Children." Added to these five special numbers, each issue of *The Dial* in 1919 contained a list of "Books of the Fortnight," with two or three dozen notices of publications issued during the previous two weeks. Most of these were of no great significance; however, in the special summer fiction number of June 28, John Galsworthy's *Saint's Progress* and Sherwood Anderson's *Winesburg, Ohio* ("a prose Spoon River Anthology. Acridly written, these interrelated studies of half-articulate people who do not know what they want deal more often than not with the pathological, but they deal understandingly and honestly. (Review later.) ") — both cited in the selected list of fiction in the same issue — were included. There was, then, to the end of Johnson's regime a recognition that his *Dial* depended on the book market, whatever the personal preferences of the publisher and his staff and supporters.

There was no settled and ongoing policy with regard to the arts and letters; that was the trouble. With much fanfare in its house advertisements, the magazine presented Bertrand Russell in its issue of May 31, with an essay on "Democracy and Direct Action," but for a man who had remarkably defied the Crown in recent years, Russell had little new to say to an American public. He would do much better by Scofield Thayer. There was an occasional article dealing with music. S. Foster Damon reviewed "The New Work of Puccini," in *The Dial* for January 11, 1919; the world premiere of Puccini's three one-act operas — *Il Tabarro, Suor Angelica,* and *Gianni Schicchi* — at the Metropolitan Opera House in New York, December 14, 1918, was "probably the most interesting musical event of the year." A month later came Paul Rosenfeld's tribute to Debussy, "Pélleas et Mélisande," in the issue for February 8. These were individually

superior pieces, but what *The Dial* needed was a regular reviewer
for musical affairs, and that it could not have, because the editors
were interested in public affairs. Similarly, an occasional piece
on the fine arts appeared, as, for example, Walter Pach's "The
Significance of Redon," in the issue for February 22, 1919; Pach
here discussed the etchings and lithographs of Odilon Redon
then being exhibited at the Ehrich Gallery in New York. Redon
and Pach later appeared in *The Dial* of Thayer and Watson; in
an essay representative of what Thayer and Watson consistently
published, Pach attempted to show why, after fifty years during
which the world ignored Redon, it was now turning to him
and to others who " 'dépassent l' objet' with more and more
understanding and certainty." What *The Dial* needed was a
regular staff member writing fortnightly such discussions of
contemporary art; again, this it failed to secure. Instead, the
staff penned advice to errant artists, as in the "Casual Comment"
for October 4, 1919, in which two paragraphs were devoted to
the question why American painters look to Europe, why they
should not look to Europe, and what they should do instead of
looking to Europe: "What the American artist needs above
everything else is to get close to nature in the largest and pro-
foundest sense, to relate himself to the plangent American life
that envelops him; to study it, absorb it, and understand it.
Only when he has done this will he begin to create." For the
artists addressed, such chiding was worse than useless; it was an
attempt to fit them to the Procrustean bed of Deweyan theory.
Thayer and Watson changed all that. At the very end, in the
issue of November 15, 1919, the editors published Eugene M.
Kayden's memorial essay on "Leonid Andreyev: 1871-1919," a
harbinger of the custom of *The Dial* of the 1920's of publishing
memorial tributes to distinguished writers and artists just deceased. Andreyev was a writer greatly admired by Thayer and
Watson; Gregory Zilboorg's translation of Andreyev's *He, the
One Who Gets Slapped* led the issue of March 1921 and was
later published by the Dial Publishing Company in pamphlet
form and advertised in *The Dial*. Yet, here again, Kayden's
tribute — that Andreyev "was never the *conscience* of Russia,

with lips touched by divine living fire, as Tolstoy was, but the *mood* of Russia, falling and rising with the dreams and hopes of the struggle" — seems to have been published as a part of the political policy of *The Dial,* because Andreyev's work adumbrated and sympathized with the Russian Revolution, not because of a fixed editorial policy of honoring great artists and writers.

The staff were hospitable to the New Movement; the poets flocked to the *Dial* office; the young men like Malcolm Cowley who were making their way as poets and critics after the war were hospitably received and given plenty of books to review anonymously for "Notes on New Books" and to sum up for "Books of the Fortnight." That Martyn Johnson had only good will toward the New Movement and the vanguard seems clear from an advertisement he gave *The Little Review.* The half-page advertisement announced *The Little Review* as a magazine of the arts, "making no compromise with the public taste" and as "publishing the current work of James Joyce, William Butler Yeats, Wyndham Lewis, Ezra Pound, T. S. Eliot, Dorothy Richardson, May Sinclair, Ford Madox Hueffer, Jean de Bosschère, William Carlos Williams, Ben Hecht, Sherwood Anderson, etc., in a cheap and convenient format." The prospective reader could obtain this work "in no other American magazine." *The Little Review,* moreover, was "not a chatty journal giving mere publicity about the arts; it is not here to increase contemporary stupidity; it defends the Artist against the Vigilanti of Common Sense; it gives him a chance to show his work with that of his peers, ungarbled in editorial rooms." Johnson's generosity toward Margaret Anderson and Jane Heap was, however, not so great as it was toward other causes neither more urgent nor more deserving but social or political or economic rather than artistic. Instead of publishing the poetry and critiques of Joyce, Yeats, Pound, Eliot, and W. C. Williams, *The Dial* in 1919 printed poems by Lola Ridge, Agnes Lee, Maxwell Bodenheim, Josephine Bell, Bayard Boyesen, and Elizabeth J. Coatesworth; to be sure, it also printed in the same year poems by Amy Lowell, Babette Deutsch, Carl Sandburg, John Gould Fletcher, and

Conrad Aiken. Yet except perhaps for Aiken, its poets were at best secondary figures, either forerunners, such as Amy Lowell, or imitators, such as Carl Sandburg, of the masters of modern American poetry. Of the writers named by *The Little Review* in its advertisement, Sherwood Anderson, T. S. Eliot, Ezra Pound, and William Carlos Williams were honored by Thayer and Watson with the Dial Award during the 1920's; the work of none of these men was published in Martyn Johnson's *Dial*. Above any other adverse criticism of Johnson's policy, that is the most telling.

With regard to its policy, the intentions of his *Dial* were good. From June 1916 through November 1919, *The Dial* attracted the nucleus of its staff of the 1920's and many of its American contributors of that decade. It stood courageously, even rashly, for causes it felt needed support. Its policy — and its intentions too — lacked steadiness, its purpose was not focused. In 1918 the magazine was at odds with Randolph Bourne's protest against the first World War and American participation in the war — only, the next year, to echo much of his attitude. Above all, it lacked aesthetic perspicacity in the most formative decade of the twentieth century, years during which attitudes toward art were being evolved and works of art were being created that half a century later remain revolutionary and seminal. These weaknesses finally brought down Martyn Johnson's *Dial,* after three and a half years of his control.

Although Johnson lacked money to run *The Dial* and thus possessed little bargaining advantage, he tried with some temporary success to change the terms of agreement by which Scofield Thayer would have given twenty thousand dollars to *The Dial* in September 1918. After a discussion over lunch at the old Brevoort one day, the two men agreed to the proposition advanced by Johnson: Thayer took ten thousand dollars' worth of Dial stock and took back from *The Dial,* or, rather, the Dial Publishing Company, notes for another ten thousand, "which were invested in paper," that is to say, in paper stock, then scarce because of military demands. The altered settlement solved nothing when, first, the forces of John Dewey captured the magazine in the fall of 1918 and, second, Randolph Bourne died in December 1918. Ostensibly because of the pro-Soviet issue of December 14, 1918, about which he protested to Johnson and Lovett, Thayer resigned from his posts as Secretary-Treasurer of the Dial Publishing Company and as an editor of *The Dial.* He generously insisted, however, on going through with his original agreement to give *The Dial* thirty thousand dollars and completed his payments with a third installment of five thousand dollars on January 1, 1919. That sum was an addition to the $25,000 he had given Johnson before November 4, 1918.

Within ten months of Thayer's resignation, the inevitable happened. Although an issue of *The Dial* cost only $750 to produce, the magazine was running at a loss of four or five thousand dollars a month. Johnson was consequently not able to meet the notes for ten thousand dollars that he had borrowed from Thayer for the purchase of paper stock, when on delivery of the paper Thayer requested payment. In the first nine or ten months of 1919, Johnson went to several persons — to Willard C. Kitchel, who had helped him originally in financing the purchase of *The Dial* from the Brownes, to Edward F. Sanderson of the People's Institute, to Helen Marot; by the middle of October 1919 they all held notes for which the Dial Publishing Company was responsible, and of course so did Scofield Thayer.

Johnson seems to have sought to attract support from the Forum Movement and perhaps from Mrs. Willard Straight's Co-operative Movement. As various house advertisements and the supplement of November 1, 1919, suggest, he attempted to align himself with parties as disparate as the Veblenian engineers, those forebears of the depression Technocrats, and *The Nation* (for example, the issue of October 4, 1919, as well as several other issues, carried a joint subscription offer, good until December 31, 1919, of "these two famous periodicals," *The Dial* and *The Nation,* which were "necessary supplements to each other. You need them both"). By the side of the joint subscription offer of *The Dial* and *The Nation,* there appeared an advertisement of the Russian Lecture Bureau, to the effect

that in "response to widespread requests, *The Dial* announces
the organization of a bureau to supply speakers to Open Forums,
churches, women's clubs, labor unions, educational institutions,
etc., on different phases of the Russian question." Requests
received would be transmitted to those known to *The Dial* as
having first-hand knowledge of conditions in Soviet Russia and
Siberia, "former Red Cross officials, Y.M.C.A. and Y.W.C.A.
secretaries, civil and military government officials, journalists,
etc." Available for this service were "men holding different
attitudes towards Russian revolutionary parties, but united in
advocating self-determination in Russia, lifting of the blockade,
and in desiring to spread before the American public the facts
as to actual conditions in present-day Russia." This was the fruit
of Johnson's flirtation with the Rev. Percy Stickney Grant and
his Forum Movement. That the speakers' bureau was not successful may be gathered from the omission of the advertisement in the
three succeeding issues, the last of Johnson's *Dial*.

Martyn Johnson had already tried the most desperate measure of all, next to selling his magazine. In the issue for May
31, 1919, there appeared a full-page house advertisement, "Keep
the Faith":

The integrity of the American people is challenged.

Fifty thousand American men are buried on the battle-
fields of France where they fell in fulfillment of the pledge
given by the American people that a war against German autocracy should end in a democratic peace.

THE DIAL remembers the high resolve with which those
men went forth. Will America forget?

The fight is won. Shall victory mock the dead?

The peace terms written by the Allied governments are
not the terms for which America entered the war. They
are terms inspired by the military imperialism against
which we fight. They are an affront and a betrayal.

What is America going to do about it? Forget and grow
fat with imperialistic prosperity? Or keep the faith?

THE DIAL will not be an accomplice in this chicanery.

THE DIAL stands for the flat rejection of these infamous

terms by the American people and demands terms and a
Covenant in accordance with our pledge.
In this crisis THE DIAL ceases to be an individual journalistic enterprise and becomes a rallying center for a movement of free men. Such a movement must have the financial and moral support of a great army of volunteers.
There is an abundance of money for the forces of reaction
and repression. Where in America is the money for freedom? For this support we turn to our readers who believe
in our editorial policy. If THE DIAL is to continue its editorial independence capital must be immediately forthcoming. For this purpose The Dial Publishing Company
is issuing two hundred shares of stock at one hundred
dollars per share. This amount is necessary to assure THE
DIAL's permanance.
Will you be one of these shareholders? If you cannot afford
one share get your friends to make a pool with you to buy
a share.

The failure of that particular appeal for $20,000 is best judged
by a look at two statements "of the Ownership, Management, Circulation, Etc.," those for the sixty-sixth volume, published in
the issue for April 19, 1919, and the sixty-seventh volume, published in the issue for October 18, 1919. The only stockholder
added between the two issues, in the six months during which
Johnson's appeal was made and should have been effective, was
Gustave K. Carus of La Salle, Illinois. It may be that the moral
and intellectual shabbiness of the appeal — "faith" indeed! — was
so obvious that potential investors shied away from the offer.

When Johnson could maneuver no farther, he offered his
stock in the Dial Publishing Company, about seventy-five percent
of the total shares issued, to bidders. In the words of Robert
Morss Lovett, *The Dial* was admittedly hanging on a shoestring,
and finally the shoestring broke. "Scofield Thayer was the only
financial resource. I had once incautiously remarked to him
on the anomaly of putting up money for a paper and letting
others have the fun of running it. Whether he remembered this
suggestion or not, he took up his option" on the paper stock and

on the shares held by Martyn Johnson. To Charles Norman, Sibley Watson said that, after he suggested to Scofield Thayer that they get hold of *The Dial*, as they "did not want to approach Martyn Johnson . . . directly," Thayer wrote a check for $10,000, Watson wrote another for $2,500, and they "gave the money to Harold Stearns, who was to act as a go-between. Time passed, and nothing happened. Harold simply disappeared. He afterwards returned the entire sum."[10] The actual negotiations for the purchase of the magazine were accomplished entirely by lawyers acting as agents for the two principals. Sibley Watson thus returned to *The Dial*, this time as Publisher and stockholder; he and Thayer divided the stock between them, with Watson holding a few more shares than his new partner. He purchased Johnson's stock in the Dial Publishing Company for more than Johnson could obtain from any other of the many people whom he had consulted before selling out to Thayer and Watson.

The staff scattered. Lovett returned to the University of Chicago. Veblen went on to teach at the New School for Social Research. Helen Marot worked again at her many good causes. Harold Stearns went on to edit *Civilization in the United States* and then went to Paris. There he became the model for Harvey Stone, one of the expatriates in *The Sun Also Rises*; Francis Taylor recalled Stearns as the man who taught him about betting, when they used to go to the track at Longchamps. Clarence Britten remained, though briefly, at *The Dial* and wrote "School and College Life" for Stearns's book. Geroid Robinson — that conscientious and able young man, in Stearns's phrase — went on to Columbia University and became another collaborator in *Civilization in the United States*, writing the essay on "Racial Minorities." Lewis Mumford also wrote for the same book, the essay on "The City," and thus began his career as the outstanding American authority on the subject. Indeed, Stearns's volume was a collective *Dial* effort, for Conrad Aiken wrote the essay on "Poetry" and Robert Morss Lovett the one on "Education." Taking his money from the new owners, Martyn Johnson disappeared with the jocular remark, "I have got my sixpence and am off for the moon" — he went first to Carmel, California, then spent a year in the diplomatic service in Norway and moved to Los Angeles.

S. Foster Damon, one of the lights of *The Dial* of the 1920's, wrote in his biography of Amy Lowell that in December of 1919, "the *Egoist* stopped publication, and the *Dial* was bought by Scofield Thayer, who transformed it into a *Seven Arts* without politics."[11] There is a modicum of truth in the description; but no more truth than in the accusations of *The Little Review* that *The Dial* was a de-alcoholized version of *The Little Review*. It is best to allow the new Publisher and the new Editor to describe their own magazine. Near the end of the "Casual Comment" for November 29, 1919, *The Dial* announced the resignation of Martyn Johnson, Oswald W. Knauth, and Helen Marot from the Dial Publishing Company and from the editorial staff, and of Robert Morss Lovett, Thorstein Veblen, Lewis Mumford, and Geroid Robinson from the editorial staff. "J. S. Watson, Jr., has been elected President, and Scofield Thayer Secretary-Treasurer of The Dial Publishing Company. With this issue Scofield Thayer becomes Editor, and Stewart Mitchell Managing Editor of the magazine." Then came the description of *The Dial* as Thayer and Watson envisioned it:

> By the merging of the two fortnightly numbers for December into a single issue, *The Dial* will become a monthly. [No issue for December 1919 was ever published, however.] It will also diverge in more important aspects from THE DIAL of the last year and a half [i.e., its political and social phase], particularly in its greater emphasis on art and literature. Or more precisely, in addition to essays we expect to publish some fiction and drawings. We can assure all concerned that our choice of materials will be independent of the conventional considerations, independent, that is, "jusques au feu exclusive." But for fear this become the occasion of a manifesto, we leave our readers to form their opinion of us from what we shall do rather than from what we say at present.

The urbanity of the announcement is admirable, so is the restraint; five months later a house advertisement of *The Dial,* in the issue for April 1920, was more forthright: "THE DIAL gives to each according to his needs. It cannot be everything to everybody. It is non-political and has no message for the million."

The old year 1919 went out for *The Dial* sped by a news item in the *New York Times* for December 29:

THE DIAL, one of the oldest literary magazines in the United States, has recently changed hands, and hereafter will be published as a monthly instead of a fortnightly magazine. The January issue, which will also be published in a new form, will appear on the newsstands this morning. The new editor in chief is Scofield Thayer of Worcester, Mass. J. S. Watson of Rochester, N.Y., is President of the Dial Publishing Company, and W. B. Marsh of this city is Secretary-Treasurer.

And the 1920's were knocking at the door that veiled the future.

William Gropper, *Tightrope* (September 1922)

Maria Uhden, *Tumbler*

Anne Merriman Peck, *The Zanfretta Circus* (September 1924)

William Gropper, *A Line Syncopation: Male Dancer* (October 1924)

arie Laurencin, *The Little Dancer* (October 1927)

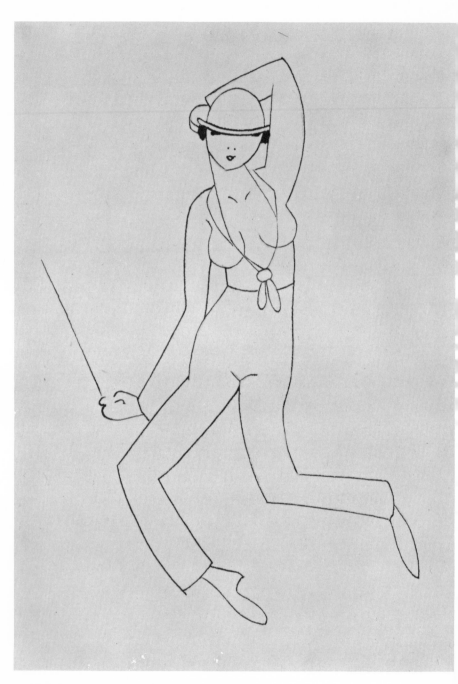

E. E. Cummings, *Girl with Swagger Stick, Dancing*

E. E. Cummings, *National Winter Garden Burlesque II* (January 1920)

Adolf Dehn, *Mura Dancing*

Adolf Dehn, *A Memory of Our Hungarian Lady* (February 1925)

Adolph Dehn 1923
Two Dancers.

Adolf Dehn, *Negress Dancing* (February 1928)

dolf Dehn, *Two Dancers* (August 1924)

William Gropper, *A Line Syncopation: Negro Dancer* (December 1923)

Frans Masereel, *The Boxer* (March 1923)

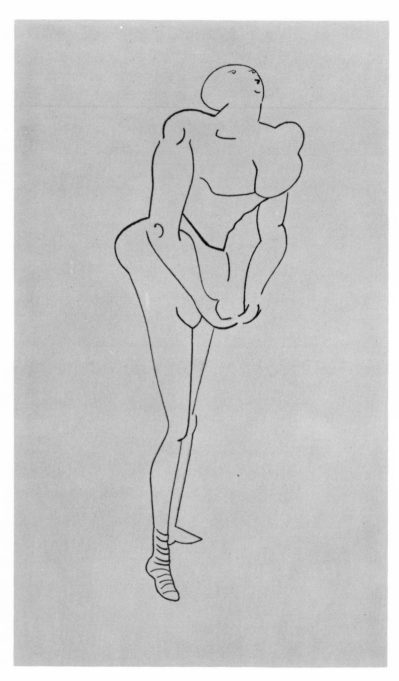

E. E. Cummings, *Acrobat* (January 1922)

Hunt Diederich, *Toreador* (April 1921)

Max Liebermann, *Polo Game* (December 1927)

VII

The end of the transition: The DIAL, *The Little Review,
and the New Movement*

ONE of the most significant relationships in the cultural
history of the period 1919-23 is that of the two chief journals
of the vanguard, *The Dial* and *The Little Review*. It is a relationship that encompasses both the achievement of the New Movement and the beginnings of an age that consolidated that victory
after a hectic revolutionary decade. In 1919, *The Dial* comple-
mented rather than rivaled *The Little Review*. By 1923, with
its political phase an uneasy and unwelcome shade, *The Dial*
outpaced *The Little Review* as the most distinguished American
magazine fostering contemporary arts and letters.

What the relationship of the two journals involved was,
on the surface of events, a kind of contest to see who published
which promising — or, to the unsympathetic observer, notorious —
author or artist first. The contest would be won by the editor
who collected the larger and more widely publicized stable of
front runners. Becoming a front runner depended on the artist's
ability and willingness to shock and often as not to affront the
larger public that consumed *The Atlantic Monthly, The Literary*

Digest, Collier's, and *The Saturday Evening Post.* Being involved in a law suit over the alleged indecency of one's prose or the recognizability of one's sculpture as art — the lots respectively of James Joyce and Constantin Brancusi — did not hurt one's chances of being published in *The Little Review* and of being defended in *The Dial.* The problem of course was a much more serious matter than mere notoriety, for the notoriety itself involved the acceptance of the vanguard, of the New Movement, by the larger public. These pages, then, while concerned primarily with the relatively narrow world of the little magazines in the early 1920's, impinge on another matter, the acceptance of works of art of a radically different kind from those traditionally brought into American homes — an acceptance that argues a fundamental change in attitudes transcending those toward art and letters.

Both relationships within the intellectual and artistic vanguard itself and of the vanguard with the public at large were made more difficult by their characterizing, conflicting traits. The millions of consumers seem to have asked for nothing else than their accustomed diet of Harold Bell Wright and Ethel M. Dell. To them the effort of the poet or novelist or artist representing the "new" was an affront, a cheap attempt to shock merely to titillate. Max Putzel says that when the component poems of Edgar Lee Masters' *Spoon River Anthology* appeared in William Marion Reedy's weekly *Reedy's Mirror* beginning with the issue for May 29, 1914, they "were at their best as they poured out in the *Mirror* with no premeditated order. Their impetuosity had the conviction of unforeseen events and the spontaneous feelings they provoke."[1] But it was those characterizing traits of impetuosity and spontaneity that provoked the mistrust and, in the event, the anger of some elements of the public outside the members of the New Movement itself. And those very traits caused the writers and reformers of the New Movement to disagree among themselves about the larger significance of their own struggle.

What was the intention, what was the direction of such a great outpouring of talent and emotional and intellectual energy?

How should one most effectively confront the critics outside the movement? In *The New Republic* for December 15, 1920, in his essay entitled "America, Listen to Your Own," D. H. Lawrence impetuously advised Americans that they "must take up life where the Red Indian, the Aztec, the Maya, the Incas left it off. . . . They must catch the pulse of the life which Cortes and Columbus murdered. There lies the real continuity, not between Europe and the New States, but between the murdered Red American and the seething White America."

To which advice Walter Lippman coolly replied in the same issue that "Americans can 'start with Montezuma' with precisely as much success as the distinguished author of Sons and Lovers can start with Sargon. That is to say, they can start by looking him up in the encyclopedia." And Lippmann made the further point that in 1920 "American artists and American writers are not being suffocated by the perfection of the past, but by the scorn of excellence in the present. . . . We have a Mayor in New York whose contempt for 'art artists' has been publicly expressed. We have a public opinion that quakes before the word highbrow as if it denoted a secret sin, and bureaucrats who will not permit Mr. Lawrence's novels to go unexpurgated through the mails. His article would please them if they read it. They would see in it still another way in which to isolate themselves from the dangerous contagion of the human race."

It is impossible to understand seminal writers like Lawrence, Masters, Joyce, Eliot, and Dreiser without viewing their work as integral to the controversy of the period: controversy between the hotheads and the more rational spirits in the New Movement; controversy with such philistines as the Mayor of New York. Primarily such controversy was engaged in by the newspapers and magazines, and among the journals of the vanguard undoubtedly the impetuous *Little Review* bore the brunt of the struggle. The cooler and more cautious *Dial* reaped the benefits of its colleague's pugnacity — and soon earned in its turn the animosity of the more daring journal. In 1919-20, the furore over the new freedom of literary expression culminated in the suppression of portions of *Ulysses*, while it was being

serialized in *The Little Review*. The sixth issue thus to be cen-
sored contained Episode XIII of *Ulysses*, the passage in which,
as Margaret Anderson explains, "Mr. Bloom indulges in simple
erotic musings about Gerty McDowell."[2] The fact that Miss
Anderson and Jane Heap, proprietors of the journal, felt themselves to be pure in heart made little difference to the executive
secretary of the New York Society for the Suppression of Vice,
John S. Sumner.

The Washington Square Bookshop was "served with papers
by the Society for the Suppression of Vice for having sold a
copy of the *Little Review* containing Joyce's Episode XIII."[3]
John Quinn, the famous lawyer and collector of modern art and
patron of Joyce and other writers, defended Miss Anderson; John
Cowper Powys and Philip Moeller testified for the defendant, at
her trial in February 1921. Scofield Thayer, both as Editor of
The Dial and almost equally as famous a patron of art and artists
as Quinn, appeared for the defense in court but, along with
the Rev. Percy Stickney Grant and Ernest Boyd, was not called
to testify. The judges were decidedly not impressed, and the
defendant lost her case.

Inevitably the effects were felt by other and more prosperous
journals, perhaps chiefly by *The Dial*, which stood to lose a large
sum if its publication were interrupted, for it was just newly
refurbished and redesigned as a journal of arts and letters and
was emerging as undoubtedly the most munificent magazine of
the time in its patronage of the vanguard. *The Dial* thus immediately became much more cautious about publishing not only
Joyce — to whom Scofield Thayer epistolarily apologized late in
October 1920 for his caution as Editor — but other writers of
the New Movement.

The apex of the era of good feeling between *The Dial* and
The Little Review was reached when, to publicize its support
of its sister journal, *The Dial* gave — gave, without doubt,
as Miss Anderson could not have afforded the cost of such a
luxury as an advertisement in *The Dial* — *The Little Review* a
full-page advertisement in its issue of April 1920. *"The Little
Review* / A Magazine of the Arts / making no compromise with

the public taste," ran the copy, adding that "THE LITTLE REVIEW is not a chatty journal giving mere publicity about the Arts; it is not here to increase contemporary stupidity; it defends the artist against the Vigilanti of Common Sense: it gives him a chance to show his uncensored work with that of his peers ungarbled in editorial rooms." Perhaps it was also at this time that James Sibley Watson gave his famous hundred-dollar bill, the first of several such gifts, to Miss Anderson when he purchased from her bookshop a copy of T. S. Eliot's *Prufrock and Other Observations.* Watson and Miss Anderson became good friends and so remained during all the attacks *The Little Review* later made on *The Dial.*

Cordial relations with the Editor of *The Dial* in 1920 further aided *The Little Review* in its defense of the artist against the Vigilanti of Common Sense, led by John S. Sumner. The editorial column of monthly "Comment" for July 1920 said that the "Comstockians have driven everything from Fanny Hill to Rabelais, from Petronius to Dreiser, from the book-shelves, and the prosecutions for new books are necessarily few." Yet the age was not one of "religious fanaticism. The persecutors of art" were not "enthusiasts for God." *The Dial* admitted that it was "inclined to sympathize with this hatred which begins in fear and selfishness. It is only by hating beauty, wherever it is found, that the dreariness and banality of common life are made tolerable." Six months later, Scofield Thayer himself wrote the "Comment" (the manuscript of which is in the Dial papers). He compared what he termed "The Case Jurgen" with the *Ulysses* affair:

> The suppression of The Little Review for printing Episode XIII of James Joyce's Ulysses has not attracted so much attention, but it is likely to be longer remembered. One does not begrudge Mr Cabell his supporters, nor is one annoyed that where money is there a certain mild freedom is also. It is very nice that Messrs Schubert [*sic*] and Ziegfeld, The International Studio, The Police Gazette, and Vanity Fair are permitted to display the simpler facts of human anatomy and even

of human physiology, but it is probably not very important to the greater glory of life. Mr Joyce, however, is an artist, and imbeciles who try to interfere with the circulation of his work are a nuisance. The thing that mattered in this kind of outrage and blasphemy, so Thayer said, was liberty, and "the police alone, as the regularly constituted guardians of liberty, should be privileged to prosecute; and they should be compelled to prove, in accordance with Plato, that the offending work constitutes an absolute menace to the public good." Like so much that *The Dial* advocated, these prophetic words were a third of a century in advance of American popular opinion. Thayer's altruism is all the more striking when one learns that by the end of 1920 *The Little Review* had already begun to snipe away at the wealthier journal that it considered an unworthy rival.

In July 1921, *The Dial* published John S. Sumner's apology for his part in the prosecution of *The Little Review,* in the course of which he attacked Ernest Boyd for calling into question the rectitude of the forces imperiling the onward march of the New Movement. As Sumner saw the matter, "the offense of the defendant is an offense against society, the placing in traffic and in circulation of something which experience has shown is detrimental to the public wellbeing. . . . He has caused no personal injury . . . but he has violated a law enacted in the interests of society in general, one which the Supreme Court of the United States places on a par with laws in the interest of public health and public safety." The immediate cause of the prosecution was a letter the District Attorney of New York County received "from a reputable citizen in business on lower Broadway":

> I enclose a copy under another cover — of a copy of 'The Little Review' which was sent to my daughter unsolicited. Please read the passages marked on pages 43, 45, 50, and 51. If such indecencies don't come within the provisions of the Postal Laws then isn't there some way in which the circulation of such things can be confined among the people who buy or subscribe to a publication of this kind? Surely there must be some way of

keeping such 'literature' out of the homes of people who don't want it even if, in the interests of morality, there is no means of suppressing it. Through the office of the District Attorney, the letter made its way to Sumner's group; a conference was held, and the upshot was a trial in which "three Justices of the Court of Special Sessions were of the . . . opinion" that the matter complained of was a violation of law — and "there was a conviction." The part that the New York Society for the Suppression of Vice played in the trial was that of complaining witness, in place of the ordinary citizen "who would have declined the honour because he had a family to support and his time was entirely taken up with the business which was his livelihood." Was the District Attorney to "wink at this violation of the law" because Ernest Boyd and "some others are hysterical on the subject of 'lynch law in the arts'?"

The Dial allowed Ernest Boyd to reply, at the conclusion of Sumner's self-justification. In a brief paragraph, Boyd merely said that as might be expected, Sumner endeavored to prove that his Society was "essential to the moral welfare of America." And Boyd could "only conclude that plain English is as incomprehensible to Mr Sumner as art, which he confounds with dirty post cards." With this confrontation, *The Dial* concluded its public defense of *The Little Review*. It had courageously committed itself as much as it could, without actual legal involvement, possible censorship and consequent confiscation of its own issues, and, eventually, considerable financial loss to Thayer and Watson.

The relation of the two magazines thus got off to an amicable start in 1920; if there was rivalry, it was a friendly rivalry. Even were there no supporting instances, the advertisement of *The Little Review* that *The Dial* for April 1920 published would, of itself, make apparent the breadth and, so to speak, the indivisibility of the New Movement: a continuum of tastes and attitudes however superficially divergent and even opposing. *The Dial* actively pursued a wider public; *The Little Review* announced that it would make no compromise with the public taste. Both

journals nevertheless sought their respective ends with remarkably similar means. Of thirty-four writers named as contributors
to *The Little Review*, in the advertisement under discussion, the
two journals shared nineteen of these contributors, from Sherwood Anderson to William Butler Yeats. And of eight artists
whose works *The Little Review* advertised itself as having reproduced, *The Dial* published five, from Jean de Bosschère to Osip
Zadkine. Moreover, *The Dial* and *The Little Review* shared a
nobler aim with their contributors. The radical changes in taste
and attitude instigated by the artists and writers and editors
of the vanguard comprehended more than the "new" freedom of
expression in the printed word; their notion of freedom was not
restricted to the abandoning of Victorian prudery. The shock
value of the work of those who participated in the New Movement was the greater and more enduring because that work incorporated, to be sure, changed attitudes toward sex and expressed
them with a new frankness and realism — but the shock value
was the greater, it endured, because that work also expressed
what was uttered in novel and shocking aesthetic forms. One
wonders what most readers of *The Dial* made of T. S. Eliot's *The
Waste Land* as it appeared in the issue for November 1922 —
printed as a collection of individual poems under a general title
and with none of its explanatory notes appended (Gilbert Seldes
refused to print the notes to the poem, although they had
arrived as a part of Eliot's typed copy). What is certain is that
the shock value of the aesthetic form of *The Waste Land,* more
than any other element of the poem, made it a *cause célèbre.*

With the publication of *The Waste Land* there arose not
only the prolonged discord of praise and dissent over Eliot's
poem but, also, the sound of another dispute, equally intense if
not as loud, between *The Dial* and *The Little Review.* The
early friendly relation of the two magazines changed for the
worse in 1921 and 1922. After less than two years as Editor, Scofield Thayer complained, in a moment of irritation with his
hypercritical confreres among the little magazines, that they all
showed a deplorable cousinship to Jane Heap. It is true, sad to
report, that Thayer had some cause for complaint; the bad feel-

ing was instigated by *The Little Review*, and, in it, chiefly by Jane Heap. Ostensibly the rather one-sided dispute — most of the harsh words were written by Miss Heap — had to do with the claim of *The Little Review* that it led the artistic vanguard. Whatever the validity of the claim, the dispute itself is most instructive, indicating as it does that the tempo of the changes brought about by the New Movement was slowing and also suggesting a wide popular acceptance of these changes.

Since its renovation in January 1920, *The Dial* had published a number of works by artists and writers whom *The Little Review* previously had published and praised. James Joyce appeared in *The Dial* only once, as he was too controversial; "A Memory of the Players at Midnight," in *The Dial* for July 1920, was innocuous in all save the name of the notorious author. More importantly for *The Little Review*, Ezra Pound, one of its chief contributors, was retained as Paris Correspondent of *The Dial*, and T. S. Eliot began a stint as London Correspondent for *The Dial* in March 1921. Margaret Anderson and Jane Heap had cause to be grateful to Dr. Watson; as Miss Heap admitted in the final number of *The Little Review* in May 1929, in some "Wreaths" to a number of persons and institutions whom she liked and here recalled, Watson, "while owner and publisher of The Dial, helped The Little Review though several tragic moments. He knew a good magazine when he saw it." Still, that their journal pretty consistently ran afoul of the law and Mr. Sumner, whereas *The Dial* remained unscathed, that their circulation was tiny, that they could not afford the luxury of payment to contributors, and that they had to be supported through the generosity of a rival who, as both ladies viewed the case, appropriated their ideas and their writers and even published reproductions of specific works of art already published and well publicized by *The Little Review*: all these were causes for reproach. Reproach indeed was their return for Dr. Watson's generosity. As early as its issue for September-December 1920 in a double-page spread advertising its own virtues, *The Little Review* sailed into *The Dial* with an exchange between reader and staff:

Of course you see the *Dial*? Why in the name of litera-
rature do they start a magazine at this date and follow
directly in your footsteps? Can't they do any pioneering of their own? I have followed your progress for the
past five years and I am very loyal to your little journal.
This loyalty may prejudice me to the extent of considering the *Dial*'s policy a literary breach.

[Yes, we have had this called to our attention many
times. The *Dial*'s contents page often reads like our
letter-head; but we don't mind, and they seem to like it.
There is room in America for any number of efforts of
this kind. And it is especially fitting, now that we have
prohibition, to have a de-alcoholized version of the
Little Review. — jh]⁵

About a year later, a similar attack, again unsigned (could
it have been written by Ezra Pound?), appeared:

As jh so admiringly says, isn't it *wonderful* to have
an organ like the Dial for refreshing the memory?

In November 1918, "The Starry Sky" by Wyndham
Lewis was reproduced in the Little Review; reappeared
in the August Dial [i.e., August 1921]. Zadkin's "Holy
Family" in December 1918 Little Review now in current [i. e., October 1921] Dial. What is it — a merry-
go-round?⁶

By this time, *The Dial* was disenchanted, though it said
little. Privately, Scofield Thayer rejoiced when he could beat
out Djuna Barnes in the reservation of pictures in Herwarth
Walden's gallery Der Sturm in Berlin; she had omitted, on the
preceding day, September 23, 1921, to ask for reservation rights,
for reproduction in *The Little Review* of Walden's holdings in
contemporary art, so Thayer took the greatest pleasure in seeing
to it that Walden agreed definitely to give no journal in America
but *The Dial* the right to reproduce the pictures its Editor chose
(he spent the entire afternoon with Walden, choosing two
dozen, among them some Chagalls now in the Dial Collection).
Only once did Miss Heap annoy *The Dial* to the point of response. In August 1922 the editorial "Comment" (perhaps writ-

ten by Gilbert Seldes) gave "publicity to her renunciation" when she suggested, apropos the attack that Gorham Munson's little magazine *Secession* made on *The Dial* for its alleged lack of "homogeneity" of contents, that she was "not rushing to the rescue of the Dial," as it had "a larger audience" than *The Little Review*.[7] The publicity thus given was an ironic reminder that, fairly recently, *The Dial* had come to the rescue of *The Little Review*. "Comment's" joshing self-defense and the reference to *The Little Review* and its proprietors were good-humored if, to Margaret Anderson and Jane Heap, irritatingly condescending. Their irritation arose, apparently, from a feeling that *The Little Review* pioneered in publishing the sort of work for which *The Dial* received most of the acclaim.

To some extent, that feeling was justifiable. *The Little Review* was, in fact, receptive to the vanguard in certain instances in which *The Dial,* to its own eventual hurt, was inhospitable. A front runner in any stable escaped when first Scofield Thayer and then Alyse Gregory rejected the poems and fiction of Ernest Hemingway. As early as March 5, 1922, Thayer told Ezra Pound that "I was interested to see the poems by Ernest Hemingway. I am however of the opinion that *The Dial* has enough young blood already to make it decidedly rough reading. I have therefore been unable to accept even those examples of Mr. Hemingway's art which you as always so perceptively point out to be the better ones." And Thayer added that he had sent "the things" directly back to the author. Hemingway may have placed these poems elsewhere; the very poems Thayer declined in March 1922 may have been among those printed in the New Orleans *Double Dealer* that June, or in *Poetry* in January 1923. The group of poems printed in *Poetry* was augmented by four more, and the ten were included in *Three Stories and Ten Poems,* the pamphlet published in Paris in 1923 that inaugurated Hemingway's career. Even more importantly, the Exiles number of *The Little Review,* for Spring 1923, began with a group of six brief images by Hemingway, entitled "In Our Time"; these became the first six vignettes of the Paris edition of *in our time* that William Bird published in January 1924.

In *The Dial* for October 1924, Edmund Wilson devoted a review of two pages, "Mr Hemingway's Dry-Points," to the Paris editions of *Three Stories and Ten Poems* and *in our time*. Wilson felt that *in our time* was the more important book and dismissed the ten poems as not particularly important; yet his review of the pamphlet of stories and poems was unique, its single criticism by a responsible American critic in a leading American literary journal. Taking what he may have viewed as a hint, Hemingway again tried his luck with *The Dial* late in 1924, but Alyse Gregory, then the Managing Editor, rejected his story in a letter of December 4, 1924.

Undaunted, Ernest Hemingway tried *The Dial* a third time; on January 21, 1925, he submitted a story. Although his accompanying holograph letter does not mention the title, it may have been "The Undefeated," that portrait of the wounded but indomitable Spanish matador Manuel Garcia. In an effort to come to a decision about Hemingway's story, someone at *The Dial* wrote Marianne Moore that since "you and Mr Thayer have discussed Hemingway, Mr Thayer thought you might be willing to give your judgement of this manuscript which Mr Thayer and Dr Watson and Miss Gregory disagree upon." Next day Marianne Moore replied that she had read Hemingway's story with great interest but that as it stood, she would "say no." Miss Gregory has recalled the story as one "about bull-fighting." She rejected it in a letter of March 10, 1925, thus taking the responsibility for declining Hemingway's story that Thayer and Watson had voted to publish. That loss for *The Dial* was all gain for *The Little Review*.[8] The *affaire* Hemingway serves to illustrate further the gap widening between *The Dial* and *The Little Review* after 1921, a divergence due to the more committed experimental spirit as well as to the reckless courage of Margaret Anderson and Jane Heap. These two qualities went with a third, their poverty. *The Dial,* as Thayer explained to James Joyce, could not afford the honorable martyrization that resulted from the publication of *Ulysses* and other such "rough reading," because of the considerable financial investment in the review of its Editor and Publisher.

Over the arts as well as literature the relations of the two magazines deteriorated still further. *The Little Review* for Autumn 1921 (actually issued early in 1922) was self-termed the "Brancusi number"; its pages were largely devoted to photographic reproductions of sculptures by Constantin Brancusi and to discussions of his work. His sculptures were as startlingly original in form and as controversial in treatment of subject as *Ulysses*; and *The Little Review* admitted no compromise in its advocacy of such pieces as *The Kiss,* various versions of *Mlle. Pogany,* and the *Golden Bird.* It was no consolation at all that in *The Dial* for November 1922, the famous issue in which *The Waste Land* was introduced to American readers, there also appeared Brancusi's brass sculpture of the *Golden Bird,* reproduced in the same photograph that the sculptor had given *The Little Review* and accompanied by Mina Loy's poetic eulogy, "Brancusi's Golden Bird." *The Dial's* customary note about a new contributor made only cursory mention of *The Little Review* and its special number: "Constantin Brancusi is a sculptor, born in Rumania and now living in Paris. He first became known in this country through the Armory Exhibition of 1913, and was recently the subject of a special number of The Little Review. He has worked in virtually every material amenable to sculpture." *The Dial* did not add, however, that *Vanity Fair,* a magazine with a much wider circulation than itself and *The Little Review* combined, had scooped *The Dial* by publishing a page of photographs of Brancusi's work entitled "New Sculptures by Constantin Brancusi" in its issue for May 1922, showing "Torso," "Mlle. Pogany," "The Kiss," as photographed by Charles Sheeler, plus a photograph of "Brancusi at Work" (something that *The Little Review* had not published).[9] The three-pronged publicity thus given to Brancusi is important to consider.

What the proprietors of *The Little Review* now were reduced to complaining about could no longer be, in fact, that they continued "really" to lead the vanguard and that other journals took the credit for doing so. The changes in taste and attitudes promulgated by the New Movement had become too widespread for such a charge to ring true had it been continued to be asserted; acceptance of artists like Brancusi and writers like Joyce and Eliot had become fashionable by 1923. The editorial complaints of *The Little Review* veered to two charges, with a third implied. The Autumn 1922 issue of *The Little Review* (published in 1923) made the two charges, one sent in by a reader-correspondent and made against *The Dial* only, the other made by Jane Heap against a group of magazines:

> Do you ever read the advertisements of the other magazines? . . . The Dial's Christmas cards described it as the only journal devoted to art and letters in America. Such deliberate dishonesty! Why doesn't jh go after them?

To which Miss Heap replied:

> I am not a professional trimmer. These magazines are business concerns. They use the advertising methods of certain grades of business. They place themselves. The *Little Review* is for and by the artist, we have no interest in confusing the public or in directing it to buy only from us. Buying and selling isn't our fun. *jh*[10]

The Dial was, of course, not being dishonest in asserting its uniqueness as the only journal devoted to art and letters in America. Its devotion to art and letters was both more comprehensive and profounder than, though perhaps not as narrowly intense as, the equally sincere devotion of *The Little Review*. In the sense in which *The Dial* announced the uniqueness of its devotion to the life of literature and the arts in America, surely the assertion has generally been granted. — As for the second accusation, it is made as a statement of fact with the implication that somehow the devotion to the public rather than to the artist is demeaning and corruptive. Whatever the validity of her implication, Miss Heap's statement is true, of course. Scofield Thayer had exploded in a letter of November 28, 1922, to his Associate Editor, Gilbert Seldes, that

> The photograph of "The Golden Bird" should of course never have been accepted. We should only have pictures in *The Dial* (Mr. Watson agreed with me as to

this question in Berlin and assured me he would see to it that such things should not further appear in *The Dial*) which at once have *aesthetic value* and are not *commercially suicidal*. The picture in question has *no aesthetic value whatever* and is *commercially suicidal*. As to the quality of "The Golden Bird," having only seen this picture I of course have no idea whatever.[11]

Thayer and Watson at this juncture in the affairs of their review were making great efforts to the end that *The Dial* would eventually break even financially. They did not aspire to make a profit from *The Dial,* but they did hope that it would cease losing money at the rate of eighty thousand dollars a year. Among the devices to which they and the *Dial* staff resorted in order to attract a wider public than that of *The Little Review* were several used by magazines as diverse as *The Atlantic Monthly, The National Geographic,* and *Vanity Fair.* Undoubtedly, it was the example of this last-named periodical that *The Dial* emulated. A house advertisement in *Vanity Fair* for March 1922 reads: "Do You Know — That Vanity Fair maintains these Six Service Departments for *your* convenience?" The six are Financial Department, Amusement Department, Book Department, Shopping Department, Automobile Department, and Travel Department; by applying to them, the reader of *Vanity Fair* might obtain, for a price or gratis, depending on the department (one bought books and theater tickets from the appropriate departments; one received advice and practical aid from the others), what he sought. *The Dial* instituted book and travel departments, duplicating those of Frank Crowninshield's magazine; it also used its house advertisements to puff "Dial Advertisers," as when in the November 1920 issue it pointed out its monthly listing of gallery exhibitions and its advertisements of publishers, book-shops, and "unusual schools." These are the "advertising methods" that Jane Heap objected to for her own journal; ironically, Miss Anderson and she advertised a book service for *The Little Review.* Perhaps theirs was a service "for and by the artist."

By 1923 the proprietors of *The Little Review* were thus reduced to the indignity of insincerities in their magnificent struggle to keep going. It is a measure of the futility of their accusations that bitterness creeps in, supplanting the old tone of feckless gaiety. True, poverty even in Greenwich Village in its heyday was difficult to bear; and the strain of the events culminating in the *Ulysses* trial tells, despite her valor, in Margaret Anderson's words in *The Little Review* for January-March 1921: "The trial of the *Little Review* for printing a masterpiece is now over — lost, of course, but if anyone thought there was a chance of our winning . . . in the United States of America . . . ." And she added: "It is the only farce I ever participated in with any pleasure."[12] Equally hard to bear was her realization that the New Movement was spreading, was slowing down, that the great and signal changes in art and letters were becoming incorporated in the mainstream of middle-class American culture, that "her" artists and writers were deserting her and her journal — though in these years one cannot separate Margaret Anderson from *The Little Review*: "she" was also "it" — and that all she stood for was now the common coin of magazines, such as *Vanity Fair*, that were, candidly, "business concerns."

How far beyond the circle of Margaret Anderson and Jane Heap the New Movement had spread by 1923 one may gather from a single instance. In its issue for June 1923, *Vanity Fair* published a group of six poems by T. S. Eliot.[13] All had been published previously; for example, "La Figlia Che Piange" had first appeared in Harriet Monroe's *Poetry* in September 1916 as one of a group of five poems sent in by the young American from his wartime exile in England[14] and then had been collected in the author's first volume of poems, *Prufrock and Other Observations* of 1917. One hazards the guess that not enough readers of *Vanity Fair* were familiar with Eliot's writing for it to matter that Frank Crowninshield and his staff were printing second- and third-hand material. The publication of Eliot's poems in the magazine refutes Cleveland Amory's assertion that "Above all, *Vanity Fair* was ahead of its time in the search for new talent." Amory's statement is hardly strengthened by his "list of American and foreign discoveries . . . unmatched by any other magazine in a similar period" — especially as he cites to support his point

Thomas Wolfe, Gertrude Stein, E. E. Cummings (who was in fact "discovered" by *The Dial*, as he once acknowledged to this writer), Edmund Wilson, Robert Sherwood, Paul Gallico, Corey Ford, Margaret Case Harriman, Clare Boothe Brokaw, Gilbert Seldes (who was Managing Editor of *The Dial* from 1921 until the close of 1923; and who had first contributed to *The Dial* in 1917!), Allan Seager, Carl Carmer, P. G. Wodehouse, Aldous Huxley, Colette, Ferenc Molnar, and "many others."[15] Aside from the quality of the contributions published in *Vanity Fair* by the writers Amory listed, the majority of them had slight connection with the New Movement and what it represented. Rather, *Vanity Fair* was, to use a social phrase, in the swim — not ahead of its time.

Observing "La Figlia Che Piange" in *Vanity Fair* in its issue for June 1923, a knowledgeable reader realizes that the writers and artists of the vanguard, those of the New Movement, had consolidated the gains of the movement and that their works of art were now becoming commercially valuable property. Thus, if the New Movement was transforming American culture during the early 1920s, by an ironical reciprocity and in the same years the New Movement itself was becoming *embourgeoisé.*

As for *The Dial* and *The Little Review,* there is little further to recount of the relationship. Realizing that her part in the New Movement had now been played, Margaret Anderson wished to allow the journal to die. Jane Heap demurred; she insisted that it continue publication, and largely by her efforts *The Little Review* endured, sporadically, through the 1920's and ended its career with an issue of farewell and summation in 1929. Miss Anderson wisely had cut her losses and had gone to France in 1923 to live with Georgette Leblanc a very differently oriented life, more private, more personal, quite away as it were from the middle of things. *The Dial,* for its part, had always been casual in its attitude toward *The Little Review* except for those months in 1920 during which Scofield Thayer defended it and James Sibley Watson supported it. As oblivious to the vicissitudes of *The Little Review* as *The Little Review* was to *The Dial*'s own less checkered years of publication, *The Dial,* too, continued to the end of the decade, expiring quietly with the issue of July 1929. The major struggle — Margaret Anderson's Thirty Years' War — had been won by the forces of the New Movement, and American tastes had changed through the popular acceptance of the kind of art and literature both *The Little Review* and *The Dial* had advocated and had published. Perhaps not the least effective element in deciding that struggle was the combative insistence by both journals on their respective freedoms to express the new themes in novel aesthetic forms. And their internecine dispute itself advertised, as no other means could, the integrity of these forces ultimately allied in America's cultural Thirty Years' War.

VIII

THE DIAL *and the Taste of the 1920's*

"THERE is very little difference between one man and another," said William James, "but what little there is, *is very important.*"[1] Much the same holds true for magazines. *The Dial* made its own mark on the taste of the 1920's. In specific ways, it molded taste in its decade, taste that has influenced American arts and letters in the decades since the 1920's. *The Dial* also was an expression of men and women living at a certain time, and it therefore has a great deal in common with other periodicals of the 1920's, reflecting, with them, contemporary attitudes and opinions.

Whatever representative quality *The Dial* ever possessed and still possesses lies in the work of its contributors; to that extent — admittedly, a major extent — the journal is a passive reflection of its decade. The fact remains that *The Dial* also differs from all its competitors and contemporaries precisely in these very contributions and, quite as importantly moroever, in their relations to one another within the context of the magazine in which they were published. The reference here is not only to the intangible aesthetic and ideational juxtapositions of texts, illustrations, and commentary but, more importantly and specifically, to the material appearance of the review and its contents and the editorial arrangement and disposition of texts and pictures in given issues month after month. To regard *The Dial* as merely a mirror of its decade is to miss the essential note of its vitality — its reason for being, the very reason that it attracts not just the student of the period but the reader fortunate or dogged enough to avail himself of the comparatively rare files of *The Dial*, Volumes 68 through 86 (January 1920 — July 1929.) The essential note of its vitality lies in the fact that *The Dial* is not a passive repository, an accumulation (though by its nature a magazine is such a mirror); nor is it essentially a technically well-arranged journalistic artifact; rather, *The Dial* was and remains, by every intention and by execution, a work of art. As a monthly review, it *is* a repository and *was* a remarkable feat of journalism; as a work of art, it incorporated both these categories and actively influenced its immediate age.

The nature of that influence lies in the conception of *The Dial* adhered to by backers, editors, and staff. One sees no controlling ideology, however; *The Dial* had no axe to grind.

Nowhere in the Dial papers or in the published work of the staff and editors and backers does one observe an emphasis on the prophetic imagination or on the organic theory as it relates to the concept of *The Dial* and of its immediate publication.[2] Scofield Thayer and James Sibley Watson purchased the stock of a periodical called *The Dial*. They took over the magazine without knowing much, if anything, of its tradition. As late as the termination of the first year of publication of the new *Dial* of Thayer and Watson, someone on the staff composed an advertising circular, fortunately never to be published, that traced the lineage of *The Dial* back to "the year of 1853" when "a group of New England intellectuals striving for the liberation of the American mind from the blight of puritanism, founded at Cambridge, a journal of arts and letters. . . . Associated in this venture were some of the finest minds that America has produced. The versatile but erratic Margaret Fuller was its first editor, and Emerson its second. Much of the work that appeared in its pages is now accounted the richest heritage of American letters." One easily dismisses such interpretation of that "richest" heritage" of *The Dial* by someone who was lucky enough to share, however misapprehendedly, in that tradition. He was, at the least, attempting to construct some bridge of continuity.

To attempt a construction on such lines is to fail to connect *The Dial* of the 1920's with its heritage. There is no "inner" continuity — at any rate, of the prophetic imagination, of organicism. The essential continuity lies, of course, in the title itself of the journal, in the loyalty of some contributors, in the continuous numbering of its volumes, in some of the journalistic devices carried over to *The Dial* of the 1920's, and in the orderly transmission of ownership of Dial stock.

Even the title of the journal conveyed no continuity of symbolic meaning. One contrasts the importance of the dial in 1840 as an ideological symbol to its complete unimportance in 1920 as any such symbol.

There is no extended editorial comment on the significance of the dial as the emblem of and the title of the periodical of the 1920's, and the only metaphorical application, in the editorial "Comment" for January 1921 and written by Scofield Thayer, describes the emergence of the renovated *Dial* in the figure of an aging lady acrobat: "more or less coming up on her more or less renovated feet, clad in reassuringly genteel tights, she smiled stiffly at the world." Thayer's satirical wit epitomizes the anti-bourgeois spirit of the 1920's with its self-conscious irony of the clown and the popular theater. Appropriately, the Dial Collection houses one of the better groups of Toulouse-Lautrec prints, and Scofield Thayer seemed to prefer that period of Picasso's work that abounds in his sad families of clowns and his ambiguous harlequins and acrobats. It is as though the editor,, attuned to the *Zeitgeist* as he was, was not to be caught admiring a nineteenth-century achievement.

What could the two *Dials* have in common? Thayer's banter does not for all its irony disguise the Editor's awareness of his formal debt to the Boston and Chicago *Dials* and their editors.

The use of the adjective "genteel" is revealing. The very fact that *The Dial* of Thayer and Watson insisted on printing "both the accepted and the unaccepted" would place it outside the pale of Bohemia despite the physical location of the editorial offices at 152 West Thirteenth Street, and Scofield Thayer's "Comment" in its metaphor tacitly acknowledged, if perhaps unwillingly so, the spiritual home of the latest *Dial*. That is to say, *The Dial* acknowledged a continuity of traditions rather than of forms.

That continuity manifested itself through the consistent publication by *The Dial* of the 1920's of work in several currents of expression. The first of these was liberalism. By this term is meant here primarily the political attitude one thinks of in connection with the Fabian socialist and Progressive political movements of the early twentieth century, but also *The Dial* was liberal in printing expressions of the most diverse opinions, e.g., Bertrand Russell versus George Santayana, Leo Stein versus Scofield Thayer.

As *The Dial*, like its backers, was nothing if not aesthetic, one hesitates to apply the term in its full range; nevertheless it was through Thayer's social and political liberalism that he became interested in *The Dial*.

The liberalism of *The Dial* was nonpolitical, however. Paradoxically, for all its inherited liberalism, even as a critical review, the new *Dial* was primarily aesthetic in its interests; it reviewed an occasional volume of philosophy, especially if the work had been written by a philosopher whom it affected such as George Santayana or Bertrand Russell; it reviewed an occasional work of anthropology, as when Edward Sapir in the November 1922 issue wrote about the collection by various hands, *American Indian Life,* edited by Elsie Clews Parsons. Even in these excursions, however, the limitation of the reviewer and review was the self-imposed one of the aesthetic attitude. When *The Dial* went on record to oppose the remarkable John S. Sumner, the head of the New York Society for the Suppression of Vice, its opposition was grounded on the principles of aesthetic freedom and sound publishing practice rather than on that of politics. Whether one deplores the general exclusion of science, sociology, and politics from the pages of *The Dial* and applauds its espousal of the belletristic and the aesthetic depends largely on whether one finds himself among, to use Emerson's pejorative phrases, the Humanity and Reform Men, "Who trample on letters and poetry,"[3] for it is generally admitted that within the self-imposed limitation of its interest, what *The Dial* did it did supremely well.

Another current of expression, besides liberalism, to which *The Dial* was responsive was shared also by Scofield Thayer and Randolph Bourne. Even before his association with *The Dial,* Bourne called it transnationalism and defined it in "Trans-national America" as "not a nationality but a trans-nationality, a weaving back and forth, with the other lands, of many threads of all sizes and colors. . . . Against the thinly disguised panic which calls itself 'patriotism' and the thinly disguised militarism which calls itself 'preparedness' the cosmopolitan ideal is set." Only America, by reason of the unique liberty of opportunity and traditional isolation for which she seems to stand, can lead in this "cosmopolitan enterprise," and for precisely the reason that she is already a world-federation in miniature.

Scofield Thayer subscribed to Randolph Bourne's thesis, and he admitted in 1920, in his correspondence with Harold Evans, that he became interested in *The Dial* as a possible vehicle for Bourne's journalistic writing. Thayer felt, however, that Martyn Johnson was using the backer's money to finance an undertaking that was essentially propaganda rather than the criticism Bourne advocated. At this point it may be well to interpret Thayer's words in the context of the previous five or six years. Thayer was never shy about propagandizing for the arts, though he preferred to do so in the tradition of the gentleman, as nearly anonymously as possible. In relation to politics, one may avail oneself of a religious term and describe Thayer's attitude as that of bearing witness, in contrast to the openly polemical attitude of some other patrons and editors of the day. Indeed, by its very indirection, propagandizing for art and letters took on the nature of the attitude of bearing witness to, i.e., of validating, the moral-religious, social-political complex of notions and biases and activities to which Thayer privately subscribed and for the advancement of which he was willing to finance Randolph Bourne's journalism.

Thayer was entirely sympathetic to the aims of the propaganda in question — that of Martyn Johnson's *Dial* — but felt such progapaganda was being handled far better by *The Liberator*, *The New Republic*, and *The Nation*. His disagreement with Martyn Johnson was based on what he considered to be the publisher's unfairness in obtaining a backer's money under a certain understanding and then spending it in a different way. As opposed to Johnson, Thayer saw his own interests as being almost purely aesthetic, and both he and his friend Bourne felt that a magazine such as they originally intended was the journalistic venture America most needed.

Transnationalism has at best the sound of jargon; perhaps the more commonly used word "cosmopolitanism" is an acceptable equivalent. Frederick J. Hoffman has identified the policy of *The Dial* of Thayer and Watson as "an intelligent eclecticism."[4] Professor Hoffman has cited two examples that support these two terms, cosmopolitanism and eclecticism, as at least in part identifying a current of expression important to *The Dial*. Answering one of the many attacks on *The Dial* — this time in *The Literary Review*, which had accused *The Dial* of saying editorially "by implication and sometimes directly — here is the way to write; these are the subjects, these are the methods of modern European literature" — the editorial "Comment" for June 1923 (probably written by Kenneth Burke in the absence in Europe of Scofield Thayer and Gilbert Seldes) asserted: "If we have already history behind us, if American letters owe us something, it is simply because we have never published anything or anybody for any reason but the one natural reason: because the work was good. We have published European work not as exotics and not as exemplars; only because we feel that Americans are at work in the same *milieu* and in the same tradition of letters as the Europeans — that we are all in the Western-civilized-Christian-European-American tradition, and that

American letters have their independent existence and their separate, precious character, within that circle, just as German and Italian letters have." "Comment" concluded: "If the work of European artists continues to be nobler in conception and more honest in execution than the work of Americans, we shall undoubtedly print the former in preference to the latter. . . . It is barely possible that our greatest service to American letters will turn out to be our refusal to praise or to publish silly and slovenly and nearly-good-enough work. The Americans we publish have at least the certainty that we publish them not because they are Americans, but because they are artists." One should view these remarks against the cosmopolitan world of the 1920's — a decade in which for the first time masses of American travelers, the Sam Dodsworths as well as the Jake Barneses, were discovering at first hand for themselves the important part of that world that was Europe. *The Dial* in its "Comment" was trying to place these discoveries in the only perspective it considered proper.

In another and equally overt way, though one of necessity less publicized, the editorial policy encouraged recognition of the cosmopolitan, eclectic spirit, through its correspondence with contributors. One letter by Malcolm Cowley exemplifies this relationship. Preparing for his review of Conrad Aiken's *Priapus and the Pool* and Carl Sandburg's *Slabs of the Sunburnt West* — published in *The Dial* for November 1922, as "Two American Poets" — Cowley wrote Scofield Thayer (August 3, 1922) that he intended to compose, of course, a review of Aiken's and Sandburg's latest, but chiefly an analysis of what the adjective "American" meant when applied to a poet:"I don't think it means much. It is a temporal rather than a spatial adjective; it belongs definitely to the generation of 1914; an earlier writer like Poe, or a later like Cummings is just a poet; Amy Sandburg Frost is an American Poet." While *The Dial* published the work of Amy Lowell and Carl Sandburg (for example, the title poem of his volume under review, "Slabs of the Sunburnt West"), though not that of Robert Frost, it consciously was publicizing the work of a newer literary generation than that of 1912-14. The

younger writers such as Malcolm Cowley and Kenneth Burke
were consciously harking back to the tradition of Poe, the tradition occasionally appealed to by Gilbert Seldes in his drama
reviews, book reviews, and editorials for *The Dial* — the tradition
that, also, T. S. Eliot was revivifying in his "London Letter"
and essays and reviews and *The Waste Land*. Malcolm Cowley's relationship with Scofield Thayer thus exemplifies the
means by which Randolph Bourne's transnationalism and Thayer's cosmopolitan attitude toward the life of art were transmitted to the readership of *The Dial*.

A third current of expression manifest in *The Dial* is aestheticism. As with the expression in *The Dial* of liberal and cosmopolitan attitudes, so with its aestheticism there arose controversy
and misunderstanding. This is not to say that there were those
who thought *The Dial* not hospitable to the arts and to artists;
the magazine existed, obviously, for the sake of the arts. In his
memoir, *The Days of the Phoenix*, Van Wyck Brooks — a contributing editor to Martyn Johnson's *Dial*, a close friend of Randolph Bourne, honored by the Dial Award for 1923 and nomi-
nated by Dr. Watson to the Editor for the post of "strong man"
(i. e., Managing Editor) in a letter to Thayer dated March 15,
1923 — ironically agreed with Thayer's self-estimate already cited,
that he saw his own interests as being almost purely aesthetic.
Brooks said that "the editors of *The Dial* were aesthetic or
nothing."[5] In its "Comment" for July 1922, the magazine went
on record as being in essential sympathy with the "New Criticism" of Joel Spingarn, whom it termed "a percursor," and,
far from disagreeing with his words, *The Dial* here took them
up and interpreted them: "We have again and again, specifically
and by our practice, indicated the irrelevance of certain terms
to the life of the spirit. We have believed that to publish the
best work available in both the accepted and the unconventional forms of expression was closer to the ideal of a journal of
art and letters than to publish work, however undistinguished,
because the author was young or old or American or European
or a member of the old school or of the new. The application of
this belief has led us to publish, with pleasure, the work of

those artists who worked in forms not yet familiar; and as a result we have been held to be defenders not of the specific works, but of the idea of 'new forms.' It has led us to publish the work of young men and women — it could not do otherwise. Yet in the silly hub-bub about the age of this second-rate poet or the youth of that insignificant novelist, we have had little or no part. We have not been interested." The editorialist was not being candid here — he either forgot or refused to acknowledge that the prime reason Sherwood Anderson was awarded the first Dial Award, for 1921, had been that he was forty-seven years old at the time, whereas the other candidate, E. A. Robinson, was fifty-two; also Anderson was definitely of the younger group of writers.[6] "Comment" continued: "it is necessary to recall these things because of the wholly illogical assumption that if one does not think physical youth a criterion of artistic excellence one must confine one's self to the works of physical age. We assume that in this connexion Mr Spingarn means what we mean, that one must confine one's self to works of art." In quoting Joel Spingarn, "Comment" said that his words were "the words of a precursor, and Mr Spingarn leaves us not long in doubt as to the source of the new inspiration, which is the outburst of Modern Idealism in Italy." This "Comment" was one of the most important editorials to be published in the magazine, not only as a statement of beliefs but also for its acknowledgement of such sources of inspiration for the aestheticism of *The Dial* as Joel Spingarn, Benedetto Croce (one assumes that he is the cause of the outburst of Modern Idealism in Italy?), Nietzsche, and Goethe.[7]

Something of that attitude was basic to the foundation of *The Dial,* and when he resigned his editorship, Scofield Thayer repeated and summed up what — as he himself said in his "Announcement" of June 1925 — he had already written in different words "and in editorial comment as well as in *Dial* advertisements." In founding a magazine to supply the absence of "any regular publication much interested in bringing out the sort of writing we like to read and the sort of pictures we like to see," Thayer and Watson had "in mind no literary or artistic propa-

ganda, no desire to urge, for example, the advantages of free
verse as opposed to regular (or of regular as opposed to free),
but also" they "depended upon no aesthetic system either of our
own or of another to guide us in selecting what should be the
contents of *The Dial.*" It "seemed worth while to set up a
journal where we and others of our way of feeling and of thinking could sit at ease; and might, when the stars should be auspicious, perhaps encounter moments of delight." This pragmatic
approach and the fact that Dr. Watson and the Editor "were possessed of no fast aesthetic dogma" made "the personality of those
members of the *Dial* staff who were to pass upon manuscripts and
pictures the decisive factor in the contents and, indeed, in the
whole life of the magazine."

The two editorial pronouncements just quoted, by Scofield Thayer, exemplify the extremes of the aestheticism of *The
Dial.* One looks forward to the theoretical and academic criticism of the 1940's and 1950's, while the other looks to the past,
to the "decadent" aestheticism of the 1890's in England, to a
time when one's personal response (those "moments of delight")
to the work of art obviated more ideological, systematic considerations.[8] Thayer's words are reminiscent of Whistler's statement: "there is no such thing as English art. You might as well
talk of English Mathematics. Art is art, and Mathematics is
Mathematics."[9] To be sure, *The Dial,* as edited by Thayer, owes
much to the aestheticism of the 1880's and 1890's — which held
that "that Nature is always right, is an assertion, artistically,
as untrue, as it is one whose truth is universally taken for
granted"[10] — at least as much as it owes to the American tradition
of *The Dial.* Yet both editorials concur in their emphasis on the
significance of the isolated work of art and of the response of
the isolated individual to it. The title of T. S. Eliot's review of
Ezra Pound's *Personae* indicates the bias of *The Dial* and its more
representative contributors: "Isolated Superiority" (January
1928). That the attitude was Thayer's and that it was consistently
held is demonstrated by his remark in the first of a series of four
monthly eulogies of Marianne Moore's poetry in the editorial
"Comment" for January 1925: "We flare not in glorification;

we flare in practical service. Service not to that Juggernaut, the Reading Public, — that Juggernaut which is well served in being served badly. Service rather to the Imaginative Individual, to him who is in our world always the Marooned Individual. The towns, the villages, the prairies and sandbars, of this North American Continent support many such. For since neither by the public pictures nor by the family radios are the hungerings of imagination appeased, therefore have these their being for ever in isolation, for ever shut and cut off. Therefore have these sharp eyes, the sharper for long fasting, eyes which, I have been encouraged to believe, are wont to pick out and follow our own irregular and unchartered sailings. And it is for these important eyes that we run . . . this name of Marianne Moore." In that emphasis one finds the justification of the aestheticism of *The Dial: The Dial* justified its aestheticism by emphasizing in these "Comments" its attitudes and editorial practice.

Through the unstinted generosity of Scofield Thayer and James Sibley Watson, Jr., *The Dial* afforded practical, material encouragement to artists, among them E. E. Cummings, Gaston Lachaise, and all those honored by the annual Dial Award of $2,000. Beyond publication of works of art and writing in their review, paid for at duly stated rates, the two patrons of *The Dial* made no demands on those whom they thus aided; there was no coterie, no entourage.

Thayer and Watson and their staff responded to and encouraged specific works of art, specific pieces of writing; they were not concerned with "the arts and letters" as a mere abstract generalization, just as they refused to concern themselves with the establishment and perpetuation of a school or coterie. Especially in the earlier years of its decade of publication, *The Dial* responded to what its Managing Editor, Gilbert Seldes, termed the Seven Lively Arts, in the phrase made famous by his book in 1924. One need not speak of a campaign that *The Dial* conducted for the acceptance as valid art forms of the popular arts Seldes praised: comic strips, motion pictures, musical comedy, vaudeville, radio, popular music, the dance. Nevertheless the most quickening aspect of the venture that was *The Dial* in the

earlier 1920's was its publication of such satirical drawings as
Cummings's *National Winter Garden Burlesque* I and II in the
very first issue, January 1920; of Eliot's *The Waste Land* with its
celebration of "that Shakespeherian Rag" in November 1922; of
Adolf Dehn's *Negress Dancing* in February 1928; and of portions
of Seldes' *The Seven Lively Arts,* for example, the chapter entitled "Toujours Jazz," in August 1923. But there were also bull-
fights and boxers by Hunt Diederich, Manolo, Cummings, Picasso, Frans Masereel; cabarets and circuses by Adolf Dehn, Duncan Grant, Picasso, George Demuth; and clowns and harlequins
by Picasso and Lipchitz and Severini. One of the three regular
notices of the arts was "The Theatre" conducted usually by Gilbert Seldes and then by Padraic Colum; it reviewed the open-
ings of the Ziegfeld Follies as enthusiastically as it noticed plays
by Eugene O'Neill. There was real excitement in the attempt
to persuade readers that the relation of the fine to the popular
arts lies in the "close intimacy between high seriousness and
high levity, the thing that brings together the extremes touching
at the points of honesty and simplicity and intensity," and that
such a relation and recognition of mutual concern will "act like
the convergence of two armies to squeeze out the bogus."[11] Certainly *The Dial* helped to form the taste of the 1920's in such a
view of the commonwealth of art. And by means of the expression and publication of its attitude toward the popular arts, the
aestheticism of *The Dial* was related by those concerned in it
to the preoccupations of the mainstream of American life of the
1920's.

Still another expression of the aestheticism of *The Dial* is
the form itself of the review. As an artifact, *The Dial* is a work of
art. This aspect of the aestheticism to which *The Dial* was responsive has to do not only with the expression of an attitude
that one recognizes as based on the attitude of *l'art pour l'art,*
the aesthetic attitude of the 1890's and *The Yellow Book.* Also it
has to do with a vital and continuing activity, the search for
aesthetic perfection, as announced by the "Comment" for August
1922, with its quotation from Santayana's "A Contrast with

Spanish Drama" and the implicit acknowledgement of intellectual indebtedness to Santayana, a debt essential for an understanding of the *raison d'être* of *The Dial*.¹²

The Dial sought to impart moments of delight embodied in artistically viable forms. Announcing the new, monthly *Dial* in the final number of the old, fortnightly *Dial*, on November 29, 1919, Thayer and Watson promised their readers that the new journal would "diverge in more important aspects from *The Dial* of the last year and a half," that is to say from the political journal that resulted from the move to New York, "particularly in its greater emphasis on art and literature," and in its eschewal of the "fumy scene of politics." The brief editorial announcement promised that "more precisely in addition to essays we expect to publish some fiction and drawings" and that "our choice of material will be independent of the conventional considerations, independent, that is, 'jusques au feu *exclusive.*'" Six months later the editorial "Comment" was wondering "whether it is necessary to reject anything, in the old forms or the new, except the dishonest and the shallow and the feeble in execution. The question is practical because *The Dial* has set itself the task of including a great many things which fall under the ban of one or the other of the challenging pontiffs of art." There follows on this rhetorical question an avowal that perhaps has not been sufficiently heeded by those who have viewed *The Dial* as, basically, advanced and experimental in its selection of contributions: "the place of a contributor in any 'movement' backward or forward does not concern us; and until we are convinced that we are in error, we shall hold to that principle."

....*The Dial*, then, was not interested in ideological controversy as such. Rather, it was centrally concerned with excellence of aesthetic form in literature and the fine arts. Moreover, the taste of the editors was equally concerned with the conception of a magazine of art and letters as itself a work of art. Leafing through the pages of *The Dial*, issue after issue, one comes to understand that the pictures and essays and stories in it are not merely juxtaposed but are interdependent. They are used, as mosaicists compose a total picture from discrete and previously unrelated pieces of stone and glass, so that the magazine itself becomes a work of art. Three examples illustrate the point. In June 1924, Roger Fry's essay, "Mr Epstein's Sculpture," is immediately followed by photographs of the sculptor's heads of *Dolores, Miriam,* and *Kathleen,* and the same number reviews Epstein's current showing in New York. In July 1922, Hans Purrmann's "From the Workshop of Henri Matisse" complements the frontispiece of Matisse's painting *Nasturtiums and "The Dance"* — in the version sold to Sergei Shchukhine and now in the Pushkin Museum in Moscow rather than in the second version purchased by Scofield Thayer a little later, during his residence in Vienna, and now housed in the Worcester Art Museum as part of the Dial Collection. On the occasion of Ezra Pound's reception of the Dial Award for 1927, the January 1928 number began with a portion of Pound's "Canto XXVII," which is followed by T. S. Eliot's appreciative review of Pound's *Personae,* "Isolated Superiority"; as a tribute to Pound and his influence, the issue also includes two pen and wash drawings by Wyndham Lewis and a review of H. D.'s volume of poems, *Hippolytus Temporizes,* as well as the "Announcement" of the Dial Award to Pound. Such a conception of the role, the appearance, and the structure of a magazine was not then new to American journalism, but never previously had it been executed with such intelligence, thorough attention to detail, dogged persistence, and good taste. The monthly columns dealing with the theater, music, and fine arts; the letters from abroad; the book reviews; the criticism of literature and the arts; the poetry; the shorter and the longer, serialized fiction; the critiques of thought and culture; the reproductions of pictures and sculptures in half tone and color; and, finally and importantly, the incisive, impudent "Comment": the rich, stimulating totality constituted a new phenomenon, sharp yet suave, international rather than provincial, though composed often enough, of individual units that were decidedly regional. Sherwood Anderson might receive its Award, yet Marcel Proust would write in extravagant terms of his "tres cher Dial qui m'a mieux compris et plus chalereusement soutenu qu'aucun journal, aucun revue." (As quoted by Gilbert Seldes to Scofield Thayer, May 15, 1922). "Toute ma reconnaissance pour tout de lumière qu'illumine la pensée et réchauffe le coeur." The magazine was, of course, designed to make an impression, and as Proust's enthusiasm attests, that it successfully did. It did not, however, overwhelm the individual contribution but rather offered itself as a brilliant showcase in which each contribution appeared all the better for also being part of an integrated ensemble.

What characterized *The Dial* as unique is the editorial search for aesthetic perfection, a struggle through which the review was transformed into a work of art. The sheer ugliness and disorder of Martyn Johnson's *Dial* contrast most instructively to the order and beauty of *The Dial* of the 1920's. Through their conception of *The Dial*, Thayer and Watson were able to impress upon the decade of the 1920's certain components of aesthetic taste that have affected American art and letters to our own day. There is the urge toward formalism, the emphasis on the work of art as primarily a unique form (which might and mostly did exist in a tradition of one kind of form, of course). There is also the accompanying urge toward a relative impersonality in the editorial regard of the artist and his created work of art. This is not to say that Thayer and Watson lost interest in their contributors as persons or that the backers of *The Dial* turned their sympathetic patronage, the essence of which was the personal empathy between artist and purchaser, into the impersonal fecundity of a foundation. Rather, the focused interest of *The Dial* and its staff and contributors was in the work of art, the form that gave moments of delight. Still another urge the magazine expressed is the urge toward what Randolph Bourne called "an intellectual sympathy which is not satisfied until it has got at the heart of the different intellectual expressions, and felt as they feel . . . the cosmopolitan ideal." The impact of *The Dial* on its decade was a strong one, and in at least these three respects *The Dial* can be seen to have influenced the taste of the 1920's — and later.

Footnotes to Introduction

1. For discussions of Browne's *Dial*, see Fredric J. Mosher, *Chicago's "Saving Remnant": Francis Fisher Browne, William Morton Payne, and the Dial (1880-1892)*, (Urbana, Illinois, University of Illinois unpublished dissertation, 1950); Fredric J. Mosher, "Report of a Conversation with Herbert S. Browne (Tuesday, March 15, 1949)" (unpublished memoir); Frank Luther Mott, *History of American Magazines* (Cambridge, 1938), III, 539-41; Bernard Duffey, *The Chicago Renaissance in American Letters* (East Lansing, Mich., 1954), pp. 66-70; Herbert E. Fleming, "The Literary Interests of Chicago," *American Journal of Sociology*, XI (1905-06), 514-19; etc. The early years of *The Dial*, 1880-92, are recounted in a *Supplement* to XIII (October 16, 1892), 14 pp., with constituent articles drawn not only from the magazine itself but from outside sources, e.g., " 'The Dial' and its Editor," *The Inland Printer*, X (1892), 33-35. See also "The Dial's Score of Volumes," *The Dial*, XX (1896) 347-48; "The Dial, 1880-1900," XXVIII (1900), 327-28: "The Dial's Quarter-Century," XXXVIII (1905), 305-07. For a description of Francis F. Browne's *Dial* and Browne's Bookstore, see Margaret Anderson, *My Thirty Years' War* (New York, 1930), pp. 27-31.

2. "The Original 'Dial,' " *The Dial*, I (May 1880), 9-11. Fredric J. Mosher to Nicholas Joost (January 3, 1958) : "I am sure that Browne intended to name his magazine after the Fuller-Emerson *Dial*, but his reasons are not stated in any document I have seen."

3. The original *Dial* is treated at length in George Willis Cooke, *An Historical and Biographical Introduction to Accompany The Dial as Reprinted in Numbers for the Rowfant Club* (Cleveland, 1902) , 2 vols.; *idem*, " 'The Dial': A Historical and Biographical Introduction, with a List of the Contributors," *Journal of Speculative Philosophy*, XIX (1885), 224-65, 322-23. See also Ralph Waldo Emerson, "Life and Letters in New England," *The Complete Writings of Ralph Waldo Emerson* (New York, 1929), II, 1043-57; and Faith Chipperfield, *In Quest of Love: The Life and Death of Margaret Fuller* (New York, 1957) , pp. 155-213 *passim;* Clarence L. F. Gohdes, *The Periodicals of American Transcendentalism* (Durham, N.C., 1931) , pp. 27-37; Frank Luther Mott, *A History of American Magazines*, I, 702-10; Ralph L. Rusk, *The Life of Ralph Waldo Emerson* (New York, 1949), pp. 275-78, 295-96; Louise Hall Thorp, *The Peabody Sisters of Salem* (Boston, 1950), pp. 133-47; Mason Wade, *Margaret Fuller, Whet-*

stone of Genius (New York, 1940), pp. 82-101; etc. See also Ralph L. Rusk, ed., *The Letters of Ralph Waldo Emerson* (New York, 1939), 6 vols., for letters to Margaret Fuller and the other Transcendentalists. I have used the unbound copies of *The Dial* at the American Antiquarian Society, Worcester, Mass., and Emerson's bound volumes of *The Dial* now in the Emerson papers at the Houghton Library, Harvard University.

4. Quoted from Perry Miller, ed., *The Transcendentalists: An Anthology* (Cambridge, Mass., 1950), p. 248.

5. T. W. Higginson, *Margaret Fuller Ossoli* (Boston, 1884), pp. 147-48. I have not found Alcott's statement, quoted by Higginson, among Alcott's papers in the Houghton Library, Harvard.

6. In Bronson Alcott's papers (p. 249 in ms.) in the Houghton Library, Harvard; used by permission of the Harvard College Library.

7. *Idem.* Pages of the ms. are numbered 47 (entry LXXXI) for February, and 56 (entries XC and XCI) for March.

8. *Idem.* p. 79 (entry CXII) for May.

9. Bronson Alcott, "The Transcendentalist Club and *The Dial*," ed. Clarence Gohdes, in "Alcott's 'Conversation' on the Transcendental Club and *The Dial*," *American Literature*, III (1931), 19.

10. *Letters of Emerson*, ed. Rusk, II, 284.

11. *The Correspondence of Thomas Carlyle and Ralph Waldo Emerson*, ed. Charles Eliot Norton (Boston, 1883), I, 285.

12. See Mario Praz, *Studies in Seventeenth-Century Imagery* (London, 1939), p. 202, for the dial as used in Webster's *The White Devil* (I, ii, 279 ff.); Praz contends that Webster's use here "is that of an emblematist." For the dial pictured as an emblem, see Paracelsus, *Selected Writings*, ed. Jolande Jacobi, Bollingen Series XXVIII (New York, 1951), fig. 133, *Sundial*, reproduced from a woodcut by Hans Holbein the Younger.

13. *Complete Writings* (New York, 1929), I, 229.

14. "Language," *Nature*, in *Complete Writings*, I, 10.

15. *Ibid.*, II, 941.

16. For Emerson's knowledge of the metaphysical poets and their work, see Norman A. Britten, "Emerson and the Metaphysical Poets," *American Literature*, VIII (1936), 1-21. See "The Garden," *Poems and Letters of Andrew Marvell*, ed. H. M. Margoliouth, 2d edn. (Oxford, 1952), I, 50.

17. William Wasserstrom, *The Time of the Dial* (Syracuse, N.Y., 1963), p. 158.

18. Rusk, *The Life of Ralph Waldo Emerson*, p. 196.

19. Thomas Carlyle, *On Heroes, Hero-Worship, and the Heroic in History* (Boston, 1907), p. 148.

20. *Wilhelm Meisters Lehrjahre,* ed. Erich Trunz, in *Goethes Werke* (Hamburg, 1950), VII, 192: "Diese geheimnisvollsten und zusammengesetztesten Geschöpfe der Natur handeln vor uns in seinen Stücken, also wenn sie Uhren wären, deren Zifferblatt und Gehäuse man von Kristall gebildet hätte, sie zeigen nach ihrer Bestimmung den Lauf der Stunden an, und man kann zugleich das Räder- und Federwerk erkennen, das sie treibt."

21. An allied use of the dial as a symbol was noted in the Chicago *Dial.* See "Casual Comment," *The Dial,* LIV (April 16, 1913), 333: "A sundial interesting to bookmen has been set up in the gardens of the Country Life Press at Garden City, Long Island; and an artistic little paper-covered book descriptive of its curious construction is issued by the same press, with the imprint of Messrs. Doubleday, Page & Co. Mr. Walter Gilliss, the designer of the dial, writes the description, and excellent illustrations are added. 'A Printers' Sun Dial' is the title of the treatise, and it tells how the dial came to be erected, how the Gutenberg Bible, as the first of printed books and the 'Book of Books,' was chosen for representation on its face, and how the marks of twelve early printers were selected for the twelve hour spaces. No expense seems to have been spared in making the dial a thing of beauty and a most solid and lasting construction. Its pedestal extends three and a half feet below the surface of the ground, to ensure against disturbance by frost, and concrete, cement, and brass are the materials used, with a perdurable composition of an unnamed sort as filling for the engraved lettering on the open pages of the Bible, which itself is said to be exactly reproduced from the fifty-thousand-dollar copy secured at the late Hoe sale by Mr. Henry E. Huntington. Appreciative visitors are welcome in the 'cedar room,' as it is called, of the beautiful garden where the Printers' Sun Dial is to be seen." In reply to an inquiry about the Doubleday sundial, Miss Helen Crosby of the publicity office of Doubleday and Company, successors to Doubleday, Page, and Company, sent a Xerox copy of "an article . . . printed in a little bound book called 'Country Life Press' 'for the friends of Doubleday, Page & Company.' The print date is 1919." Doubleday no longer has copies of the pamphlet issued in 1913. Walter Gilliss, "The Sun Dial," *Country Life Press* (Garden City, 1919), pp. 73-87, is undoubtedly a second edition of the pamphlet to which *The Dial* referred; it is an elaborately illustrated description of the Doubleday sundial, in the terms of the *Dial* note. Miss Crosby added: "As you know we no longer have a printing plant in Garden City (all offices now).

The Sun Dial was moved to one of our printing plants located in Berry-ville, Virginia, and makes an attractive addition to the grounds there": Helen Crosby to Nicholas Joost (May 18, 1966).

Also, see Don Marquis, "Confessions of a Reformed Columnist," *Saturday Evening Post*, CCI (December 29, 1928), 59-62 (the second part of a two-part serial), in which Marquis recounts the way in which he came to write his famous daily column for *The New York Evening Sun*, "The Sun Dial." In the spring of 1913, Marquis found himself "editing a magazine page in the New York Evening Sun." The page "blew up, as it deserved to," and the proprietors set Marquis "to writing editorials for the Evening Sun. Then they gave me the short editorial paragraphs to do, as well as occasional longer editorials." He saw his chance at last and "stole that column when they weren't looking." The editorial paragraphs in the *Sun* followed the editorials "under a small separate headline: Notes and Comment. I deliberately wrote more Notes and Comment every day than they had ever had before, and after a few weeks, suggested that the Notes and Comment Department be lifted to another part of the page." Marquis recalled that he moved his new column to the right, under the daily cartoon. He gradually began to run more and more verse, more and more comment, and features of a different kind from that traditionally run in "Notes and Comment." But Marquis was still dissatisfied: "It was set in nonpareil type. It had this deadly dull headline over it, Notes and Comment. It had no signature. I ran it for ten months in that fashion and as far as I could make out nobody ever paid any attention to it. It didn't catch on at all . . . . I was not permitted to do stunts with it; I was obliged to make it conform more or less closely to the editorial policy of the paper itself. What I wanted was my own editorial policy." Then one day "the late George M. Smith became managing editor of the paper, and almost the first thing he did was give me the column I had been after so long with a fixed spot in the editorial page every day, with an attractive heading, The Sun Dial, with a signature, and with permission to go as far as I liked in the way of personal expression. . . . The Sun Dial — that was George Smith's name and not my invention — caught on with the town almost from the first week." While "The Sun Dial" was not a separate periodical, it became a part of the lore of American journalism and of American humor; it was in Marquis's column that much of his writing about "archy and mehitabel" appeared in the years during which Marquis conducted his column six days a week, 1913-22. The first time Don Marquis's byline appeared with "Notes and Comment" in *The New York Evening Sun* was Friday, April 4, 1913, p. 12 (editorial page). The following Monday, there first appeared Don Marquis, "The Sun Dial," *ibid.,* April 7, 1913, p. 12 (editorial page). The important and indeed essential connection of "The Sun Dial" with the tradition of the various *Dial* periodicals lies in the obvious symbolism of the name itself.

22.   Conway to Emerson (November 17, 1859); among the Emerson papers at the Houghton Library, Harvard University; used by permission of the Trustees of the Ralph Waldo Emerson Memorial Association and the Harvard College Library.

23.   I have used the terms of Monroe C. Beardsley, *Aesthetics* (New York 1958), pp. 288-93, in discussing the categories of symbol.

24.   Fredric J. Mosher, "Report of a Conversation with Herbert S. Browne," p. 6. My thanks go to Mr. Mosher for making his manuscript available to me.

25.   For two studies of *The Dial* (1920-29) of which Scofield Thayer (1920-26) and Marianne Moore (1926-29) were successively Editors and James Sibley Watson, Jr., was Publisher, see Nicholas Joost, *Scofield Thayer and The Dial* (Carbondale, Ill., 1964), and William Wasserstrom, *The Time of The Dial.* Also F. J. Hoffman, Charles Allen, and Carolyn Ulrich, *The Little Magazine,* 2d edn. (Princeton, N.J., 1947), pp. 196-206.

Footnotes to Chapter I

1.   For discussion of Browne's *Dial,* see references, p. 278, *n*1.

2.   "Francis Fisher Browne, 1843-1913," LIV (June 1, 1913), 437-41; "From Those Who Knew Him," pp. 441-43. Besides the signed statement of Howells, the only signed eulogies are a sonnet by Wallace Rice and two paragraphs by John Burroughs.

3.   *Autobiography,* I, 306, 312.

4.   See the *Supplement* to XIII (October 16, 1892) and the unsigned article by Waldo Ralph Browne (Fredric J. Mosher's ascription, *Chicago's "Saving Remnant,"* p. 170) , "Francis Fisher Browne," LIV (June 1, 1913), 437-43, for this material on the early years of *The Dial.* For *The Lakeside Monthly* and Browne, see the unsigned article by John M. Binckley (Fredric J. Mosher's ascription, *Chicago's "Saving Remnant,"* p. 486) and annotated by the Editor of *The Dial,* "The Life-Story of a

Magazine," *The Dial,* LIV (June 16, 1913), 489-92. The Editor was probably Waldo R. Browne.

5.   Hon. Charles F. Carpentier, Secretary of State, State of Illinois, to
      Nicholas Joost (December 13, 1957): "I have checked my files care-
fully, and, sorry as I am to say so, I find no record of any corporation in
this State bearing the name 'Chicago Dial' or 'The Dial' during the years
you mention (1880 to 1892). Apparently this magazine must have been
published by some individual or partnership rather than a corporation
or it could have been published by a corporation having an entirely different
name." For Browne's history of the founding of the Dial Company, see
"The Dial, 1880-1900," XXVIII (May 1, 1900), 327-28; see the new headpiece, XXXVIII (May 16, 1905), 343. According to Mott, *History of American Magazines,* III, 539, *n*1, after the sale of *The Dial* by A. C. McClurg
& Co. to Browne in 1892, the publisher was the Dial Co., 1892-1914; and
Mott is corroborated by Fredric J. Mosher to Nicholas Joost (January 3,
1958): "The Dial Company was incorporated in Illinois in the summer of
1892. The exact date I don't know, but I suppose it's a matter of record
in Illinois." According to Herbert S. Browne (in Mosher, "Report of a
Conversation with Herbert S. Browne," pp. 3-4), at the time of the
founding of Browne's Bookstore in 1907 the directors of the Dial Company were Francis F. Browne, Waldo R. Browne, Herbert S. Browne, John
Stuart Coonley, and Avery Coonley, and the "two largest stockholders in
The Dial Company were the Coonleys, and they were creditors of the Company to the extent of about $22,000" in 1912 when Browne's Bookstore
failed. Herbert S. Browne also remarked to Fredric Mosher (*ibid.,* p. 7)
that Edward Gilpin Johnson — an associate editor during the 1890's, along
with William Morton Payne — bought some shares of Dial Company stock
in 1892 and that after his sudden and inexplicable break with *The Dial,*
Johnson still held on to his stock, which Herbert S. Browne "later" purchased. By 1912 the legal ownership of this stock was not altogether that
of the Dial Company directors named by Herbert Browne, but rather of their
wives and female relatives. See "Statement of Ownership, Management, etc.,
of The Dial," LIII (November 1, 1912), 354, for the stockholders as given
in the text. With the issue of May 16, 1914, the Dial Company ceased
to exist, and the sole owner as well as the publisher of *The Dial* became
the Henry O. Shepard Company.

6.   Mott, *History of American Magazines,* III, 540; Ralph Fletcher Sey-
      mour, *Some Went This Way* (Chicago, 1945), p. 55.

7.   "The Dial's Score of Volumes," XX (June 16, 1896), 348.

8.   (1898) p. 159; (1908) p. 181. Ayer's *American Newspaper Annual*

and Directory never gave any figures for the Chicago *Dial's* circulation. See Fredric J. Mosher's unpublished "Report of a Conversation with Herbert S. Browne," p. 9, for Herbert S. Browne's statement regarding circulation figures for the Chicago *Dial.* The nearest Francis F. Browne ever came to revealing the growth of his circulation was in an announcement, "The Dial — Its Work and Influence," XVI (January 16, 1894), 64, and repeated in several subsequent issues; here the Editor wrote that "The circulation has rapidly increased, and its geographical distribution shows the national character and influence attained by the journal. . . . the new subscriptions (76) recently received in a single day came from *twenty-four States.* Encouraged by the success of 1893, the conductors of THE DIAL intend that 1894 shall witness even greater gains and progress." This growth, according to the announcement, marked a distinct epoch in the magazine's history, the first complete year since *The Dial* had become a "semi-monthly with enlarged scope and character." About the closest *The Dial* of Chicago ever seems to have come to admitting a total circulation figure was the indirect hint it gave by quoting from *Publisher's Weekly* (n.d.) in a small box that appeared a couple of times in XLIX (September 16, 1910; October 16, 1910), 204, 296: "In studying circulation remember quality is equally important with quantity. Ten thousand readers, and every one a tentative buyer of your books, is better than 100,000 scattered circulation where you 'may hit somebody.' Publishers can't afford 'general publicity.' " The quotation is especially apposite in its initial appearance, when it is juxtaposed with a one-column half-page advertisement for *The Dial* as an indispensable aid to librarians and libraries. That his father's *Dial* attained a consistent circulation of 10,000 one may doubt on the authority of Herbert S. Browne.

9.   "The New Dial," XIII (September 1, 1892), 127: "When THE DIAL was established in May, 1880, it was the intention of the editor and publishers to make of it a critical review of the first rank, which should occupy in this country a field somewhat similar to that occupied in England by such papers as 'The Athenaeum' and 'The Academy.' " In 1900 Browne evidently considered *The Dial* to be complementary to *The Atlantic;* see the combination offer of *The Dial* and *The Atlantic,* in the former, XXIX (October 16, 1900), 279. Presumably by 1900 Browne believed that *The Dial* had reached its plateau of circulation. In 1894, when he was campaigning to increase the circulation, he was much less discriminating, for an advertisement in XVII (December 1, 1894), 358, informs readers that "WHATEVER PERIODICAL you take next year, you will need THE DIAL also. Send your cash order through us, with *one dollar addi-*

tional, and we will mail you THE DIAL one year for the extra dollar. This is of course intended only for *new* subscribers." Despite its energetic campaign, *The Dial* was a rarity; see an advertisement, "For Sale at a Bargain," XVII (November 16, 1894), 305: "Any Public or Private Library not possessing a complete set of THE DIAL (May, 1880 to June 16, 1894) can secure the 16 volumes at a favorable price by addressing the undersigned, who has recently been able to pick up copies of the very rare issues of January, October, and November, 1882, and January, 1883 (numbers now *entirely out of print*), thus completing a file from the beginning. The set of 16 volumes, newly bound in THE DIAL's regular style, dark brown cloth, side and back lettered in gold, is offered for $40. Each volume has a full index. The publishers cannot supply another set at any price." Signed E. R. K., the advertisement was repeated in the following number of *The Dial* (December 1, 1894), p. 348 — the very issue in which, a few pages later, the editor made his offer to send *The Dial* and any other magazine for a year in return for a cash order to the desired periodical plus a dollar for *The Dial*. But Browne's struggle to attract subscribers, of the class that regularly read *The Athenaeum* and *The Atlantic,* did succeed, within limits: the magazine survived — and on the editor's terms.

10. *Chicago's "Saving Remnant,"* pp. 260-61.

11. Duffey, *The Chicago Renaissance in American Letters,* p. 67.

12. "The Dial's Contributors," Supplement, XIII (October 16, 1892), 6. See also "The Dial, 1880-1900," XXVIII (May 1, 1900), 327-28.

13. See, e. g., A. C. Miller, "Problems of Railway Finance" (review of S. F. Van Oss, *American Railroads as Investments* [New York, 1893]), XV (October 1, 1893), 185-89.

14. See XV (November 1, 1893), 278, for the first of these announcements; each number through XVI (June 1, 1894) carried this announcement in either the original or in a slightly abbreviated version. Also see Mosher, *Chicago's "Saving Remnant,"* pp. 134-35.

15. Hoffman *et. al., The Little Magazine,* p. 235. For other discussions of *The Chap-Book,* see Duffey, *The Chicago Renaissance in American Letters,* pp. 70-73; Herbert E. Fleming, "The Literary Interests of Chicago," *American Journal of Sociology,* XI (1905-06), 797-804; Sidney Kramer, *A History of Stone & Kimball and Herbert S. Stone & Company* (Chicago, 1940); Mott, *History of American Magazines,* IV, 450-52; etc. Also see *The Chap-Book,* IX (July 15, 1898), n.p.; this number, printed in lieu of a regular issue, consisted of an announcement stating that "Instead of the July 15th issue of THE CHAP-BOOK the subscribers to that magazine will receive the issue of The Dial for the same date." *The Dial,* XXV (July

16, 1898), 37, published an announcement related to *The Chap-Book*'s closing statement; it gave much the same account.

16.   *The Chap-Book,* VI (1896-97) , 192.

17.   But probably used in Paris, not in America. Cf. Loys Delteil, *H. de
       Toulouse-Lautrec* (Paris, 1920), Second Part, fig. 362, *Irish and Amer-
       ican Bar, Rue Royale* (*The Chap-Book*). Of this print of 1896, Delteil
       notes that "On lit en H.: THE CHAP, et au B.: BOOK. *Imp. CHAIX...*
       etc. puis: *Affiches Artistiques de LA PLUME, 31 rue Bonaparte, PARIS,"*
       and also that "Cette affiche a été exécutée par H. de Toulouse-Lautrec
       pour faire connaître la revue américaine: The Chap Book." Stone and Kim-
       ball and Herbert S. Stone and Company never advertised this poster in
       The Chap-Book with the "American Posters" advertised by the publishers in
       the magazine during 1895-97. See III (October 1, 1895), 406-09, for "A
       LIST OF SOME FRENCH POSTERS TO BE HAD OF STONE &
       KIMBALL CHICAGO," which itemizes 162 French posters, with prices as
       low as forty cents and as high as six dollars. This alphabetical list in-
       cludes, besides the *Chap-Book* poster twelve other works (Nos. 109-21)
       by Toulouse-Lautrec; otherwise his poster for the magazine remained un-
       publicized, yet he was "the only foreign artist selected to do work for *The
       Chap-Book"* (Sidney Kramer, *A History of Stone and Kimball,* pp. 34-35) .
       As an advertisement, the *Irish and American Bar* was the second state of
       the colored lithograph; in its first state it advertised nothing and carried
       no lettering.

18.   Mott, IV, 451; Mott's circulation figures averaging "less than twenty
       thousand" seem too generous.

19.   See II, 486; Sidney Kramer specifies a high circulation of 16,500
       for *The Chap-Book,* "According to a trade circular issued during
       the course of Volume V" (Kramer, *A History of Stone & Kimball,* p. 53,
       *n*39) ; this circular I have not seen. II (April 15, 1895), 486, is a full-page
       advertisement soliciting advertisers for the second year, which would
       begin "with the next issue"; "AVERAGE CIRCULATION FOR THREE
       MONTHS, 12,206" is Stone and Kimball's claim. Also they specify that
       "Advertisers may have access to our subscription list and circulation ac-
       counts at any time." But this figure is lower than the number of copies
       printed during at least some portion of the three-months period referred
       to; every number of II from December 1, 1894, through February 15, 1895,
       carried the announcement on the colophon page that *"The Edition of the
       CHAP-BOOK this week is 12,500 copies."* The *American Newspaper Direct-
       ory* does not list *The Chap-Book,* and Ayer's *American Newspaper Annual
       and Directory* (1898) gives circulation figures of 14,500 for 1897 only.

According to Herbert E. Fleming, who gained his information from Herbert Stone himself, the format changes Stone made "did not help sales and circulation" ("The Literary Interests of Chicago," *American Journal of Sociology*, XI [1905-06], 802); moreover, contradicting the explicit advertisement of Stone and Kimball, Fleming states that the magazine never made an effort to secure a list of annual subscribers, so that it could not improve its position as regards general adveertising (p. 803). *The Chap-Book's* famous posters sent to the news-stands, ran up sales "as high as 50,000 and averaged 20,000," but with the fashion for buying these posters, "prospective readers often competed in keen bidding for them without buying the periodical they were intended to advertise" (Fleming, p. 801). These posters were sold separately from copies of the magazine; for example, an advertising page for V (May 15, 1896), xiii, carried the Herbert S. Stone and Company's own advertisement for "American Posters," numbered from 1 to 12, plus four other unnumbered posters listed, with each poster selling for twenty-five cents, fifty cents, or a dollar. Again, VI (December 1, 1896), xviii, advertised a partly different list of fourteen numbered posters plus three unnumbered ones, at the same range of prices. Would it not be impossible to gauge sales of the magazine by sales of these posters? Dependence on unstable newsstand sales, then, largely destroyed *The Chap-Book;* it did not keep track of a dependable core of subscribers to rely on when Stone moved "toward getting the *Chap-Book* out of the class of ephemerals and into that of magazines firmly established on a sound business basis" (Fleming, p. 802). In his efforts to increase sales, Stone did offer a combination subscription of *The Bookman* ($1.50) and *The Chap-Book* ($1.00) for $2.00; when with IV (February 15, 1896) the subscription became $2.00, this combination was raised to $3.25, for *The Bookman* also now cost $2.00 annually. And through advertisements in *The Chap-Book,* from the issue for V (August 1, 1896) to that for V (October 1, 1896), Herbert S. Stone and Company offered "to any person securing two hundred and fifty (250) new subscribers to THE CHAP-BOOK, free tuition for one year" at Harvard, Yale, Princeton, Columbia, Cornell, University of Pennsylvania, University of Michigan, University of Chicago, or Leland Stanford University "and one hundred ($100.00) dollars in cash"; for 150 new subscribers the energetic and presumably youthful salesman was offered "free tuition as above." Those less successful were offered a commission of twenty-five percent of each subscription. These three offers expired by January 1, 1897. None of the devices employed seems to have worked effectually.

20. Fredric J. Mosher has treated the fiasco of Browne's Bookstore at

length in his dissertation, pp. 137-44. My brief account is largely based on Mosher's discussion, and on his "Report of a Conversation with Herbert S. Browne," pp. 3-7, further elaborated in Mosher to Nicholas Joost (January 3, 1958). Grant Carpenter Mason, *Frank Lloyd Wright to 1910* (New York, 1958), p. 167, and fig. 110, gives some account of Browne's Bookstore.

21.   Duffey, p. 66.

22.   *Ibid.*, p. 69.

23.   "Literary Cosmopolitanism," XXXIII (October 1, 1902), 204.

24.   "Recent Fiction," XX (February 1, 1896), 80.

25.   "Recent Fiction," XX (June 1, 1896), 336.

26.   *My Thirty Years' War* (New York, 1930), pp. 27-31.

Footnotes to Chapter II

1.   Ralph Fletcher Seymour, *Some Went This Way* (Chicago, 1945), pp. 49-50. While Seymour's accuracy is intermittent at best, his account is useful if only because it is based on his own experience; in quoting him, I have silently corrected the spelling and the punctuation in an effort to avoid the constant use of *sic*. See the obituary of Seymour, *The Prairie School*, III (First Quarter, 1966), 26.

2.   *Ibid.*, pp. 54-55.

3.   LV (December 16, 1913), 511-12. Attributed to Payne by Frederick J. Mosher, *Chicago's "Saving Remnant,"* p. 483.

4.   Mosher, "Report of a Conversation with Herbert S. Browne," pp. 2, 5. As both Herbert and Waldo Browne edited Mr. Mosher's transcript, it has unique authority regarding "the somewhat complicated story of what happened to The Dial after the death of Francis Fisher Browne on May 11, 1913" (p. 1). Also see Mosher, *Chicago's "Saving Remnant,"* pp. 229-35, for a discussion of the first sale of *The Dial.*

5.   According to "Statement of Ownership, Management, Circulation, etc., of The Dial," LVI (April 16, 1914), 359, stockholders of the Dial Co. were the Estate of Francis F. Browne, Waldo R. Browne, Mrs. Avery Coonley, Mrs. Sarah F. Gane, W. M. Payne, and Mrs. Coonley Ward. The new headpiece for LVI (May 16, 1914) announced the Henry O. Shepard Co. as the new publisher; that this company also became sole owner

one gleans from "Statement of Ownership, Management, Circulation, etc., of The Dial," LVIII (April 1, 1915), 314, which lists as "Owners — Trustees of the Estate of Henry O. Shepard, Deceased." Mosher, "Report of a Conversation with Herbert S. Browne," p. 2, says that the Henry O. Shepard Company was controlled by the founder's widow and daughter.

6.   See George A. Test, "Francis Hackett: Literary Rebel without Portfolio," *Midcontinent American Studies Journal*, V (Fall 1964, 24-37; Bernard Duffey, *The Chicago Renaissance in American Letters* (East Lansing, Mich., 1954), 172-82; G. Thomas Tanselle, "Floyd Dell in the 'Friday Literary Review,'" *Papers of the Bibliographical Society of America*, LVII (1963), 371-76; G. Thomas Tanselle, "The 'Friday Literary Review' and the Chicago Renaissance," *Journalism Quarterly*, XXXVIII (Summer 1961), 332-36. William J. Burke and Will D. Howe, *American Authors and Books*, rev. edn., ed. Irving R. Weiss (New York, 1962), p. 122, contains data pertaining to Lucian Cary.

7.   See J. J. Healy, *"The Dial and the Revolution in Poetry: 1912-1917,"* *"Bulletin of the British Association for American Studies,* New Series, Number 10 (June 1965), pp. 48-60. Healy misdates the appearance of the piece on Lindsay and completely overlooks Cary's editorship and, alas, generally misinterprets the evidence. For the background of the present chapter, I have found three general studies both complementary and indispensable: Dale Kramer, *Chicago Renaissance* (New York, 1966); Bernard Duffey, *The Chicago Renaissance in American Letters,* previously referred to; and Hugh D. Duncan, *The Rise of Chicago as a Literary Center from 1885 to 1920* (Totowa, N. J., 1964). My paper entitled *"The Dial* in Transition, the End of the Browne Family's Control, 1913-1916," *Journal of the Illinois State Historical Society,* LIX (Autumn 1966), 272-88, passes over the problems raised by Lucian Cary's editorship of *The Dial.*

Footnotes to Chapter III

1.   Mosher, "Report of a Conversation with Herbert S. Browne," p. 5; and Waldo R. Browne to William Morton Payne (February 1 [1915]), from the Francis Fisher Browne Collections, Newberry Library, Chicago; this and Browne's letters to Payne of February 23, August 20, and October 6, 1915, are used by the courtesy of the Newberry Library, Chicago.

See colophon, LX (June 8, 1916), 563, listing the Editor and his Associate and giving Herbert S. Browne as President of the Dial Company and Paul G. Smith as Secretary. Contrary to Frank Luther Mott, *History of American Magazines* (Cambridge, Mass., 1938), III, 541, Charles Leonard Moore was not listed as an Associate on *The Dial* in these years, although he was a contributor of importance and frequency.

2.   Browne to Payne (February 1 [1915]), Browne Collection, courtesy of the Newberry Library.

3.   Browne to Payne (February 23 [1915]), Browne Collection, courtesy of the Newberry Library.

4.   Browne to Payne (February 1 [1915]).

5.   Browne to Payne (August 20, 1915), Browne Collection, courtesy of the Newberry Library.

6.   Browne to Payne (October 6, 1915), Browne Collection, courtesy of the Newberry Library.

7.   "Cosmic Systems and Philosophical Imagination" (rev. Edwin B. Holt's *The Concept of Consciousness*), LX (February 3, 1916), 120-21.

8.   Waldo R. Browne to Payne (February 23, 1915).

9.   See Raymond M. Alden, "Recent Poetry," LIX (June 24, 1915), 26-30; LIX (September 30, 1915), 271-76; LX (January 6, 1916), 24-30; LX (March 30, 1916), 330-35; and LXI (July 15, 1916), 59-65.

10.   For a full discussion of the impact of the publication of *Spoon River Anthology*, see Duffey, "Edgar Lee Masters: The Advent of Liberation," Ch. IX of *The Chicago Renaissance in American Letters*, pp. 143-70; and Max Putzel, "Crossing Spoon River," Ch. XVII of *The Man in the Mirror* (Cambridge, Mass., 1963), pp. 193-216; the next chapter, "The War of the Imagists and Their Antagonists," pp. 217-25, discusses much of the struggle with which my present chapter is concerned.

11.   For an account of the Monroe-Lowell relationship, see S. Foster Damon, *Amy Lowell* (Boston, 1935), pp. 182 ff; the letter protesting the attitude of *Poetry* was written by Amy Lowell in consequence of a visit by Harriet Monroe to Miss Lowell in the week of April 4, 1916, Damon, pp. 356-57.

12.   See J. J. Healy, "*The Dial* and the Revolution in Poetry: 1912-1917; A Study in Controversy," *Bulletin of the British Association for American Studies*, n. s., No. 10 (June 1965), pp. 48-60; quoted here, p. 53; pp. 53-56 are given to a discussion of the controversy over "Cousin Nancy." Healy must be used with care; he fails entirely to distinguish the basic shifts in editorial policy that occurred in the years 1913-16, and for that

reason I have explored the question of just what *The Dial* did expound editorially as well as what it did publish.

13. This drawn-out correspondence began as a result of Hervey's letter in "Communications," headed "Bryant and the New Poetry," LIX (August 15, 1915), 92-93. It continued for the rest of the year, and in "Communications," LX (January 6, 1916), 16, Miss Monroe's letter was hopefully headed "The Last of the Bryant Controversy." See also: LIX (October 14, 1915), 314-15; LIX (October 28, 1915), 361-63; LIX (November 28, 1915), 479-80; LIX (December 9, 1915), 555-57.

14. There is no standard biography of Arthur Davison Ficke. For the most notorious event of his career, see William Jay Smith, *The Spectra Hoax*, (Middletown, Conn., 1961), which deals with the publication in 1916 of the Spectrist poems of Emanuel Morgan and Anne Knish, the pen names of, respectively, Witter Bynner and Ficke; this will be discussed in the next chapter. Ficke's *Chats on Japanese Prints* (he was a well-known collector) was reviewed by Frederick W. Gookin, "The Fascination of Japanese Prints," LIX (October 28, 1915), 373-76; but a reading of Gookin's review fails to show that it has a connection with the Imagist controversy in *The Dial*.

15. See Putzel's discussion of the Loomis-Irwin correspondence, pp. 212, 225. See "Communications," LX (March 30, 1916), 325; LX (April 27, 1916), 415; LX (May 25, 1916), 498; and LXI (June 22, 1916), 14.

16. "A Word on 'the Genteel Critic,'" LIX (October 28, (1915), 303-05. Followed by Boynton's "Some American Novelists and the Lame Art," LIX (December 9, 1915), 548-49.

17. *Artist and Public* (New York, 1914), pp. 97-98. Showerman's reference is to Cox's earlier *The Classic Point of View* (New York, 1911).

18. See advertisements for *Books of the Month*, in LVII (September 16, 1914), 178; LVII (November 16, 1914), 400; LIX (September 2, 1915), 130; LIX (September 30, 1915), 294; LIX (November 11, 1915), 438.

19. Seymour, p. 55.

20. "Holiday Publications," LIX (November 25, December 9, and December 23, 1915), 497-506, (to which is appended a bibliography of "The Season's Books for the Young," 507-10), 575-80, 618-23. See Joseph Pennell, "Four Etchings," *The Dial*, LXXVII (December 1924), ff. 474; Maxim Gorki, "Reminiscences of Leonid Andreyev," tr. S. S. Koteliansky and Katherine Mansfield, *The Dial*, LXXVI (June 1924), 481-92, LXXVII (July 1924), 31-43, 105-20, and "Notes on Tolstoy and Other Recollections," tr. William A. Drake and Max Stetsky, LXXVIII (February 1925), 96-106.

21. "Announcements of Fall Books," LIX (September 16, 1915), 228;

the list extends to p. 243 of this issue, and the next issue (September 30, 1915), pp. 284-88, listed "Books for School and College" and "Books for the Young."

22.   LIX (September 2, 1915), 165. See, e. g. , "List of New Books," LIX (September 16, 1915) , 243-44, and "Topics in Leading Periodicals," LIX (November 11, 1915) , 430; the former appeared with each issue, the latter once a month.

23.   Seymour, pp. 55-56.

24.   Besides Seymour's memoir, see Hoffman, *The Little Magazine*, p. 380, for an identification of *Art* and *The Trimmed Lamp*. Laird Bell, a stockholder of the period 1916-18, had no recollections and "could not recall anything about his dealings with the magazine," according to Harley A. Stephenson to this author (December 4, 1957). Herbert Browne's reminiscence is in Fredric Mosher's unpublished "Report of a Conversation with Herbert S. Browne," p. 6. The stockholders of the newly formed Dial Publishing Company are listed in the "Statement of the Ownership, Management, Circulation, Etc., Required by the Act of Congress of August 24, 1912," LXI (October 5, 1916), 287. Graham Aldis died in April 1966, and William H. Doughty wrote to this author (June 24, 1966) that no member of the Aldis family nor any of his surviving contemporaries could be of assistance in determining the part played by Mary Aldis in establishing *The Dial* of Martyn Johnson. For a detailed account of *The Trimmed Lamp*, see my forthcoming study *Howard Vincent O'Brien, Art, and the Trimmed Lamp: A Little Magazine of the Chicago Renascence, 1912-16*. For the obituary of Waldo R. Browne, see the *New York Times*, January 27, 1954, p. 27, col. 1.

Footnotes to Chapter IV

1.   [Anonymous,] "An Announcement," LXII (January 25, 1917), 45-46.

2.   Besides the obvious bibliographical tools, this account of Johnson is based chiefly on his obituary: "Martyn Johnson, / Ex-Publisher Dies // Former Owner of The Dial / Its Fortnightly Form — Once / Aide to Envoy of Norway," the *New York Times*, Friday, January 26, 1934, p. 17, col. 4. For one of his magazine articles see "A Day with the Circus," *The World To-Day*, XIX (1910), 709-15 (ill.). For his play, see "Mr. and

Mrs. P. Roe," *Drama*, XIII (December 1922), 92-95. For other references used, see Nicholas Joost, *Scofield Thayer and The Dial*, p. 271, *n*1.

3.   LXI (September 21, 1916), 236. "Notes and News," p. 198, of the issue, directed attention to this advertisement: "Further particulars regarding the future plans of THE DIAL may be found on page 236 among the advertisements."

4.   Lionello Venturi, *Art Criticism Now* (Baltimore, 1941), pp. 28-33, summarizes this development but not with direct reference to *The Dial*.

5.   Stearns, *The Street I Know* (New York, 1935), pp. 154-55.

6.   LXIII (December 20, 1917), 650.

7.   The most detailed account of the Spectra hoax is by William J. Smith, *The Spectra Hoax* (Middletown, Conn., 1961). Smith does not note either Bynner's review of Robert W. Service's *Rhymes of a Red Cross Man* or the exposure of the Spectra hoax by "Casual Comment" in *The Dial*. Max Putzel, *The Man in the Mirror: William Marion Reedy and His Magazine* (Cambridge, Mass., 1963), devotees Ch. XIX, pp. 226-42, to a discussion of the Spectra hoax and cites the exposure in "Casual Comment," p. 239. Also see S. Foster Damon, *Amy Lowell*, pp. 454-55.

8.   Claude Bragdon, *More Lives than One* (New York, 1938), pp. 274-76. James Sibley Watson, Jr., to Nicholas Joost (June 9, 1966), gives the details of his introduction to *The Dial* in 1916-17. William Wasserstrom, *The Time of the Dial*, p. 64 and p. 169 *n*10, mentions Watson's years at Groton. Portraits of him are in Alyse Gregory's *The Day Is Gone* (New York, 1948), pp. 181-213 *passim*; Marianne Moore's *"The Dial*: A Retrospect," *Predilections* (New York, 1955), pp. 103-04; Llewelyn Powys's *The Verdict of Bridlegoose* (London, 1927), pp. 114-16. See also the intimate portrait of Dr. and Mrs. Watson and her family, the Lasells and the Whitins, of Whitinsville, Mass., a mill town just south of Worcester: Virgil Thompson, *Virgil Thompson* (New York, 1966), pp. 72, 127-42, and *passim*. For a portrait of Elaine Orr Thayer, Scofield Thayer's bride in 1916, see John Dos Passos, *The Best of Times* (New York, 1966), pp. 82-85, 131-32.

9.   Ivan Opffer, "Gilbert Cannan" and "Gilbert Cannan after Reading the Following Article [Evelyn Scott's essay]," LXVIII (February 1920), ff. 168; Evelyn Scott, "Gilbert Cannan: Inquisitor," *ibid.*, 173-86; and Gilbert Cannan, "The Authoress of The Way of All Flesh" (review of Henry Esting Jones, *Samuel Butler: A Memoir*), *ibid.*, 248-52.

10.   For Moore's first "Conversation" published in *The Dial*, see "An Imaginary Conversation," LXV (October 5 and 19, November 2, 1918), 253-56, 297-302, 254-61. See also "A Second Imaginary Conversation:

Gosse and Moore," LXVI (March 22, April 5 and 19, 1919), 287-92, 347-54, 394-401. In *The Dial* in the early 1920's, George Moore published such pieces as "How Héloïse Passed the Winter 1117," LXIX (November 1920), 448-54, published admittedly as a selection from the soon-to-be-published *Abélard and Héloïse*; an essay, "The Decline of the Drama," LXX (January 1921), 1-11; and a poem, "La Réponse de George Moore," LXXI (July 1921), 62. Also see Marianne Moore, "A Portrait of George Moore" (rev. John Freeman, *A Portrait of George Moore in A Study of His Work* [New York, 1922]), LXXIII (December 1922), 664-68; "Histrionic Seclusion" (rev. *Conversations in Ebury Street* [New York, 1924]), LXXVIII (March 1925), 225-27.

11.   See Jerome Mellquist and Lucie Wiese, eds., *Paul Rosenfeld: Voyager in the Arts* (New York, 1947), a memorial volume from which is taken Edmund Wilson's "Paul Rosenfeld: Three Phases," *Classics and Commercials* (New York, 1950), pp. 503-19; see also *ibid.*, "Imaginary Dialogues. I. The Poet's Return: Mr. Paul Rosenfeld and Mr. Matthew Josephson," *The Shores of Light* (New York, 1952), pp. 125-40; "The All-Star Literary Vaudeville," *ibid.*, p. 236; Van Wyck Brooks, *The Days of the Phoenix* (New York, 1957), pp. 7-11; Llewelyn Powys, *The Verdict of Bridlegoose*, pp. 94-97; etc.

12.   For "Trans-national America," see *The Atlantic Monthly*, CXVIII (July 1916), 86-97, and collected posthumously in Randolph Bourne, *The History of a Literary Radical*, ed. Van Wyck Brooks, reprint edn. (New York, 1956), pp. 260-84.

13.   Titles of these reviews and of Bourne's two essays in *The Dial* are listed in Michael D. True, "The Achievement of an American Literary Radical: A Bibliography of the Writings of Randolph Silliman Bourne (1886-1918)," *Bulletin of the New York Public Library*, LXIX (October 1965), 523-36. Also see Michael D. True, "The Social and Literary Criticism of Randolph Bourne: A Study of His Development as a Writer," *Dissertation Abstracts*, XXV (1964), 6639, a brief summary of True's unpublished dissertation (at Duke University). See True's dissertation, pp. 158-59, for mention of Bourne's "guides." Christopher Lasch, *The New Radicalism in America (1889-1963)* (New York, 1965), discusses Randolph Bourne as a principal figure, pp. 74-103, and also discusses the liberals and the first World War, pp. 181-224. I have used Lasch, pp. 77-81, especially Bourne's letter to Elizabeth Shepley Sergeant (June 9, 1915).

14.   See James Oppenheim, "The Story of The Seven Arts," *American Mercury*, IX (1930), 156-64; Van Wyck Brooks, *The Days of the Phoenix* (New York, 1957), pp. 17-36; *Paul Rosenfeld: Voyager in the Arts, passim.* Hoffman, *The Little Magazine*, pp. 86-92, sketches its history.

15. Waldo Frank to John Moreau, interview, October 31, 1963; in John
Moreau, *Randolph Bourne: Legend and Reality* AWashington, D. C.,
1966), pp. 163-64, 222 *n*6. Among the Dial papers available to me occurs
no such reference to Thayer and *The Seven Arts.*

Footnotes to Chapter V

1. Stearns, *The Street I Know,* p. 145.
2. Robert Morss Lovett, "George Bernard Donlin," *The Dial,* LXIX
   (August 1920), 150.
3. "Contributors," LXVI (January 11, 1919), 54.
4. The ensuing account of Stearns's editorship is based on his account
   in *The Street I Know,* pp. 145-80 *passim,* with duly noted references
   to other sources.
5. *Ibid.,* pp. 156-57.
6. *Ibid.,* p. 180.
7. While this information about Scofield Thayer is based on information in the Dial papers — most importantly, Scofield Thayer to Harold
   Evans (December 24, 1920) — it also is based on scattered hints in various
   memoirs of the period and on conversations with Mr. Hermann P. Riccius
   of Worcester, Mass. See also Nicholas Joost, "Report of a Conversation
   with Henry McBride, March 11, 1958." No accurate record of Scofield
   Thayer's life has ever been published.
8. Stearns, p. 152.
9. Reference here is to the correspondence between Thayer and Harold
   Evans (December 9, 15, 17, 24, and 30, 1920, and January 3. 1921).
   In this correspondence the Editor gave his version of the negotiations for the
   purchase of *The Dial* by Watson and himself, and these letters remain the
   fullest first-hand contemporary account. They are supplemented by a
   typed *Memorandum of a Conference concerning the Investments of Mr.
   Thayer and Mr. Watson in The Dial* (May 24, 1920), 3 pp. plus charts.
   The Thayer-Evans correspondence has peculiar significance: Harold Evans
   wrote to the Editor in reply to a subscription-soliciting circular from *The
   Dial* and said that he could not under any circumstances subscribe to *The
   Dial* because of certain apparently well-grounded allegations about the
   Editor and his purchase of *The Dial* that had been repeated to him. Thayer

proceeded to answer Evans point by point and in so doing gave a closely circumstantial account of his affiliation with *The Dial*. Evans had written of the holders of some notes mortgaging as it were *The Dial* stock that their "interest seemed to be to cut short the existence of a liberal magazine such as *The Dial* was under Mr. Johnson's management" (Dec. 17, 1920). Thayer replied (Dec. 24, 1920): "As to my desiring to cut short the existence of a liberal magazine, that is the greatest rot I have ever heard. I gave bail for one of the staff of the Masses during the war" — could this have been Merrill Rogers? — "and most of my friends are socialists. I have always voted the socialist ticket. My disagreement with Mr. Johnson's DIAL was based merely on what I considered Mr. Johnson's unfairness to myself, [he] having gotten my money under a certain understanding and having spent it in a different way." Evans apologized (January 3, 1920) for a criticism that, he acknowledged, was perfectly sincere on his part but that fortunately was not founded on fact. For the meeting of Thayer with Bourne, the evidence is Merrill Rogers' unpublished memorandum, "Concerning Randolph Bourne" (December 24, 1963), used by the courtesy of the Columbia University Library and the donor, John A. Moreau. Otherwise, this account is based on Thayer's correspondence, as cited in this note. See the *New York Times*, Wednesday, November 11, 1964, p. 43, for the obituary notice of Merrill Rogers; its date (1916) given for Rogers' appointment as Business Manager of *The Dial* is inaccurate. For some reason, Rogers was never listed in *The Dial* as its Business Manager, although when Johnson held the same post, he listed himself. For a contemporary account of the indictment of the staff of *The Masses*, see "*The Masses* Staff under Arrest," *The Survey*, XXXIX (November 24, 1917), 207; besides Merrill Rogers, those indicted were Max Eastman, Floyd Dell, John Reed, Josephine Bell, Henry J. Glintenkamp, and Arthur (the famous "Art") Young. The bail for Rogers was fixed at $3,000 and was "promptly paid," reported *The Survey*.

10.   As quoted in Charles Norman, *E. E. Cummings, The Magic-Maker* (New York, 1959), p. 160.

11.   LXV (June 20, 1918), 28; ms in the Dial papers.

12.   LXV (July 18,1918), 73-74; ms. in the Dial papers.

13.   LXV (September 5, 1918), 170-71; ms. in the Dial papers.

14.   LXIV (June 6, 1918), 536-38; ms. in the Dial papers.

15.   The Pléiade edition of Molière, *Oeuvres Complètes*, ed. Maurice Rat (Paris, 1956), I, 802-04. For the quotation from Stearns, see *The Street I Know*, p. 152; for the quotation from Powys, see his memoir, p. 115; for the quotations from Alyse Gregory, see *The Day is Gone*, (New York,

1948) pp. 178, 209; for the quotation from Margaret Anderson, see her memoir, pp. 188-89.

16. "Passionate Puppets" LXV (June 20, 1918), 22-23; ms. in the Dial papers.

17. LXV (July 18, 1918), 61-63; ms. in the Dial papers.

18. LXV (August 15, 1918), 117-18; ms in the Dial papers.

19. "James Joyce," LXV (September 19, 1918), 200-03; ms. in the Dial papers.

20. This account has been based on the following authorities. B. W. Huebsch to James Joyce (10 June 1919), *Letters of James Joyce,* ed. Stuart Gilbert (New York, 1957), p. 125. Scofield Thayer to James Joyce (October 1920). Mary Colum, *Life and the Dream* (Garden City, N. Y., 1947), pp. 383-84. See the same episode retold in Padraic and Mary Colum, *Our Friend James Joyce* (New York, 1958), pp. 110, 114.

21. "Compton Mackenzie," LXV (November 30, 1918), 473-79; ms. in the Dial papers.

22. "Mr. Mackenzie's Jest" (rev. Compton Mackenzie, *Poor Relations* [New York, 1920]), LXVIII (May 1920), 611-13; "Briefer Mention" (rev. Compton Mackenzie, *The Vanity Girl* [New York, 1920]), LXX (January 1921), 107.

23. John Dewey's essays in *The New Republic,* here quoted and summarized, were reprinted in his *Characters and Events,* ed. Joseph Ratner, 2 vols. (New York, 1929): "Conscience and Compulsion," I, 576-80; "The Future of Pacificism," I, 581-86; and "What America Will Fight For" (collected as "America and War"), I, 561-65. See Randolph Bourne, *The History of a Literary Radical,* ed. Van Wyck Brooks (New York, 1920); I have used the reprint edn. (New York, 1956) for quotation and summary: "The War and the Intellectuals," pp. 205-22; and "Conscience and Intelligence in War," pp. 197-204.

24. For the relation of Eliot, Bourne, and Thayer, I am indebted to the unpublished dissertation of Michael D. True, "The Social and Literary Criticism of Randolph Bourne: A Study of His Development as a Writer" (Duke University, 1964), pp. 152-53 *n*l. For the quotation from Eliot, see "The Perfect Critic," *The Sacred Wood* (New York, 1921), p. 4; the essay was first published in *The Athenaeum,* July 9 and 23, 1920, pp. 40-41, 102-04. Mr. True has also suggested that the Thayer family had known Bourne for some time before his connection with *The Dial*; his friends the Gerald Thayers (whom he met abroad in 1913-14) visited friends in Worcester during the war years. Both the Gerald Thayers and the Abbott Thayers were hospitable to Bourne in Dublin, N.H., in the

summer of 1915. For the letter by Randolph Bourne to Elizabeth Shepley
Sergeant (October 10, 1915), see *The World of Randolph Bourne,* ed.
Lillian Schlissel (New York, 1965), p. 309. For Brooks's comments on
Bourne and the first World War, see *Days of the Phoenix,* pp. 19-36 (the
quotation from Brooks, p. 34).
25.   See Alyse Gregory, *The Day Is Gone,* pp. 136, 175-79, for her memoir
         of the meeting with Thayer; this account is supplemented by letters
of Alyse Gregory to Nicholas Joost during the course of 1965.
26.   *Ibid.,* pp. 136, 153, 165-67. The letters of Bourne to Alyse Gregory
         (July 1918) and to Bourne from Paul Rosenfeld (Oct. 7, 1918) are
in the Bourne Collection at Columbia University, donated by Mrs. Agnes
de Lima in 1955, and used with the permission of the Director of Libraries,
Columbia University. I have used the Bourne Collection as a further check
on the accuracy of my present account as well as of published sources I
have used. Paul Rosenfeld's unpublished letter is quoted by permission of
his literary executor, Mrs. Edna Bryner Schwab. See *The World of Randolph Bourne,* pp. 324-25, for Bourne's letters of October 12 and November
4, 1918, to his mother. Mrs. Agnes de Lima asked Vernon Sternberg in a
letter dated February 3, 1965, that the locale of the death of Randolph
Bourne (placed in *Scofield Thayer and the Dial,* p. 11, as Paul Rosenfeld's
apartment) be given correctly in a future account. See Van Wyck Brooks,
"Randolph Bourne," *Fenollosa and His Circle* (New York, 1962), pp. 318-
21, for the Bourne-Cornell relationship and Bourne's death. Moreau, pp.
198, 227 *n*46, says that Bourne's earnings for January 1 to November 2,
1918, amounted to only $679.11, on the evidence of Bourne's "Bibliography"
notebook in Box 4 of the Bourne Papers at Columbia University. According to Bourne himself (to his mother, November 4, 1918), he was paid by
The Dial just as though he were one of the contributing editors; he was
not desperate for funds.

Footnotes to Chapter VI

1.   Robert Morss Lovett, *All Our Years* (New York, 1948), pp. 151-56.
        Also Stearns, pp. 172-75, for his opinion of the "Reconstruction" *Dial.*
2.   For the record, here are the changes, as they occur. *The Dial,* LXV
         (September 19, 1918) : George Bernard Donlin, Editor; Harold E.

Stearns, Associate; Conrad Aiken, Randolph Bourne, Robert Dell, Van Wyck Brooks, Padraic Colum, Henry B. Fuller, H. M. Kallen, Clarence Britten, and Scofield Thayer, Contributing Editors; Martyn Johnson, President, the Dial Publishing Company; Willard C. Kitchel, Secretary-Treasurer. LXV (October 5, 1918): Clarence Britten, George Donlin, Harold Stearns, and Scofield Thayer (Editors, presumably) ; John Dewey, Thorstein Veblen, Helen Marot, "In Charge of the Reconstruction Program"; on the publisher's staff Scofield Thayer replaces Willard C. Kitchel as Secretary-Treasurer. "Statement of the Ownership, etc." LXV (October 19, 1918), 327, lists as editors Britten, Stearns, Thayer, and Donlin; as Dial stockholders Frederick Lynch, W. C. Kitchel, Martyn Johnson, Scofield Thayer, Agnes Brown Leach, Henry Goddard Leach, and Marion C. Ingersoll; and Martyn Johnson as publisher and business manager. "Statement of Ownership, etc.," LXV (November 16, 1918), 439, is identical with the preceding statement except that it lists W. C. Kitchel as "Agent." "Contributors," LXV (December 14, 1918), 578, publicized the withdrawal of Scofield Thayer as an editor and as Secretary-Treasurer of the Dial Publishing Company: "THE DIAL announces the resignation of Mr. Scofield Thayer as Associate Editor." "Contributors," LXVI (January 11, 1919), 54, announced the editorship of Robert Morss Lovett, and George Donlin's demotion to associate editor. "Statement of the Ownership, etc.," LXVI (April 19, 1919) , 437, makes only one change in the statement given in the issue of November 16, 1918, substituting Robert Morss Lovett fer Editor in place of Britten, Stearns, Thayer, and Donlin. LXVII (July 12, 1919), 29, omitted the previously used editorial masthead and placed in a small box in the lower right corner as "EDITORS" John Dewey, Martyn Johnson, Robert Morss Lovett, Helen Marot, and Thorstein Veblen, and Clarence Britten as Associate; "Contributors," p. 30, noted that "Geroid Robinson, . . . has recently joined the staff of THE DIAL," but Robinson's name was not yet placed in the editorial box. "Casual Comment," LXVII (September 6, 1919), 208, announced "the resignation of John Dewey from the editorial board. . . . Lewis Mumford and Geroid Robinson join the editorial staff," and Oswald W. Knauth was appointed as Secretary-Treasurer of the Dial Publishing Company. A box just beneath this announcement listed as Editors Martyn Johnson, Robert Morss Lovett, Helen Marot, and Thorstein Veblen; as Associates Clarence Britten, Lewis Mumford, and Geroid Robinson; and as Secretary-Treasurer Oswald W. Knauth. The next issue, for September 20, 1919, listed Knauth in the editorial box as an editor instead of as Secretary-Treasurer. "Statement of the Ownership, etc.," LXVII (October 18, 1919), 357, listed the officers of the magazine as Martyn

Johnson, Publisher; Martyn Johnson, Oswald W. Knauth, Robert Morss
Lovett, Helen Marot, and Thorstein Veblen, Editors; and Business Manager, Oswald W. Knauth. The same statement added Gustave K. Carus
to the Dial stockholders. Except for Johnson, these stockholders remained
unchanged through the subsequent history of *The Dial*. And the statement listed as bondholders and mortgagees holding securities of the Dial
Publishing Company Scofield Thayer, Martyn Johnson, Edward F. Sanderson, Willard C. Kitchel, and Helen Marot. Finally "Casual Comment,"
LXVII (November 29, 1919), 486, "announces the resignation of Martyn
Johnson, Oswald W. Knauth, and Helen Marot from The Dial Publishing Company and from the editorial staff; and of Robert Morss Lovett,
Thorstein Veblen, Lewis Mumford, and Geroid Robinson from the editorial
staff. J. S. Watson, Jr., has been elected President, and Scofield Thayer,
Secretary-Treasurer of The Dial Publishing Company. With this issue
Scofield Thayer becomes Editor, and Stewart Mitchell Managing Editor,
of the magazine." In the editorial box at the bottom of the same page,
Clarence Britten was listed as Associate, beneath Thayer and Mitchell.

3.   *Creative Impulse in Industry* (New York, 1918), pp. xix, xxi.
4.   Joseph Dorfman, *Thorstein Veblen and His America* (New York,
       1934), pp. 379, 410, gives the preliminary account. Dorfman deals
with Veblen's wartime experiences, pp. 356 ff., and with his writing for
The Dial in great detail, pp. 411-49; I have pretty consistently followed
Dorfman's interpretations and have used his summaries as being authorita-
tive.
5.   In the following passage on Veblen and *The Dial*, the authority relied
       on is Dorfman. Other sources used will be mentioned in these notes.
6.   Lovett, p. 152, gives the account of his relations with Veblen. Dorf-
       man, p. 395, mentions Veblen's job offer with the War Labor Board.
7.   I have used the expanded version of "Prof. Veblen and the Cow"
       that appeared as "Professor Veblen," *Prejudices: First Series* (New
York, 1919), pp. 59-82. See H. L. Mencken ed., *A Mencken Chrestomathy*
(New York, 1949), p. 265, for the editorial note prefacing his reprint of
"Professor Veblen."
8.   *The Innocents at Cedro* (New York, 1944), pp. 150-51. For Dewey's
       stay in the Orient, see John Dewey and Alice Chapman Dewey,
Letters from China and Japan, ed. Evelyn Dewey (New York, 1920).
9.   Lovett's signed contributions not named in the text were "The
       American Soldier" (rev. Frederick Palmer, *America in France* [New
York, 1918] and Floyd Gibbons, *And They Thought We Wouldn't Fight*
[New York, 1918]), LXVI (January 11, 1919), 33-35; "Cobden, the Inter-

nationalist" (rev. J. A. Hobson, *Richard Cobden* [New York, 1919]), LXVI (April 19, 1919), 399-401: "A Parasitic Novel" (rev. Sir Harry Johnston, *The Gay-Dombeys* [New York, 1919]), LXVI (June 28, 1919), 641-42.

10. Charles Norman, *The Magic-Maker, E. E. Cummings*, p. 150. Details of the purchase of *The Dial* are to be found in Nicholas Joost, *Scofield Thayer and The Dial*, pp. 10-20. For Stearns's own comments on *Civilization in the United States*, see *The Street I Know*, pp. 191-206.

11. *Amy Lowell*, p. 519.

Footnotes to Chapter *VII*

1. *The Man in the Mirror* (Cambridge, Mass., 1963), p. 202.

2. *My Thirty Years' War* (New York, 1930), p. 212; references to the history of *The Little Review* occur throughout this memoir; Miss Anderson's later life in Europe, with Georgette Leblanc, is the subject of Margaret Anderson, *The Fiery Fountains* (New York, 1951). *The Little Review* is the subject of an unpublished doctoral dissertation by Jackson R. Bryer, " 'A Trial-Track for Racers': Margaret Anderson and the *Little Review*" (University of Wisconsin, 1965); I have generally relied on Bryer for accuracy without using his material. Bryer's excellent and detailed essay on the trial of Misses Anderson and Heap — "Joyce, *Ulysses*, and the *Little Review*," *South Atlantic Quarterly*, LXVI (Spring 1967), 148-64 — fails to consider Sumner's apology in *The Dial*, a piece of evidence that contradicts John Quinn's account of the instigation of the case, nor is Bryer accurate in assuming that Scofield Thayer offered to print portions of *Ulysses*. See Bryer, pp. 159-60, and *The Letters of James Joyce*, ed. Richard Ellmann (New York, 1966), III, 27-28; Joyce to Ezra Pound (November 5, 1920): "I knew nothing of the affair till yesterday when Mr. Thayer of the *Dial* wrote to me offering two cents a word more in exceptional case and saying that he was sorry about the *Little Review*. This explained nothing and I had heard nothing from Miss Anderson, Miss Heap or Mr. Rodker."

3. *Ibid.*, pp. 214-15. I have also followed the *New York Tribune*, February 15, 1921, p. 5, in its account of Margaret Anderson's trial.

4. *Ibid.*, pp. 44-45, 188-89.

5. "jh" was of course Jane Heap; the item is headed "Loyalty" and

subheaded "The Reader Critic" in the department "The Reader
Critic," *The Little Review*, VII (September-December 1920), 93.

6.   "Art Circus," *ibid.*, VIII (Autumn 1921), 112.

7.   See jh, "Exposé," *ibid.*, VIII (Spring 1922), 46-47.

8.   William Wasserstrom, "Hemingway, the *Dial*, and Ernest Walsh,"
      The South Atlantic Quarterly, LXV (Spring 1966), 171-77, has dis-
cussed in detail Hemingway's resentment of his rejection by *The Dial*,
which he aired during his life to many persons and posthumously indicated in *A Moveable Feast* (New York, 1964), in the unnumbered chapter
entitled "The Man Who Was Marked for Death." Wasserstrom does not
cite any specific letter rejecting a poem or story by Hemingway and argues
that there was only one submission, with one rejection. In this respect he
follows the recollection of Alyse Gregory and quotes her assumption of
responsibility (a responsibility she has acknowledged to this author too,
in correspondence). The correspondence between *The Dial* and Marianne Moore on this occasion is quoted from Wasserstrom, pp. 175-76.
Thayer's letter to Hemingway is in the Dial Papers housed in the Worcester Art Museum; the correspondence of Alyse Gregory with Hemingway is in the Beinicke Library, Yale University, and is used with permission
of the Yale University Library and Donald C. Gallup, Curator, Collection of
American Literature.

9.   Jeanne Robert Foster, "New Sculptures by Constantin Brancusi," *Van-
      ity Fair*, XVIII (May 1922), 68.

10.   IX (Autumn 1922), 46-47; this number was published in 1923, despite
      its date.

11.   As quoted in Nicholas Joost, *Scofield Thayer and The Dial* (Carbon-
      dale, Ill., 1964), p. 106.

12.   " 'Ulysses' in Court," *The Little Review*, VII (January-March 1921),
      22-25.

13.   "A Group of Poems by T. S. Eliot," *Vanity Fair*, XX (June 1923), 67;
      in the box of editorial description one reads: "Since the publication
of *The Waste Land*, Mr. T. S. Eliot has become the most hotly contested
issue in American poetry. . . . But if one has read Mr. Eliot's earlier poems
(published by Alfred A. Knopf) from which the present selection is made,
one gets the key to both his technique and his ideas."

14.   VIII (1916), 292-95.

15.   "Introduction — AFair Kept," *Vanity Fair: Selections from America's
Most Memorable Magazine, A Cavalcade of the 1920's and 1930's*, ed. Cleveland Amory, Frederic Bradlee, and Katharine Tweed (New York, 1960),
p. 7.

Footnotes to Chapter VIII

1. F. O. Mattheissen, *The James Family* (New York, 1948), p. 673.
2. William Wasserstrom, *The Time of the Dial,* unlike myself emphasizes the alleged "organicism" of *The Dial.*
3. *Journals of Ralph Waldo Emerson,* ed. Edward Waldo Emerson and Waldo Emerson Forbes (Boston, 1911), VI, 164.
4. "American Culture in a Trick Mirror," *Antioch Review,* XXIV (Fall 1964), 405.
5. *The Days of the Phoenix,* p. 66.
6. Joost, pp. 64-65, from correspondence of Thayer and Watson at the time when the first Dial Award was being considered. Watson had cabled Thayer (at the Hotel Bristol in Vienna): "Find Robinson aged fifty-two [.] Anderson forty-five but definit[e]ly of younger group stop prefer Anderson but willing either" (undated).
7. Wasserstrom discusses the pertinence of Spingarn's New Criticism in his book on *The Dial,* pp. 17-19.
8. Kenneth Burke's emergence as a major aesthetician in the 1940's and 1950's was prepared for by his work on *The Dial:* the editorial "Comment" just cited adumbrates much of Burke's work for the review. Thayer was famously an aesthete, *Le Byron de Nos Jours,* of Adolf Dehn's caricature in *The Dial* (June 1926), and he was interested enough in the aestheticism of the 1890's to become a major collector of Aubrey Beardsley drawings, now housed in the Fogg Art Museum. Thayer's predilection for line drawings and prints was a practical matter: they could best and most cheaply be reproduced in *The Dial.* Also he seems temperamentally to have been drawn to such art, inasmuch as he cut his teeth as a collector with his purchases of the Beardsley drawings.
9. *Artists on Art,* ed. Robert Goldwater and Marco Treves, 2d edn. (New York, 1947), p. 351.
10. *Ibid.,* p. 350.
11. From the concluding chapter, "Before a Picture by Picasso," of Gilbert Seldes, *The Seven Lively Arts,* 2d edn. rev. (New York, 1957), p. 303. "Before a Picture by Picasso" was first published in *The Dial,* LXXV (October 1923), 406-12.
12. See Joost, *op. cit.,* pp. 174-77, for mention of this point; also Wasserstrom, *op. cit.,* pp. 63, 65-66, 128.